Exploring Christian Spirituality

An Ecumenical Reader

Kenneth J. Collins (Ph.D., Drew University) is professor of historical theology and Wesley studies at Asbury Theological Seminary and has written extensively on the life and theology of John Wesley and the history of spirituality. Among his many books are *A Real Christian: The Life of John Wesley*, *The Scripture Way of Salvation: The Heart of John Wesley's Theology*, and *Soul Care: Deliverance and Renewal through the Christian Life*.

Exploring Christian Spirituality

An Ecumenical Reader

Edited by
Kenneth J. Collins

Baker Books

A Division of Baker Book House Co
Grand Rapids, Michigan 49516

Published by Baker Books
a division of Baker Book House Company
P.O. Box 6287, Grand Rapids, MI 49516-6287

Second printing, September 2001

Printed in the United States of America

Library of Congress Cataloging-in-Publication Data

Exploring Christian spirituality : an ecumenical reader / edited by Kenneth J. Collins.
    p.   cm.
   Includes bibliographical references and index.
   ISBN 0-8010-2233-9 (pbk.)
   1. Spirituality. I. Collins, Kenneth J.
   BV4501.2.E87   2000
   248—dc21   00-023079

For information about academic books, resources for Christian leaders, and all new releases available from Baker Book House, visit our web site:
http://www.bakerbooks.com

Contents

Contributors

Charles André Bernard, S.J., is emeritus professor of spiritual theology at the Pontifical Gregorian University, Rome.

Anne E. Carr is professor of theology at the University of Chicago Divinity School, Chicago, Illinois.

Joann Wolski Conn is professor of Christian spirituality and religious studies at Newmann College, Aston, Pennsylvania.

Ewert Cousins is professor of theology at Fordham University in New York and director of the Center for Contemporary Spirituality. He is general editor of the Crossroad Encyclopedia of World Spirituality.

David S. Dockery is president and professor of Christian studies at Union University, Jackson, Tennessee.

Keith J. Egan is professor at Saint Mary's College, Notre Dame, Indiana.

John L. Gresham, Jr., is head of information services at John Paul II Library—Franciscan University of Steubenville, Steubenville, Ohio.

Harvey H. Guthrie is professor of Old Testament and dean of Episcopal Divinity School in Cambridge, Massachusetts.

Howard G. Hageman is past president of New Brunswick Theological Seminary, New Brunswick, New Jersey.

Bradley C. Hanson is professor of religion at Luther College, Decorah, Iowa.

J. Steven Harper is vice president and dean of the Florida campus of Asbury Theological Seminary, Orlando, Florida.

Bengt Hoffman, a Lutheran priest and native of Sweden, was for many years professor of ethics and ecumenics at Lutheran Theological Seminary in Gettysburg, Pennsylvania.

Catherine Mowry LaCugna is the late professor of systematic theology at the University of Notre Dame, Indiana.

Lawrence L. LaPierre is director of chaplains at the Department of Veterans Affairs Medical Center in White River Junction, Vermont.

Richard F. Lovelace is professor of church history at Gordon-Conwell Theological Seminary, South Hamilton, Massachusetts.

John Macquarrie is emeritus Lady Margaret Professor of Divinity at the University of Oxford.

Eugene H. Peterson is former James Houston Professor of Spiritual Theology at Regent College, Vancouver, British Columbia.

Walter H. Principe is the late professor at the Pontifical Institute of Medieval Studies, Toronto, and at the Graduate Center for Religious Studies and the Graduate Center for Medieval Studies of the University of Toronto.

Sandra M. Schneiders, I.H.M., is professor of New Testament studies and spirituality at Jesuit School of Theology, Berkeley, California.

Philip Sheldrake is editor of *The Way*, co-director of the Institute of Spirituality, and lecturer in pastoral theology at Heythrop College, London.

James B. Torrance is former professor of theology at the University of Aberdeen, Scotland.

David Lowes Watson, former professor at Wesley Theological Seminary in Washington, D.C., is currently director of the Nashville Area Office of Pastoral Formation in the United Methodist Church.

Introduction

One of the truly remarkable stories of the second half of the twentieth century has been the resurgence of religion. Earlier prognosticators had seen the increasing secularization of American society as an indication that religion would soon be in serious decline. It is not. If fact, even Harvey Cox, one of the earlier doomsayers, has noted that during the 1980s a revival of religion was underway everywhere and that "the old secular city just wasn't what it used to be."[1] By the 1990s the hard demographic data were impressive: "94 percent believe in God. 90 percent pray, and 88 percent of Americans believe that God loves them."[2] Moreover, two out of every three adults (67 percent) say that "they have made a personal commitment to Jesus Christ that is still important in their life today."[3]

With this resurgence of American religion has come a flowering of spirituality as well: from the boardrooms of major corporations to farmhouses in the Dakotas, from charismatic Protestants to advocates of Marian devotion, many people are enthusiastic—indeed eager to learn—about what they call "spirituality." This cultural movement, so unlike the complacency of the 1950s, is marked by elements of dissatisfaction and even protest. George Gallup, for instance, notes a shift from the mainline churches to more conservative ones, with evangelicals and Pentecostals among the winners. In fact, in his book *The People's Religion* Gallup notes that "one of the top three reasons why Americans leave the church is that they want deeper spiritual meaning."[4] Moreover, he points out that "Americans have become more critical of their churches and synagogues over the past decade. A large majority believes the churches are too concerned with internal organizational issues and

9

not sufficiently concerned with spiritual matters."[5] So significant is the rise of spirituality in American society that one leading observer has maintained that "failure to understand the role of spirituality in our culture renders a social analyst incapable of completely comprehending the dynamics of American life."[6]

But just what is spirituality? To what does this significant term refer? Here there is far less agreement. Indeed, of late spirituality has become a buzzword in American society: it describes evangelical Protestant fervor in responding to God's offer of redemption in Jesus Christ as equally as it does New Age enthusiasm for crystals and Eastern religious notions. It depicts Roman Catholic and Jewish concern for their respective traditions as equally as it does the interests of humanistic psychology or the passions of secularists and agnostics. The term, then, as used by some, is largely amorphous, lacking definitional precision, and it often refers vaguely to some interior state or heightened awareness or perhaps to participation in a project, however conceived, greater than oneself.

One of the principal reasons I have collected the essays of this anthology is to bring greater clarity and depth to our understanding of spirituality, Christian spirituality in particular. Here two elements must ever be held in tension. On the one hand, our definitions must be broad and inclusive enough to embrace, at least in a descriptive way, both the general nature of spirituality and the diversity of spiritualities that actually exist. Thus, Christian tendencies toward triumphalism, even arrogance (as if Christian spirituality were the only spirituality), must be quietly put aside in the recognition of the spiritualities of Jews, Muslims, Buddhists, agnostics and others. On the other hand, if we are to explore *Christian* spirituality, then our definitions must be specific enough to show the distinct place that Christian insight, experience, and teaching play in this larger arena.

Interestingly enough, our English word *spirituality* is actually a derivative of the Latin term *spiritualitas,*[7] and, like its cognates *spiritus* and *spiritualis,* is a suitable translation of the original Greek terms *pneuma* and *pneumatikos.*[8] This means, then, that the "adjective 'spiritual,'" as one scholar puts it, "is a Christian neologism, coined apparently by St. Paul to describe that which pertained to the Holy Spirit of God."[9] Again, though the Christian origins of the term *spirituality* are clear, this fact must not blind us to the reality of other spiritualities. Sandra Schneiders, reflecting this broader usage, indicates that contemporary spirituality is best explored in terms of three main referents: "(1) a fundamental dimension of the human being, (2) the lived experience which actualizes that dimension, and (3) the academic discipline which studies that experience."[10] And it is precisely an exploration of the first two elements that will help us to understand not only spirituality in general but also the distinct contribution that Christian spirituality has to make.

Spirituality as the Nature of Human Beings

The first referent of the term spirituality, "a fundamental dimension of the human being," suggests that Homo sapiens is a species of distinctly spiritual beings, *homo spiritualis;* that is, beings who are capable of transcendence, not simply cognitively in terms of intellectual abstractions, but also and more importantly in terms of person and being. Put another way, human beings are capable of receiving a call, an address from a transcendent "subject," whether that subject be understood as God, nature, an undifferentiated unity, or an aesthetic experience.[11] Therefore, to ignore or to deny outright this dimension can only result in existential and spiritual atrophy. A clear depiction of the spiritual nature of human beings, so necessary in our empiricist and reductionistic age, emerges in the work of Ewert Cousins, who in describing Crossroad Books' grand publishing project, World Spirituality, wrote:

> The series focuses on that inner dimension of the person called by certain traditions "the spirit." This spiritual core is the deepest center of the person. It is here that the person is open to the transcendent dimension.[12]

Some evangelical Protestants may have difficulty here with the notion that spirituality necessarily pertains to a fundamental dimension of a human being. They, perhaps, would like to insist that every discussion of spirituality necessarily presupposes divine activity in the form of grace. In this setting, Arminians would undoubtedly champion the salutary effects of prevenient grace and Calvinists those of common grace.[13] But the capacity for transcending oneself, of receiving a call to some higher value or meaning, is not evidenced by theists alone. An atheist, for instance, who intentionally rejects or repudiates the grace of God may lose him or herself in some lofty goal or purpose, experience transcendence, as well as a measure of integration, and thereby develop a genuine spirituality, broadly understood. In other words, inextricably linking spirituality, divine activity, and grace presupposes theism, an assumption that is able to describe only a particular kind of spirituality as the term is used today. Atheists and agnostics will simply employ other categories to describe their own experience, and the notion of divine grace is not one of them. Nevertheless, this is not to suggest that human beings, by themselves, have a *natural* ability for transcending *into God,* which is quite a different matter. And theists, no doubt, will continue to insist that atheists or agnostics fail to acknowledge what grace is truly present. And so the dialog continues.

Spirituality as Experience

The second referent of spirituality, "the lived experience which actualizes that dimension," is best explored in terms of a number of definitions that scholars have offered to come to terms with spiritual *experience*. Following, in some respects, the seminal work of Zaehner, with some slight modifications, I will employ the categories of naturalistic, monistic, and theistic spirituality to describe the particular flavor expressed in each definition due to its respective ultimate or transcendent subject.[14] Put another way, the chief evoking value toward which one is directed determines, to a significant degree, the nature and contours of a particular spirituality.

Naturalistic Spirituality

Examples of the first category, naturalistic spirituality, abound. Gordon Wakefield, for example, defines spirituality as follows: "This is a word which has come much into vogue to describe those attitudes, beliefs, and practices, which animate people's lives and help them to reach out towards super-sensible realities."[15] Here "super-sensible realities" can be interpreted in terms of a theistic dimension, to be sure, but this is not absolutely necessary. Indeed, "super-sensible realities" can be understood to include any of a number of values that are beyond the purview of empiricism, such as participation in human love, an experience of rapturous beauty, or knowledge of the good. To illustrate, the aesthetic experience, the loss of a sense of self in the encounter of something "more," may, at times, only have nature itself as its goal, as expressed, for example, in the writings of the Scottish poet James Thomson or in the works of Samuel Taylor Coleridge, a key leader of the Romantic movement.[16] Again, the transcendental referent need not be understood in a theistic way, but there must be a real sense in which that referent is "beyond" us or is at least suggestive of an "other" toward which we are drawn. Accordingly, the phrases "atheistic spirituality" and "agnostic spirituality" are not oxymorons.

Monistic Spirituality

If, on the other hand, the transcendent dimension is conceived of not as an evoking "subject" at all but as an undifferentiated unity that is beyond the subject/object distinction, then this kind of spirituality is most suitably described as monistic. Such an understanding is exemplified in Hinduism, in its central premise that "Atman (self) is Brahman (unity),"[17] and in Buddhism, in terms of its teaching that "undifferentiated unity" is not a *something* at all, but sheer nothingness.[18] In this context, it is the oneness of all that is that calls us forth, that lures us to abandon false conceptions of the self, autonomous and isolated, and to actualize in a thoroughgoing way a unity that already *is*.

Theistic Spirituality

Theistic spirituality, our third category, views the transcendent subject as a *personal* God as expressed, for example, in the great monotheistic faiths of Judaism, Christianity, and Islam. Consequently, Christian spirituality today represents a subset of theistic spirituality, not its entirety, and theistic spirituality itself is a part of a broader phenomenon that includes the naturalistic and monistic varieties.[19] Thus, Haddad's definition (and others like it) that "spirituality is therefore the whole of human life in its efforts at being open to God,"[20] is not quite accurate and, according to contemporary usage, is even presumptuous. Thus, if Haddad had wished to define *Christian* spirituality—which I believe was her intention—then she should have parsed the category of spirituality in general (naturalistic, monistic, and theistic) and then further specified the particular type of theistic spirituality she had in mind. Christian spirituality, in other words, in contradistinction to other kinds, is not simply the attempt to encounter an amorphous personal God, but represents, more specifically, the revelation of God manifested *in Jesus Christ* through the Holy Spirit. To avoid, therefore, the problem of unwarranted generalization, McGinn defines Christian spirituality as "the lived experience of Christian belief,"[21] and Schneiders, for her part, specifies the subject as follows:

> We might define Christian spirituality as that particular actualization of the capacity for self-transcendence that is constituted by the substantial gift of the Holy Spirit establishing a life-giving relationship with God in Christ within the believing community.[22]

Nevertheless, this process of particularization is offered not to suggest that Christian spirituality is limited, incapable of addressing a universal realm, but only to indicate, on the one hand, that such spirituality is distinct, unique in its understanding of the transcendent, and, on the other hand, that other varieties of spirituality exist as well, some of which are quite unlike Christianity. The process is offered, in other words, for the sake of both accuracy as well as for the task of ongoing dialog.

Though there are obviously a variety of spiritualities in existence, many of them with a significant history, there is nevertheless a common thread that unites them all—the elements of *transcendence* and personal *integration*. Indeed, whether one is considering the spiritual path of Mahayana Buddhism or that of Christian monasticism, each underscores the importance of surpassing oneself into a wider circle of meaning with its resultant enlightenment or greater knowledge of God. The four degrees of love enunciated by Bernard of Clairvaux, for example, chronicle the transition from a self-centered love, with all its limitations, to a love of self for the sake of God, which is the highest love of all. John Toltschig, an eighteenth-century Moravian leader, undertook the practice of pastoral care in order "to lead people out of themselves, so that the word of power might break in on them and pierce them through."[23] And on a more contemporary note, Donald Evans explores this same dynamic in the following way:

> [What is necessary] is a letting go of my narcissism so that I am lived by the Source in all that I do and all that I experience. This contrast between self-separation and self-surrender is a contrast between two fundamental ways of being and of being conscious in the world. This contrast is the essential core of spirituality.[24]

For his part, John Macquarrie describes "spirit" as the "capacity for going out of oneself and beyond oneself. . . . Human beings are not closed or shut up in themselves."[25] In fact, so concerned is this British author with displaying this key characteristic of spirituality that he has even coined a new word, "exience" (which means "going out"), in order to capture the essential dynamic of spiritual existence.[26]

The element of transcendence, however, must not be viewed simply in an individualistic way. For the transcendence involved in spirituality not only involves going beyond egocentric commitments, but sociocentric ones as well. Thus, on the social level, spirituality is an invitation, a call, to forsake selfish group commitments and the ethnocentrism that deflects the actualization of the very highest values in life, such as the universal love of God and neighbor. Put another way, spirituality, as it is defined today, goes beyond the "tribalisms" of group life to enjoy a broader horizon of meaning.[27]

The Flow of the Anthology

In order to display the promise as well as the genius of Christian spirituality I have gathered twenty-three of the very best pieces drawn not only from my many years of reading on this subject but also in consultation with other scholars. I have organized this material into seven major sections (which are preceded by brief introductions), each one illustrating a vital aspect of the Christian contribution. These sections, though very useful in *exploring* and *defining* Christian spirituality, are by no means exhaustive and are indicative of both space limitations as well as my editorial judgment. In a larger work, other topics (such as one on "Spirituality and the Sacraments") would, no doubt, have been included. At any rate, the first two sections, "Historical Considerations" and "Contemporary Modulations," set the tone of the book and offer working definitions of Christian spirituality in light of both history and current concerns.

The largest section of the anthology is "Christian Traditions." Here breadth is necessary in order to highlight the spiritual diversity within the Christian household as well as to underscore the promise of ecumenism. To be sure, the discipline of spirituality is bringing together Christians of various traditions who might not otherwise talk to each other. And since spirituality, as just noted above, calls not only for personal transcendence, but also social transcendence whereby the provincialism and ethnocentrism of group life can be thrown off, then the discipline of spirituality itself holds promise for ecumenism, for going beyond our limited group commitments to see the Christian "other"— perhaps for the first time.

One of the truly exciting things about Christian spirituality is that its parameters as a discipline are currently being reworked and carved out. Thus, numerous scholars, from several different traditions, are detailing the method of spirituality as well as its area of expertise. These and similar concerns are reflected in the "Spirituality and Theology" section where not only is the relation between spirituality and theology addressed, but also the connection between spirituality and other academic disciplines. In this setting, Christian spirituality emerges as an interdisciplinary subject par excellence—what some scholars have called "a field encompassing field." A key question here is whether Christian spirituality as an area of human knowledge and research has a rightful place in the secular academy, or must it, due to its method and interests, be limited to church-related colleges and seminaries.

Now at the heart of Christian spirituality is revelation and a distinct understanding of God. Indeed, Christians affirm through word and sacrament not an amorphous, generalized, ill-defined understanding of the Most High, but more particularly God as revealed in Jesus Christ through the Holy Spirit. Accordingly, in part 5, "Spirituality and the Trinity," the late Catherine LaCugna, John Gresham, and James Torrance all display the richness and beauty of the Trinitarian understanding of God in which the Three in One is revealed as none other than holy love, as persons in relation, each of which is ever other directed. This understanding of God, then, at the very heart of Christian revelation, naturally holds promise for spirituality. That is, the "exience" or other-directedness of the divine being, to borrow Macquarrie's term, is emblematic of the very ethos of spirituality which calls for a similar direction and emphasis. This fact alone suggests something of the kind of generous contribution that Christianity can make, especially in terms of its doctrine of God, to any discussion of spiritual concerns.

No exploration of Christian spirituality would be complete without a serious discussion of Scripture and the role it has played in norming Christian experience. For evangelical Protestants, Scripture is the touchstone of belief and practice; it is the standard that brings illumination and order to an array of human activity. For Roman Catholics and Eastern Orthodox, Scripture's norming role is seen in concert with Holy Tradition, the entirety of which cannot be accepted, nor given equal weight, by faithful and earnest Christians in other corners of the universal church. Nevertheless, all communions of Christians agree, in a way that honors the headship of Christ, that the language of Scripture, that is, the clear presentation of the history of Israel as well as the gospel *story*, is at the very heart of Christian spirituality. Put another way, all Christians, in one way or another, are "people of the Book," and the selections of the "Spirituality and Scripture" section help us to understand not only just why this is so, but also what difference it makes for spiritual thought and practice.

The anthology concludes with the contributions of contemporary Christian feminists who invite the church to a larger vision that is truly universal and that breaks out of the provincialism of patriarchy. Indeed, insofar as feminists call the church to transcend the ethnocentrism of male privilege and prerogative, their agenda is very much in accord with the hope and promise of Christian spirituality. However, insofar as some feminists would like to make women's experience a new and competing *orienting center*, they revert to parochialism, mistake the penultimate for the ultimate, and thereby retreat from the vision of transcending gender in the universal love of God and neighbor. This means, of course, not only that the work of feminists is crucial, since it runs along the fault lines of what Christian spirituality is all about in terms of its inclusive possibilities, but also that it remains one of the best windows on the future prospects of the discipline. As with Christian spirituality, the very best of feminist writing calls us all to something more, to a larger vision of self and community.

One final word is in order. A work such as this anthology not only requires years of preparation in research, reading, conferencing, and writing, but it also entails the labors of others, all of whom I would like to thank at this time. I am especially appreciative of the work of John Demarco, Blake Langston, Paul Clifford, and Margot Thompson, my student assistants. Without their efforts, this work would have been impossible.

Notes

1. Harvey Cox, *Religion in the Secular City: Toward a Postmodern Theology* (New York: Simon & Schuster, 1984), 19.

2. George Gallup Jr. and Jim Castelli, *The People's Religion: American Faith in the 90's* (New York: MacMillan, 1989), 45.

3. George Barna, *The Index of Leading Spiritual Indicators* (Dallas: Word, 1996), 3.

4. Gallup, *People's Religion*, 144.

5. Ibid., 88.

6. Barna, *The Index*, x.

7. Sheldrake contends that the abstract noun *spiritualitas* did not make its appearance until the fifth century. He maintains that a letter once ascribed to St. Jerome exhorts the reader so to act as "to advance in 'spirituality.'" Cf. Philip Sheldrake, *Spirituality and History: Questions of Interpretation and Method* (New York: Crossroad, 1992), 35.

8. Walter H. Principe, "Toward Defining Spirituality," *Studies in Religion/Sciences religieuses* 12.2 (1983): 130.

9. Sandra M. Schneiders, "Theology and Spirituality: Strangers, Rivals, or Partners?" *Horizons* 13.2 (1986): 257.

10. Sandra M. Schneiders, "Spirituality in the Academy," in *Modern Christian Spirituality: Methodological and Historical Essays*, ed. Bradley C. Hanson (Atlanta: Scholars Press, 1990), 17. Emphasis added.

11. I use the phrase "transcendent subject" rather than "transcendent object" because the former suggests that it is God, or nature, or beauty that is active and that calls us out of our mundane existence to something "more." The phrase "transcendent object," on the other hand, suggests that the self is ever in control, the chief reference point, and that the transcendent dimension, then, is simply another object of its interests. Here one could rightly ask if transcendence occurs at all.

12. Ewert Cousins, preface to *Christian Spirituality: Origins to the Twelfth Century*, ed. Bernard McGinn, John Meyendorff, and Jean Leclercq, World Spirituality 16 (New York: Crossroad, 1985), xi–xiv.

13. Charles Ryrie confuses spirituality with maturity and so denies that human beings are by nature spiritual. He maintains, for example, that "a new Christian cannot be called spiritual simply because he has not had sufficient time to grow and develop in Christian knowledge and experience." Cf. C. C. Ryrie, "What Is Spirituality?" *Bibliotheca Sacra* 126 (1969): 204–13.

14. Cf. R. C. Zaehner, *Mysticism: Sacred and Profane* (London: Oxford University Press, 1957). I have altered Zaehner's categories somewhat from "panenhenic, monistic, theistic," to "naturalistic, monistic, theistic." Moreover, Zaehner works within the specific context of mysticism; I am working, on the other hand, within the broader category of spirituality.

15. Gordon S. Wakefield, ed., *The Westminster Dictionary of Christian Spirituality* (Louisville: Westminster/John Knox, 1983), 361.

16. Although Evans's definition is properly placed under the heading of "monistic spirituality," there are elements of it that resonate with the "naturalistic" one as well. He writes: "Spirit is the desire for nonphysical ecstatic intimacy with others: with the nonphysical aspect of other persons, works of art and nature. . . ." Cf. Donald Evans, *Spirituality and Human Nature* (Albany: State University of New York Press, 1993), 75.

17. For two valuable pieces that compare Christian and Hindu spirituality, cf. Ian D. L. Clark, "Ananda [concepts of joy, bliss, and spirit in Christianity and Hinduism]," *Theology* 86 (1983): 15–19; and Gerald J. Pillay, "Ritualistic Hinduism and Popular Pen-

tecostalism: Two Religious Worldviews in Dynamic Relation," *Religion in Southern Africa* 6.1 (1985): 29–45.

18. For two of the more helpful works that explore the spirituality of Christianity and Buddhism, cf. John Steffney, "Compassion in Mahayana Buddhism and Meister Eckhart," *Journal of Religious Thought* 31 (1974–75): 64–77; and Scott Cowdell, "Buddhism and Christianity," *Asia Journal of Theology* 4 (April 1990): 190–98.

19. For an example of theistic spirituality, Christianity in particular, see Kenneth J. Collins, *Soul Care: Deliverance and Renewal through the Christian Life* (Wheaton: Victor, Bridge-Point, 1995).

20. Frieda Haddad, "Orthodox Spirituality: The Monastic Life," *The Ecumenical Review* 38.1 (1986): 64.

21. McGinn, Meyendorff, and Leclercq, eds., *Christian Spirituality*, xv.

22. Schneiders, "Theology and Spirituality," 266.

23. Frank C. Senn, ed., *Protestant Spiritual Traditions* (New York: Paulist, 1986), 220.

24. Evans, *Spirituality and Human Nature*, 3. One of the most extensive popular treatments on the theme of spirituality and narcissism is found in the work of Earl Jabay, *The Kingdom of Self* (Plainfield, N.J.: Logos Press International, 1974). Bracketed material is mine.

25. John Macquarrie, *Paths in Spirituality* (Harrisburg, Pa.: Morehouse, 1992), 44.

26. Ibid., 45.

27. Collins, *Soul Care*, 52–54. For more on the concept of social transcendence, see Marsha Sinetar, *Ordinary People as Monks and Mystics* (New York: Paulist, 1986), 51ff.

Part 1

Historical Considerations

The following two selections from Philip Sheldrake and the late Walter Principe will give greater definitional precision to the term *spirituality* by exploring its etymological roots and by tracing its fascinating history. Along the way, both of these authors will offer a valuable and informative contemporary definition which should enable readers to grapple seriously with this increasingly important subject.

In his piece "What Is Spirituality?" Sheldrake highlights three major periods as necessary for our understanding of spirituality. The first explores New Testament usage and reveals that the apostle Paul employed the term *pneumatikos*, or "spiritual person," not as someone who turns away from material or physical reality, but as one "in whom the Spirit of God dwells." The second period of the twelfth century, crucial in many respects, evidences a number of changes in the use of the term *spirituality*, such as a division of spirituality from theology and liturgy, of affectivity from knowledge, of the personal from the communal, as well as a gradual limita-

tion of interest to "interiority or subjective spiritual experience." And finally, the third period, the contemporary setting, underscores a holistic, inclusive view of spirituality that embraces human life at its depth as well as the life of the whole person directed toward God and transcendence.

For his part, Principe, in his essay "Toward Defining Spirituality," not only deftly explores some of the same territory as does Sheldrake, especially as he chronicles the shifting meaning of the term *spirituality* throughout the history of the church, but he also notes a "certain fluidity" and "vagueness in the use of the term." In fact, the first *English* title that he discovered that employed the specific term *spirituality*, was the translation in 1922 of the first volume of Pierre Pourrat's work. Beyond this, Principe offers a well-conceived contemporary definition that includes three levels: (1) a real or existential level, (2) formulation of a teaching about the lived reality, and (3) study of the preceding levels, elements that many scholars are grappling with today in their own creative formulations.

What Is Spirituality?

Philip Sheldrake

Spirituality, as an area of study, must be capable of definition. If it has no conceptual limits, effectively it means nothing. In recent years the criticism has sometimes been levelled at spirituality that it is an artificial entity that relies for its existence on a variety of other disciplines without having anything that it can call its own, or that it "enjoys an unlimited wealth of resources but possesses no tools for getting those resources organised."[1] Undoubtedly a cursory glance at the different kinds of writing which appear under the label "spirituality," whether popular or more scholarly, reveals that it may cover history, psychology and theology as well as devotional works. It appears that spirituality is one of those subjects whose meaning everyone claims to know until they have to define it. At the very least, contemporary spirituality has emerged as a cross-disciplinary subject which, on the face of it, has considerable problems of coherence.

The reference to "contemporary" spirituality highlights an important issue. Throughout Christian history, "spirituality" has changed shape, often subtly but sometimes substantially. The word itself, as we shall see, has a relatively short pedigree. Our understanding of what the word broadly seeks to express (that is, the theory and practice of the Christian life) has evolved as individuals and historical or cultural environments change. Because our thinking about God, Church and the human person necessarily develops under the influence of theology as well as human knowledge and historical

This essay first appeared in *Spirituality and History: Questions of Interpretation and Method* (New York: Crossroad, 1992), 32–56. Used by permission.

events, every generation has to redefine what precisely spirituality is meant to encompass. The approach of traditional ascetical-mystical theology, or spiritual theology, over the last hundred years or so implied an agreed theological language in reference to the Christian life which no longer applies. The universal categories of the old theology textbooks were based largely on an approach to the truths of the Christian faith that was framed within logical and rigorously constructed theses. In other words, theology was a stable body of knowledge, rich in the tradition of the past and secure enough to answer the questions of the present and future. This detached, and a priori, approach to doctrine gave birth to a similarly structured theory of the spiritual life which was separated from the core of human experience and consequently was largely alienated from, for example, nature, the body and the feminine.

In recent decades, there has been a paradigm shift in the general approach to theology towards a greater reflection on human experience as an authentic source of divine revelation. Not surprisingly, this has brought about substantial changes in the way that the study of the Christian life has been conducted and, in particular, has facilitated a movement from the static concept of "spiritual theology" to the more fluid "spirituality." If the frontiers of theology increasingly seek articulation in a process and method that is experiential, spirituality has followed suit by becoming more of a dialectical tension. On the one hand, there is the historical concreteness of revelation in Jesus and subsequent Christian tradition, and, on the other, there is the personal assimilation of salvation in Christ by each person within changing historical, cultural and social circumstances that demand new approaches to Christian conduct.

As a result of these shifts of perspective, the realisation has emerged that specific spiritual traditions are initially embodied in people rather than doctrine and grow out of life rather than from abstract ideas. Thus they may be described as secular-dialogic—secular because they take the everyday world as the proper starting place for spiritual experience and reflection; dialogic because spiritual theory and practice operate on the frontier between contemporary experience and the tradition and do not simplistically apply the latter as the measure of the former.[2] In short, part of the contemporary problem with defining "spirituality" is associated with the fact that it is not a single, transcultural, phenomenon but is rooted within the lived experience of God's presence in history—and a history which is always specific. Indeed, our basic understanding of what is "spiritual" and what is "the Christian life" depends, in part at least, on particular experiences rather than merely on a theological language given for all time.

I propose, first of all, to survey briefly the history of the word "spirituality." Then the way will be open for us to examine how the theory and practice of Christian living (or what we nowadays refer to as spirituality) has been differently understood and defined over the centuries. Because it is difficult to define "spirituality as such" in abstract terms, apart that is from historical questions and attention to changes in theological presuppositions, the remainder of this chapter as a whole may be understood as a discussion of what spirituality is. However, the final section, "From Spiritual Theology to Spirituality," offers a brief discussion of contemporary approaches to questions of definition and a summary conclusion.

The History of the Term "Spirituality"

The word "spirituality" is used so frequently nowadays that it comes as a surprise to find that its pedigree is very short both in theological and secular writing.[3] A comparison of *The Catholic Encyclopedia*, published between 1912–15, with the revised New Catholic Encyclopedia of the 1970s is revealing. In the first there are no references to "spirituality," while in the second there are eight articles that employ the word. Secular usage, however, remains conservative. In the *Oxford Dictionary* and in the *Webster's International Dictionary* of 1961, six meanings are given. Five of these do not correspond to "spirituality" as a religious area of study: three definitions refer to incorporeal beings or volatility, and two to the obsolete social class of "persons spiritual," that is, ecclesiastics. The sixth definition, while related to the contemporary religious meaning, is firmly dualistic: the condition of being spiritual, or regard for things of the spirit as opposed to material interests.

The Latin root of the word "spirituality," *spiritualitas*, attempts to translate the Greek noun for spirit, *pneuma*, and its adjective *pneumatikos* as they appear in the New Testament Pauline letters. Thus, "to be united to Christ is to enter into the sphere of the Spirit" (1 Cor. 6:17), or "faith in the Lord is from and in the Spirit" (1 Cor. 2:10f.). This is not the place to enter into debate about more complex issues of Pauline scholarship. However, at the risk of simplification, it is important to grasp that, in Pauline theology, "Spirit" and "spiritual" are not contrasted with "physical" or "material" (for which the Greek *soma*, in Latin *corpus*, is the root) but rather with *all that is opposed to the Spirit of God* (for which the word *sarx*, in Latin *caro*, is used). What is opposed to the Spirit may as well be the mind or the will as the body or material reality. The contrast that emerges is therefore between two ways of life or attitudes to life. The "spiritual" is what is under the influence of, or is a manifestation of, the Spirit of God. A dualistic contrast between "spiritual" and "physical," or body and soul, is not part of the Pauline understanding of the human person or of created reality in general. There is therefore no justification for using the Pauline

contrast as the basis for a denial of the flesh or a rejection of materiality
as some classical Christian spirituality subsequently did. The "spiritual
person" (e.g. 1 Cor. 2:14–15) is *not* someone who turns away from material reality but rather someone in whom the Spirit of God dwells.[4]

In fact the abstract Latin noun *spiritualitas* (spirituality), as opposed to
the adjective *spiritualis* (spiritual), did not make its appearance until the
fifth century. A letter once ascribed to St Jerome exhorts the reader so
to act as to advance in "spirituality" (*ut in spiritualitate proficias*). As the context is living within the power of the Holy Spirit, this continues to reflect
the basic theology of the Pauline letters. The reference to life in the Spirit
is constant in further usage of the word up to the twelfth century.

It was the influence of a new philosophical trend in theology, known
as scholasticism, which began in the twelfth century, that led to a sharper
distinction between spirit and matter. The word "spiritual" began to be
applied to intelligent creatures (that is, humankind), as opposed to nonrational creation. Thus it lost its Pauline moral sense and took on a meaning more radically opposed to corporeality. Here, then, lie the intellectual roots of that disdain for the body that sometimes appeared in later
spiritual writing. However, the new meaning of "spirituality" did not completely replace the former Pauline emphasis. In the thirteenth century
the two meanings stood side by side. Thus Thomas Aquinas used both
the Pauline and the anti-material senses. A third juridical sense, "spirituality" as the clerical estate, also came into being at this time and, from
the thirteenth to sixteenth centuries, is in fact the most frequent usage.

It was only in the seventeenth century that the word became once again
established in France in reference to the spiritual life. In a positive sense
it was used to express a personal, affective relationship with God. However, this new meaning was also used pejoratively of enthusiastic or
quietistic movements and here it was contrasted with words such as
"devotion," which seemed to preserve a proper emphasis on human cooperation. For example, Voltaire used the word in his violent attacks
on the "salon mysticism" of Madame Guyon and Fénelon, which appeared
too refined, rarified and separated from ordinary Christian life. In fact a
variety of words were used in the seventeenth and eighteenth centuries
to express life in the Spirit: "devotion" in Francis de Sales or the Anglican
mystic William Law; "perfection" in John Wesley and the early Methodists;
"piety" among Evangelicals. The word "spirituality" virtually disappeared
from the religious and theological vocabulary of Roman Catholic circles
in the early eighteenth century and this undoubtedly had a great deal to
do with a suspicion both of religious enthusiasm and quietism. In the nineteenth century the use of the word "spirituality" was confined mainly to
free religious groupings outside the mainline Churches.

In the early decades of the present century, "spirituality" once again appeared among Roman Catholics in France and then passed into English through translations of French writings. The use of "spirituality" was closely tied to the debate concerning the nature of the spiritual life in itself. Those who saw a continuity between the "ordinary" and "extraordinary" (that is, mystical) dimensions of Christian living preferred the word "spirituality" because of its comprehensiveness. Its increased use was also associated with attempts to distinguish between dogma and the study of the spiritual life as well as with an increasing emphasis on religious consciousness and the experiential. The foundation of the much respected *Revue d'Ascetique et de Mystique* in 1920, and the beginning of the continuing *Dictionnaire de spiritualité* in 1932 further established the respectability of the term. In the years after the Second Vatican Council, the theological dictionary *Sacramentum mundi*, and its one-volume popular edition, included a comprehensive article on the subject. More recently a dictionary and a general introduction to the subject have been published in English as the result of ecumenical collaboration.[5]

The History of "Spirituality," as a Subject for Reflection

Precisely because the word "spirituality," in its present sense, has a relatively short history, we are faced with a problem of "translation" when we attempt to explore how spirituality was viewed in different periods of Christian history. What precisely should we look for and how can we avoid an unhelpful imposition of contemporary assumptions on the evidence we find? If we look back merely over the last hundred years, it soon becomes apparent that "spirituality" is not simply coterminous with older concepts such as "spiritual theology" or "ascetical-mystical theology." If we extend our exploration further into the past, we will soon realise that defined concepts of any kind with regard to "the spiritual life," let alone with reference to a distinct discipline, have a limited history. Translation, therefore, is not merely a question of looking for terminology equivalent to "spirituality" in different ages.

Yet to write in any way about "spirituality" in the history of the Christian tradition means that we must have some working model or framework for interpretation. I would suggest that what the word "spirituality" seeks to express is the conscious human response to God that is both personal and ecclesial. In short, "life in the Spirit." Within this simple working definition, we may then approach particular periods with a number of questions in mind. Was there in fact a body of literature that dealt specifically with the "spiritual" life? More broadly, how was the relationship between the intellectual, affective and ethical dimensions of Christian existence viewed and was there, in practice, a distinction between what we now think of as doctrine, spirituality and ethics? This necessarily brief overview will be limited to three major periods: the patristic, the High Middle Ages in the West, and finally the (mainly Roman Catholic) concern for an explicit theology of the spiritual life in the period from the late nineteenth century to Vatican II. I will also consider some particular emphases in the Anglican tradition and point, in broad terms, to the major differences in approach between the Eastern Orthodox tradition and that of the West.

The Patristic Period

There is disagreement about how long this period may be considered to have lasted. Some would limit it to the earliest centuries of the Christian era—so, for example, the Protestant tradition has tended to accept the Council of Chalcedon in 451 C.E. as an approximate end. The Eastern Orthodox would include such figures as Gregory Palamas who lived from 1296–1359. Others use the term, somewhat broadly, to describe the whole period up to the development of the "new theology" of scholasticism in the West in the twelfth century. While we may feel that such a broad definition of the term "patristic" raises awkward questions, there is some validity in it, at least as far as the general *style* of theology in the West is concerned. Until the rise of scholasticism, "life in the Spirit" continued to be viewed as something which was applicable to all the baptised, even though there was already a *de facto* division between "states of life" in the Church. Theology was also conceived as a unity to which later divisions (into, for example, doctrine, ethics and spirituality) were entirely foreign. The unifying feature was the Bible, and theology was generally what we nowadays think of as biblical theology—that is to say, an exegetically-based interpretation of Scripture aimed at producing both a fuller understanding of Christian faith and a deepening of the Christian life in all its dimensions.

Thus, patristic theology encapsulates an idea of Christian knowledge in which biblical exegesis, speculative reasoning and mystical contemplation are fused into a synthesis. Because patristic theology was primarily a way of looking at the Bible, the most common written genre was scriptural commentary. The "Fathers" did not neglect a methodical study of texts within the limits of their time, but their interest was primarily theological and their theology, while rigorous, was fundamentally pastoral. In other words, they placed the Bible in the context of the Christian life and their theology was involved in the life of the Church.

The patristic period, in the limited sense of the early Christian centuries, was a formative time both for the fundamentals of doctrine and for what has been called "mystical theology." It is no accident, therefore, that the two aspects of Christian knowledge are intimately bound up with each other. "The basic doctrines of the Trinity and Incarnation, worked out in these centuries, are mystical doctrines formulated dogmatically."[6] In other words, "mystical theology" aimed to provide a context for the direct apprehension of God who is revealed in Christ and within us as the Spirit. Doctrinal theology attempted to incarnate these apprehensions in precise and objective language which in turn inspired a mystical understanding of the God who has been revealed. Thus the polemical writings of this period, for example, should not be separated from the homilies and scriptural commentaries. A more fruitful approach would be to study the "mysticism" of the Fathers as the very *heart of their theology.*[7]

When we talk of the "mystical theology" of this period, we must be careful not to confuse it with the later medieval fascination in the West with subjective experience or with the development of a detailed itinerary for the spiritual journey. Patristic "mysticism" is neither abstract nor systematic. It refers to the personal life of the Christian who knows God as revealed in Christ by belonging to the fellowship of the "mystery." This means the mystery of Christ as expressed in the Bible and the liturgy as well as in personal Christian living. Living the mystery begins with our incorporation into Christ in baptism and comes to fruition in us through the sacramental life and by growth in virtue. In this sense, all believers are mystics in that they are plunged into the mystery of Christ.

In the late fifth or early sixth century, this fundamental insight flowed together with certain Neo-Platonic elements in the writings of a theologian commonly known as Pseudo-Dionysius who, for many centuries, was thought to be the Pauline convert known as Denis (or Dionysius) the Areopagite. However, even though this author does appear to offer a "mystical theology" that is closer to later western emphases, he in fact sums up the patristic tradition. His *Mystical Theology* was not concerned with enumerating the means towards spiritual progress or with the technicalities of mystical union but rather explored the nature of the soul's surrender to God as the person passed beyond sign and concept to be fully grasped by the mystery of love and so transformed. The later interest in subjective experience is not present, for "the mystery" is still the objective fact of God in Christ into which all are drawn through Scripture and liturgy. To take the writer's *Mystical Theology* out of the context both of his other writings and of his overall theological horizons would be to ignore the fact that he continued the general patristic understanding of "mystery" and "mysticism."[8]

What is the context within which the Fathers created their synthesis? There seem to be four important factors. First of all, the general setting for the spiritual message of the Fathers is the atmosphere created by the doctrinal polemics of the early centuries, as the Christian community worked out the central features of its understanding of God, Christ and redemption. It is these same Fathers whose style of theology chiefly contributed to the Orthodox formulation of the data of faith. So, for example, Athanasius' rejection of the Arian view of salvation may appear biased in some respects, but it was the medium through which he became a champion of the renewed doctrine of the incarnation and its spiritual implications. It is Augustine's refutation of Pelagian ethics which was the medium for the forceful exposition of his own spirituality.

Secondly, nearly all of the major writers were bishops. Therefore, it was entirely natural that their theology should be involved in the life of the Church. In a real sense, all of their theology was pastoral—that is to say, for the upbuilding of the community. Their pastoral work put them in contact with the life of ordinary Christian communities. Preaching was understood as the action of the living Word of God in the congregation. So the explanation of the sacraments had a privileged place in their teaching.

Thirdly, a large proportion of the writers had been monks or were responsible for encouraging the development of celibate community life (for example, John Chrysostom, Basil, Jerome and Augustine). It is not surprising, therefore, that they saw theological speculation and contemplation as closely associated nor that they placed a strong emphasis on the Christian life as a call to holiness and on themes drawn from the ascetical trends of their time.

Finally, the intellectual pattern of the patristic theologians was necessarily forged, in part, by their social origins and education. In fact, apart from Athanasius and Augustine, all the outstanding spiritual and theological leaders seem to have been born into the élite classes and all were men. So their spirituality which was inherited and relied upon by succeeding generations for almost a thousand years needs to be relocated within its social milieu—that is, the estates of landowners or the sophisticated upper-class circles of the leading cities of the Roman Empire. In practice, this meant a grafting on to the biblical vision of Christianity of the humanistic values and traditional philosophical attitudes of the contemporary upper-class and male élites.[9]

The High Middle Ages

F)   In the West, from the seventh to the twelfth centuries, theology developed almost exclusively within the confines of male religious houses. Although one might expect some interest in spirituality as a familiar area of experience and therefore reflection, in practice the patristic synthesis continued to dominate. There seems little evidence, from the sources, for any interest in mysticism as a subjective experience, or in the kind of spiritual-mystical states which dominated the lives of many saints as well as the treatises of the High and late Middle Ages.[10] The monastic style of theology, as it continued until overtaken by that of the schools from the twelfth century onwards, drew its inspiration from the traditional meditative reading of Scripture, or *lectio divina*, and monastic liturgy. Indeed, it was this fact that led the new breed of thinkers to criticise the proponents of the old theology. That is, that their theological method was limited to reading, reflecting and commenting on traditional sources. In contrast, the new theologians were concerned to develop a more systematic and precise method of research based upon the increasing availability of the Greek philosophy of antiquity. So the twelfth century, and even more strikingly the thirteenth, witnessed the birth of a more "scientific" understanding of the theological enterprise.[11]

Until the twelfth century, therefore, what we might call "spiritual theology" or "mystical theology" had continued, in the main, to appear in the context of collections of homilies or scriptural and patristic commentaries. There were some exceptions to this general rule. Firstly, some writings appeared that were associated specifically with religious life, particularly with the new monastic or canonical communities which arose in the eleventh and twelfth centuries. These promoted a series of reflections on the way to God appropriate to reformed religious life. For example, there were the *Customs* of Guigo I composed for the Grande Chartreuse during the years 1121–28 as well as his *Reflections* on the interior life of the solitary. There were also Cistercian texts, such as the *Cara Caritatis* of Citeaux in 1114 and St Bernard's *Apologia* for the Cistercian emphasis on detachment and spiritual simplicity. Secondly, there were a small number of treatises on specifically spiritual topics which, however, also came into existence predominantly within the context of monastic renewal. For example, Guigo II of Chartreuse produced the *Scale of Perfection* which was a fairly systematic approach to the traditional monastic *lectio divina*. William of St Thierry, a Benedictine turned Cistercian, wrote his *Letter to the Brethren of Mont-Dieu* (often known as the *Golden Epistle*) for the Carthusians but it also encapsulates a vision of mystical theology. Although St Bernard wrote on prayer and asceticism, and saw his teaching as valid for all Christians, we need to remember two things: that his spiritual doctrine cannot be separated from his overall theology, which is all of a piece; that he took for granted that the monastery was the best place to put his teaching into practice. He remains, as Jean Leclercq describes him, essentially a *doctor monasticus*.[12]

2)   From the twelfth century onwards, writing on the spiritual life began
to take new directions as the result of several factors. Firstly, there was
the gradual separation of considerations about the spiritual life from the
rest of theology, although this process took some time. This related to
the fact that theology as a whole began to be organised into its different components. For example, in the thirteenth century, St Thomas
Aquinas (who tried to retain the unity between loving contemplation
and theological speculation) divided his *Summa theologiae* into parts. The
first dealt with God as first principle, the second with God as the "end"
of creation, the final part with the Incarnate Word as the way to that
"end." In other words, he effectively established the classical scholastic
divisions of theology into dogma and moral theology. Most of what he
had to say about the Christian life appeared in the second part as an
aspect of moral theology.[13] Secondly, there was a recovery of interest in
the mystical theology of Pseudo-Dionysius.

A combination of these two factors bore fruit in the writings produced
by the school of theology associated with the Canons Regular at St Victor in Paris, especially Hugh of St Victor and Richard of St Victor, which
exercised such an influence on subsequent directions in medieval spiritual
theory. Richard of St Victor, in particular, seemed equally at home with
speculation and contemplation and made a distinct spiritual theology his
speciality. He condensed his spiritual doctrine especially into two works,
Benjamin minor and *Benjamin major*, which describe the journey of the soul
towards contemplation. Although, like Hugh, he was influenced by Scripture, Richard and his disciples in the Victorine school increasingly opened
the way to an emphasis on the teachings of Pseudo-Dionysius as the yardstick by which to judge the spiritual and specifically mystical way of life.
Some commentators would now consider this emphasis to be unbalanced
and, in any case, to be based on a selective reading and understanding of
Pseudo-Dionysius, taken out of context. Richard had considerable subsequent influence, not least on St Bonaventure's *Journey of the Mind/Soul into
God*, and the fourteenth-century English text, *The Cloud of Unknowing*.[14]

A third factor was the growth of affective mysticism and subjective mystical experiences and the birth of a new literary genre based upon these.
The shift of emphasis in medieval mysticism away from a participation in
the objective mystery of Christ towards the experiences of *mystics*, as an
identifiable group, was clearly, in part, a result of the interest in Pseudo-
Dionysius. However, there seem to be other reasons for this development.
Some medievalists have noted the emergence, from about the twelfth century onwards, of a new religious sensitivity of which practical, experiential mysticism was merely the most marked expression. The major intellectual and cultural movement, known as the "twelfth-century Renaissance,"

which divides the early from the High Middle Ages also involved a shift of feeling and sensitivity which was at least as important as its new intellectual content. Peter Dinzelbacher, for example, writes of "the nearly synchronous discovery of divine and of human love as expressed in experienced mysticism on the one hand and courtly love on the other." In general terms, the twelfth century witnessed a striking increase in the cultivation of the theme of love both in religious circles and in secular culture. The degree to which the latter influenced religious writing or developments in mysticism cannot be settled definitively. Whatever the case, a preoccupation with the romantic love of men and women, its emotions and gentle expression, was encouraged by the poetry and song of troubadors, by the Arthurian myths and other romances. At the same time, love became a central theme for religious writers, particularly in the new Cistercian order. Many, like St Bernard, turned their attention to the Old Testament book, the Song of Songs, as a contemplative text which offered a ready expression for a spirituality of intimacy. The Song of Songs became a major source of imagery for mystics and writers of mystical theology.[15] Other medievalists have concentrated their attention on an increasing interest in the individual and in the realm of subjective feelings where individuality was most apparent. However, this needs careful qualification. The individual, in the modern sense of a unique person in isolation from group membership, was not discovered at this time. Yet there does seem to have been a new sense of *the self*, or of the inner mystery and "inner human landscape."[16] The development of spiritual guidance was another phenomenon associated both with the rise of affective mysticism and with the proliferation of new forms of Christian life, eremitical or community-orientated. Several important texts on the mystical way, such as *The Cloud of Unknowing*, were written (or purported to be) as treatises by directors for those under their guidance. Much of the writing which is known as the Rhineland school of mysticism arose from the developing ministry of guidance by Dominican friars among communities of contemplative women.[17]

A further factor, in the growth of interest in a distinct body of knowledge associated with the spiritual life, was the gradual systematization of meditation and prayer. Although people such as John of Fécamp and St Anselm, in the eleventh century, produced collections of meditations, these were still aimed at providing material for traditional monastic *lectio divina*, or free-flowing ruminative and prayerful reading of Scripture. There was no attempt to be methodical. It was really the Canons of St Victor in the twelfth century, already noted for their promotion of the influence of Pseudo-Dionysius, who tried to describe and formalize meditation, as one of the activities of prayer, with much greater precision than the monastic tradition up to that date. This gradually led to several ways of classifying meditation which became more and more systematic but which, as yet, did not include a *method* in the strict sense. However, it was as a result of these distinctions and schemes that there later developed the interest in methods of prayer and meditation.[18] Writings on methods of prayer rapidly increased, from the fourteenth century onwards, in the context of the movement of spiritual renewal in Germany and the Low Countries known as the *devotio moderna*. Its leading figure, Gerard Groote, composed a systematic treatise on "the four kinds of things to be meditated." Other representatives of this movement, such as Florent Radewijns, Gerard of Zutphen and Jan Mombaer, further developed the "science" of meditation and structured prayer, arranging it into groups of exercises day by day, week by week and month by month. This tradition of methodical prayer gave rise to a considerable literature over the next few centuries—not merely in the Roman Catholic Church but, after the Reformation, in some Reformed communities as well.[19]

In summary, the period from the twelfth century onwards in the West saw a process of development in the approach to the spiritual life which may be characterized as one of separation and division. There was, first of all, a division of spirituality from theology, of affectivity from knowledge. Secondly, there was a gradual limitation of interest to interiority or subjective spiritual experience. In other words, spirituality became separated from social praxis and ethics. And finally, although it has been touched upon only indirectly, there was a separation of spirituality from liturgy, the personal from the communal, expressed most graphically by a new attention to the structures of personal prayer and meditation. The practical context, of course, for the late-medieval believer was not to face God in isolation, but through communal experience, for example in the numerous religious confraternities. Through these divisions and separations, an interest developed in specific experiences and activities: prayer, contemplation and mysticism. This was increasingly linked to theories about spiritual progress and growth. And growth was conceived more and more in terms of ascent, whereby the active life was merely a preparation for the contemplative and was thus viewed as a "lower" way. By the end of the Middle Ages, the "spiritual life" had increasingly moved to a marginal position in relation to culture as a whole. A more internalized, personal religious practice assumed an existence of its own and therefore demanded a new, specialized language.

Towards a Systematic Spiritual Theology

To some extent the division between a "science" of the spiritual life and doctrine or ethics, begun in the later Middle Ages, was already well-entrenched by the sixteenth and seventeenth centuries. We only have to contrast the approaches of Thomas Aquinas and Bonaventure, on the one hand, and the Carmelites Teresa of Avila and John of the Cross, Ignatius of Loyola and Francis de Sales, on the other, to realise that, while the latter did not use the precise terms "ascetical" or "mystical" theology, they certainly showed clear signs of subscribing to a new discipline, separated from academic theology.

It was the intense interest in the life of Christian perfection that developed in the course of the seventeenth century, especially in France, that led to this becoming an object of detailed study in the eighteenth and nineteenth centuries. It appears that the Jesuit Giovanni Battista Scaramelli (1687–1752), with his *Direttorio ascetico* (1752) and *Direttorio mistico* (1754), was the first to establish the titles of "ascetical" and "mystical" theology in a way that subsequently became firmly established in Roman Catholic circles. During the following hundred and fifty years or so the vocabulary of "Christian perfection" stabilized and a field defined as "spiritual theology" became well-established. This was classically divided into ascetical theology, which dealt with the form and progress of the Christian life up to the beginnings of passive contemplation, and mystical theology which analysed further stages up to mystical union.

The approach of the manuals of ascetical and mystical theology was to seek to reduce the study of the Christian life to manageable categories, precise distinctions and reliable definitions. This accorded with the static approach to theology in general which applied during the period up to the Second Vatican Council. The method used was primarily deductive because divine revelation and rational knowledge were assumed to be its principal sources. Unless universal principles governed the study of the spiritual life it could not claim to be scientific, within a scientific theology. The classical works of this gerre tended to be divided between "principles" and "applications." Although defended as a distinct branch of theology, spiritual theology was in practice subordinate to dogmatic theology, from which it derived its principles, and was frequently thought of as a subdivision of moral theology. The latter was primarily concerned with what was "of obligation" for all Christians, and the subdivision of spiritual theology went on to discuss what was "additional."

There were, in fact, a large number of different manuals of spiritual theology in this period. Perhaps the most familiar were those written by A. A. Tanquerey (the most common textbook in Roman Catholic seminaries in the period before Vatican II), J. de Guibert and R. Garrigou-Lagrange.[20] There was a difference of opinion with regard to whether the spiritual life was fundamentally a unity or not. In the debate about the distinction or continuity between the "ordinary" (ascetical) way of Christian living and the "extraordinary" (mystical) way, Tanquerey and Garrigou-Lagrange may be taken as representatives of the two contrasting views. For Tanquerey there was a fundamental division between ordinary growth in the moral life and the extraordinary gifts of mystical prayer. Ordinary life passed through stages, in a gradual progression towards the fulfilment of the counsels of perfection, by means of observing the commandments and of ascetical practices. The mystical state was reserved for a very few and the study of it focused on special experiences and extraordinary phenomena. In contrast, Garrigou-Lagrange emphasized the unity and continuity of the Christian life in all its aspects. Mystical prayer was thus a goal to which all were called and for which they were offered God's grace. He agreed that mystical phenomena were extraordinary, but was not happy with the limitation of mysticism merely to these.[21]

The phrase "spiritual theology" came into vogue, for example with de Guibert, precisely to bypass this controversy about continuity or discontinuity. Such a term appeared more comprehensive than "ascetical" and "mystical" and yet it is questionable whether it does justice to what most people understand by spirituality today. Whether distinguished as ascetical and mystical theology or united as spiritual theology, the approach to the spiritual life which held the field up to the Second Vatican Council had several features with which a contemporary theology would be uncomfortable. Firstly, while not crudely dualistic, this approach often conceived of the supernatural life as distinguishable from, or grafted onto, the natural. As a consequence it was possible to identify specifically spiritual areas for exclusive treatment. Secondly, while differing on the classifications and distinctions in the spiritual life, spiritual theologians saw the journey towards perfection in terms of degrees and consecutive or separate stages. Thus, the ultimately mysterious nature of human experience and existence was reduced to detailed analysis according to predetermined general laws. Finally, there was a tendency to be individualistic, to ignore the social dimensions of Christian spiritual life and to reduce the ecclesial aspects of spirituality to participation in the sacraments. Although in general, this approach withered after Vatican II, there appeared as late as 1980, rather surprisingly, an English-language volume of spiritual theology on the old model which differed little from Tanquerey and which, apart from some references, appeared to ignore any developments in theology since the Vatican Council.[22]

A writer such as Louis Bouyer must be distinguished carefully from this kind of manual theology. His approach is illustrated mainly through *An Introduction to Spirituality*.[23] Bouyer differed substantially from the older manuals in recognizing developments in liturgical theology and biblical study, and in his impatience with a multitude of classifications and distinctions. He was also more open to the spirituality of traditions other than the Roman Catholic one. Although Bouyer's approach is now dated, it formed an important bridge between the constraints of a narrow neo-scholastic theological approach to spirituality and a more scriptural, liturgical and ecumenical approach after Vatican II.[24]

The Anglican Tradition

Many people would single out the Anglican tradition as different from the Churches of the Reformation as a whole because it continued to take an interest in the spiritual guidance of individuals. As a consequence, it produced a body of literature which sought to frame a pattern for the development of the Christian life. Much of this guidance was not systematic but was dispersed in sermons, collections of prayers or devotions and even poems. Equally, because the Anglican tradition was based so strongly on a collective liturgical life, inspired by the Book of Common Prayer (which itself may be considered a work of "spiritual guidance"), many of the writings which dealt explicitly with the spiritual life were, in effect, companions to the Prayer Book and were strongly liturgical and sacramental in flavour. Until the twentieth century, it seems fair to say, there was no real attempt to compile a coherent spiritual theology which precisely paralleled the ascetical-mystical theology of the Roman Catholic tradition. However, from the seventeenth century through to the twentieth, there were various attempts to provide guidance in the life of prayer or Christian virtues. One of the most notable aspects of this Anglican approach to the spiritual life was that it was frequently linked to moral theology.

There is some evidence for the continued popularity among Anglicans of such late medieval English spiritual treatises as Walter Hilton's *Ladder of Perfection* which was reprinted several times in the seventeenth century. In the seventeenth century, a number of books appeared on meditation or on practical rules for prayer, such as Bishop Hall's *The Arte of Divine Meditation*. There were also pastoral treatises on the Christian life as a whole, such as Bishop Bayley's *The Practice of Piety: Directing the Christian how to Walk that he may Please God*, Jeremy Taylor's highly influential *Rules and Exercise of Holy Living*, and the anonymous *Whole Duty of Man* with its emphasis on proper conduct and "the plain way of holiness." Importantly, there were also attempts to provide some guidance for clergy in the art of spiritual direction. George Herbert, in his treatise on the priestly life, *The Country Parson*, included some hints in chapters 15 and 34, but these are not much developed. A major work in this area was Gilbert Burret's *Discourse on Pastoral Care* and Jeremy Taylor also addressed the practicalities of spiritual direction in *Doctor Dubitantium*.

Of the eighteenth-century works, undoubtedly the best known is William Law's *A Serious Call to a Devout and Holy Life*, a guide to the counsels of perfection addressed to all "serious" Christians. The nineteenth century continued to see new treatises on the life of prayer and virtue such as *A Treatise on Prayer* by the Evangelical, Edward Bickersteth, which included a summary theology of prayer. Strangely perhaps, the Tractarians did not on the whole write spiritual treatises but frequently confined themselves to translating contemporary French Roman Catholic works on confession. Arguably, the Tractarians tended not to distinguish their treatment of a theology of the Christian life from other theological considerations such as the liturgy, the sacraments and the nature of the Church.

It was only in the 1930s that the beginnings of a school of spiritual theology emerged with the work of F. P. Harton. In his *The Elements of the Spiritual Life*, Harton provided Anglicans with a structured treatise similar in some respects to contemporary Roman Catholic ascetical theology, though with a somewhat greater emphasis on liturgy and sacraments and a less legalistic approach. This development corresponds to a period when Anglo-Catholicism, once barely tolerated, was becoming a central force within the Church of England and when a revival of Thomism offered an attractive new theological ground plan. At much the same time there appeared the authoritative classic by Evelyn Underhill, *Mysticism*, and Bede Frost's *The Art of Mental Prayer*. Finally, in the 1950s and 1960s, Martin Thornton attempted a properly Anglican approach to the theory of spirituality with his *Pastoral Theology, Christian Proficiency* and *English Spirituality*. More recently, it seems fair to say, the Anglican contribution to the theory of the spiritual life has, like its Roman Catholic counterpart, blended into a more ecumenical, multi-disciplinary approach to spirituality.[25]

The Eastern Orthodox Tradition

The Eastern Orthodox tradition, unlike western Christianity in the Middle Ages, did not suffer a separation between theology and spirituality or mysticism. In other words, when the Eastern tradition uses the phrase "mystical theology," it does not mean a division of practical theology as in the West, but something which, on the patristic model, closely relates the Christian moral life and experience of God with doctrine. Because the subjective spiritual experience of individuals is comparatively hidden in eastern Christianity, it possesses very few autobiographical accounts of the interior life in contrast to the development of a certain spiritual individualism or interest in subjective experience in the West.

The classical treatment of Eastern mystical theology by Vladimir Lossky defines it as a spirituality which expresses a doctrinal attitude. On one level, all theology is mystical in that its aim is to show forth the divine mystery. There is therefore no opposition between theology and a mysticism that is something inaccessible to understanding or lived rather than known. Mysticism and theology support and complete each other. On the one hand, mystical experience, while personal, is nevertheless the working out of a common faith. Theology, on the other hand, is an articulation of something which can be experienced by everyone. Theology could not be merely a rational deduction from revealed premises because *theologia* was inseparable from *theoria* or contemplation. Rather, theology is a vision experienced by saints whose authenticity was checked against the witness of Scripture and tradition. True theologians were those who saw and experienced the content of their theology.[26]

From Spiritual Theology to Spirituality

It was suggested at the beginning of this chapter that there has been a major shift in western theology towards a more serious reflection on human experience in its cultural particularity and therefore pluriformity. This in turn provoked a movement away from a static approach to the Christian life, embodied in an analytical and abstract spiritual theology, and towards a more dynamic and inclusive concept, namely "spirituality." I would also add that this new concept has gained considerable ecumenical acceptance and so spirituality now tends to be eclectic in its approach as it seeks to draw upon the riches of a shared Christian heritage rather than to limit itself to a sectarian understanding of "life in the Spirit." Spirituality, in other words, is a far better expression of Catholicity than any previous spiritual theology.

The differences between the spirituality that has emerged in the last twenty years within western Christianity and the older spiritual theology may therefore usefully be summarized by four central characteristics. Firstly it is not exclusive—certainly not associated exclusively with any one Christian tradition, nor even necessarily with Christianity as a whole. Secondly, while if anything more, rather than less, associated with solid theology than in the recent past, it is not simply the prescriptive application of absolute or dogmatic principles to life. Thirdly, it does not so much concern itself with defining perfection as with surveying the complex mystery of human growth in the context of a living relationship with the Absolute. Finally, it is not limited to a concern with the interior life but seeks an integration of all aspects of human life and experience.

The last characteristic underlines the importance of issues of life-style within Christian spirituality. While not pointing to a return to the categories of scholastic theology, this has stimulated some reflection on the relationship between spirituality and ethics or moral theology. Moral theology has moved away from a concern primarily with the quality of actions to a much greater interest in people's dispositions of character. In other words, there has been a shift from human actions to human agent and the beginnings, at least, of an awareness of the basic unity of the moral and spiritual life. Many would now consider that the joint task of spirituality and contemporary moral theology is to explore renewed definitions of "virtue" (that is, what enables a person to become truly human within a commitment to Christ and the action of grace) and "character" (or what we should *be* if we are to become fully human persons).[27]

These changes in perspective are at the heart of questions of definition. The broader the perspective, the greater the issue of coherence and the danger of subsuming spirituality into an interest in religion in general.[28] Many contemporary writers would explicitly reject the limitation of spirituality to interiority. Rather, "the spiritual life is the life of the whole person directed towards God."[29] The British theologian Rowan Williams rejects the notion that spirituality is merely the science of interpreting exceptional private experiences and suggests that "it must now touch every area of human experience, the public and social, the painful, negative, even pathological byways of the mind, the moral and relational world."[30] Contemporary theorists accept that once we cease to drive a wedge between sacred activities and the secular, or between the spiritual dimension of human existence and materiality, the issues become more complex. However, whatever the problems, contemporary spirituality is characterized more by an attempt to integrate human and religious values than by an exclusive interest in the component parts of "spiritual" growth such as stages of prayer.

A notable liberation of women's spiritual experience has been associated with the shift towards a more human, inclusive and experiential approach to spirituality. This is important not only for women but ultimately for Christian spirituality as a whole. A disembodied spirituality which had problems not only with the body and material reality but with the feminine in particular (that most potent symbol of embodiment, not to say of sexuality), was firmly rooted in theological concepts. These, as we have seen, were dogmatic and thus free from emotion, objective, rational and logical in contrast to the muddy waters of personal experience. To say that women's religious experience was caged within a male theology is more than to note that theological teaching was for so long dominated by men. Although, theoretically, theology was a priori, in practice the categories and tone expressed a male mentality.

The result was a spirituality whose values included the individual and separateness and the quest for achievement, self-determination associ-

ated with dominance, control and conquest—of the self and of the world.
Such values inevitably led, it seems to me, to a hierarchical conception
of the human and spiritual life. Consequently the language of traditional
spiritual theology tended to prefer images of ladders of perfection, the
language of "stages" and detachment achieved by rules and formulae. The
end in view was undivided love of God which, in fact, implied being
divided from large parts of the self and separated from created reality.

In contrast, the liberation of women's experience has meant the rein-
forcement of other values such as subjectivity, feelings, the relational,
nurture, reverence, compassion, the sacredness of all life and the earth.
Although the shift in contemporary spirituality is not simply the result
of this liberation (indeed is, to a degree, a precondition of it) there is no
doubt that the explicit contribution of women to the debate about spirituality has offered a great deal to the whole field.[31]

For some, the emphasis on experience as the starting point for spirituality is associated with what is perceived as a tendency to define it in generic
terms, that is, "spirituality as such" or "in general." In practice, spiritualities
are specific and have particular religious or doctrinal referrents. This is
what makes it possible to sift the authentic from the inauthentic in spirituality. Every religious tradition has tests for the authenticity of spiritual
experience based not only on human considerations but also on the revelation or foundational beliefs of the tradition. Without specific points of
reference, it is difficult to say precisely what is spirituality and what is not,
and what is appropriate or not. Criticisms of generic definitions of spirituality are undoubtedly valid because spirituality is unavoidably conditioned by historical and religious contexts and embodies thematically
explicit commitments and distinctive symbols—in other words, the language of a tradition. However, it is not clear that the vagueness of some
contemporary definitions in Christian circles (for example, "one typical
way of handling the human condition" or "becoming a person in the fullest
sense") indicates more than a recognition that there are people who live
consciously within a horizon of absolute value, or who seek genuine self-
transcendence, but who do not describe this in specifically Christian terms
or even within religious language as traditionally conceived.[32]

Certainly, when it comes to defining contemporary Christian spirituality, the emphasis on the experiential does not in practice exclude
specific reference to tradition. Even if there is common ground between
different faith traditions regarding the meaning of spirituality, that is,
the development of the human capacity for self-transcendence in relation to the Absolute (however this is named), nevertheless the specifically Christian approach is increasingly related to theological themes
rather than otherwise. While spirituality, in Christian terms, is not about

some other *kind* of life but about *the whole of human life at depth,* our understanding of what this might mean cannot avoid questions posed specifically by the Christian tradition of revelation about the nature of God, human nature and the relationship between the two. Spirituality is understood to include not merely the techniques of prayer but, more broadly, a conscious relationship with God, in Jesus Christ, through the indwelling of the Spirit and in the context of the community of believers. Spirituality is, therefore, concerned with the conjunction of theology, prayer and practical Christianity. A central feature is that spirituality derives its identity from the Christian belief that as human beings we are capable of entering into a relationship with God who is both transcendent and, at the same time, indwelling in the heart of all created things. This relationship is lived out, not in isolation, but in a community of believers that is brought into being by commitment to Christ and sustained by the active presence of the Spirit of God in each and in the community as a whole. In Christian terms, the self-transcendence involved in referring life to something beyond is a gift of the Spirit of God which establishes a life-giving relationship with God, in Christ, within a believing community. In other words, contemporary Christian spirituality is explicitly Trinitarian, Christological, and ecclesial.[33]

Notes

1. See Edward Kinerk, "Towards a Method for the Study of Spirituality," *Review for Religious* 40.1 (1981): 3.

2. See Avery Dulles, *Models of the Church* (Dublin: Gill and Macmillan, 1974), 86.

3. For surveys of the history of the word, see Walter Principe, "Towards Defining Spirituality," *Studies in Religion/Sciences Religieuses* 12.2 (1983): 130–35; Sandra Schneiders, "Theology and Spirituality: Strangers, Rivals or Partners?" *Horizons* 13.2 (1986): 257–60; and "Spirituality in the Academy," *Theological Studies* (December 1989): 680–84; Jon Alexander, "What Do Recent Writers Mean by Spirituality?" *Spirituality Today* 32 (1980): 247–56; Jean Leclercq, introduction to *The Spirituality of Western Christendom,* ed. E. Rozanne Elder, Cistercian Studies 30 (Kalamazoo, 1976).

4. For a good summary of the issues, see Thomas Deidun, "Beyond Dualims: Paul on Sex, *Sarx* and *Soma,*" *The Way* (July 1988): 195–205.

5. See Josef Sudbrack, "Spirituality," in *Encyclopedia of Theology: A Concise Sacramentum Mundi,* ed. Karl Rahner (London, 1975); Gordon Wakefield, ed., *A Dictionary of Christian Spirituality* (London, 1983); Cheslyn Jones, Geoffrey Wainwright, and Edward Yarnold, eds., *The Study of Spirituality* (London and New York, 1986).

6. See Andrew Louth, *The Origins of the Christian Mystical Tradition* (Oxford, 1981), xi (introduction).

7. See Louth, ibid., for a general background to the origins of the Christian mystical tradition in the patristic period.

8. For a development of this point see, Louis Bouyer, "Mysticism—an Essay on the History of the Word," in *Understanding Mysticism,* ed. Richard Woods (London, 1981), 52–53.

9. For a brief overview of the meaning of patristic theology, see J. Daniélou, "Patristic Literature," in *The Pelican Guide to Modern Theology*, vol. 2, ed. J. Daniélou, A. H. Couratin, and John Kent (Harmondsworth, 1971), 30–32. For a survey of the main lines of patristic spirituality, see Charles Kannengeisser, "The Spiritual Message of the Great Fathers," in *Christian Spirituality: Origins to the Twelfth Century*, ed. Bernard McGinn and John Meyendorff (London and New York, 1986), 61–88. A good introduction to the theology of Pseudo-Dionysius is provided by Paul Rorem, "The Uplifting Spirituality of Pseudo-Dionysius," in *Christian Spirituality*, ed. McGinn and Meyendorff, 132–51. Bouyer, "Mysticism," offers a corrective to an unbalanced approach to Dionysian mysticism.

10. For some illuminating suggestions concerning the origins of an interest in subjective mystical experiences, see Peter Dinzelbacher, "The Beginnings of Mysticism Experienced in Twelfth-Century England," in *The Medieval Mystical Tradition in England*, ed. Marion Glasscoe, Exeter Symposium 4 (Woodbridge, Suffolk, 1987).

11. The classic analysis of monastic theology is Jean Leclercq, *The Love of Learning and the Desire for God* (ET, London, 1978), chap. 9. For comparisons between this and the "new" scholastic method, see E. Rozanne Elder, ed., *From Cloister to Classroom: Monastic and Scholastic Approaches to Truth*, Cistercian Studies 90 (Kalamazoo, 1986), especially essays by Thomas Renna, Michael Strasser, Jean Leclercq, and Luke Anderson.

12. A useful summary of writings associated with the new religious orders is in Jean Leclercq, "The New Orders" (chap. 6) and "The School of Citeaux" (chap. 8), in *A History of Christian Spirituality*, ed. Louis Bouyer et al., vol. 2, *The Spirituality of the Middle Ages* (ET, London, 1968). See also John Sommerfeldt, "Bernard of Clairvaux: The Mystic and Society"; E. Rozanne Elder, "William of St Thierry: Rational and Affective Spirituality"; and Keith Egan, "Guigo II: The Theology of the Contemplative Life," in *The Spirituality of Western Christendom*, ed. Elder.

13. For a recent edition of the *Summa*, with English translation, see that published by Eyre & Spottiswoode/McGraw-Hill from 1963 onwards.

14. On the Victorine school and its influence, see François Vandenbroucke, "The Schoolmen of the Twelfth Century," in *The Spirituality of the Middle Ages*, ed. Bouyer, chap. 1; and Grover A. Zinn, "The Regular Canons" in *Christian Spirituality*, ed. McGinn, 218–27. *Benjamin Major* and *Benjamin Minor* were commonly referred to in the medieval period as *The Mystical Ark* and *The Twelve Patriarchs* respectively. Recent English translations have appeared in the volume on Richard of St. Victor, edited by Grover Zinn, in the series The Classics of Western Spirituality (London/New York, 1979).

15. Dinzelbacher, "The Beginnings of Mysticism," 126. On the popularity of the Song of Songs in monastic, and, particularly, Cistercian circles and on the importance of the imagery of the book in contemplative and mystical works, see Jean Leclercq, *The Love of Learning and the Desire for God* (New York, 1974; London, 1978), 106–9; and Caroline Walker Bynum, *Jesus as Mother: Studies in the Spirituality of the High Middle Ages* (Berkeley, 1982), chap. 4. For a brief sketch of the cultivation of the theme of love in both secular and religious circles in the twelfth century, see the preface by Ewert Cousins in *Bernard of Clairvaux: Selected Works*, ed. G. R. Evans (New Jersey, 1987), 7–8. For a selection of sermons on the Song of Songs by St. Bernard, see the same volume, 209–78.

16. See Bynum's illuminating survey of this question in *Jesus as Mother*, chap. 3, "Did the Twelfth Century Discover the Individual?" 82–109. She also has many fresh insights on mysticism in chap. 5, "Women Mystics in the Thirteenth Century," 170–262. A good general collection of essays on mysticism would be Paul Szarmach, ed., *An Introduction to the Medieval Mystics of Europe* (New York, 1984); and see also Alois Maria Haas's chapter, "Schools of Late Medieval Mysticism," in *Christian Spirituality: High Middle Ages and Reformation*, ed. Jill Raitt et al., 140–75.

17. See Haas, 143–55.

18. See Jean Leclercq, "Prayer and Contemplation: 2, Western," in *Christian Spirituality*, ed. McGinn, 427ff. For the development of an approach to imaginative prayer using Scripture, see Ewert Cousins, "The Humanity and Passion of Christ," in *Christian Spirituality*, ed. Raitt, 375–91.

19. For two modern overviews of the *devotio moderna* and its approach to prayer, see Otto Gründler, "Devotio Moderna," in *Christian Spirituality*, ed. Raitt, 176–93; and John Van Engen, ed., *Devotio Moderna: Basic Writings* (New York, 1989).

20. A. A. Tanquerey, *The Spiritual Life* (ET, Tournai, 1930); J. de Guibert, *The Theology of the Spiritual Life* (ET, London, 1954); R. Garrigou-Lagrange, *Christian Perfection and Contemplation* (ET, St. Louis, 1937).

21. Tanquerey, 5–6; Garrigou-Lagrange, 27–43.

22. J. Aumann, *Spiritual Theology* (London, 1980).

23. Louis Bouyer, *An Introduction to Spirituality* (ET, New York, 1961).

24. For a survey of developments in spiritual theology from the High Middle Ages to the immediate aftermath of Vatican II, see Eugene Megyer, "Spiritual Theology Today," *The Way* (January 1981): 55–67.

25. For references and general background, see John Moorman, *The Anglican Spiritual Tradition*, (London, 1983); Kenneth Leech, *Soul Friend* (London, 1977), chap. 3; and the appropriate sections in Jones, *Study of Spirituality*. For background on the advance of Anglo-Catholicism, see Adrian Hastings, *A History of English Christianity, 1920–1985* (London, 1986), chap. 11.

26. For summaries of the nature of "mystical theology" in the Eastern tradition, see Vladimir Lossky, *The Mystical Theology of the Eastern Church* (ET, London, 1973), chap. 1; John Meyendorff, *Byzantine Theology* (London, 1975), introduction.

27. For a brief summary of the overlap between ethics and spirituality and the issues facing them, see the review essay by James A. O'Donohoe, "A Return to Virtue," *Church* (spring 1987): 48–54.

28. See comments on this problem in Principe, "Towards Defining Spirituality," 137–41.

29. See Leech, *Soul Friend*, 34.

30. Rowan Williams, *The Wound of Knowledge* (London, 1979), 2.

31. See, for example, Margaret Brennan, "Women and Theology: Singing of God in an Alien Land," *The Way Supplement* 53 (summer 1985): 93–103.

32. For critical surveys of contemporary attempts to define spirituality, see Principe, "Towards Defining Spirituality"; Alexander, "What Do Writers Mean by Spirituality?" 247–56; Sandra Schneiders, "Theology and Spirituality," 253–74; and idem, "Spirituality in the Academy," 687–97.

33. For a useful attempt to define the Christian understanding of spirituality in contemporary terms, see Joann Wolski Conn, *Spirituality and Personal Maturity* (New York, 1989), chap. 1.

Toward Defining Spirituality

Walter Principe

T wenty-two years ago the Italian historian Gustavo Vinay expressed the malaise felt by his fellow historians and to some extent by himself over the term "spirituality." "Che cosa è dunque questa 'spiritualità'?" he and they asked. His own contribution was to pinpoint some problems for historians using the term in their research, give his own provisional working definition of it, and invite others to discuss the problem.[1] One response to his invitation was Jean Leclercq's article on the history of the word *spiritualitas*, a study that will be used to supplement research already completed before discovery of the article.[2]

At about the same time Louis Bouyer's *Introduction à la vie spirituelle* and Jean Daniélou's review of it, together with Bouyer's spirited reply, renewed discussion of the question whether there is one Christian spirituality or whether there are many Christian spiritualities.[3] In 1965 and 1966 Hans Urs von Balthasar, François Vandenbroucke and Josef Sudbrack addressed this and related questions.[4] In 1974 B. Fraling expressed his astonishment that the ninth volume of the *Lexikon für Theologie und Kirche* (1964) contained no article on "Spiritualität" but simply referred the reader to the article on "Frömmigkeit."[5]

While these discussions were taking place, many other authors seemed to have little difficulty understanding or at least using the term. The card catalogue of my university's library under the head-

This essay first appeared in *Studies in Religion/Sciences religieuses* 12.2 (1983): 127–41. Used by permission.

ing "spirituality" shows that from the 1950s on the term "spirituality" began to be and increasingly became a more popular word than terms such as "spiritual teaching," "spiritual life," "devout life," "interior life," or "piety" that had been used earlier.

Studies began to appear on the spirituality of many individuals, ranging from Chrétien de Troyes, Margaret of Hungary, Ignatius of Loyola and John Calvin through Saint-Cyran, Bossuet and Rosmini to von Hügel, Bergson, Blondel, and Teilhard de Chardin.[6] Biblical spirituality as a whole or of particular sections of the Bible was also presented.[7] The spirituality of different periods of history came under review as well as the spirituality of various Christian groups.[8] The term was extended to studies of non-Christian groups: there exists, for example, a collection entitled "Spiritualités vivantes" with subsections on Islamic, Hindu, and Buddhist "spiritualité."[9]

Monographs have appeared on the spirituality of the liturgy, the sacraments, baptism, and the Mass,[10] and on spirituality of the family, the laity, and of all Christians in relation to secularity.[11] A spirituality for missions was developed as well as a spirituality of the land for Christian farmers.[12] The spirituality of the human voice has been examined, and even the spirituality of matter.[13] The 1960s saw a book entitled *Offbeat Spirituality* whereas a book called *On the Run* had as its subtitle *Spirituality for the Seventies*.[14] Reaching its forty-eighth volume in 1972, the *Revue d'ascétique et de mystique* changed its name to *Revue d'histoire de la spiritualité*, and a periodical that began in 1949 as *Cross and Crown* chose *Spirituality Today* for its new title in 1977.[15]

In all this one can sense a certain fluidity, not to say vagueness, in the use of the term.[16] To sharpen the notion of spirituality, it will be useful briefly to survey the history of the term from its beginnings and to see the developments in its use that took place.

History of the Use of the Term

The Latin term *spiritualitas*, which stands behind the different vernacular cognates, is an abstract word derived from the noun *spiritus* and the adjective *spiritalis* or *spiritualis*. In Latin translations of Pauline letters one finds *spiritus* and *spiritualis* as translations of *pneuma* and *pneumatikos* respectively. In Pauline theology *pneuma* or *spiritus* are set over against *sarx* or *caro*—not, it should be noted, in opposition to *soma* or *corpus*—and *pneumatikos* or *spiritualis* are contrasted with *sarkikos* or *carnalis* and not with *somatikos* or *corporalis*.[17] For Paul, the "spirit" within the human person is all that is ordered, led, or influenced by the *Pneuma Theou* or *Spiritus Dei*, whereas *sarx* or *caro* or "flesh" is everything in a person that is opposed to this influence of the Spirit of God. Thus *caro* or "flesh" could be the person's mind or will or heart as much as or even more than the physical flesh or the body if the mind, will, or heart resist the influence of the Spirit. For Paul the opposition is not between the incorporeal or nonmaterial and the corporeal or material, but between two ways of life. The "spiritual" person (*pneumatikos, spiritualis*) is one whose life is guided by the Spirit of God; the "carnal" person (*sarkikos, carnalis*) is one whose life is opposed to the working and guidance of the Spirit of God.[18]

Thus far, the abstract word *spiritualitas* has not been found earlier than the first part of the fifth century when an anonymous author, in a letter formerly ascribed to Jerome and then to Faustus of Riez, urges the person addressed: "Age ut in spiritualitate proficias," that is, "So act as to advance in spirituality."[19] The context makes it clear that the author is urging a life according to the Spirit of God. Thus the Pauline sense of *spiritus* and *spiritualis* stands behind this first appearance of the word.[20]

This general Pauline meaning of *spiritualitas* is found in Dionysius Exiguus' translation of Gregory of Nyssa, in Avitus (bishop from 490 to 518), and in authors from the ninth to the thirteenth century.[21] A rare ninth-century use of *spiritualitas* by Candidus, probably a monk of Fulda, foreshadows a new meaning that would be given the word in the twelfth century and that would become increasingly important in later centuries. By opposing *spiritualitas* to *corporalitas* or *materialitas*, this new use of the word changed its Pauline moral sense to an entitative-psychological sense.[22] In this shift one can foresee the confusion of spirituality with disdain for the body and matter that was to mark many later movements dealing with spiritual life.[23]

This new use was introduced with evident hesitation by Gilbert of Poitiers in the twelfth century; it is also found in Gundissalinus and Gerard of Cremona, and then in many thirteenth-century authors. At the same time the earlier meaning endures, especially in theologians.[24] In Roberto Busa's computerized concordance of Thomas Aquinas' writings the word *spiritualitas* occurs about seventy times (by comparison with the word *spiritualis*, which is found some five thousand times). In the majority of Thomas' texts *spiritualitas* is related to the Pauline notion of life according to the Holy Spirit or life according to what is highest in the human person; in a good number of texts, however, it is set in opposition to corporeity or to matter.[25]

In the meantime the word took on another nuance when it came to be used of ecclesiastical jurisdiction or of persons exercising such jurisdiction: they were the *spiritualitas* or "lords spiritual" as opposed to the *temporalitas* or "lords temporal" who exercised civil jurisdiction.[26] From this came a further development whereby *spiritualitas* designated ecclesiastical property by contrast with the property of king or prince, designated as *tempo-ralitas*.[27] Usage thus moved rather far from the original Pauline background!

In the mediaeval vernacular the Latin word *spiritualitas* gave rise to such forms as *esperitalité, espiritualité, espirituauté,* and *espérituaulté* in French and *spiritualty* or *spirituality* in English.[28] In both languages these words were first used for the spiritual-religious realm or for ecclesiastical persons or properties;[29] only in the seventeenth century did the philosophical senses sometimes seen in twelfth- or thirteenth-century Latin appear in French and English cognates.[30] Descartes, for example, speaks of "la spiritualité de l'âme" by contrast with the extension of matter; Spenser in his *Logick* (1628) opposes "spiritualitie called life" to "a corporall substance"; in 1644 Digby speaks of "the heat and spirituality of the blood."[31]

In seventeenth-century France "spiritualité" seems to have been used more frequently than before in its religious sense of the devout life; however, it was also used pejoratively by authors such as Bossuet, Saint-Simon, and Voltaire to attack "la nouvelle spiritualité" of Madame Guyon and Fénelon.[32] Voltaire found the word both novel and distasteful when he says of Madame Guyon: "Devenue veuve dans une assez grande jeunesse, avec du bien, de la beauté et un esprit fait pour le monde, elle s'entêta de ce qu'on appelle la spiritualité."[33]

This pejorative sense of the word may have accounted for its relatively infrequent use in the later eighteenth and the nineteenth centuries. Littré, it is true, gives an example from Chateaubriand's *Génie du christianisme* (1802),[34] and Henri Brémond quotes Abbé Michel Houssaye's study of Bérulle (1875) in which Houssaye says of Oratorian and Jesuit spiritualities: "De là deux écoles de spiritualité, l'une plus théologique que morale."[35] But it was only in the earlier decades of this century that "spiritualité" began to be used rather frequently in France. Auguste Saudreau had already used it in the extended title of his *La vie d'union à Dieu* (1900), but it was more likely his popular *Manuel de spiritualité* (1916) together with Pierre Pourrat's four-volume *La spiritualité catholique* (1918–1928) that gave the term *droit de cité* among French authors.[36] We have already mentioned the use of the term in the influential *Revue d'ascétique et de mystique* beginning in 1920.[37] In 1927 a study by René Daeschler used it in his *La spiritualité de Bourdaloue,* and in 1932 the *Dictionnaire de spiritualité ascétique* began publication, while in 1943 the Institut Catholique de Paris established a chair in "Histoire de la spiritualité," whose inauguration was marked by a brilliant lecture on the subject given by Étienne Gilson.[38]

There followed the numerous studies of spirituality already mentioned. All these usages undoubtedly influenced Paul Robert to include in his *Dictionnaire . . . de la langue française* (1964) these new definitions: "l'ensemble des croyances, des exercises qui concernent la vie de l'âme," a definition that links spirituality with the soul in evident opposition to the body, and "ensemble des principes qui règlent la vie spirituelle d'une personne, d'un groupe," of which an example is "la spiritualité de saint François."[39] This last meaning is noteworthy because it reflects the growth of historical studies of "spirituality" or of "spiritualities."

In English the religious or devotional sense of "spirituality" continued into the nineteenth century but seems to have gradually become archaic and to be less frequently used.[40] In the later nineteenth and early twentieth centuries, however, a special interest by some in modern Hinduism and the resulting exchange between such Hindus as Swami Vivekananda (1862–1902), Sister Nivedita (Margaret Elizabeth Noble) (1867–1911), Annie Besant (1873–1933), and others with persons of Western culture saw the frequent use of "spirituality" to designate what was considered to be the superiority of Indian religion to the so-called Western "materialism."[41]

This usage, however, remained within a relatively small if important group of students and adepts of religion and piety, so that the word had lost currency among the generality of English-speaking persons. Thus when some of my colleagues at Toronto heard that I was giving a course in the history of spirituality, they asked the same question as that raised by Vinay and his colleagues: "What is this 'spirituality'?" It seems that, except within the Indian-Western cultural-religious milieu and interchange, the revived use of the term in English has been mainly the result of translation into English of French studies using the word "spiritualité." The first English title I have been able to find using the term is the translation in 1922 of the first volume of Pierre Pourrat's work; in English it bore the title *Christian Spirituality*.[42]

Gradually—still under French influence, it seems—the word came to be applied more and more to all kinds of particular spiritualities. But whereas Robert's dictionary recognized in 1964 the newer general meaning of *spiritualité* and its application to a particular person or group, no English dictionary has been found that gives anything more than "the quality or condition of being spiritual; attachment to or regard for things of the spirit as opposed to material and worldly interests."[43] Nor do either the French or English dictionaries give the even more recent use of "spirituality" to designate a branch of study within religious studies, theology, and history of religion. Yet one now finds many courses in spirituality or history of spirituality, and even institutes or faculties specializing in the study of spirituality *tout court*.

Toward a Definition of Spirituality

A search for a definition of spirituality should distinguish three different if related levels.[44] The first is the *real* or *existential* level. This is the quality—the lived quality—of a person. It is the way some person understood and lived, within his or her historical context, a chosen religious ideal in sensitivity to the realm of the spirit or the transcendent. For Christians such a life would be one influenced, as Paul taught, by the Holy Spirit or Spirit of God incorporating the person into Jesus Christ as Head, through whom he or she has access to the Father in a life of faith, hope, love, and service. A formulation of this level of spirituality might be the following: spirituality is life in the Spirit as brothers and sisters of Jesus Christ and daughters and sons of the Father. Such an explicit link of spirituality with the Holy Spirit was rather uncommon among writers first using the term in this century but it has come to the fore owing to greater attention to studies of Pauline theology.

Can a definition of spirituality be formulated that could be applied more universally, that is, to the lived spiritual life and reality of persons who are not Christians? Jean Leclercq expressed hesitation about this, but Hans Urs von Balthasar and others see no problem so long as one is conscious of what one is dealing with.[45] The following might be suggested as such a universally applicable definition of spirituality: the way in which a person understands and lives within his or her historical context that aspect of his or her religion, philosophy or ethic that is viewed as the loftiest, the noblest, the most calculated to lead to the fullness of the ideal or perfection being sought.[46]

The second level of spirituality is the *formulation of a teaching about the lived reality,* often under the influence of some outstanding spiritual person.[47] Sometimes the way of life and example of such a person becomes a pattern for others; sometimes it is the writings of a person judged to be gifted in providing insight or guidance that furnishes the doctrine. Here history has seen the rise of many traditions or schools of spirituality by reason of differing teachings or emphases in teachings. Such doctrines have been worked out either in more formal theological presentations or more often in practical works designed for practical instruction of those interested in spiritual growth.

A third level of spirituality is the *study* by scholars of the first and especially of the second levels of spirituality. Here spirituality has become a discipline using the methods and resources of several other branches of knowledge. Within such study of Christian spirituality a special question has arisen. Is there not for Christians only one spirituality, that of the gospel lived after the pattern of Christ's own life, death, and resurrection? If some have held this, students of the history of spirituality have countered that in fact there have been many variations in the way Christians have interpreted and lived the gospel. They have identified schools or traditions of spirituality labelled Pauline, Johannine, Oriental, Western, Benedictine, Franciscan, Dominican, Jesuit, lay, clerical, Lutheran,

Calvinist, Anglican, etc., each of which seeks to live the gospel but stresses different aspects or groups of components while leaving others in a less prominent position.[48] The study of these varieties is especially found in the history of spirituality, whether one proceeds as a historian of theology or uses the methods of religious studies.[49]

The Breadth of Spirituality

On this third level of spirituality as the study of various doctrines or traditions (second level) or as the analysis of different practices and examples (first level), the question arises as to what should be included in such study and analysis. Here there is a marked difference of opinion, depending on how each scholar understands "spirituality."

A frequent tendency has been to concentrate on an examination of a person's or group's practice and teaching about virtues and vices, about prayer, about religious and mystical experiences, about laws of growth or barriers to growth in life in the Spirit. This tendency is in part a legacy of the separation first of moral theology or Christian ethics from systematic or dogmatic theology (to use later terms) and then of spiritual, ascetical, and mystical theology from all of these but especially from moral theology or Christian ethics; this separation was already evident in the fourteenth century.[50] Pourrat's study reveals such a narrow concentration, at least in its introduction; Bouyer notes that he did sometimes range farther afield into dogma, moral doctrine, and psychology.[51] The earlier volumes of the *Dictionnaire de spiritualité* also showed this narrow concentration, whereas its later volumes have often but not always broadened their view.

In his introduction to the first volume of the *Histoire de la spiritualité chrétienne* Louis Bouyer sought a wider perspective. He insisted that spirituality, and so the history of spirituality, must take account of the link between the objects of faith and the reactions aroused by these objects in the religious consciousness. Thus the belief-systems or theologies implied in any spirituality must, he held, be at least referred to. Yet for him spirituality and its study only presupposes these elements; it concentrates especially on the results they produce in the religious consciousness and stresses acts immediately related to God.[52]

Bouyer's statement was valuable for broadening the implications of spirituality, but his refusal to include this broader field in the study of spirituality seems to be still too narrow an approach. One may ask whether any person's or group's spirituality—or the dynamics and causes of that spirituality—can be grasped without understanding that person or group in their total context. Having advocated such a broader approach for some time, this author was happy to find a similar view expressed by André Vauchez in his *La spiritualité du moyen âge occidental* and by Jean Leclercq in a recent essay.[53]

If this broader view of spirituality is correct, the total context has to be studied. The total context, first, of the person's or tradition's theological and religious attitudes. In every person's way of living by the Spirit or teaching about it many theological and religious attitudes are involved even if only implicitly. To bring these out it has proved useful to lead students to ask many questions about each author, person or school they study—questions about the view of God expressed or implied, about the view of the human person's relationship to God and God's relationship to the person, about the role seen for Christ and the Spirit if a Christian doctrine is being examined. Other leading questions suggested are: What view of anthropology is expressed or implied? What role is given to liturgy and sacraments? What proportionate role is assigned to knowledge and to love? How are evil and sin thought of? What is said or implied about the interaction of nature and grace? What role is assigned to the community, to work, to cultural activities, to recreation? All these are meant to illumine the theological and religious implications of any doctrine or person's life.

The total context, secondly, of psychological, historical, anthropological, sociological, philosophical, linguistic, and other influences: these also must be considered because in some way each fashions the person's or the tradition's spiritual ideal and response to that ideal. What does the person reflect of his or her period? What is his or her psychological temperament? One might compare, for example, three Spaniards living at roughly the same time: Ignatius of Loyola, Teresa of Avila, and John of the Cross. In them one sees a considerable difference in temperament and response to the Christian ideal of holiness. Sociology and history likewise explain a great deal: the spiritualities of Francis of Assisi or of Francis de Sales, for example, cannot be understood apart from the sociological, historical, and religious movements of their times. Thus the history of spirituality or comparative spirituality should make use of every branch of religious studies and apply each to the area of spirituality. Otherwise one runs the danger of presenting a partial, truncated, and disincarnate view of a spirituality as lived or taught; one is in danger of failing to understand all that is implied in any spirituality, of failing to understand some of the most important causes of diverse spiritualities.

But, it might be asked, does not such a broad perspective turn the history of spirituality into simply the history of religious sensibility or religious consciousness, or even into the history of religion or the history of mentalities? This objection might be made against André Vauchez' definition of spirituality as "l'unité dynamique du contenu d'une foi et la façon dont celle-ci est vécue par des hommes historiquement déterminés."[54] Although Vauchez is to be commended for broadening methodology in the study of spirituality and for examining the spirituality of all Christians rather than only that of an elite found in monasteries, he seems to cast his net too wide.

Spirituality, in this author's opinion, points to those aspects of a person's living a faith or commitment that concern his or her striving to attain the highest ideal or goal. For a Christian this would mean his or her striving for an ever more intense union with the Father through Jesus Christ by living in the Spirit. Although *all* elements of theology, psychology, sociology, history, and other disciplines must be examined if one is to understand religion under the aspect of spirituality, there are many other aspects of religion and of religious life and practice that are less directly related to this spiritual ideal and striving and that may even be opposed to it. This would be especially true if one were examining the history of religion within some time period, some geographical area, or some particular and differing groups. Such matters as ecclesiastical structures and politics, popular practices, superstitious activities, conflicts, basely-motivated activities, human tyranny, and violence do have some connection with spirituality, but the viewpoint of a commitment to live by the Spirit according to the highest ideals gives a special perspective within the more general history of religious experience or history of religion.[55]

A final question can be examined only briefly. It is a question raised by Professor Joseph Kitagawa at the Fourteenth Congress of the International Association for the History of Religions in Winnipeg in 1980, one whose complexities have been discussed in several meetings of the Canadian Society for the Study of Religion and the Canadian Theological Society, often in joint sessions. Within research into the history of spirituality, is there a difference to be observed between the methodology of religious studies and that of theology? Although there is some convergence of religious studies and theology, I think it can be argued that they still remain distinct in their objectives and methodologies.

In such a view the theologian studying the history of spirituality seeks—or should seek, for there have been many failures here—as accurate and objective a grasp of the historical data as possible, one as accurate and objective as that sought by the religious studies scholar. At this level there should be no difference. But the theologian, after doing research in history, psychology, sociology, and other related areas, would seek to examine and judge the results in the light of theological principles—this theology itself being derived from a community or ecclesial experience of faith responding to a revelation accepted as normative although its conceptualization and verbal expression would be subject to constant scrutiny and development. He or she would tend to seek patterns of God's ways of acting and of human response, to weigh or judge different spiritualities in the light of revelation and the ideal of life developed in the understanding of the community and its theology. While using, as any good theologian should, the findings of philosophy, psychology, anthropology, sociology, linguistics, and history, he or she would use theological judgments as a basis for selecting what is significant and important in any spirituality and for assessing its historical impact or lack of it. An even further extension of inquiry would be to examine the powerful role exercised by secular ideologies in recent centuries, ideologies that might be studied under the rubric of "transposed dogmas" threatening or perverting authentic spirituality.

On the other hand, the religious studies scholar, having done his or her research in the areas of history, psychology, sociology, and other related areas, would seek to produce a description of different spiritualities, a presentation that would be derived from the sources, widely conceived, that have been studied. These sources would frequently include a faith-content and the response to it as an important and perhaps decisive element, but these would be given a descriptive analysis. A further step would be comparison of different spiritualities within the same religious tradition or as found in different religious backgrounds. This in turn could lead the scholar toward discovery of fundamental principles common to all the spiritualities studied and of reasons for variations in spiritualities. All this would be done without reference to an accepted belief or theological system.

If, however, such a scholar then consciously applies philosophical, psychological or sociological categories to the data, he or she has entered the realm of philosophy, psychology, or sociology of spirituality and is as much beyond the strict history of spirituality as is the theologian of spirituality working on the same data. The difference would be that the theologian has developed principles of interpretation and judgment within a faith-oriented discipline whereas the philosopher, psychologist, or sociologist of spirituality would be using principles of interpretation and judgment derived from human reason alone as developed, often hypothetically, within the respective disciplines.

A nagging question remains, however, for the approach of both the theologian and the religious studies scholar even on the primary level of description and comparison prior to use of other disciplines. At this first level of historical inquiry and analysis, is there not already an implicit judgment of values? Why, in examining history, do we select some evidence as more weighty, more crucial, more influential than other? Can one judge the data or select the materials to be examined without implicitly invoking one's own categories and one's own value-systems? Is there not in every historical study a judgment of causalities by analogy with what one today considers decisive in human development?

Someone has said that we can learn more from a historical study about the historian's own period than about the period studied by the historian. Can someone who wishes to be only a strict historian of religion and not a historical theologian or philosopher, psychologist, or sociologist of religion be a completely detached, objective, "scientific" observer? Or does not each bring to historical study a value-system, a philosophy and perhaps even an implicit and sometimes unconscious theology, that finally betrays the search for pure objectivity in the history of religion or in that special area, the history of spirituality, whose object and method we have tried to define? If this be true or even open to question, we are better off acknowledging the fact and trying to reckon with it than pretending it does not exist.

Notes

Originally the topic of a seminar of professors and students at the Graduate Centre for Religious Studies, University of Toronto, this paper was reworked and presented at the Fourteenth Congress of the International Association for the History of Religions in Winnipeg, August 17–22, 1980, in the Christianity section.

1. Gustavo Vinay, "'Spiritualità': Invito a una discussione," *Studi medievali* 2 (1961): 705–9; the quotation is from 705.

2. Jean Leclercq, "Spiritualitas," *Studi medievali* 3 (1962): 279–96. See also Jon Alexander, "What Do Recent Writers Mean by Spirituality?" *Spirituality Today* 32 (1980): 247–56, which has some brief historical remarks and interesting observations on present usage.

3. Louis Bouyer's *Introduction à la vie spirituelle: Precis de théologie ascétique et mystique* (Paris: Desclée, 1960), was reviewed by Jean Daniélou, "A propos d'une introduction à la vie spirituelle," *Études* 94 (1961): 170–74, to which Bouyer replied (*Études* 94 [1961]: 411–15). See also Maurice Giuliani's analysis of Bouyer's book, "Une introduction à la vie spirituelle," *Christus* 8 (1961): 396–411. An earlier discussion of the same topic was carried on between F.-X. Maquart, "Écoles de spiritualité," *Vie spirituelle* 14 (1926): 310–14, and Ferdinand Cavallera, "Écoles de spiritualité," *Revue d'ascétique et de mystique* 7 (1926): 313–15; see also Lucien-Marie de Saint-Joseph, "École de spiritualité," *Dictionnaire de spiritualité* 4 (1960): 116–28.

4. Hans Urs von Balthasar, "The Gospel as Norm and Test of All Spirituality in the Church," in *Concilium*, vol. 9, *Spirituality in Church and World* (New York: Herder & Herder, 1965), 7–23; F. Vandenbroucke, "Spirituality and Spiritualities," in ibid., 45–60; J. Sudbrack, "Vom Geheimnis christlicher Spiritualität: Einheit und Vielfalt," *Geist und Leben* 39 (1966): 24–44.

5. B. Fraling, "Überlegungen zum Begriff der Spiritualität," *Zeitschrift für katholische Theologie* 92 (1970): 183–98, see 183. See the *Lexikon* 9 (1964): 995; and A. Auer, "Fröm-

migkeit," *Lexikon* 4 (1960): 398–405 (Auer uses "Spiritualität" three times in cols. 404–5). See n. 43 below for further on German usage.

6. John Bednar, *La spiritualité et le symbolisme dans les oeuvres de Chrétien de Troyes* (Paris: Nizet, 1974); Astrik Gabriel, "The Spirituality of St. Margaret of Hungary," *Cross and Crown* 3 (1951): 298–309; Hugo Rahner, *The Spirituality of St. Ignatius Loyola* (Westminster, Md.: Newman, 1953); Lucien J. Richard, *The Spirituality of John Calvin* (Atlanta: John Knox, 1974); Jean Orcibal, *La spiritualité de Saint-Cyran avec ses écrits de piété inédits* (Paris: Vrin, 1962); Jacques Le Brun, *La spiritualité de Bossuet* (Paris: Klincksieck, 1972); Enrico Verondini, *Lettere sulla spiritualità rosminiana* (Milan: Marzorati, 1966); Alfeo Valle, *Momenti e valori della spiritualità rosminiana* (Rome: Città Nuova, 1978); Joseph P. Whelan, *The Spirituality of Friedrich von Hügel* (London: Collins, 1971); René Violette, *La spiritualité de Bergson . . .* (Toulouse: Privat, 1968); Chrysologue Mahame, *Spiritualité et philosophie chez Maurice Blondel, de 1883 à 1893* (Paris: Beauchesne, 1972); Thomas Corbishley, *The Spirituality of Teilhard de Chardin* (London: Collins, 1971).

7. E.g., Paul Marie de la Croix, *Spirituality of the Old Testament*, trans. Elizabeth McCabe, 3 vols. (St. Louis: Herder, 1961–63); Diva Barsotti, *Spiritualité de l'Exode*, trans. by Claude Poncet (Bruges: Desclée de Brouwer, 1959); Louis Bouyer, *The Spirituality of the New Testament and the Fathers*, trans. Mary P. Ryan (London: Burns & Oates, 1963); Willem K. M. Grossouw, *Spirituality of the New Testament*, trans. Martin W. Schoenberg (St. Louis: Herder, 1961).

8. E.g., Jean Gautier et al., *Some Schools of Catholic Spirituality*, trans. Kathryn Sullivan (New York: Desclée, 1959); Hilda C. Graef, *The Light and the Rainbow: A Study in Christian Spirituality . . .* (London: Longmans, 1959); James Walsh, ed., *Spirituality through the Centuries: Ascetics and Mystics of the Western Church* (New York: Kenedy, 1964); Thomas M. Gannon, *The Desert and the City: An Interpretation of the History of Christian Spirituality* (New York: Macmillan, 1969); Irénée Hausherr, *Études de spiritualité orientale* (Rome: Universitas Gregoriana, 1969); E. Rozanne Elder, ed., *The Spirituality of Western Christendom* (Kalamazoo, Mich.: Cistercian Publications, 1976); Félix Vernet, *Mediaeval Spirituality*, trans. Benedictines of Talaire (London: Sands, 1930); Léopold Génicot, *La spiritualité médiévale* (Paris: Fayard, 1958); Jean Leclercq et al., *The Spirituality of the Middle Ages*, trans. Benedictines of Holme Eden Abbey, Carlisle (London: Burns & Oates, 1968); Edmond-R. Labande, *Spiritualité et vie littéraire de l'Occident, Xᵉ–XIVᵉ s.* (London: Variorum Reprints, 1974); *Spiritualità cluniacense* (Todi: Centro di Studi sulla Spiritualità medievale, 1960); Louis Bouyer, *La spiritualité orthodoxe et la spiritualité protestante et anglicane* (Paris: Aubier, 1965); Jean Vitrier, *Spiritualité franciscaine en Flandre au 16ᵉ siècle* (Geneva: Droz, 1971); Stephanus Axters, *The Spirituality of the Old Low Countries*, trans. Donald Attwater (London: Blackfriars, 1954); James Walsh, ed., *Pre-Reformation English Spirituality* (London: Burns & Oates, 1965); Louis Cognet, *La spiritualité moderne* (Paris: Aubier, 1966); William A. Kaschmitter, *The Spirituality of Vatican II . . .* (Huntington, Ind.: Our Sunday Visitor Press, 1975); René Voillaume, *Spirituality from the Desert: Retreat at Beni-Abbès*, trans. Alan Neame (Huntington, Ind.: Our Sunday Visitor Press, 1975); John Macquarrie, *Paths in Spirituality* (London: SCM, 1972).

9. *Spiritualités Vivantes*, Collections publiées sous la direction de Jean Herbert (Paris: Éditions Albin Michel): Série Bouddhisme; Série Hindouisme; Série Islam. See also Roger Le Déaut et al., *The Spirituality of Judaism*, trans. Paul Barrett (St. Meinrad, Ind.: Abbey, 1977), and Daisetz Teitaro Suzuki, *Japanese Spirituality* (n.p.: Japan Society for the Promotion of Science, 1972).

10. Gabriel M. Brasó, *Liturgy and Spirituality*, trans. Leonard J. Doyle (Collegeville, Minn.: Liturgical Press, 1971); Bernard Bro, *The Spirituality of the Sacraments*, trans. Theodore DuBois (New York: Sheed & Ward, 1968); Pierre-Thomas Camelot, *Spiritualité du Baptême* (Paris: Cerf, 1960); Adolph D. Frenay, *The Spirituality of the Mass in the Light of Thomistic Theology* (St. Louis: Herder, 1952).

11. *Anneau d'or: Cahiers de spiritualité conjugale et familiale* (Paris: Éditions du Feu Nouveau, 1945–); H. Oger, *Spiritualité pour notre temps* (Paris: Spes, 1962); Raphaél Oechslin, *The Spirituality of the Layman*, trans. Michael C. O'Brien (New York: Desclée, 1964); *Concilium*, vol. 9, *Spirituality in Church and World* (New York: Herder & Herder, 1965); *Concilium*, vol. 19, *Spirituality in the Secular City* (New York: Herder & Herder, 1966); *Concilium*, vol. 49, *Secularization and Spirituality* (New York: Herder & Herder, 1969); Alfons Auer, *Open to the World: An Analysis of Lay Spirituality*, trans. Dennis Doherty and Carmel Callaghan (Baltimore: Helicon, 1966).

12. Michel Menant, *Spiritualité missionnaire* (Paris: Éditions Ouvrières, 1963); Michael C. Reilly, *Spirituality for Mission: Historical, Theological, and Cultural Factors for a Present-Day Missionary Spirituality* (Manila: Loyola School of Theology, 1976); Alban Du Laurens, *La spiritualité de la terre* (Paris: Éditions la Cordelle, 1963).

13. Lucie de Vienne, *Spiritualité de la voix* (Paris: Cerf, 1960); Robert Linssen, *Spiritualité de la matière* (Paris: Éditions Planète, 1966). Although a scientific examination of matter and energy, this latter work also embraces "spirituality" in the sense examined here.

14. See Pamela M. Carswell, *Offbeat Spirituality* (New York: Sheed & Ward, 1961), and Michael F. McCauley, ed., *On the Run: Spirituality for the Seventies* (Chicago: Thomas More, 1974).

15. The first number of the *Revue* (1920) contained an important essay on our topic by Joseph de Guibert, "Les études de théologie ascétique et mystique: Comment les comprendre?" 5–19. He uses the term "spiritualité" frequently and in a broader sense than "théologie ascétique et mystique." *Spirituality Today* is published by the Dominicans of the Province of St. Albert the Great, 1909 South Ashland Avenue, Chicago, IL 60608.

16. A similar fluidity and vagueness is evident in the widespread use of the term "mysticism." See Walter Principe, "Mysticism: Its Meanings and Varieties," in *Mystics and Scholars: The Calgary Conference on Mysticism 1976*, ed. Harold Coward and Terence Penelhum (Waterloo, Ontario: Wilfrid Laurier University Press, 1977), 1–15.

17. See Gal. 3:3; 5:13, 16–25; 1 Cor. 3:1–3; Rom. 7–8.

18. For a summary of Paul's doctrine, see Xavier Léon-Dufour, ed., *Dictionary of Biblical Theology*, 2d ed., trans. P. Joseph Cahill et al. (London: Geoffrey Chapman, 1973), s.v. "Flesh" (X. Léon-Dufour), 187–88, and s.v. "Spirit of God" (Jacques Guillet), 575–76.

19. Pseudo-Jerome, Epist. 7 (PL 30, 114D–115A), quoted by Leclercq, "Spiritualitas" (see n. 2 above), 280. Georges de Plinval, *Pélage, ses écrits, sa vie et sa réforme* (Lausanne: Payot, 1943), 44, held that Pelagius was the author, and his opinion was accepted by others, including Leclercq and Eligius Dekkers, *Clavis patrum latinorum*, 2d ed. (Bruges: Beyaert, 1961), no. 740, p. 168. But Bonifatius Fischer, *Vetus latina* 1/1, 2d ed. (Freiburg: Herder, 1963), 308, joins C. Caspari in rejecting the letter as belonging to Pelagius; for them it belongs to some semi-Pelagian writer of the fifth century in Gaul but not (as had also been suggested) Faustus of Riez. Although several dictionaries quote Tertullian as the first to use the word (with reference to his *Adversus Marcion* 5.8), the correct reading is not *spiritalitate* but *specialitate*. See the edition by Aem. Kroymann, *CCSL*, vol. 1 (Turnhout: Brepols, 1954), 687 (no variants are given).

20. See Leclercq, "Spiritualitas" (see n. 2 above), 280–81.

21. See ibid., 281–86.

22. See ibid., 282–83, 286.

23. Thus the *Oxford English Dictionary* (hereafter abbreviated as *OED*), vol. 10 (Oxford: Clarendon, 1933), 622, gives as first definition of the related term "spiritual" the following: "Of or pertaining to, affecting or concerning, the spirit or higher moral qualities, esp. as regarded in a religious aspect. (Freq. in express or implied distinction to *bodily, corporal, or temporal.*)" (*OED*'s emphasis.) See also below on the contrast between Hindu "spirituality" and Western "materialism."

24. See Leclercq, "Spiritualitas" (see n. 2 above), 286–92.

25. See Robertus Busa, ed., *Index thomisticus: Sancti Thomae Aquinatis operum omnium indices et concordantiae*, sectio II, *Concordantiae operum thomisticorum: Concordantia prima* (Stuttgart: Frommann-Holzboog, 1975), 21:111, s.v. "spiritualitas."

26. See C. Du Cange, *Glossarium mediae et infimae latinitatis*, 2d ed. by Léopold Favre (Paris: Librairie des Sciences et des Arts, 1938), 7:558; and Leclercq, "Spiritualitas" (see n. 2 above), 291–92.

27. See ibid., 292.

28. For the French, see ibid., 292, and Walther V. Wartburg, *Französisches Etymologisches Wörterbuch*, vol. 12 (Basel: Zbinden, 1966), 191. Here and elsewhere Leclercq refers, for the evolution of the French terms and their use, to Lucy Tinsley, *The French Expressions for Spirituality and Devotion: A Semantic Study* (Washington, D.C.: Catholic University of America Press, 1953), which was unavailable to me. For the English, see *OED*, 10:625, s.v. "Spirituality," and 10:624, s.v. "Spirituality."

29. For the French, see Leclercq, "Spiritualitas" (see n. 2 above), 292–93; and the examples given by Wartburg, *Französisches Etymologisches Wörterbuch*, 191. For the English, the *OED* gives examples from the fourteenth century for "spiritualty" in the devotional sense (e.g., 1377: Langland, *Piers Plowman* B. v. 148) and for ecclesiastical properties, while the first example of its use for ecclesiastical persons is dated 1400 (10:625).

30. Wartburg, *Französisches Etymologisches Wörterbuch*, 191, does give one example from the sixteenth century for *espirituelleté*, but all his other examples are later. The *OED* gives no examples for "spirituality" in this sense and only seventeenth-century examples for "spirituality."

31. For Descartes (and Bossuet, who also uses the word in this sense) see É. Littré, *Dictionnaire de la langue française*, vol. 4 (Paris: Hachette, 1883), 2035, s.v. "spiritualité." For Spencer and Digby see the *OED* 10:624, s.v. "spirituality," 4 and 5.

32. See Littré, *Dictionnaire de la langue française*, and Leclercq, "Spiritualitas" (see n. 2 above), 293.

33. Quoted in Littré, *Dictionnaire de la langue française*. Professor Pierre Savard, Director of the Centre de Recherches de Littérature canadienne-française de l'Université d'Ottawa, kindly called my attention to the nineteenth-century Canadian historian, François-Xavier Garneau, who, in his *Histoire du Canada depuis sa découverte jusqu'à nos jours*, 3 vols. (4 editions: Québec, 1845–48; 1852; 1859; Montréal, 1882), uses "spiritualité" in a similar pejorative sense of certain groups in Canada. In the study of the first three editions by Charles Bolduc, *Métamorphoses de l'Histoire du Canada de F.-X. Garneau* (Ottawa: Éditions de l'Université d'Ottawa, 1966), 149–50, the first two editions have the same following statement (slightly modified in the third edition): "Cette secte, car on lui a donné ce nom, se jeta dans la *spiritualité*. . . . [Emphasis his.] Le tremblement de terre de 1663 fut le plus beau temps du Quiétisme en Canada. Ce phénomène mit en mouvement l'imagination ardente et mobile de ses adeptes: les apparitions furent nombreuses, singulières, effrayantes . . . ; les prophéties se multiplièrent. . . . La supérieure de l'Hôtel-Dieu et la célèbre Marie de l'Incarnation, supérieure des Ursulines, partagèrent ce délire de la dévotion; mais la dernière est celle qui donna le plus d'éclat dans ce pays au culte de la spiritualité, pieuse chimère qui s'affecta pendant longtemps plusieurs intelligences tendres et romanesques. . . ." Bolduc suspects the "influence possible de Bossuet" in this passage that "ne fait pas trop honneur à l'historien non plus qu'au croyant" (149 n. 6).

34. Littré, *Dictionnaire de la langue française* (see n. 31 above), s.v. "spiritualité."

35. M. Houssaye, *La vie du cardinal de Bérulle*, vol. 2: *Le Père de Bérulle et l'Oratoire de Jésus, 1611–1625* (Paris: Plon, 1874), 588–89, quoted in Henri Brémond, *Histoire littéraire de l'expérience religieuse en France* (Paris: Bloud et Gay, 1923), 3:198. Houssaye's work was unavail-

able to me: it may have influenced the increased use of "spiritualité" among French writers that we now describe.

36. A. Saudreau, *La vie d'union à Dieu et les moyens d'y arriver d'après les grands maîtres de la spiritualité* (Angers: Germain et G. Grassin, 1900); A. Saudreau, *Manuel de spiritualité* (Paris: Amat, 1916; 3d rev. ed., Paris: Téqui, 1933). Pourrat's work had many "éditions" (= reprintings) within a few years, the first volume appearing in 1918 and a third edition already in existence in 1919 (Paris: Gabalda).

37. See n. 15 above.

38. Daeschler's study was published at Louvain: Museum Lessianum, 1927, the *Dictionnaire* at Paris: Beauchesne, 1932ff. Gilson's lecture is entitled *Théologie et histoire de la spiritualité*, Leçon inaugurale de la Chaire d'Histoire de la Spiritualité prononcée à l'Institut Catholique de Paris, le 15 novembre 1943 (Paris: Vrin, 1943).

39. See Paul Robert, *Dictionnaire . . . de la langue française*, vol. 6 (Paris: Société du Nouveau Littré, 1964), 531.

40. Interesting information on North American usage is given by Alexander, "What Do Recent Writers Mean by Spirituality?" (see n. 2 above).

41. See Ursula King, "Indian Spirituality, Western Materialism: An Image and Its Function in the Reinterpretation of Modern Hinduism," *Social Action* (New Delhi) 28 (1978): 62–86; she traces the history of this cultural-religious exchange and use of the term "spirituality" (see 83 for her list of its meanings). I am grateful to Dr. King for calling my attention to this special development.

42. Pierre Pourrat, *Christian Spirituality*, trans. W. H. Mitchell and S. P. Jacques (vol. 1), S. P. Jacques (vol. 2), W. H. Mitchell (vol. 3) (London: Burns, Oates and Washbourne, 1922–27); the fourth volume, translated by Donald Attwater, appeared only in 1955 (Westminster, Md.: Newman). A. Saudreau's *Vie d'union* (see n. 36 above) was translated (from the 3d ed.) by E. J. Strickland only in 1927 (London: Burns, Oates and Washbourne) under the title *The Life of Union with God, and the Means of Attaining It, according to the Great Masters of Spirituality*.

43. This is the *OED* definition (10:624), s.v. "Spirituality," 3. The revision of the *OED* (Oxford: Clarendon, 1972–) has not yet reached the letter "S." Similar definitions are found in *Webster's Third New International Dictionary*, vol. 3 (Toronto: Encyclopaedia Britannica, 1971), 2198–99, and in *The Random House Dictionary of the English Language* (New York: Random House, 1966), 1372. *Webster's* definition of "spiritual" contains a meaning that is noteworthy for its linking this term to the Pauline doctrine of the Spirit: "*a:* influenced or controlled by the divine Spirit; having a nature in which a concern for the Spirit of God predominates (~man) *b:* proceeding from or under the influence of the Holy Spirit; concerned with religious values; seeking earnestly to live in a right relation to God (a ~Christian)" (3:2189). The *OED* and the *Random House Dictionary* lack such definitions.

The German language was slower in accepting "Spiritualität." Evidently aware that they were using a new term, both Hans Urs von Balthasar and F. Wulf used "Spiritualität" in titles of articles in 1958 (see n. 44 below for references to their articles and other studies mentioned here). As has been said (above), the *Lexikon für Theologie und Kirche* in 1964 listed "Spiritualität" but referred readers to "Frömmigkeit" (in which "Spiritualität" was used several times). In the same year and also in 1966 Sudbrack used the term in titles of articles. In 1966 *Der Grosse Duden* (Mannheim: Bibliographisches Institut, Dudenverlag), 668–69, still included the word in its vol. 5: *Fremdwörterbuch* (2d ed.), giving the meaning as "Geistigkeit."

In 1969, in response to this growing trend, the encyclopedia *Sacramentum Mundi*, vol. 4 (Freiburg: Herder) included an article entitled "Spiritualität" (674–97). In 1972 the *Theologische Revue* began to use "Spiritualität" as a title indexing its own reviews. Its index titles in the bibliography section went through interesting changes. In the 1950s and 1960s, works in this area were classed under "Religiöses Leben und Brauchtum." In vol. 67 (1971) appeared a new title: "Theologie des geistlichen Lebens," now put immediately after "Moraltheologie" rather than, as before, being put farther back; this has continued to the present except for vol. 73.6 (1977), where the title became "Theologie christlicher Spiritualität," which was quickly dropped in the next issue.

 Langenscheidts Enzyklopädisches Wörterbuch, vol. 2.2 (London: Hodder & Stoughton, 1975), 1434, gives "Spiritualität . . . (geistiges Wesen)," whereas Gerhard Wahrig, *Deutsches Wörterbuch* (Gutersloh: Bertelsmann, 1978), 3464, gives "Spiritualität: Geistigkeit; Ggs. Materialität." This last contrast confuses the issue.

 "Spiritualität" now appears as a German and not a foreign word in the new edition of *Duden: Das grosse Wörterbuch der deutschen Sprache* (Mannheim: Dudenverlag, 1981), 6:2449: "Spiritualität: . . . *Geistigkeit, inneres Leben, geistiges Wesen* (Ggs.: Materialität)."

 44. For discussions of the notion of spirituality, spiritual theology, spiritual life, etc., see the studies already referred to in n. 1 above (Vinay), n. 2 above (Leclercq and Alexander), n. 3 above (Bouyer, Daniélou, Giuliani, Maquart, Cavallera, Lucien-Marie), n. 4 above (Balthasar, Vandenbroucke, Sudbrack), n. 5 above (Fraling), n. 15 above (de Guibert), n. 38 above (Gilson), and Hans Urs von Balthasar, "Spiritualität." *Geist und Leben* 31 (1958): 340–52, reprinted in his *Verbum Caro: Skizzen zur Theologie* (Einsiedeln: Johannesverlag, 1960), 1:226–44; F. Wulf, "'Monchsspiritualität'?" *Geist und Leben* 31 (1958): 460–63; Josef Sudbrack, "Um den Stellenwert der Spiritualität im Gesamt der Theologie," *Geist und Leben* 37 (1964): 387–93; Hans Urs von Balthasar, "Theologie und Spiritualität," *Gregorianum* 50 (1969): 571–80: Josef Sudbrack et al., "Spirituality," in *Sacramentum Mundi* (English ed.; Montreal: Palm, 1970), 6:147–67; *Spiritualität in Geschichte und Gegenwart* (Linz: Oberösterr. Landesverl., 1974); Josef Weismayer, "Spirituelle Theologie oder Theologie der Spiritualität?" in *Spiritualität in Moral: Festschrift für Karl Hörmann*, ed. Günter Virt (Vienna: Dom-Verlag, 1975), 59–77; Roberto Moretti, "L'unità della conoscenza teologica e il compito della teologia spirituale," *Seminarium*, n.s., 14 (1974): 41–60; Albaro Huerga, "El metodo de la teología espiritual," *Seminarium*, n.s., 14 (1974): 231–49; Roberto Zavalloni, "L'apporto della scienze dell'uomo alla vita spirituale," *Seminarium*, n.s., 14 (1974): 249–65 (important for the relation of spirituality to anthropology and religious studies); P. Simeone, "Per lo studio della teologia spirituale . . . ," *Seminarium*, n.s., 14 (1974): 266–91 (bibliographical study); Jean Leclercq, introduction to E. Rozanne Elder, ed., *The Spirituality of Western Christendom* (Kalamazoo, Mich.: Cistercian Publications, 1976), xi–xxxv. Here I have been unable to give an account of or react to all these varying studies and opinions; what follows are more personal reflections.

 45. See Leclercq, "Spiritualitas" (see n. 2 above), 295–96, and Balthasar, "The Gospel as Norm" (see n. 4 above), 7–13.

 46. Cf. the general definitions given by Balthasar (ibid., 7), and by Vinay, "Spiritualità" (see n. 1 above), 706.

 47. In his inaugural lecture cited above (n. 38), Étienne Gilson seems to distinguish the lived reality (our first level) from doctrinal formulation (our second level) by calling the first "spiritualité" or "spiritualités" (also "la vie spirituelle" or "les vies spirituelles") and the second "la théologie de la vie spirituelle" (see 21–23). Subsequent usage has tended to group these two together under the name "spirituality" and to add the third level we shall distinguish. On the second level one can and, I believe, should distinguish two types of doctrine or theological knowledge called by Jacques Maritain "savoir spéculativement pratique" and "savoir pratiquement pratique." For him the former is the doctrine of a speculative or systematic theologian like Thomas Aquinas concerning life in the Spirit and union with God, whereas the latter is the body of practical teaching coming from a spiritual guide such as John of the Cross. See his *Distinguer pour unir, ou*

Les degrés du savoir, 4th ed. (Paris: Desclée de Brouwer, 1946). chap. 8 (615–97), translated under the supervision of Gerald B. Phelan as *Distinguish to Unite or The Degrees of Knowledge* (New York: Scribner, 1959), chap. 8 (310–51).

48. See the studies referred to above, nn. 3–4, and the variety of studies listed in nn. 6–14.

49. There are some who would distinguish a theological approach from the religious studies approach by calling the latter a "humanistic approach." I should like to suggest that a study of the history of Western culture would show that, to the time of Aufklärung, theology was considered very much a part of the humanities. One has only to think of Erasmus, Marsilio Ficino, Pico della Mirandola, Thomas More, Colet, and others to recall that the great humanists of the past were often theologians as much as philologists, philosophers, scientists, etc. On humanism and theology, see Yves Congar, *A History of Theology*, trans. Hunter Guthrie (Garden City, N.Y.: Doubleday, 1968), 147–50.

50. See ibid., 131–54.

51. Pierre Pourrat, *La spiritualité chrétienne*, vol. 1 (Paris: Gabalda, 1918), v, says: "La Spiritualité est cette partie de la théologie qui traite de la perfection chrétienne et des voies qui y conduisent. On distingue la *théologie dogmatique* qui enseigne ce qu'il faut croire, la *théologie morale* qui apprend ce qu'on doit faire ou éviter pour ne pas pécher mortellement ni véniellement, et, au-dessus des deux mais basée sur elles, la *spiritualité* ou *théologie spirituelle*. Celle-ci se subdivise en *théologie ascétique* et en *théologie mystique*." For Louis Bouyer's comments, see his *Spirituality of the New Testament* (see n. 7 above), vii.

52. Ibid., viii–ix.

53. The subtitle of Vauchez' study (*La spiritualité du moyen âge occidental* [Paris: Presses Universitaires de France, 1975]) is *VIIIᵉ–XIIᵉ siècles*. See his introduction, 5–8. Leclercq's essay is his introduction (see n. 44 above).

54. Vauchez, *La spiritualité du moyen âge occidental*, 7.

55. The difference can be seen by comparing what we have said with the important study by Raoul Manselli, *La religion populaire au moyen âge: Problèmes de méthode et d'histoire*, Conférence Albert-le-Grand 1973 (Montréal: Institut d'Études Médiévales Albert-le-Grand; Paris: Vrin, 1975). See for example his chap. 4, sec. 4: "'Ecclesia spiritualis' et 'ecclesia carnalis'" (177, 204–15), where popular movements of spirituality are seen in opposition to the outlook, policy, and activities of the hierarchy. The hierarchy's outlook, etc. might in these cases reflect a certain type of "spirituality," but to define or describe them as such seems to make the word vague and practically meaningless.

Part 2

Contemporary Modulations

Aware of the history and etymology of the term *spirituality* as well as its shifting definitions throughout history, several scholars have labored to define spirituality for a contemporary setting where a number of new factors must be brought into play. Indeed, since an important element of spirituality has to do with human *experience*, then any understanding of spirituality which is static, not open to fresh insights as human beings explore and increasingly understand their world, will be wide of the mark. Accordingly, prayer offered up in the twelfth century, with the belief that the earth was the center of the universe, would have a somewhat different flavor than a prayer which is informed by twenty-first-century cosmology and which stands in awe before the Creator in terms of the sheer size, the magnitude, of the creation.

In the first essay of this section, John Macquarrie explores spirituality in terms of what it means to be a human being: he believes that "spirituality has to do with becoming a person in the fullest sense." In his work "spirit" is understood in a general way, under-scoring some common human elements, as "an active, formative, life-giving power." As such "spirit" is elusive in that it describes that "extra dimension" of human beings which makes them more than mere physical organisms. Moreover, in a critique of twentieth-century estimates of what a human being is (which have been remarkably reductionistic), Macquarrie cautions us that "reality is not exhausted by the things we discern by the senses." So important is the notion of "transcending oneself" in this conception of spirituality that he has coined the term "exience," a word which points to the dynamic form of a spiritual being as "continually going out from itself."

Lawrence LaPierre, in the second essay, offers a constructive and imaginative model that contains six components (journey, transcendence, community, religion, mystery of creation, and transformation) that illuminate many of the elements of contemporary spirituality. Drawing on a distinction between spirituality and religion, LaPierre observes that the spiritual dimension of a person is broader than institutional religion, a truth that demographers such as George Gallup, in their studies of American religion, have been underscoring as well. Beyond this, LaPierre demonstrates a broad, inclusive definition of spirituality in his discussion of the personal transformation that often emerges in such contemporary movements as Alcoholics Anonymous and other twelve-step programs.

In the final piece of this section, Ewert Cousins considers spirituality against the backdrop of growth in human consciousness through three major phases: (1) Primal Period (prior to 800 B.C.E.), (2) First Axial Period (800–200 B.C.E.) and (3) the Second Axial Period (twentieth century). In the first period, the dominant form of consciousness was "cosmic, collective, tribal, mythic and ritualistic." The next period, the First Axial, emerged in the Middle East with the work of the great Jewish prophets Elijah, Isaiah, and Jeremiah; in China through the teachings of Lao-tze and Confucius; and in India with the transformation of Hinduism through the rise of the Upanishads. Whereas Primal consciousness was tribal, Axial consciousness was individual. The last period, the Second Axial, marks an important shift from individual consciousness to global consciousness. While not neglecting the insights of the First Axial Period, the Second Axial Period, which Cousins maintains has many implications for Christian spirituality, seeks to incorporate the "collective and cosmic dimensions" of pre-Axial consciousness. It does this in order to articulate a vision of a community and spirituality that is not only truly inclusive and global but also ecologically sensitive.

Spirit and Spirituality

John Macquarrie

In this chapter we take up the meaning of spirituality. The word "spirituality" is used in a broad way, and includes prayer, worship and whatever other practices are associated with the development of the spiritual life. But just as prayer and worship have become suspect, so too "spirituality" has become a word of doubtful repute. To some it suggests a kind of hot-house atmosphere in which people are unduly preoccupied with their own inward condition. To others it suggests a pale ghostly semi-existence in which the spiritual is contrasted with the bodily and material. To others again, the word has connotations of unctuousness and pseudo-piety. Yet, in spite of all misunderstandings, the word "spirituality" still has a certain fascination and it has been rediscovered by some of the young people. This is because it points to something so important that no amount of distortion and perversion can ever quite destroy it. I believe that fundamentally spirituality has to do with *becoming a person in the fullest sense*, and the rest of the chapter will be devoted to exploring what this means.

We begin by pushing the problem further back. To talk about "spirituality" would seem to imply that we already understand what is meant by the word "spirit." Yet the word "spirit" is notoriously difficult and ambiguous. It is a word which (except in the expression "Holy Spirit") I have usually avoided in my own theological writings, precisely because of the difficulty of attaching a clear meaning to it.

This essay first appeared in *Paths in Spirituality*, 2d ed. (Harrisburg, Pa.: Morehouse, 1992), 40–52. Used by permission.

But I can scarcely avoid it in a writing devoted to spirituality! Let us begin then by noting that the term "spirit," like many other items in the religious vocabulary, was originally an image or picture rather than a concept. The image was, of course, that of the stirring of the air: the breath or the breeze.[1] The breath is the invisible though none the less palpable characteristic that distinguishes a living man from a dead one; the breeze is the equally invisible force that stirs around man in the world and that manifests itself in many effects there. Walther Eichrodt remarks: "No wonder, then, that in the blowing of the wind and in the rhythm of human respiration the ancients detected a divine mystery, and saw in this element in Nature, at once so near to him and yet so incomprehensible, a symbol of the mysterious nearness and activity of the divine."[2]

The general significance of the imagery is clear enough. It was already bringing to expression the conviction that to reality there belongs a depth, a complexity and a richness that are not exhausted by the visible and material objects presented to the senses. Man is more than his physical body, and man's environment is more than the physical universe. But if "spirit" is understood as more than the physical, it is not separated from the material world in some "beyond," but shows itself in the world and even enters into the body of man.

Furthermore, the biblical imagery of spirit is essentially dynamic. The breath and the breeze are in motion. Spirit is the active, formative, life-giving power. Language about the "indwelling" spirit is inadequate if it suggests a merely passive inhabiting. The Old Testament idea of spirit, in Oliver Quick's words, "represents an invasive, rather than a pervasive, power."[3]

It is a far cry from the early Hebrew imagery of the breath and the breeze to the subtle concepts of spirit which have been developed in Western philosophy, both ancient and modern. Some of these philosophical concepts of spirit stand in rather sharp opposition to the Old Testament ideas, especially when they have set up a dichotomy between spirit and matter and have conceived these as different kinds of substance. At the same time, it must be remembered that possibly the greatest of all European philosophies of spirit, that of Hegel, agreed with the Old Testament in refusing to isolate the spiritual from the physical and in seeing the former as the dynamic reality which expresses itself in the latter: "Nature is far from being so fixed and complete as to subsist without spirit. And similarly spirit on its part is not merely a world beyond nature and nothing more; it is really and with full proof seen to be spirit only when it involves nature as absorbed in itself."[4]

No concept of spirit can be adequate to the reality. Spirit is "incomprehensible," in the sense in which that adjective is used in the English version of the Athanasian creed. It does not mean that we can have no understanding of the matter at all, but it does mean that the full significance of spirit always breaks out beyond the grasp of our concepts. This is clearer when we remember that "incomprehensible" is a not very felicitous translation of the Latin *immensus*, meaning that which cannot be measured or contained in the categories of finite thought. Spirit has an elusive character. "The wind blows where it will, and you hear the sound of it, but cannot tell whence it comes or whither it goes."[5]

The imagery of the biblical language, evocative rather than precisely descriptive, well suggests the elusiveness of spirit itself. But we do need to clarify our language as much as possible, especially if we have any intention of commending spirituality to those who have become uncertain or even suspicious about it. And it should not be impossible to reach some clarification. From the beginning, the Spirit of God has been understood as God amidst humanity, God present and active in the world, God in his closeness to us as a dynamic reality shaping human lives and histories. The Spirit, in this sense, is not something other than God, but God in that manner of the divine Being in which he comes closest, dwells with us, acts upon us. When one considers the matter from this point of view, it would seem much more difficult to form any interpretative concept of the Father than it would of the Spirit, among the Persons of the Trinity. For although the image of the Father seems more concrete and definite than the image of the Wind or Breath, yet the mysterious source of all beings, the deepest and ultimate region of the God-head, is surely more remote and inaccessible than the Spirit who moves among us and whose spiritual being is somehow shared by us. The New Testament declares that it is through the Spirit that we have access to the Father[6] and that it is by the "Spirit of adoption" that we are empowered to cry "Abba, Father."[7]

More than that, as mentioned in the last paragraph, "spirit" names a kind of being that is somehow shared by man with the Spirit of God. Spirit is present in and constitutive of man, as well as God. The word points to the mysterious affinity that binds man to God, an affinity that has to be affirmed just as strongly as the otherness which differentiates God from man. When God had made man a creature of the dust, he "breathed into his nostrils the breath of life and man became a living soul."[8] Thus man, alone among all the beings on earth, was granted a share of spirit. He has not only learned to perceive the Spirit of God without; he recognizes that there is spirit within. Thus, because of our share in spirit given in creation, we should be able to find within ourselves, in the very structure of our being, some clue to the nature of the divine Spirit. It is true, of course, that man's spiritual endowment is often sadly obscured because he immerses himself in sensual indulgences or in amassing possessions. It is true also that spirit itself can become perverted so that we can speak of "evil spirit" and of "spiritual evil," and these represent a pitch of sin beyond sensuality. Yet the true potentialities of spirit are never quite abolished. So long as there is a recognizably human experience, there can be discerned the lineaments of spirit as given by God in creation.

Let us proceed then to consider what it is that makes us spiritual beings. What can we say about spirit as the most elusive and mysterious constituent of our human nature, yet the one that seems most distinctive when we think of man in relation to all the other beings on earth? If we can form a clearer idea of spirit as we are aware of it on the level of our own experience, then we should be able in turn to attain a clearer understanding of the Spirit of God and finally of the meaning of spirituality.

We have already taken note that when we talk of "spirit" in man, we are pointing to that extra dimension of being that belongs to him and that makes him more than a mere physical organism or a highly complicated animal. We do not relate to other people as if they were only objects that we could see and hear and touch or even as if they were simply living organisms from which reactions could be evoked. We relate to them *as persons*, and we talk about them or talk to them in a language appropriate to persons. What makes the difference between a person and a thing or between a person and an animal is not itself something that can be seen. It is the invisible "extra dimension" as I have called it, and we know this at first hand in our experiences of thinking, willing, feeling, experiences which we attribute to other human beings as well. It is this range of experience that is distinctive of the human being and that we call "spirit."

We need not suppose, as some philosophers have done, that spirit is some kind of substance, to be contrasted with physical substance. Nowadays at least, to talk of anything as a "substance" almost inevitably suggests that it is some kind of "thing." But to reify spirit is surely to commit a category mistake. Furthermore, to reify spirit tends to reduce it to the ontological level of that very thinghood beyond which, as we have suggested, the image of spirit was meant to point to a different dimension of reality. Talk of "spirit" was meant to express the perception that reality is not exhausted by the things we discern by the senses. However, our minds are so much under the domination of the category of thinghood that we immediately tend to convert spirit itself into another thing. But spirit is not another thing, not another substance parallel to the substance of physical entities. Spirit belongs to a different category. It is, we might say, a dynamic form, just as life, for instance, is not a thing but a special form and a distinct mode of being.

What then is this dynamic form or mode of being which we call "spirit" and which we know in the human experience? It may be described as a capacity for going out of oneself and beyond oneself; or, again, as the capacity for transcending oneself. Human beings are not closed or shut up in themselves. They are not just objects among the objects that make up the world, with a given nature and destiny. To them there belong essentially freedom and creativity, whereby they are able to shape (within limits) both themselves and their world. It is this openness, freedom, creativity, this capacity for going beyond any given state in which they find themselves, that makes possible self-consciousness and self-criticism, understanding, responsibility, the pursuit of knowledge, the sense of beauty, the quest of the good, the formation of community, the outreach *fruits* of love and whatever else belongs to the amazing richness of what we call the "life of the spirit." And, as already said, though sin severely impairs this life, it never destroys it or humanity would cease to be.

The kind of openness and self-transcendence of which I have been writing is what existentialist philosophers have called "existence," in the strong sense of that word as an "ex-sisting" or "standing out." It is this "ex-sisting" that is the peculiar characteristic of man's mode of being, and clearly it is closely related to "spirit," as described above. But perhaps the dynamic character of spirit could be even better expressed if, instead of talking of "existence" as "standing out," I were to coin a new word and say that spirit is *exience*, that is to say, "going out."[9] The word "exience" would better express the essentially dynamic form of spiritual being as continually going out from itself.

The more man goes out from himself or goes beyond himself, the more the spiritual dimension of his life is deepened, the more he becomes truly man, the more also he grows in likeness to God, who is Spirit. On the other hand, the more he turns inward and encloses himself in self-interest, the less human does he become. This is the strange paradox of spiritual being—that precisely by going out and spending itself, it realizes itself. It grows not weaker but stronger, for it is not a quantifiable thing.

It is worth noting that the Greek word cognate with "existence" is "*ek-stasis*." The life of the spirit is therefore the "ecstatic" life, precisely the life that goes out of itself. But just as I have claimed that "exience" would be a more dynamic term than "existence," so I think we can find a better word than "ecstasis." The adjective "ecstatic" is especially too strongly reminiscent of "static," the very opposite of "dynamic." I suggest we might do better to speak of "ecbasis" and "ecbatic" to capture the notion of a genuine surging forth of spirit.[10]

In saying that the life of the spirit is ecbatic (or ecstatic), I do not mean by this that it is a life marked by sporadic periods of intense experience. One might get this impression, admittedly, from passages in the Old Testament which tell of prophets who were, so to speak, "beside themselves" in their moments of prophesying, and the Hebrew word for such a prophet, *nabi*, means one who raves or speaks ecstatically. Even in the New Testament we read about such intense moments of Spirit-possession as issued in "speaking with tongues." It is hardly surprising that today, in a world that has been starved of spirituality, many people are turning to the intense spirit-experiences of the Pentecostalist sects. However, the main tendency in the New Testament is to see the work of the Spirit and thus a truly spiritual life for man as manifested in the less sensational but ethically more important "gifts" or "fruits" of the Spirit—love, joy, peace, patience, kindness, goodness, faithfulness, gentleness, self-control.[11] These gifts are not confined to exceptional spirit-filled individuals but are distributed throughout the body of Christ. To those who make up that body, St Paul can say that "to each is given the manifestation of the Spirit for the common good."[12] Yet while there is nothing sensational or psychologically abnormal about these *charismata*, as compared with the more frenzied manifestations of possession by the Spirit, the gifts are none the less ecstatic (or ecbatic) in the strict sense. They draw the recipient out of himself into a new manner of life. He goes out from a self-centred mode of being into a new openness. The merely "natural" life is broken open and the "spiritual" man is born. This is the spiritual rebirth. "That which is born of the Spirit is spirit."[13] It is not a rebirth once for all but a continuing process of rebirth and renewal.

In stressing that the highest fruits or gifts of the Spirit are not sensational performances but ethical qualities, I am also stressing the personal character of spirit, both in God and man. Some early ideas of the Spirit of the Lord seem to have supposed that this was some impersonal force that might take possession of a man and cause him to do extraordinary things quite apart from his own volition. But the Christian understanding of the Spirit thinks of his action as the personal action of God upon men. Such action does not force men into strange patterns of behaviour, and it does not suspend their exercise of reason and will. Rather, it heightens whatever in man is spiritual—his rationality, freedom and creativity. The approach is on the personal level through reason and conscience, and the response is no involuntary submission to a strange power but rather a willing and fully personal going out to join in the life of a Spirit greater than man's.

The words "spirit" and "person" are not synonymous. Obviously, for instance, a human person is not simply a spirit. He is also a creature of flesh and blood. Yet person and spirit, though not identical, are closely connected. Spirit is the most distinctive constituent of personhood. We might say that spirit is the form of the personal.

Personal rebirth is the work of the divine Spirit, but it is also the fulfilling and perfecting of the basically spiritual constitution of man, the "existent" being who has a freedom and a creativity that make him more than just another item in the inventory of created things. Man "stands out" from all other creatures on earth and has the possibility of exience, of going out and transcending himself into a fuller form of life. This possibility was his from the moment that breath or spirit was breathed into him by God, bestowing on him the divine image and the possibility of closeness to God and participation in the divine life. Already then we have gone far toward establishing the thesis announced at the beginning of this chapter, that spirituality is, in simple terms, the process of becoming a person in the fullest sense.

But now that we have spent a little time exploring the meaning of spirit as we know it in human life, let us see whether what we have learned can provide an analogy, however fragmentary, by which we may arrive at a better understanding of the Spirit of God and so finally at a still more adequate understanding of spirituality.

We have learned that when we talk of "spirit" in man, we refer to his capacity for going out beyond himself. It would seem then that we must also think of the divine Spirit in terms of God's openness, of his exience or going out. And at once we must be struck with the fact that the language we use about the Holy Spirit is precisely the language of "going out," of "procession." He is "the Spirit of truth, who proceeds (ekporeue-tai) from the Father."[14] In the familiar words of the Nicene Creed in its Western form, the Holy Spirit "proceeds from the Father and the Son."

Although the important point for my argument is simply the notion of procession, I should perhaps pause for a moment to say something about the vexed question of a single or a double procession. I mention the matter because it has implications for spirituality as well as for systematic theology.

It is well-known that in the original version of the Nicene creed, the Holy Spirit was said to proceed from the Father, without any mention of the Son. In this respect, it agreed with the verse from St John's Gospel, quoted above. But some early theologians (mostly, but not all, in the West) began to teach that the Spirit proceeds from the Father and the Son, the doctrine now known as that of the double procession. St Cyril of Alexandria, for instance, wrote: "For though the Holy Spirit has a personal subsistence of his own and is conceived of by himself, in that he is the Spirit and not the Son, yet he is not therefore alien from the Son. For he is called 'the Spirit of Truth' and Christ is 'the Truth,' and he is poured forth from him (Christ) just as he also is from God the Father."[15] This doctrine came to be accepted in the West and was incorporated into the creed by the addition of the filioque clause. The Eastern Church, however, has continued to maintain belief in a single procession. We have not yet heard the end of the controversy, for in this ecumenical age some in the West think that we should go back to the original form of the creed, and the East stands firm by its position. Though I naturally lean to the Western view myself, I would be glad to see some compromise such as "from the Father through the Son." But let me now point out the implications for spirituality of the two points of view.

The Western view insists that the Spirit must be understood in the closest relation to the Son. Christ is the one in whom the Spirit dwelt in fulness, he is the one who went out from himself to the point of emptying himself, and, in accord with the paradox of the spiritual life, he is the one who manifests a full, mature, spiritual humanity. Hence the spirit of Christ and the Holy Spirit are scarcely distinguishable, and indeed they were not distinguished among some of the earliest Christians.

The advantage of this way of looking at the matter is that the Spirit and spirituality are interpreted in thoroughly christocentric terms. The Holy Spirit is understood concretely in terms of Christ as the unique bearer and embodiment of that Spirit, and the goals of spirituality are set in terms of the Christ who has transcended to a new level of spiritual existence. Our Lord's teaching that "God is Spirit" is inseparable from his own revelation of God; and likewise the consequence he draws that "those who worship him must worship in spirit and truth" is inseparable from his own self-offering to the Father as the highest mode of spiritual worship and the spiritual life. Men are spiritualized, so to speak, to the extent that they become capable of following Christ in a self-outpouring of love and obedience. It is this that deepens and confirms them in their spiritual being.

On the other hand, the Eastern doctrine of a single procession has the advantage that it draws attention to something which, though not denied in the Western doctrine, has become over-shadowed—namely, the relation of the Spirit to all creation. Dale Moody comments: "Western theology has tended to confine the activity of the Creator Spirit to the redemptive realm of the Church, but Eastern Orthodoxy has vigorously challenged this confinement, and contended for both a creative and a redemptive work of the Spirit. At least on this point, the West can learn from the East, for creation cannot be excluded as a realm in which the Spirit works."[16]

The whole creation is the domain of the Spirit. In the creation story, the Holy Spirit is associated with the Father and the Logos in the creative work. In the beginning, "the Spirit of God was moving over the face of the waters."[17] Some modern translations have "wind of God" rather than "Spirit of God" as a rendering of the Hebrew, but this makes little difference, for what may have at first been understood literally as a wind blowing over the face of the chaotic deep was interpreted in later times as the

Creator Spirit, bringing shape and unity into the creation. Though we can only speculate on what the action of the Spirit might be on the lower or inanimate levels of creation, must we not interpret this too in analogy with his action on human spirits? This would mean that just as he brings men out of themselves, making them spiritual as he is himself Spirit, so he is breaking open those lower levels of creation in order to bring forth their potentialities for fuller development. Such a breaking open and bringing forth would be the theological equivalent of what in the empirical sciences is called "evolution," the unfolding of the rich possibilities of nature.

But we are chiefly interested for the present in the question about the consequences for spirituality of this association of the Spirit with all creation. The point here is that, just as spirit belongs to all men, so the working of the Holy Spirit is not confined to the Church or even to the religious community in the broadest sense but may operate powerfully beyond its borders. Christian prayer and spirituality have their secular counterparts outside of the Christian community. Surely Christians must gladly recognize that the Holy Spirit may work in very unexpected places, outside of the "normal channels." The Church is certainly the community of the Spirit, but it is not the exclusive field of the Spirit's working. Here again the ancient metaphor of the wind, as a clue to the meaning of "spirit," is fruitful. "The wind blows where it will."[18] The wind cannot be channelled along set courses, and refuses to be shut up within limits. Likewise the divine Spirit cannot be restricted to narrow limits. The entire creation is the domain of the Spirit, and also the whole of time and history. No single community of persons, no particular geographical area or race of human beings, no specially privileged century or epoch can claim the Spirit for itself alone.

One might even come to believe that the more men attempt to restrict the operation of the Spirit to what they take to be the "approved" channels, ecclesiastical or traditional, the more vigorously the same Spirit will manifest himself outside of these channels. The contemporary churches seem to get themselves increasingly involved in bureaucracy and look less and less like the community of the Spirit. It is hard to believe that they provide an ideal medium through which the Spirit can work, though neither can they exclude him. The Church has always needed its share of rebels and "far out" people to save it from a legalism and institutionalism that can be deadening and unspiritual. It has needed also the stimulus of writers, artists and philosophers who, though not themselves Christians, have been voices through which the Spirit can speak to the churches and, indeed, to all men and women.

But while it is important to remind ourselves that the work of the Holy Spirit is as wide as creation and that aspiration to spirituality is as wide as humanity, we would certainly be wrong if we supposed that the Spirit is quite arbitrary in his working, or that we would be most likely to attain to the fulness of a spiritual existence if we were to turn our backs altogether on structures and institutions. That has been the mistake of the enthusiasts and fanatics of all ages, our own included. We have seen that the life of the spirit is indeed an "ecstatic" life, but not in the bad sense of a disordered existence, swayed by irrational emotions and uncritical enthusiasms.

The Church is the community of the Spirit not in the sense of having a monopoly of the Spirit or of having the Spirit in its possession, but in the very real sense of having been called into existence by God, and having entrusted to it the Word and Sacraments. In the beginning, the Spirit had brooded over the creation. At Christ's baptism, the Spirit had descended in fulness upon our Lord. At Pentecost, the same Spirit was poured out on the Church. Those three events form a series which teaches us what is meant by calling the Church "the community of the Spirit." This expression does not refer to an exclusive characteristic of the Church, but asserts that in the Church there is going on in a concentrated manner that work of the Spirit which, in a more diffuse way, is also going on throughout the whole creation. The Church is—at least, ideally—the growing point where the upbuilding work of the Spirit proceeds most intensely. We ought to be able to see in the Church a true spirituality, that process of breaking open and bringing forth the new qualities of a truly spiritual humanity. The Church, as community of the Spirit, should be the environment for the developing of full personhood. However imperfectly, the Church should be already exhibiting the eschatological kingdom of God, that final community of the Spirit toward which not only the Church but all creation is headed.

But there is still more to be said about the Church and spirituality. However difficult the road to spiritual maturity may be, we have all met some individuals who have made some progress along it and who are able to come out of themselves and give themselves in ways that often surprise us. Such individuals restore our faith, both in human nature and in the reality of the Spirit's work among us. But it is an important objection to traditional spirituality that it has been largely conceived in individualistic terms. Much of life nowadays is determined not by the actions of individuals but of groups, and often of large groups. The measure of spiritual achievement which we sometimes see in individuals seems to be impossible for groups. If, with difficulty and practice and divine grace, an individual may learn to go out from himself in a truly spiritual way, it seems that groups remain hard, self-regarding, unspiritual, unable to break out beyond their narrowly conceived interests. We have only to think of the social conflicts that surround us today between, say, unions and employers or between different racial and ethnic groups, to realize how self-regarding and unspiritual the life of society really is. Is this a situation that can never be changed, so that even if spirituality represents a possibility in the lives of individuals, social morality will always be a matter of power politics? I suppose that if one is realistic, one must acknowledge that groups will rarely give up any power or privilege unless forced to do so. But surely Christian spirituality envisages a broader strategy than the spiritualization of the individual. In calling the Church "the community of the Spirit," we are implying that here there is a *corporate spiritual entity*, a society with the capacity to go out from itself. It has been said that the Church is the only society which exists primarily for the benefit of the non-member. To be sure, the Church has been often just as defensive, self-regarding and unspiritual as any other group. But whenever and wherever it is learning to be truly the Church, the community of the Spirit, it is introducing a new dimension into the social situation, one that gives hope for an eventual transformation.

Notes

1. This seems to have been true of a great many languages—not only English but Latin, Greek, Sanskrit, Hebrew, and others.
2. W. Eichrodt, *Theology of the Old Testament* (London: SCM; Philadelphia: Westminster, 1967), 2:46.
3. O. C. Quick, *Doctrines of the Creed* (London: Nisbet; New York: Scribner, 1938), 275.
4. G. W. F. Hegel, "Logic," in *The Encyclopedia of the Philosophical Sciences* (Oxford: Clarendon, 1892), 180.
5. John 3:8.
6. Eph. 2:18.
7. Rom. 8:15.
8. Gen. 2:7.
9. The word "ex-ience" is formed in analogy with "trans-ience" from Latin *ire*, to go.
10. The word "ec-basis" is formed in analogy with "ana-basis" from Greek *basis*, a going.
11. Gal. 5:22f.
12. 1 Cor. 12:7.
13. John 3:6.
14. John 15:26.
15. C. A. Heurtley, ed., *On Faith and the Creed* (Oxford: Parker, 1886), 172.
16. Dale Moody, *Spirit of the Living God* (Philadelphia: Westminster, 1968), 28.
17. Gen. 1:2.
18. John 3:8.

A Model for Describing Spirituality

Lawrence L. LaPierre

Abstract: A model for describing the spiritual dimension of life is presented. The model consists of six factors or dimensions along which life can be experienced as a spiritual person. These factors are identified as those of the journey, transcendence, community, religion, "the mystery of creation," and transformation. Evil is described as a lack of progress and/or regression in any of these six dimensions. Recent literature is cited to indicate some of the diversity of understanding of spirituality and in support of various parts of the author's model.

Whatever else I learned in seminary, it was clear that, as a pastor, I would be expected to deal with spirituality. Of course, no one told me exactly what spirituality was. Nor did I realize how vital it was to work on my own spiritual needs. I did realize, however, that I was expected to help with the spiritual needs of parishioners and non-parishioners alike.

The importance of focusing on their spiritual needs was emphasized in a variety of ways in the communities where I pastored. Sometimes the reminders were gentle. For example, requests for home and hospital visits, nursing-home worship services, prayers for healing, Bible studies, and pastoral counseling were usually made with consideration for my schedule. On a few occasions, particularly when my sermons ventured too far into the realm of politics, the reminders were harsh. Those were times when a parishioner would advise me to "stick with the spiritual things, Reverend, and leave the rest to us."

This essay first appeared in *Journal of Religion and Health* 33 (summer 1994): 153–61. Used by permission of Plenum Publishing Corporation.

No one, however, offered to identify what they thought belonged in the spiritual realm. Nor did I ask. Worse yet, my reading had introduced me to a bewildering variety of insights and opinions about what "spirituality" included. Only lately have I realized that I have not had a very clear definition of what I have meant when I have used the word.

Nor did the situation improve when I became a chaplain at a Veterans Affairs Hospital. In that capacity I minister to people in varying stages of illness or rehabilitation, or dying. I do this as a member of several health-care teams concerned with the well-being of the whole person. Each member of these teams approaches a patient from the perspective of his or her discipline while trying to enhance the team's impact on the healing process.

The focus for this paper is the description of a conceptual basis for assessing a patient's spiritual needs. This is especially relevant for chaplains and other clergy who want to offer the most effective pastoral care in response to those needs. It may also prove helpful in assisting the rest of the health-care team to understand that specific facets of patients' spirituality may affect their healing.

Ideally, one would already have an unambiguous definition of spirituality in place as the foundation for such a conceptual model. There is no agreement, however, about what spirituality includes. Elkins et al. discovered in their search of the literature that "none of the writers provided a clear, comprehensive definition of spirituality."[1] Yet, they also noticed that

> certain elements of spirituality began to emerge; we found there was a great deal of convergence and overlap among the various writers in their usually implicit descriptions of spirituality. Eventually, we were able to make a preliminary list of several factors that seemed to constitute core dimensions of what is meant by "spirituality." It became increasingly clear that spirituality could not be defined simply and that it was a complex, multidimensional construct composed of several major factors. . . .[2]

My own reading and experience confirm the conviction that spirituality is multidimensional. Six clear factors turn up in the literature, however, with enough frequency to make them appear to be fundamental aspects of spirituality. These are identified in this paper as those of the journey, transcendence, community, religion, "the mystery of creation," and transformation.

In this model I draw mostly upon contemporary authors in the fields of religion or spirituality. Most of them write from a Judaeo-Christian perspective. Some insights also come from writers in the health-care field.

The composite model described here may be useful in attempts to describe the state of a person's spirituality qualitatively. It might provide the foundation for an instrument to detect changes in various aspects of the spirituality of an individual or a group. It may even be useful in institutional settings as diverse as local parishes, hospitals, religious communities, and retreat houses.

Journey

The search for purpose, direction, or meaning in our lives often consumes a great deal of energy. Elkins et al. acknowledge the importance of this dimension in their paper on humanistic-phenomenological spirituality:

> The spiritual person has known the quest for meaning and purpose and has emerged from this quest with confidence that life is deeply meaningful and that one's own existence has purpose. The actual ground and content of this meaning vary from person to person, but the common factor is that each person has filled the "existential vacuum" with an authentic sense that life has meaning and purpose.[3]

Once an individual decides to respond to a discovery of meaning and purpose, then a journey begins—a journey of the spirit. That journey may lead to deeper understanding of meaning and purpose in life. Or it may lead to exploring other aspects of the spiritual life.

Even suffering and delays do not necessarily prevent one from experiencing life as a spiritual journey. As Gordon Allport notes in the preface to Victor Frankl's book *Man's Search for Meaning: An Introduction to Logotherapy*, "Frankl is fond of quoting Nietzsche, 'He who has a why to live can bear with almost any how.'"[4] However, without a sense of "why," that is, without meaning, purpose, or direction, life becomes less a journey and more an aimless wandering. B. C. Johnson adds that "spirituality in persons is the form which that instinctual search for meaning takes."[5]

Even with a clear purpose, a spiritual journey is not always direct. The tortured paths we sometimes follow along our spiritual journeys were alluded to three centuries ago by John Bunyan in *Pilgrim's Progress*.[6] His allegory describes the odyssey of a person named "Christian" who sets out to leave the "Earthly City" and travel to the "Eternal City." In other words, it narrates a journey toward lasting relationship with God as well as describing the obstacles and sources of assistance along the way.

St. Augustine argued that this decision to seek relationship with God is fueled by the experience of restlessness in a person's spirit. Wood, Britt, and Jackson discuss this:

> The restless heart—a sense of an inner restlessness that prevents inner peace—is a universal, timeless, phenomenon. Life is a rhythm of discovering needs and pursuing satisfaction of those needs. . . . The questing heart looks for a resting place. But each satisfaction in life leads to another, perhaps previously undefined, longing. . . . Augustine of Hippo expressed our heart's desire in the opening words of his autobiography when he wrote, "Thou has made us for thyself and restless is our heart until it comes to rest in thee."[7]

Thus, spirituality, according to Augustine and Bunyan, involves a life-long journey that culminates when the traveler encounters God. Perhaps it continues even further in the next life.

Some people who are on a spiritual journey are not looking for God, however. In fact, some seekers are searching for an ideal of truth rather than the person of God. R. S. Goldberg, a psychiatrist, details this alternative search: "spirituality is a search for universal truth. . . . our conception of spirituality must be broad enough to include the strivings of all seekers of universal truth, and not only those we encounter on Saturday or Sunday morning."[8]

Encounter with Transcendence

A second dimension of spirituality deals with the belief that there is a transcendent dimension to life. Many human beings recognize the existence of a level of reality that exceeds the limits of ordinary human experience. As the Elkins group notes,

> But whatever the content, typology, metaphors, or models used to describe the transcendent dimension, the spiritual person believes in the "more"—that what is "seen" is not all there is. . . . The spiritual person is one who has experienced the transcendent dimension, often through what Maslow referred to as "peak experiences," and he or she draws personal power through contact with this dimension.[9]

S. L. Granstrom also believes that the experience of the transcendent is a vital element in spirituality, suggesting that "spirituality involves a personal quest to find meaning and purpose in life and a relationship to the Mystery/God and the rest of the universe."[10] It is not clear whether or how the quest for meaning or purpose is connected to the search for a relationship with the Mystery or God.

By citing these writers I am not arguing that God is experienced as transcendent as opposed to immanent. Rather, my claim is that however we experience God, God is clearly greater than our human capacity to comprehend or to control. Whether it is the account of Abraham being instructed to leave his homeland (Gen. 12:1ff), the narrative of Moses being drawn to the burning bush (Exodus 3:1ff), the call of Isaiah (Isaiah 6:1ff), the story of Jonah being sent to Nineveh (Jonah 1:1ff), or the report of God sending Jesus into the world (Luke 1:26ff), the Biblical lesson is that God reaches out to us. We are not able to reach across the gulf between us and God.

Community

While the search for God can be a very private affair, members of religions such as Christianity, Judaism, and Islam often find that being in community with like-minded believers is important to their spirituality. Groeschel stresses the importance of community:

> Whatever the individual's life, one must grow with others if one is to grow spiritually. It was Harry Stack Sullivan's insight that we learn to be and remain functioning individuals only in relation to others; this is an important concept in the spiritual life.[11]

Hay also identifies the struggle to overcome limits as a process for experiencing spirituality as community:

> Spirituality is experienced as a capacity for transcending one's working realities, (physical, sensory, rational and philosophical), in order to love and be loved within one's communities, to give meaning to existence and to cope with the exigencies of life.[12]

Perhaps the formation of a sufficient number of such loving communities will eventually stimulate the rest of the human race to work at overcoming the factors that inhibit something approaching a more global experience of spiritual community.

Soeken and Carson, members of the nursing profession, define spirituality in a paper that deals with the needs of people who are chronically ill: "Thus spirituality can be considered a conscious or unconscious belief that relates the individual to the world and gives meaning and definition to existence."[13] Their definition recognizes the importance of the stage I am calling "journey." It also seems to affirm an experience of connectedness with the world and thus of being in community.

Religion

One does not have to be a religious person to recognize that religion has an enormous impact on the lives of billions of people. It is not an exaggeration to note that for many people religion helps make life bearable. S. M. Jourard acknowledges this:

> Man needs reasons for living and if there are none, he begins to die . . . man is incurably religious. What varies among men is what they are religious about. Whatever a person takes to be the highest value in life can be regarded as his God, the focus and purpose of his time and life.[14]

Relationships in the realms of "spirituality" and "religion" are sometimes ambiguous, and it is worth attempting to clarify what is meant by religion.

Religion is often experienced as a collection of rituals, rules, patterns of life, and other behavior to which one must adhere in order to be accepted in particular religious groups. There is often an attendant array of theologies, beliefs, and a polity to defend, explain, connect with, or to implement the rituals, rules, and other recommended or required behavior. In popular use, however, religion is often understood as what a person does in response to specific personal beliefs about a divine being or beings.[15] On the other hand, a person's individual spirituality may or may not incorporate the rules, rituals and behaviors of a particular religious group. Soeken and Carson see a difference between spirituality and religion: "The spiritual dimension of a person is broader than institutionalized religion, although for some persons spirituality is expressed and developed through formal religious activities such as prayer and worship services."[16]

Goldberg distinguishes religion from spirituality by reminding us that religion presupposes the existence of a supreme being.[17] His definition of spirituality asserts that the ultimate truth for which all of us search is "simply the realization that one's separateness from everything else in the universe is an illusion."[18] One may differ with his understanding of ultimate truth, of course, but it seems broad enough to include the restlessness and searching of which Augustine of Hippo spoke nearly fifteen centuries ago.

The Mystery of Creation

Gerald May sees a connection between spirituality and the environment in which it is to be found. In his book *Will and Spirit,* he says straightforwardly that "spirituality consists of an experienced and interpreted relationship among human beings and the mystery of creation."[19] This "mystery of creation" could include both the natural world and its creator. As such, it may be a spiritual reality with which many of the patients at the Veterans Affairs hospital where I am a chaplain would identify. The overwhelming majority of them (some 98% male) claim that they "find God out in the woods." This statement is usually accompanied by the remark that "I don't need to go to church to find God."

Is the natural world, then, another place where one can actually "find" or experience God? Might the most basic facet of spirituality, at least for some people, be found in a relationship with God as encountered in the objects, creatures, views, and forces of the natural world—within "the mystery of creation"? The experience of many people, including this author, points to the natural world as a place where God is to be encountered.

A specific locale in the natural world may be significant in identifying or fostering spiritual experience. Even the ancient Biblical writers took note of locations as particular elements in the experience of God's presence (the desert for the wandering Israelites, the mountain to which Elijah fled, the ground near the burning bush, the mountain top for Peter, James, and John, etc.). It was in specific places or environments that God was somehow present to God's people.

I myself can speak of knowing the ocean as a place where God is present at specific times. Other persons may respond to different aspects of their environment—sunsets, mountains, the colors of autumn in the Northeastern United States, waterfalls, the Grand Canyon—as occasions when the mystery of creation is evoked and with it the presence of God.

Transformation

Perhaps nowhere outside of organized religion is it more obvious how important personal transformation is to spirituality than in the Twelve-Step programs that began with Alcoholics Anonymous. Each step is intended to lead to greater personal change than those before. The process of change begins with an admission of helplessness over alcohol or some other substance or force. By the time one is actively involved with step 12 a person is sharing with others how the program can help to change one's behavior and leading assumptions.

In an article entitled "Spirituality in the Recovery Process," F. A. Prezioso defines spirituality as a dynamic process that leads to change as one becomes increasingly involved with others.

> Spirituality is a quality that belongs exclusively to the human animal. . . . It's the life energy, the restlessness, that calls us beyond "self" to concern for, and relationships with, others and to a relationship with the mysterious "other." Spirituality is our ability to stand outside of ourselves and consider the meaning of our actions, the complexity of our motives and the impact we have on the world around us. It is our capacity to experience passion for a cause, compassion for others and forgiveness of self. Spirituality is a process of becoming, not an achievement; a potential rather than a possession. . . .[20]

One may examine specific elements of Prezioso's definition, each of the steps in the 12 Steps, or various facets of other definitions of spirituality and discover the same result. One is almost always having to face at least the implicit need for transformation as an element in spiritual growth. Spirituality almost always involves the ongoing process of becoming.

Evil

The reality, however, is that we all face times when we are not involved in the "process of becoming." Instead, we find ourselves enmeshed in something that may undo some part or much of what we have become. That is, our words, thoughts, and actions may be spiritually destructive rather than constructive. It is then that we are involved with evil.

That raises the question of what we mean when we use the word "evil." Theories abound in attempts to answer that question. Morton Kelsey reminds us of the widespread belief in a bipolar spiritual reality where one pole is a good God and the other an evil spirit known as Lucifer or Satan.[21] There are also experiences of destructiveness in nature, both of disease and violent upheavals like earthquakes and volcanic explosions, that can be thought of as evil because so much good is undone and so many people suffer. There are collective experiences of evil such as the Holocaust and wars. There is also the experience of individual evil which results from personal failings of many kinds.

Another way to describe the existence of evil is to suggest that it is anything that contributes to a lack of progress, or even to regression, in one or more of the six dimensions of spirituality. This can happen whenever a person, force, or group directly interferes with an individual's or a group's progress in any of the six dimensions. It can also result from a reluctance to grow through the experience of any one or more of these dimensions. Discovering how to cope with evil begins with identifying as clearly as possible how the evil developed and where the resistance originated, most importantly whether the forces are within or beyond oneself. Identifying the potential for evil or its actual existence at some level would only require noting the fact that one has regressed or that one is resistant to developing oneself in one or more of the six dimensions of spirituality.

Summary

This six-part model of spirituality is proposed as a model for describing the spirituality of individual people. Further reflection may demonstrate the need for refinement of the model. For the moment, however, it may offer a starting-point for developing qualitative and even perhaps some quantitative ways to describe a working spirituality and changes in it. It is flexible in allowing an investigator to utilize only as many dimensions as are applicable to the experience of a particular person or a group. It is not necessarily limited to those who claim a Judaeo-Christian heritage.

Notes

1. D. N. Elkins, L. J. Hedstrom, L. L. Hughes, J. A. Leaf, and C. Saunders, "Toward a Humanistic-Phenomenological Spirituality: Definition, Description, and Measurement," Journal of Humanistic Psychology 28 (1988): 9.

2. Ibid.

3. Ibid., 11.

4. Gordon Allport, preface to V. Frankl, *Man's Search for Meaning: An Introduction to Logotherapy* (New York: Pocket Books, 1959), xi.

5. B. C. Johnson, "Spirituality and the Later Years," *Journal of Religion and Aging* 6.3/4 (1985): 128.

6. J. Bunyan, *The Pilgrim's Progress* (Old Tappan, N.J.: Revell, 1985).

7. *Augustine: Confessions and Enchiridion*, trans. and ed. A. C. Outler (Philadelphia: Westminster, 1955), 31. Cited in C. Wood, C. Britt, and J. Jackson, *Spiritual Life—Book One: Spiritual Hunger, Transformation, Discipline* (Nashville: Graded Press, 1986), 6–7.

8. R. S. Goldberg, "The Transpersonal Element in Spirituality and Psychiatry," *Psychiatric Residents' Newsletter* 10 (1990): 9.

9. Elkins et al., op. cit., 10.

10. S. L. Granstrom, "Spiritual Nursing Care for Oncology Clients," *Topics in Clinical Nursing* 7 (1985): 41. Cited in M. A. Burkhardt and M. G. Nagai-Jacobson, "Dealing with Spiritual Concerns of Clients in the Community," *Journal of Community Health Nursing* 2 (1985): 192.

11. B. J. Groeschel, *Spiritual Passages: The Psychology of Spiritual Development* (New York: Crossroad, 1984), 53.

12. M. W. Hays, "Principles in Building Spiritual Assessment Tools," *The American Journal of Hospice Care* (September–October 1989): 25.

13. K. L. Soeken and V. J. Carson, "Responding to the Spiritual Needs of the Chronically Ill," *Nursing Clinics of North America* 22 (1987): 604.

14. S. M. Jourard, *Health Personality* (New York: Macmillan, 1974), 305–7. In R. I. Stoll, "Guidelines for Spiritual Assessment," *American Journal of Nursing* (1979): 1574.

15. Scott Hinrichs, personal communication to the author during an extended clinical pastoral education unit at the Dartmouth Hitchcock Medical Center, Lebanon, N.H., October 1991–April 1992.

16. Soeken and Carson, op. cit., 603.

17. Goldberg, op. cit., 1.

18. Ibid.

19. G. May, *Will and Spirit* (San Francisco: Harper & Row, 1982), 22. Cited in *Spirituality and Pastoral Care*, ed. D. S. Browning (Philadelphia: Fortress, 1985), 55.

20. F. A. Prezioso, "Spirituality in the Recovery Process," *Journal of Substance Abuse Treatment* 4 (1987): 233.

21. M. Kelsey, *Discernment: A Study in Ecstasy and Evil* (New York: Paulist, 1978), 97ff.

A Spirituality for the New Axial Period

Ewert Cousins

At the recent Parliament of the World's Religions in Chicago, Diana Eck of Harvard University introduced the opening plenary address. The speaker was Robert Müller, former Deputy Secretary General of the United Nations, who addressed the topic "Interfaith Harmony and Understanding: Why the Parliament?" In her introduction Diana Eck painted a picture of how different the 1993 gathering was from the original parliament held in Chicago a hundred years before. In 1893 when Swami Vivekananda arrived after traveling for some months to the parliament, there were no Hindus living in Chicago. A Buddhist speaker at the parliament named Dharmapala asked the huge assembly how many had read or heard of the life of the Buddha. Only five raised their hands.

How different it is today! Religious pluralism, which was novel then, has now become part of our familiar environment. Diana Eck described the dramatic shift in our population that occurred after Congress changed our immigration laws in 1965, opening the door for thousands of Asians to take up residence here. This new pluralism has been the object of a major research project under her direction. It is unlike the wave of Zen masters and gurus who came in the 1950s and early 1960s to awaken Westerners to the spiritual

This essay first appeared in *Christian Spirituality Bulletin* 2.2 (fall 1994): 12–15. Used by permission.

quest. Like our earlier Italian and Irish immigrants, the Asians bring their families with them and set up the equivalent of parishes in Christian and Jewish neighborhoods. Instead of ashrams and Zendos, temples and mosques dot our landscape. Global pluralism has entered our back yard.

Multiculturalism

The 1993 Parliament was a symbol of the emerging global community. More than six thousand participants—representing the broad spectrum of religions—gathered in Chicago for eight days of interreligious dialogue, ritual celebration, and artistic expression. The mood was predominantly irenic although dissension did erupt, usually fueled by political issues.

In his keynote address Robert Müller expressed hope for the future, but made an impassioned plea to religious leaders to channel their spiritual wisdom into the solution of world problems. Like many informed observers, Müller believes that the human community is undergoing an enormous transformation. As I will develop shortly, I believe that this is the greatest and most far-reaching transformation in human history. The challenges are overwhelming; the stakes are high—either survival and flourishing or disintegration and destruction. At this moment the need for penetrating and far-sighted wisdom is imperative. It has never been greater in human history.

Each of the wisdom traditions of the world—individually and collectively—must tap the richness of its spiritual heritage and at the same time awaken a new creativity to meet the challenges of this decisive moment in history. By wisdom I mean not any kind of knowledge, but a deep knowledge accompanied by discernment of what is true and right. It seeks ultimate values and the orientation of all of life to these values. Wisdom is the term most often applied to the teachings of the world's religions: of the sages and prophets, the priests and saints, the gurus and shamans.

What can the West offer in the search for a global wisdom? It has just recently witnessed the disintegration of its cherished paradigm of modernity. The emergence of post-modernism seems hardly capable of reaching a level of spiritual wisdom that could compare with that of Hinduism, Buddhism, or Confucianism. Does this open the way for the West to recover its own classical spiritual heritage? In dialogue with the other traditions? In collaborative creative transformation?

In the meantime the process moves forward. New voices are being heard, the voices of those who have been oppressed for centuries: women, the poor, primal peoples, racial and ethnic minorities around the world, the economically and politically oppressed peoples of the southern hemisphere. This chorus has ushered in the phenomenon of multiculturalism.

At its best multiculturalism can manifest the rich diversity of the human community. At its worst it can create a cacophony of discordant voices, stimulating and perpetuating violence throughout the world. It can become so politicized that power substitutes for wisdom and social identity for spirituality. Ethnic concerns can blind groups to the global common good. In the midst of these human strivings, the earth itself is being threatened. Our life support systems are being undermined as prophetic voices seek to halt and reverse the forces of ecological destruction that are escalating each day. In this tumult the question arises: What is the relevance of the wisdom of the past? Is there new wisdom emerging in our times?

The Axial Period

I will now present my own interpretation of the global transformation that the human community is going through. In this I draw heavily from Teilhard, but supplement his understanding of the evolution of consciousness with the thought of the German philosopher and intellectual historian Karl Jaspers.

In order to view the present and the past transformations, we must disengage ourselves from any particular culture or religion, situating ourselves at a viewing point from which we can see clearly both cultures and religions in a global perspective. In doing this we will be like the astronauts who travelled into outer space and looked back on the earth. What they saw overwhelmed them! For the first time in history, humans actually saw the earth as a whole. This image of the beautiful blue globe, shining against the black background of the universe, moving in its orbit in space, can concretely symbolize the emergence of global consciousness on the eve of the twenty-first century.

From our astronaut's position, let us look back in history to another period when the world religions were fundamentally shaped into their present form. If we look at the earth from our distant vantage point during the first millennium B.C.E., we would observe a remarkable phenomenon. From the period between 800–200 B.C.E., peaking about 500 B.C.E., a striking transformation of consciousness occurred around the earth in three geographic regions, apparently without the influence of one on the other. If we look at China, we will see two great teachers, Lao-tze and Confucius, from whose wisdom emerged the schools of Chinese philosophy. In India the cosmic, ritualistic Hinduism of the Vedas was being transformed by the Upanishads, while the Buddha and Mahavira ushered in two new religious traditions. If we turn our gaze farther west, we observe a similar development in the eastern Mediterranean region. In Israel the Jewish prophets—Elijah, Isaiah, and Jeremiah—called forth from their people a new moral awareness. In Greece Western philosophy was born. The pre-Socratic cosmologists sought a rational explanation for the universe; Socrates awakened the moral consciousness of the Athenians; Plato and Aristotle developed metaphysical systems.

It was Karl Jaspers who some 45 years ago pointed out the significance of this phenomenon in his book *The Origin and Goal of History*.[1] He called this period from 800–200 B.C.E. the Axial Period because "it gave birth to everything which, since then, man has been able to be." It is here in this period "that we meet with the most deepcut dividing line in history. Man, as we know him today, came into being. For short, we may style this the 'Axial Period.'"[2] Although the leaders who effected this change were philosophers and religious teachers, the change was so radical that it affected all aspects of culture; for it transformed consciousness itself. It was within the horizons of this form of consciousness that the great civilizations of Asia, the Middle East, and Europe developed. Although within these horizons many developments occurred through the subsequent centuries, the horizons themselves did not change. It was this form of consciousness that was spread to other regions through migrations and explorations, thus becoming the dominant, though not exclusive, form of consciousness in the world. To this day, whether we have been born and raised in the culture of China, India, Europe, or the Americas, we bear the structure of consciousness that was shaped in this Axial Period.

What is this structure of consciousness and how does it differ from pre-Axial consciousness? Prior to the Axial Period the dominant form of consciousness was cosmic, collective, tribal, mythic, and ritualistic. This is the characteristic form of consciousness of primal peoples. The consciousness of the tribal cultures was intimately related to the cosmos and to the fertility cycles of nature. Thus was established a rich and creative harmony between primal peoples and the world of nature. Just as they felt themselves part of nature, so they experienced themselves as part of the tribe. It was precisely the web of interrelationships within the tribe that sustained them psychologically, energizing all aspects of their lives. To be separated from the tribe threatened them with death, not only physical but psychological as well.

The Axial Period ushered in a radically new form of consciousness. Whereas primal consciousness was tribal, Axial consciousness was individual. "Know thyself" became the watchword of Greece; the Upanishads identified the *atman*, the transcendent center of the self. The Buddha charted the way of individual enlightenment; the Jewish prophets awakened individual moral responsibility. This sense of individual identity, as distinct from the tribe and from nature, is the most characteristic mark of Axial consciousness. From this flow other characteristics: consciousness that is self-reflective, analytic, and that can be applied to nature in the form of scientific theories, to society in the form of social critique, to knowledge in the form of philosophy, to religion in the form of mapping an individual spiritual journey. This self-reflective, analytic, critical consciousness stood in sharp contrast to primal mythic and ritualistic consciousness. When self-reflective *logos* emerged in the Axial Period, it tended to oppose the traditional *mythos*.

Although Axial consciousness brought many benefits, it involved loss as well. It severed the harmony with nature and the tribe. Axial persons were in possession of their own identity, it is true, but they had lost their organic relation to nature and community. They now ran the risk of being alienated from the matrix of being and life. With their new powers, they could criticize the social structure and by analysis discover the abstract laws of science and metaphysics, but they might find themselves mere spectators of a drama of which, in reality, they were an integral part.

The emergence of Axial consciousness was decisive for religions, since it marked the divide in history where the major religions emerged and separated themselves from their primal antecedents. The great religions of the world as we know them today are the product of the Axial Period. Hinduism, Buddhism, Taoism, Confucianism, and Judaism took shape in their classical form during this period; and Judaism provided the base for the later emergence of Christianity and Islam. The common structures of consciousness found in these religions are characteristic of the general transformation of consciousness effected in the Axial Period.

Axial and Primal Spirituality

The move into Axial consciousness released enormous spiritual energy. It opened up the individual spiritual path, especially the inner way in which the new subjectivity became the avenue into the transcendent. It allowed the deeper self to sort out the difference between the illusion of the phenomenal world and the authentic vision of reality. On the ethical level it allowed individual moral conscience to take a critical stand against the collectivity. And it made possible a link between the moral and the spiritual aspects of the self, so that a path could be charted through virtues toward the ultimate goal of the spiritual quest.

Although Axial consciousness opened many possibilities, it tended to close off others and to produce some negative results. The release of spiritual energy thrust the Axial person in the direction of the spirit and away from the earth, away from the life cycles and the harmony with nature which the primal peoples experienced and which they made the basis of their spirituality. In some traditions this emergence of spiritual energy caused a radical split between the phenomenal world and true reality, between matter and spirit, between earth and heaven. Although in a number of traditions this separation was not central, nevertheless the emergence of Axial consciousness, with its strong sense of subjectivity, made that separation not only possible, but a risk and a threat. From the time of the Axial Period, the spiritual path tended to lead away from the earth and towards the heavenly realms above.

Note that I am placing the radical transformation of consciousness in the first millennium B.C.E. and not at the rise of Western science in the Renaissance and the Age of Enlightenment. It is, of course, true that Western science was innovative, even radical. Yet I believe that it developed within the horizons of Axial consciousness and represents one of its possible trajectories. In fact, at the same time that science enlarged the understanding of matter, it progressively narrowed Western Axial consciousness by employing exclusively a mechanical model and by limiting human knowledge to what can be grasped only by an empirical method. In Western science the earlier Axial split between matter and spirit was intensified. Descartes ignored spirit and saw mind as a detached observer of mechanical forces. Although this paradigm yielded enormous knowledge of the physical world, its narrow perspective only added to the fragmentation latent in the original Axial transformation.

The Second Axial Period

If we shift our gaze from the first millennium B.C.E. to the eve of the twenty-first century, we can discern another transformation of consciousness. It is so profound and far-reaching that I call it the Second Axial Period. Like the first it is happening simultaneously around the earth, and like the first it will shape the horizon of consciousness for future centuries. Not surprisingly, too, it will have great significance for world religions, which were constituted in the First Axial Period. However, the new form of consciousness is different from that of the First Axial Period. Then it was individual consciousness, now it is global consciousness.

In order to understand better the forces at work in the Second Axial Period, I will draw from Teilhard. In the light of his research in evolution, he charted the development of consciousness from its roots in the geosphere and biosphere and into the future. In a process which he calls "planetization," he observed that a shift in the forces of evolution had occurred over the past hundred years. This shift is from divergence to convergence. When human beings first appeared on this planet, they clustered together in family and tribal units, forming their own group identity and separating themselves from other tribes. In this way humans diverged, creating separate nations and a rich variety of cultures. However, the spherical shape of the earth prevented unlimited divergence. With the increase in population and the rapid development of communication, groups could no longer remain apart. After dominating the process for millennia, the forces of divergence have been superseded by those of convergence. This shift to convergence is drawing the various cultures into a single planetized community. Although we have been conditioned by thousands of years of divergence, we now have no other course open to us but to cooperate creatively with the forces of convergence as these are drawing us toward global consciousness.[3]

According to Teilhard this new global consciousness will not level all differences among peoples; rather it will generate what he calls creative unions in which diversity is not erased but intensified. His understanding of creative unions is based on his general theory of evolution and the dynamic which he observes throughout the universe. From the geosphere to the biosphere to the realm of consciousness, a single process is at work, which he articulates as the law of "complexity-consciousness" and "union differentiates." "In any domain," he says, "whether it be the cells of a body, the members of a society or the elements of a spiritual synthesis—*union differentiates*."[4] From subatomic particles to global consciousness, individual elements unite in what Teilhard calls center to center unions. By touching each other at the creative core of their being, they release new energy which leads to more complex units. Greater complexity leads to greater interiority which, in turn, leads to more creative unions. Throughout the process, the individual elements do not lose their identity, but rather deepen and fulfill it through union.

In the light of Teilhard's thought, then, we can better understand the meeting of religions on the eve of the twenty-first century. The world religions are the product of the First Axial Period and the forces of divergence. Although in the first millennium B.C.E., there was a common transformation of consciousness, it occurred in diverse geographical regions within already differentiated cultures. In each case the religion was shaped by this differentiation in its origin, and developed along differentiated lines. This produced a remarkable richness of spiritual wisdom, of spiritual energies and of religious-cultural forms to express, preserve, and transmit this heritage. Now that the forces of divergence have shifted to convergence, the religions must meet each other in center to center unions, discovering through interreligious dialogue what is most authentic in each other, releasing creative energy toward a more complexified form of religious consciousness.

This global consciousness, complexified through the meeting of cultures and religions, is only one characteristic of the Second Axial Period.

The consciousness of this period is global in another sense: namely, in rediscovering its roots in the earth. At the very moment when the various cultures and religions are striving to create a new global community, our life on the planet is being threatened. The very tools which we have used to bring about this convergence—industrialization and technology—are undercutting the biological support system that sustains life on our planet. The future of consciousness—even life on the earth—is shrouded in a cloud of uncertainty by the pollution of our environment, the depletion of natural resources, the unjust distribution of wealth, the stockpiling of nuclear weapons. Unless the human community reverses these destructive forces, it may not survive far into the twenty-first century.

In this Second Axial Period we must rediscover the dimensions of consciousness of the spirituality of the primal peoples of the pre-Axial Period. As we saw, this consciousness was collective and cosmic, rooted in the earth and the life cycles. We must rapidly appropriate that form of consciousness or perish from the earth. However, I am not suggesting a romantic attempt to live in the past; rather that the evolution of consciousness proceeds by way of recapitulation. Having developed self-reflective, analytic, critical consciousness in the First Axial Period, we must now, while retaining these values, reappropriate and integrate into that consciousness the collective and cosmic dimensions of the pre-Axial consciousness. We must recapture the unity of tribal consciousness by seeing humanity as a single tribe. And we must see this single tribe related organically to the total cosmos.

This means that the consciousness of the twenty-first century will be global from two perspectives: (1) from a horizontal perspective, cultures and religions are meeting each other on the surface of the globe, entering into creative encounters that can produce a complexified collective consciousness; (2) from a vertical perspective, they must plunge their roots deep into the earth in order to provide a stable and secure base for future development. This new global consciousness must be organically ecological, supported by structures that will insure justice and peace. In the Second Axial Period this twofold global consciousness is not only a creative possibility to enhance the twenty-first century; it is an absolute necessity if we are to survive.

What I am suggesting is that the real challenge of the global community is a spiritual one. This gives a strategic place to theology and religious studies. From an educational point of view it can be seen as a challenge in the realm of wisdom—for each of the world's religions to retrieve its spiritual wisdom, to enter into deep dialogue with the other bearers of wisdom, and together creatively seek the collective wisdom so vitally needed for the future of the human community.

More specifically, within the wisdom traditions we must be creative and imaginative, for example, asking questions about the ultimate roots of human identity in a global context. Beyond racial, ethnic, gender, and cultural identity, is there a deeper spiritual identity? Can this be a basis for the global community? Teilhard, for example, answers yes, in terms of the grounding of all humans in Omega. One strategy in our courses would be to explore the different models, within the world's religions, for establishing the unity of the human community.

Finally, we must address in an equally creative way those common problems that are challenging the human community as a whole: poverty, violence, destruction of the environment, the oppression of races, ethnic groups, and women. These are the common challenges facing all the wisdom traditions, urging them to develop a transformed spirituality of the human and of matter. We must listen to the contemporary prophetic voices but situate their message in a larger wisdom—viewing them from our astronaut's perspective, seeing the earth as the home of a human community striving for a new ecologically sound, holistic humanism.

Notes

1. Karl Jaspers, *The Origin and Goal of History,* trans. Michael Bullock (New Haven: Yale University Press, 1953). For a study of Jaspers on pluralism in religion, see John F. Kane, *Pluralism and Truth in Religion: Karl Jaspers on Existential Truth* (Chico, Calif.: Scholars Press, 1981).

2. Jaspers, *The Origin and Goal of History,* 1.

3. Pierre Teilhard de Chardin, *The Phenomenon of Man* (New York: Harper & Row, 1965), 242–43.

4. Ibid., 262.

Part 3

Christian Traditions

What is truly refreshing about the study of Christian spirituality today is that it is often marked by an ecumenical spirit. Presbyterians attend workshops with Roman Catholics and Methodists. Evangelicals and mainline Lutherans dialog energetically with the Eastern Orthodox. Nuns chat over coffee with Anglican priests, and the Society for the Study of Christian Spirituality, a group that arose out of the American Academy of Religion in the early 1990s, is genuinely ecumenical in its programs as well as in its membership.

It is doubtful, however, if the same kind of cooperation, even affinity, would have emerged among members of such diverse denominations if the focus had been either doctrine or liturgy. But it seems that the discipline of spirituality has the uncanny ability to bring people together and remove some of the doubts and fears that separate believers from one another. Indeed, the discipline of Christian spirituality is broad enough and contains so many elements of common interest that people from quite diverse religious traditions can come together and

participate in a common conversation. What follows, then, are the "voices," the "dialects," of that larger conversation. And though the accents of the speakers are all different, they give evidence of an inclusive, universal language.

In the first selection, Keith Egan displays the themes of Carmelite spirituality in the Roman Catholic church. A religious order that from its beginnings stressed solitude, silence, prayer, asceticism, and daily Eucharist, the Carmelite community emerged in the Holy Land near Mount Carmel around 1200. Two important transitions occurred in the life of this spiritual order: First, what was once a semi-eremitic community, with members living in individual cells, in time became a cenobitic, communal one. And second, a papal bull in 1452 created a Carmelite order for women from which emerged some of the more prominent leaders of Christian spirituality, namely, Theresa of Avila, with her emphasis on prayer and contemplation, and Thérèse of Lisieux, who portrayed in both life and teaching the beauty of humility. Both women, interestingly enough, looked to the famous

Carmelite divine John of the Cross as both mentor and guide.

The next chapter, which examines Orthodox spirituality, was written anonymously by "a monk of the Eastern church." Here the author carefully displays the major themes of this tradition, including union with God (*henō-sis*), deification (*theōsis*), synergy (divine/human cooperation in redemption), *hēsychia* (silent prayer), and an emphasis on the Holy Trinity in devotion and life. The writings of Pseudo-Dionysius (who was most probably a Syrian monk in the fifth or early sixth century) inform the discussion at key points, especially in terms of the distinction between asceticism and mysticism and in terms of the description of the stages of the spiritual life as purgation, illumination, and union, a typology, by the way, that has had an enormous impact not only on Eastern spirituality but on Western spirituality as well.

In a work that attempts to clear up some misunderstanding, Bengt Hoffman elucidates Lutheran spirituality largely in terms of the great sixteenth-century Reformer himself. Maintaining that Luther held together both the Christ-for-us of Lutheran orthodoxy and the Christ-in-us of later Lutheran pietism, Hoffman criticizes those views that fail to recognize not only that Luther quoted with approval the mystical theology of Bernard of Clairvaux, but also that his teaching on justification by faith must not be seen as a repudiation of the Christ-in-us themes so important to an understanding of sanctification. For Hoffman, Luther's spirituality was a balanced one; it held together the justifying *for*-you and the sanctifying *in*-you motifs, even if later Lutheran tradition did not.

In a similar fashion, Howard Hageman attempts to dispel some erroneous notions concerning his own tradition, Reformed spirituality, by affirming at the outset that this characteristic spirituality was in place prior to the ministry of John Calvin through the work of Ulrich Zwingli in Zurich. Nevertheless, Hageman is genuinely appreciative of the significant— and in some sense unique—contribution that Calvin has made to Reformed spirituality. For one thing, it was the Genevan Reformer who underscored and developed "mystical union with Christ" as the leading theme of Reformed spirituality. In this setting, justification and sanctification are seen as dual gifts that come from our relationship with Christ in the communal context of the church where the believer is united to the one Word through the proclamation of the gospel and through receiving the Lord's Supper. Thus, "the lonely pious *individual* striving to become more like Christ," Hageman cautions, "has little or no place in the spirituality of Calvin."

In exploring another great communion of the Reformation, Harvey Guthrie rightly recognizes that he must first of all describe the essence or ethos of Anglicanism itself before he can consider its spirituality. To that end, Guthrie offers three basic manifestations of the church: (1) confessional (affirming the faith held by the church), (2) experiential (experiencing a distinct conversion), and (3) pragmatic (participating in what the church does liturgically, sacramentally, and empirically). Now Anglicanism is best understood, Guthrie contends, in terms of the third manifestation of the church (pragmatic) with an emphasis on participation, that is, on taking part in the life of the church in its round of activities and duties. Anglican spirituality, then, which finds its basis in the Book of Common Prayer as a *Regulum*, is corporate, liturgical, and sacramental. It is grounded in "participating with the church in what the church does in the Eucharist, in the Office, [and] in the various sacraments and ordinances."

In the longest essay of this section, David Lowes Watson displays the nature of historic Methodist spirituality as the confluence of three key elements: (1) "Anglican holiness of intent," (2) "Puritan inward assurance," and (3) a context of "accountable discipleship." Concerning the first element, Watson considers the work of Jeremy Taylor, a Caroline divine of the sev-

enteenth century, and William Law, the Non-Juror and one-time mentor of John Wesley, extremely influential, as each wrote on heart religion in terms of purity of intention and devotion to God. Watson attributes the second aspect of Wesley's spirituality, that of inward assurance, largely to Puritan influence and even points out that numerous authors from this tradition (such as Samuel Clarke, Robert Bolton, John Preston, Richard Alleine, John Bunyan, Richard Baxter, and Edmund Calamy) all appeared in Wesley's *A Christian Library*, though it would perhaps have been better to underscore the Moravian contribution as well. The last emphasis of "accountable discipleship" reveals how seriously Wesley took the formal elements of spiritual growth such as the means of grace (prayer, reading the Bible, receiving the Lord's Supper, fasting, and Christian conference), as well as the various groups such as classes, bands, and the select societies that provided the context for mutuality, support, and accountability in the Christian life.

The last essay of this section displays the substance of evangelical spirituality throughout history. Richard Lovelace points out the engaging and at times controversial nature of Reformation spirituality in its polemic against all of the following: monasticism, the notion that "infused contemplation" is only for a spiritual elite, and the basic typology of Pseudo-

Dionysius as purgation, illumination, and union. Far more irenic were the Puritans of a later age who identified regeneration with conscious conversion and who sought to graft patristic and medieval spirituality onto the Reformation base of justification by faith. Indeed, Lovelace considers Puritanism as a bridge movement in which modern evangelicals and Roman Catholics may find spiritual common roots, though contemporary evangelicals must first of all attend to some of their own problems such as "a sanctification gap," sentimentality in promoting assurance "under any circumstances," and "cheap grace."

Carmelite Spirituality

Keith J. Egan

The name *Carmelite* derives from the mountain range Mount Carmel in the Holy Land, where the Carmelite Order originated about A.D. 1200. A group of lay penitent hermits at the wadi ʿain es-Shiah received a formula of life from Albert, patriarch of Jerusalem, between 1206 and 1214. This formula of life gave the Carmelites their basic spiritual orientation in the Church. The themes of this formula were solitude (individual cells located around a chapel), silence, continual prayer (chiefly the psalms), with life centered on the following of Jesus and an uncommon eremitic element of daily Eucharist when possible, and a life of the usual asceticism common to hermits. Albert's formula of life did not envisage pastoral ministry to those outside the community. In 1229 Pope Gregory IX imposed corporate poverty on the hermits of Mount Carmel.

The deterioration of the Latin kingdom soon made it imperative for the hermits to emigrate from the Holy Land. The Carmelite hermits began to move westward about 1238. They migrated to Cyprus, Sicily, England, and southern France. Within a short time the Carmelites found that their eremitic lifestyle was ill-suited to contemporary religious life in Western Europe. At the very time that the Carmelites were founding eremitic houses in Europe, the Dominicans and Franciscans were meeting the pastoral challenges of the Fourth Lateran Council with extraordinary success.

This essay first appeared in *The New Dictionary of Catholic Spirituality*, ed. Michael Downey (Collegeville, Minn.: Liturgical Press, 1993), 117–25. Used by permission.

Faced with this dilemma, the Carmelites acted expeditiously. They sought from the papacy approval for a revision of their formula of life that would make it possible for them to follow in the footsteps of the extremely popular friars. The Carmelites received from Innocent IV approval for slight changes in the wording of their formula of life. Through Innocent's action the formula became an official Rule (*regula*), and the Carmelites became friars. Minor as were the textual changes in the Rule, they had an enormous impact on Carmelite spirituality. The hermits from Mount Carmel were now allowed to settle in towns as well as in the wilderness locations formerly permitted by the formula of life. They were to live in a dormitory (though still with individual cells), eat together in a refectory, and participate in the choral Office. The once semi-eremitic community thus became more cenobitic.

These changes meant, in effect, that the Carmelite hermits were now mendicants like the Dominicans and the Franciscans. They resolutely and immediately acted as such by making foundations in the towns of Europe where the Dominicans and the Franciscans were already ministering to the new urban dwellers. To prepare themselves for the ministries of preaching, teaching, and administering the sacraments, the Carmelites took steps that made them, like the other friars, a student order. By the end of the 13th century the Carmelites were well established at the universities of Cambridge, Oxford, and Paris. During the rest of the Middle Ages the Carmelites moved to the other universities of Europe. The Carmelites became and have remained a major mendicant order in the Church. With constitutions modeled on those of the Dominican Order, the Carmelites were thoroughly appropriated into the friars' way of life with a mendicant spirituality: mobility in place of monastic stability, corporate as well as personal poverty, the following of modified monastic prayers and practices, and a commitment to pastoral ministry. They entered the ranks of the mendicants despite internal and external opposition in the 13th century. Yet, the Carmelite friars retained a memory of their eremitic origins, sometimes vivid, sometimes obscured by other preoccupations. Their eremitic origins and their appropriation of cenobitic mendicancy created the fundamental tension in Carmelite spirituality: solitude and (ministerial) community. Vital Carmelite reforms must always return to this tension in order to recover a form of Carmelite life faithful to the order's origins yet responsive to contemporary circumstances.

Elijah

The prophet Elijah occupies a significant place in Carmelite spirituality. Long before the Carmelites came on the scene, Elijah had been a model for monks and especially for hermits. When the Carmelites settled on Mount Carmel, they were well aware of the association of Elijah with this mountain range. The fountain at their original hermitage on Mount Carmel mentioned in the formula of life was later identified as the fountain of Elijah.

The extant constitutions of the 13th century contain a prologue that saw Carmelite life as modeled on the example of Elijah and Elisha. In the 14th century a literary tradition was initiated that looked to Elijah as the inspiration and the founder of the Carmelite Order. Through the centuries, however, much energy was wasted on a literalist interpretation of this myth. However, the modern retrieval of the Elian tradition emphasizes Elijah as an archetype of Carmelite spirituality. When the French Discalced Carmelites consulted Carl Jung, he assured them that Elijah is, in fact, a genuine "living archetype." The motto on the Carmelite shield is an Elian quotation taken from the Vulgate rendition of 1 Kgs 19:10, 14: "I am zealous with zeal for the Lord God of hosts." Teresa of Jesus and John of the Cross had a profound respect for the tradition that saw Elijah as a primal inspiration for Carmelite life. Both saints refer to Elijah as "our father." The Carmelite liturgical calendar has long celebrated a feast in honor of Elijah (July 20).

Retrievals of the Carmelite tradition must take into account the central role that Elijah has had in shaping Carmelite consciousness. That the Carmelites had no known founder, let alone a charismatic founder like Dominic or Francis, predisposed them to emphasize Elijah and Mary when they were competing with other religious orders for stature. These two figures—one from the Hebrew Scriptures and the other from the Christian Scriptures—have had a fundamental role in the evolution of Carmelite spirituality.

Mary

The chapel around which the hermits on Mount Carmel situated their hermitages was dedicated to Mary, an ancient tradition says, and by the mid–13th century the Carmelite friars bore the title that, in one version or the other, they have preserved since that time: "Brothers of the Blessed Virgin Mary of Mount Carmel." Toward the end of the 13th century, the Carmelites stated that their order had been founded to honor Mary. In the order's struggle for identity during the Middle Ages, Carmelite literature looked more and more to Mary as the order's claim to preeminence.

In the 15th century, devotion to Mary crystalized around the vision of Mary allegedly accorded in the mid–13th century to Simon Stock, a figure about whom little is known once the late medieval legends about him are discarded. Nonetheless, the wearing of the (brown) scapular became a sign of dedication to Mary and of reliance on her promise to Simon Stock of salvation for those who die wearing the scapular. The scapular has also symbolized affiliation with the Carmelite Order. The wearing of the scapular became especially widespread in the 19th and early 20th century and is still a practice among first, second, and third members of the Carmelite Order as well as among those who belong to the Confraternity of Our Lady of Mount Carmel.

In the 17th century there developed within the Carmelite Order a Marian mysticism. Mary, the mother of Jesus, has been and continues to be a central figure in Carmelite spirituality. Although there have been times when this regard for Mary tended toward devotionalism, the Carmelite saints have nurtured a vigorous dedication to the patroness of the order, whose feast as Our Lady of Mount Carmel is July 16. Teresa of Jesus in various places calls herself "a nun of Our Lady of Mount Carmel," and she speaks warmly of wearing Mary's habit. John of the Cross writes in *The Ascent of Mount Carmel* (3.2.10) of Mary's mystical experience. The Carmelites, in addition, continue the medieval custom of making their profession of vows not only to God but also to Blessed Mary. Carmelite identity has been profoundly shaped by a consciousness of the intimacy with the Blessed Virgin that has pervaded the order's history and literature.

Institution of the First Monks

Second only to the Carmelite Rule, the most important medieval text in Carmelite spirituality was the *Institution of the First Monks*. This document appeared about 1370 among a set of texts which were allegedly from an earlier era but which were, in reality, the work of the provincial of Catalonia, Philip Ribot. Otger Steggink has called the *Institution* "the principal book of spiritual reading" among Carmelites until the 17th century. This text, probably studied by Teresa of Avila (in a Castilian translation) and by John of the Cross, laid the groundwork for the mystical orientation of Carmelite spirituality that would be articulated by the two Spanish mystics and the Touraine Reform. The *Institution* sees the life of the Carmelite as a withdrawal from the usual preoccupations of life, a purification of the heart, and the gift of perceived union with God in love. The Carmelite, moreover, according to this document, lives this spiritual journey in the spirit of the prophet Elijah. An edition of this text is being prepared by Paul Chandler and deserves to be much better known by those who seek inspiration in Carmelite spirituality and who wish to understand the roots of the Carmelite mystical tradition.

Reforms and the Origins of the Carmelite Nuns

Like other religious orders in the late Middle Ages, the Carmelites made numerous efforts to return to a more dedicated way of life. By the early 15th century Carmelites in northern Italy initiated a reform that came to be known as the Congregation of Mantua. This group set aside the mitigation of the Carmelite Rule permitted in 1432 by Eugene IV. The Mantuan reform sought a return to the solitude of the Rule and a restoration of both community life and poverty. The latter two elements were at the time concerns of many religious orders seeking reform. The search for solitude, on the other hand, had special significance for Carmelite renewal.

The most important Carmelite reformer before the sixteenth century was the Frenchman Blessed John Soreth, prior general of the order from 1451 until 1471. Soreth, like other reformers of the era, fostered a return to the spirit of the Rule; in fact, he composed an important commentary on the Carmelite Rule. After Soreth's death his reform was not sustained. Yet, the late Middle Ages produced other saintly Carmelites, among them Baptist of Mantua, Angelus Mazzinghi, Frances d'Amboise, Aloysius Rabata, Joan Scopeli, Bartholomew Fanti, and Arcangela Girlani. Baptist of Mantua died in 1516, while the rest of these holy women and men died during the 15th century, not a time known for an overabundance of outstandingly holy religious women and men.

From the time of the entry of the Carmelites into the mendicant ranks, lay women and men associated themselves with the order and on a variety of levels shared fellowship with the Carmelite friars. Unlike the Dominicans and Franciscans, however, the Carmelites did not develop a second order of women in the 13th century. In fact, it was not until A.D. 1452 that a papal bull gave approval for the incorporation of women into the Carmelite family as a second order. This new evolution in Carmelite history had a permanent and profound effect on the Carmelite Order and its spirituality. These Carmelite women were not only the predecessors of Teresa of Jesus but also of all women who became Carmelites after this event of the mid–15th century. With Teresa of Jesus in the next century, women assumed a central role in the living and articulation of Carmelite spirituality. Though women came belatedly to this status in the Carmelite Order, they have been at the heart of Carmelite spirituality since the time of Teresa of Jesus. This introduction of nuns into the Carmelite Order was the achievement of Blessed John Soreth.

Like other orders struggling with reform at the end of the Middle Ages and in the early 16th century, the Carmelites encountered one frustration after another. Nicholas Audet, prior general from 1524 to 1562, made valiant and energetic efforts to reform the Carmelites. However, success eluded him and others. Not until Teresa of Jesus did there emerge an inspired reading of the original Carmelite charism, a reading that brought true and lasting reform to the Carmelite family.

Teresa of Avila (1515–1582)

A midlife conversion experience of Doña Teresa de Ahumada, a nun at the Carmelite monastery of the Incarnation in Avila, was the catalyst for the most significant reform in the history of the Carmelite Order. For Teresa it was the beginning of a whole "new life" when God began to manifest a loving divine presence to her. Reform for the Carmelite women and then the men came when Teresa recalled the fervor and solitude of the 13th-century hermits on Mount Carmel. Solitude had not been available for Teresa in the large and crowded monastery of the Incarnation, so she shaped a new model of Carmelite life at her first foundation of San José in Avila, where she limited the number of nuns to a small enough community to support a life of solitude and prayer. From the time of this foundation Teresa symbolized her new life with a change of name. From then on Teresa never used the formal title "Doña" but signed herself simply as Teresa of Jesus.

In response to the requests of her nuns for instruction in prayer, Teresa composed *The Way of Perfection*, in which she explores relationships in community, the prayer of recollection, and growth in prayer. In her *Book of Foundations* Teresa shows herself a gifted storyteller, providing spirited vignettes of the establishment of her foundations and of the lives of those involved in these foundations. For her confessors Teresa wrote her *Life*. Here Teresa, with some autobiographical details as the framework, describes God's mystical manifestations in her life and also the beginnings of her reform. It is in this book, chapters 11 to 22, that her treatise on prayer appears, with its imagery of water to describe God's growing mystical presence. These chapters can be read as a separate tract once the rest of the book is read as a unit. While her *Life* was in the hands of the Inquisition, Teresa wrote her classic exposition of the mystical journey to God, *The Interior Castle*. With her experience of the mystical life, she leads the reader through the seven mansions—the first three as prelude to the mystical life, and the last four as the journey to the mystical union of spiritual marriage.

In her writings Teresa of Jesus, architect of the Carmelite reform that resulted, after the death of John of the Cross, in the creation of the Discalced Carmelite Order, gives classic expression to the mystical fruition of the Carmelite contemplative tradition. What she describes is the limit of human effort and the unlimited scope of God's loving action in a human person willing to let God love one fully. Her exposition of Carmelite mysticism is down-to-earth, a story told with compassion and humor.

She is clear that what counts is love of God, but she is adamant that the only genuine sign that one loves God is love of neighbor. Her letters show the earthy context of her interests and activities. Teresa's dying words reveal the ecclesial context of her life of Carmelite spirituality. She died calling herself over and over again "a daughter of the Church."

Teresa of Jesus was beatified in 1614, less than thirty-two years after her death, and she was canonized in 1622. In 1970 she was declared the first woman Doctor of the Church. Her warm personality, so evident in her letters and other writings, attracts people of all faiths.

John of the Cross (1542–1591)

Teresa of Jesus handpicked a friar to be her collaborator in the reform of the Carmelite Order. Her choice was the newly ordained John of Saint Matthias, who consented to collaborate in this reform only if Teresa acted quickly. He was already thinking of transferring to the Carthusians for the sake of greater solitude. With Teresa's guidance, John thoroughly committed himself to the radical living of the Carmelite charism. As Teresa had done, her collaborator symbolized the newness of his life by changing his name to John of the Cross.

John's single-minded, God-centered life earned him the animosity of his brothers, who imprisoned him in a tiny closet at the Carmelite monastery in Toledo. There he composed some of his poems, especially many stanzas of his "Spiritual Canticle." After his escape John shared poetry with his directees, especially the Carmelite nuns, who then wanted him to explain the meaning of the poetry that had emerged from his mystical experience. These explanations constitute John of the Cross's four commentaries. *The Ascent of Mount Carmel* and *The Dark Night* comment on the poem "Dark Night," while the following commentaries explain poems with the same names as the commentaries: *The Spiritual Canticle* and *The Living Flame of Love.*

In the past, too little attention has been paid to the poetry of John of the Cross. To understand the spiritual doctrine of John of the Cross, it is necessary to be thoroughly familiar with the poetry upon which he comments. In addition, his letters provide a way of appreciating his relationships with women and men. A better understanding of the doctrine of John of the Cross is available to one who comes to his texts with a thorough acquaintance with his mystically based poetry, his dependence upon the Bible, especially on the Song of Songs, and some knowledge of his compassionate personality. The principal ministry of John of the Cross was spiritual direction, but he was actively involved in other ministries, including his role as an able administrator.

For John of the Cross, the goal of the contemplative life is the transformation of the soul in God, that is, union with God in love. This intensification of love presumes that one has been liberated from the attachments that keep one unfree. The dark-night experience is God's loving action that liberates one in a way that only God can accomplish. John of the Cross calls for radical freedom so that one may be fully open to God's love and love God and neighbor in return. Freed from disordered attachments, the one who is transformed in God, living in union with God, is now free to embrace others and creation as one was formerly unable to do.

In the late 17th century, fear of quietism pushed the spiritual doctrine of John of the Cross into the background. Scholasticism, moreover, robbed John's doctrine of its poetic, biblical, and experiential foundations. The Spanish poets of the 20th century rediscovered the poetry of John of the Cross and brought him to the attention of a wider modern audience. Presently there is a concerted effort to recover his spiritual teachings.

In 1982 the fourth centenary of the death of Teresa of Jesus was an occasion for focusing on the dynamism of Teresa's Carmelite spirituality. The celebration of the fourth centenary of the death of John of the Cross in 1991 offered the same opportunity for the retrieval of the spiritual doctrine of John of the Cross. The writings of Teresa of Avila and John of the Cross are, in fact, the classical expression of the mystical dimension of Carmelite spirituality. In the post–Vatican II era, especially from the 1980s onward, the emphasis has been on learning how to read the writings of these Spanish mystics on their own terms, in their historical context, and with an appreciation of their importance for the Christian life of mystical experience and mystical theology.

John of the Cross was beatified in 1675 and was canonized in 1726. He was declared a Doctor of the Church in 1926. John's poetry and doctrine offer an important opportunity for the healing of the long-standing divorce between mysticism and theology.

Touraine Reform

With the establishment of the Discalced reform as a separate order in 1593, the original branch of the order had to face the need for reform. A congenial climate for reform was found in the renewed interest in the interior life of 17th-century France. The most lasting and influential reform of the original branch took place in the Carmelite province of Touraine. Spearheaded by Peter Behourt (d. 1633), the reform was led by Philip Thibault. The spiritual inspiration of the reform was the blind lay-brother John of St. Samson (d. 1636), who was the source of spiritual guidance for many members of this reform. The Touraine reform was another renewal of the Carmelite contemplative tradition that included a mystical expression of the order's charism. Current research into figures of the reform like John of St. Samson promises a new appreciation of the importance of the Touraine reform, which has had a far-reaching influence on the spirituality of the Carmelite Order down to the 20th century.

Thérèse of Lisieux (1873–1897)

Along with Teresa of Avila and John of the Cross, the most widely known Carmelite is Thérèse Martin, whose name in the monastery was Sister Thérèse of the Child Jesus and of the Holy Face. The popular designation "Little Flower" derives from her love of flowers and her use of flower imagery, especially in her references to herself as a "little flower," but indeed as a "little winter flower" who passed through the harshness of suffering. Despite her use of a spiritual idiom of her day that sounds, at times, coy and sentimental, Thérèse of Lisieux lived and wrote about a spirituality matured in the crucible of suffering. For the last eighteen months before she died, the young nun endured a terrible darkness marked by temptations against faith. Yet, she admitted that it was faith that protected her against suicide.

Though Thérèse never used the phrase "spiritual childhood," she lived and spoke of a little way of trust and love that cut through to the heart of gospel simplicity. Her message, like that of Teresa of Jesus and John of the Cross, has a ring of gospel authenticity, as is evident in the emphasis of all three on the love of God and love of neighbor. For Thérèse, "it is love alone that counts." Thérèse of Lisieux had a playful spirit and an infectious sense of humor. Even amid her sufferings she remained very human, as demonstrated by her request from her sickbed for a chocolate éclair. For Thérèse, God was everywhere or, as she said, "Everything is a grace."

The sources of Thérèse's spirituality were, in particular, the Bible (note the impact of Isaiah's suffering servant texts on her), and especially the Gospels. She was also much influenced by the writings of John of the Cross, which she read avidly over a period of several years and whose doctrine she profoundly appropriated. She looked also to the *Imitation of Christ* and to the Carmelite tradition as it was mediated to her in the monastery at Lisieux.

The Church beatified Thérèse in 1923 and canonized her two years later. In 1927 Pope Pius XI named St. Thérèse, with St. Francis Xavier, principal patroness of the missions. Pius XII in 1944 declared Thérèse to be, with Joan of Arc, the secondary patroness of France. Though she did not write for publication, Thérèse, like Teresa and John, had a gift for expressing her spiritual experience in a telling way. Her *Story of a Soul* quickly became a modern spiritual classic. Moreover, devotion to her was intense and phenomenal until the 1960s, when a waning in her cult took place. Her doctrine and life are presently being recovered with a growing appreciation of the soundness of her spiritual perception.

Modern Carmelite Figures

There are a number of 20th-century Carmelites who have lived the Carmelite charism in a gifted way. Three of them have become particularly well known and have been beatified. Blessed Elizabeth of the Trinity (1880–1906), a French Discalced Carmelite nun, died at age twenty-six in the Carmelite monastery at Dijon. Blessed Elizabeth's Trinitarian spirituality offers to contemporary theologians an opportunity to reflect upon the mystery of the Trinity as revealed in the life and prayer of a modern Carmelite woman. Elizabeth's spirituality, like that of Teresa of Avila, John of the Cross, Thérèse of Lisieux, and the *Institution of the First Monks*, is a mysticism of love—a love of God and neighbor lived in the solitude of the monastery but extended to the neighbor everywhere.

The second modern Carmelite chosen for inclusion here is Edith Stein (1891–1942), a Jew who converted to Catholicism and became a Carmelite nun in her native Germany. She was known in her order as Sister Teresa Benedicta of the Cross. Edith Stein was a brilliant philosopher who served as an assistant to the phenomenologist Edmund Husserl. As a Catholic, Edith became a teacher. She lectured and wrote especially about issues concerning the education of women. As a Carmelite nun in Cologne, she published an important study of John of the Cross. Her writings, philosophical and otherwise, are being translated into English. As a Jewish, Catholic, Carmelite philosopher and educator, Edith Stein's life and writings have the potential for drawing together what appear to be the irreconcilable paradoxes of her life and also of her death. She was executed in the Nazi concentration camp at Auschwitz. The naming of Edith Stein as a blessed is, indeed, a puzzle for Jews, who view her as a victim of the extermination of the Jews by the Nazis rather than as a Catholic martyr. As a woman intellectual from the Carmelite contemplative tradition, Edith Stein may yet prove to be an inspiration for the reconciliation of Jews and Christians. The beatification of Edith Stein took place in 1987.

Titus Brandsma (1881–1942), a Carmelite friar of the Ancient Observance, was a professor at the University of Nijmegen and a journalist. In his branch of the order, Titus Brandsma was a pioneer in articulating a modern interpretation of Carmelite spirituality. An institute of spirituality has been named in his honor at the University of Nijmegen. Brandsma's opposition to the Nazis and his work with the Catholic journalists of the Netherlands caused him to be taken to the Nazi camps. He was martyred in 1942 at the concentration camp at Dachau. Pope John Paul II named Titus Brandsma a blessed in 1985.

Conclusion

For almost eight hundred years Carmelite spirituality has been a vital way of following Jesus. This spirituality, which originated with simple hermits on Mount Carmel, places a special emphasis on solitude and prayer. A pastoral orientation was introduced into this spirituality when the Carmelite Order entered the mendicant ranks in the middle of the 13th century. Especially well known and formative has been the contribution of the cloistered Carmelite nuns to the evolution of Carmelite spirituality. However, Carmelite spirituality is the common property of the Christian Churches in a day when there is a widespread desire to retrieve a more contemplative approach to the living of the Gospels.

Bibliography

Egan, K. "The Spirituality of the Carmelites." In *Christian Spirituality: High Middle Ages and Reformation*, ed. J. Raitt, 50–62. New York: Crossroad, 1987.

Mulhall, M., ed. *Albert's Way: The First North American Congress on the Carmelite Rule*. Barrington, Ill.: Province of the Most Pure Heart of Mary, 1989.

The Rule of Carmel. Ed. and trans. B. Edwards. Aylesford and Kensington, England, 1973.

Saggi, L. *Saints of Carmel*. Trans. G. Pausback. Westmont, Ill., 1975.

Saggi, L., ed. *Santi del Carmelo: Biografie da vari dizionari*. Rome: Institutum Carmelitanum, 1972.

Smet, J. *The Carmelites: A History of the Brothers of Our Lady of Mount Carmel*. 4 vols. Darien, Ill.: Carmelite Spiritual Center, 1975–85.

The Essentials of Orthodox Spirituality

A Monk of the Eastern Church

We have seen the successive growths which have, in the course of history, shaped the spirituality of the Orthodox Church. We shall now try to extricate what is common to these various elements and thus, delving beyond accidental diversities of attitude and expression, reach the essential foundations of Orthodox spirituality.

(1) Aim and Means of Christian Life

The aim of man's life is union (*henōsis*) with God and deification (*theōsis*).

The Greek Fathers have used the term "deification" to a greater extent than the Latins. What is meant is not, of course, a pantheistic identity, but a sharing, through grace, in the divine life: ". . . Whereby are given unto us exceeding great and precious promises: that by these ye might be partakers of the divine nature . . ." (2 Pet. 1.4).

This participation takes man within the life of the three Divine Persons themselves, in the incessant circulation and overflowing of love which courses between the Father, the Son and the Spirit, and which expresses the very nature of God. Here is the true and eternal bliss of man.

This essay first appeared in *Orthodox Spirituality: An Outline of the Orthodox Ascetical and Mystical Tradition* (Crestwood, N.Y.: St. Vladimir's Seminary Press, 1996), 22–40. Used by permission.

Union with God is the perfect fulfilment of the "kingdom" announced by the Gospel, and of that charity or love which sums up all the Law and the Prophets. Only in union with the life of the Three Persons is man enabled to love God with his whole heart, soul and mind, and his neighbour as himself.

Union between God and Man cannot be achieved without a Mediator, who is the Word made Flesh, our Lord Jesus Christ: "I am the Way . . . no man cometh unto the Father but by Me" (John 14.6).

In the Son we become sons. "We are made sons of God" says St. Athanasius.[1] Incorporation into Christ is the only means to reach our supernatural end.

The Holy Ghost operates and perfects this incorporation. St. Irenaeus writes: "Through the Spirit one ascends to the Son and through the Son to the Father."[2]

The fact that the object of Christian spirituality is the *supernatural* life of the soul and not the natural effects, either normal or supernormal, obtained by human disciplines, even when they are called "religious," cannot be overemphasized. What is here in question is the action of God on the soul, and not the human actions on the soul itself. The basis of spiritual life is not psychological, but ontological. Therefore an accurate treatise on spirituality is not the description of certain states of the soul, mystical or otherwise, but the objective application of definite theological principles to the individual soul. The redeeming action of our Lord constitutes the alpha and omega as well as the centre of Christian spirituality.

(2) Divine Grace and Human Will

The incorporation of man into Christ and his union with God require the co-operation of two unequal, but equally necessary, forces: divine grace and human will.

Will—and not intellect or feeling—is the chief human instrument of the union with God. There can be no intimate union with God if our own will is not surrendered and conformed to the divine will: "Sacrifice and offering Thou wouldest not. . . . Lo, I come to do Thy Will, O God" (Heb. 10.5, 9).

But our weak human will remains powerless if it is not anticipated and upheld by the grace of God. "Through the grace of the Lord Jesus we shall be saved" (Acts 15.11). It is grace that achieves in us both the willing and the doing.

The Christian East did not experience the controversies which raged in the West around the notions of grace and predestination (Augustinianism, Pelagianism and semi-Pelagianism, Thomism, Calvinism, Jansenism, Molinism). In the Orthodox Church the idea of grace has kept something of the vernal freshness which the word *charis* evoked to the Greek minds: an idea of luminous beauty, free gift, condescension and harmony.

The Greek Fathers emphasized human freedom in the work of salvation. This emphasis strikingly contrasts with St. Augustine's language. St. John Chrysostom writes: "We must first select good, and then God adds what appertains to His office; He does not act antecedently to our will, so as not to destroy our liberty."[3] These words have almost a semi-Pelagian flavour. We ought to remember that the Greek Fathers had not to deal with the Pelagian heresy. On the contrary, their fight was directed against an oriental fatalist gnosis. Chrysostom fully acknowledged antecedent grace and its necessity. He writes elsewhere: "You do not hold of yourself, but you have received from God. Hence you have received what you possess, and not only this or that, but everything you have. For these are not your own merits, but the grace of God. Although you cite faith, you owe it nevertheless to call."[4] Origen had already taught that grace reinforces voluntary energy without destroying freedom. St. Ephraim wrote on the necessity of the divine help.

Clement of Alexandria coined the word "synergy" (cooperation) in order to express the action of these two conjoined energies: grace and human will. The term and idea of synergy have remained and represent, until to-day, the doctrine of the Orthodox Church on these matters.

(3) Asceticism and Mysticism

Both the distinction between the human will and divine grace, and their interpenetration, help us to understand how, in the spiritual life, the ascetical and mystical elements can differ and mingle.

Asceticism is generally understood as an "exercise" of human will on itself, in order to improve itself. As to the term "mysticism," modern language has sadly misused it. "Mystical" is confused with "obscure," "poetic," "irrational," etc. Not only unbelieving psychologists, like Delacroix and Janet, but Christian writers, such as von Hügel, and Evelyn Underhill, exhibit a lack of precision in their conception of mysticism. To define it as an experimental knowledge of divine things gets near the truth, but still remains too vague. The masters of the spiritual life and, following them, recent Roman writers (Garrigou-Lagrange, de Guibert, Maritain) have had the merit of giving precision to this terminology. They give to the words "ascetical" and "mystical" a very strict technical meaning. The "ascetical life" is a life in which "acquired" virtues, i.e. virtues resulting from a personal effort, only accompanied by that general grace which God grants to every good will, prevail. The "mystical life" is a life in which the gifts of the Holy Spirit are predominant over human efforts, and in which "infused" virtues are predominant over the "acquired" ones; the soul has become more passive than active.

Let us use a classical comparison. Between the ascetic life, that is, the life in which human action predominates, and the mystical life, that is, the life in which God's action predominates, there is the same difference as between rowing a boat and sailing it; the oar is the ascetic effort, the sail is the mystical passivity which is unfurled to catch the divine wind.

This view of asceticism and mysticism is excellent. It coincides perfectly with the theology of the Greek Fathers. These do not give technical definitions of asceticism and mysticism, but they distinguish very sharply between the state in which man is "acting" and the state in which he is "acted upon." The pseudo-Dionysius remarks that divine love tends to ecstasy (*ecstatikos ho theios erōs*), i.e. conduces to a state in which man is taken out of himself and his normal condition.

One must be careful, however, not to raise a wall of separation between mystical and ascetic life. The prevalence of the gifts does not exclude the practice of acquired virtues, any more than the prevalence of acquired virtues excludes the gifts. One of these two elements, of course, predominates over the other. But the spiritual life is generally a synthesis of the "ascetical" and the "mystical."

To the mystical life belong the charisms and the extraordinary phenomena which accompany certain states of prayer: inner locutions, visions—stigmatization seems to be a property of the West. Neither these phenomena nor the charisms constitute the essence of the mystic life. However great may be their significance, they are only accidents. Mystical life consists in the supreme reign of the gifts of the Holy Spirit over the soul. Graces of the mystic order are not necessary to salvation. Mystical life is not synonymous with Christian perfection: this last consists in charity or love, and may be reached by souls who will never know any other way than the simple and loving keeping of the commandments. But most of the Greek Fathers, with their sanctified optimism, seem to favour the thesis nowadays defended by the Dominicans and Maritain: that the mystical graces, far from being the privilege of a few elect, are offered to all souls of good will. Their empirical rareness comes from the fact that not many people answer the call. They are nevertheless the normal—though not necessary—blossoming of a genuine Christian life. The King wishes that all should sit at the table of the Messianic feast. Our Lord came to kindle a fire upon earth; what does He wish but to see this living flame burning in everyone?

(4) Prayer and Contemplation

Prayer is a necessary instrument of salvation. Cassian, whose voice is the echo of the Desert Fathers, distinguishes three ascending degrees of the Christian prayer: supplication (for oneself), intercession (for others), thanksgiving or praise. These three degrees of prayer constitute in themselves a whole programme of spiritual life. It matters little whether prayer is vocal or mental; the most loving prayer, either vocal or mental, is always the best.

In contrast with prayer, contemplation is not necessary to salvation. But, as a general rule, assiduous and fervent prayer becomes contemplative.

What is contemplation?[5] It is not synonymous with high intellectual speculations or extraordinary insight, which are the property of certain rare and chosen souls. According to the "classics" of the spiritual life, contemplation begins with the "prayer of simplicity" or "prayer of simple regard." The prayer of simplicity consists in placing yourself in the presence of God and maintaining yourself in His presence for a certain time, in an interior silence which is as complete as possible, while you concentrate upon the divine Object, reduce to unity the multiplicity of your thought and feelings, and endeavour to "keep yourself quiet" without words or arguments. This prayer of simplicity is the frontier and the most elementary degree of contemplation. It is not difficult. Anyone who is even to a slight degree accustomed to pray is sure to have experienced this form of contemplation, for a few minutes at least. It is marvelously fruitful. It is like a welcome shower of rain falling on the garden of the soul. It gives most powerful assistance to the efforts which we make in the moral order to avoid sin and to accomplish the divine will.

It is good to make acts of contemplation. But to live a contemplative life is better still. We must not imagine that the contemplative life means a life in which one does nothing but contemplate. Were that so, the contemplative life would be possible only in the desert or the cloister, while it is, as a matter of fact, open to all. The contemplative life is simply a life orientated towards contemplation, a life arranged in such a way that acts of contemplation are fairly often possible in it and form its summit. If each day you give some moments to the prayer of simplicity; if you know how to separate yourself interiorly, in some degree, from persons and things in order to enter into yourself, and not allow yourself to be dominated by them; if, in your thinking and reading, you bring with you a certain preoccupation with God and attentiveness to His presence; you are already beginning to lead the contemplative life, even if you are still in the world.

Contemplation is *acquired* if the acts of contemplation are the results of personal effort. It is *infused* if these acts are produced by divine grace without, or almost without, human effort. Acquired contemplation belongs to the ascetical life. Infused contemplation belongs to the mystical life. This last is the normal culmination of the contemplative life.

There is a correspondence between classification of the stages of contemplation in the West and their classification in the East. St. Theresa established the classification of the states of contemplative prayer prevalent in the West. She distinguished four aspects of it: (1) the prayer of quiet, silent concentration of the soul on God, which however does not exclude distractions; (2) full union, in which there are no longer distractions, and which is accompanied by a feeling of "ligature of the powers" of the soul; (3) ecstatic union, in which the soul "goes out of itself"; (4) transforming union, or spiritual marriage. We find in the Greek Fathers, if not such a precise classification as St. Theresa's, at least certain parallel distinctions. The prayer of simple regard, the prayer of quiet, and the full union are degrees of the *hēsychia*, which is, in some form or other, the introduction to Eastern contemplation. Above the *hēsychia* comes the ecstatic union, of which instances are found in the New Testament and which is described exactly by the Fathers of the Desert and the pseudo-Dionysius (in their theory of the *ekstasis* and of the circular movement, *kyklikē kinēsis*, bringing the soul back to God). The transforming union or spiritual marriage is described both by those who conceive spiritual life as a deification (*theōsis*) and by those who lay stress on the nuptial relationship between the soul and her Lord (Origen, Methodius of Olympus). An imperceptible transition, an unbroken chain of intermediate shades, links these states one to the other. Thus it happens, in Orthodox practice, that the Name of Jesus (which is really the heart and the strength of the "Jesus-prayer") may be used, not only as the starting point, but also in continuous support of mystical states ranging from *hēsychia* to *ekstasis*.

What has been said about the mystical life must be repeated about the contemplative life. They are not the privilege of certain exceptional souls. It is indeed true that monasticism offers specially favourable conditions for the practice of contemplation. Nevertheless, contemplation is open to all. Marriage, family life, a profession or a trade in no way excludes contemplative prayer and mystical graces. On the contrary, the contemplative or the mystic is a very special source of blessing for the medium in which he lives (though this will frequently not prevent that medium from causing him to suffer). Leaving aside some of the more elevated mystical states, such as ecstasy and the spiritual marriage, we hold that the prayer of simplicity and the mystical stages that follow it, namely, the prayer of quiet and the non-ecstatic prayer of union—we would, according to the Eastern terminology, say, rather, the initial hesychast states— are the normal end of any habitual and loving prayer-life that has as its object the keeping of the Saviour's precepts, and is accompanied by faithfulness to them. Contemplation is often the best means of becoming faithful to those precepts. For contemplation increases love, and love makes us able to keep the commandments: we can pass from love to the keeping of the commandments, but the converse is hardly possible.

Again and again it must be said that contemplation, no more than mysticism, should be identified with perfection—which is charity (love). But a contemplation which would be the utmost exercise of charity, *culmen caritatis*, would also be the acme of perfection, *culmen perfectionis*. Such a contemplation would constitute an end to which it would indeed be worth subordinating all human life.

(5) The Holy Mysteries

The Orthodox Church calls *mystērion* (mystery) what the Latin Church calls *sacramentum*. The holy mysteries are neither the end nor yet the essence of spiritual life. They are means of grace, and only means. But these means have, in the life of the Orthodox Church, an importance which must be exactly understood and measured.

One might call the Orthodox Church a "mysteric" Church in several senses.

First, the Orthodox Church adopts, in regard to the sacraments, a realist attitude. She believes that the sacraments are not mere symbols of divine things, but that the gift of a spiritual reality is attached to the sign perceptible by the senses. She believes that, in these mysteries, the same graces are present nowadays which were formerly imparted in the Upper Room, or at the waters where the disciples of Jesus baptized, or in the declarations of forgiveness that sinners received from our Lord, or in the descent of the Dove, and so on. In each of those divine gifts there is a mystical as well as an ascetical aspect. The mystical aspect consists in the fact that sacramental grace is not the outcome of human efforts, but is objectively bestowed by our Lord. The ascetical aspect consists in the fact that the holy mysteries bring forth their fruit in the soul of the grownup recipient only if that soul is assenting to, and prepared for, it.

The Orthodox Church is also "mysteric" in another way. She is somewhat reticent concerning her intimate treasures. She keeps in the word "mysterion" its meaning of "secret." She fears familiarity. She veils and covers what the Latin Church lays open and exhibits. She feels reluctant to regulate the approach to the holy mysteries by precise disciplinary canons and to utter too detailed statements on the nature of such or such a mystery (e.g. on the Eucharistic Presence). She avoids giving officially too many strict definitions. This indefiniteness has a very simple explanation. The Orthodox Church wants a mystery to remain a "mystery," and not to become a theorem, or a juridical institution. For the Orthodox Church is not only "mysteric," but "pneumatic," and the *Mystērion* is conditioned by the *Pneuma*, the Spirit.

There is "one greater than the Temple" (Matt. 12.6), and greater than the Holy Mysteries. The scholastic axiom *Deus non alligatur sacramentis*— "God is not bound to the sacraments"—may have a Western origin, but expresses quite well the Eastern mind. What Orthodox would dare to assert that the members of the Society of Friends are deprived of the graces that the sacraments represent? The angel went down at regular times into the pool, and whosoever stepped in first after the troubling of the waters was made whole; but our Lord directly healed the paralytic who could not step in (John 5). This does not mean that a man could disregard, or slight, or despise, the channels of grace offered by the Church without endangering his soul. It means that no externals, however useful, are *necessary to God*, in the absolute sense of this word, and that there is no institution, however sacred, which God cannot dispense with.

Nothing that could be called a sacramental materialism will be found among the Greek Fathers. They remind us that to keep God's Word is quite as important as to approach the Holy Mysteries. Origen, speaking of the precautions surrounding the Eucharist, writes: "Now, if you exercise so much caution when guarding His body, and rightly, how is it that you consider it a lesser fault to have neglected the Word of God than His Body?"[6]

(6) The Communion of Saints

In a vision of the *Shepherd*, Hermas saw Rhoda whom he had loved and who, affectionately reproaching him and also smilingly comforting him, manifested to him, from heaven, that she was helping him by the Lord. This second-century vision shows what is the Communion of Saints (*Koinō-nia tōn hagiōn*)—a sharing of the prayers and good works of the heavenly and earthly Christians and a familiar intercourse between ourselves and the glorified saints. The spiritual life of an Orthodox would not be complete without this brotherly relationship.

As we have already indicated, the worship of the saints is not *latreia*, the adoration due to God, but *douleia*, service, or *sebasmos*, veneration. It is also called *proskynēsis timētikē*, i.e. the veneration "paid to all that is endowed with some dignity," as St. John Damascene soberly says.[7] But our relationship with the saints implies more than certain marks of honour. Just as a living Christian can beg the intercession of another living Christian, so we commend ourselves to the prayers of the Saints.

Among the Saints, the Apostles and the Martyrs hold an eminent place according to primitive Christian tradition. The Orthodox Church prepares by a special Lent for the feast of the Holy Apostles Peter and Paul,

St. Gregory Nazianzen had a special devotion to St. Cyprian, St. Basil towards St. Mammas, St. Gregory of Nyssa towards St. Theodore. St. Ephraim writes: "Remember, O Lord, the tears I have shed before Thy holy martyrs." The Orthodox Church gives a great place in her calendar to the patriarchs, prophets, and just men of the Old Testament, contrary to the practice of the Latin Church. High above all are the Angels, classified into hierarchies by the pseudo-Dionysius. The detail of the classification matters little, but its underlying ideas are agreeable to Scripture. The Greek Fathers laid a particular stress on guardian angels. Origen already taught their existence. The pseudo-Dionysius said that they not only watch over us, but convey to us light and perfect us. Chrysostom called his guardian angel his "pedagogue," Basil and Cyril of Alexandria called theirs "fellow wayfarer" and "preceptor" respectively. There are local angels. Gregory Nazianzen prayed, in a moving way, to the angel protectors of Constantinople.[8] Bishop Theophane the Recluse advises "listening to the thoughts which come during prayer, especially in the morning," which he ascribes to the influence of a guardian angel.

Bulgakov has built up interesting theories about the guardian angels; he sees in them something like the "idea" (in the Platonic sense) and the "pattern" of each man. But we may abide in the Biblical conception according to which angels are more than the bearers of divine messages and the guides of men: they are bearers of the very Name and Power of God. There is nothing rosy or weakly poetical in the Angels of the Bible: they are flashes of the light and strength of the Almighty Lord. The early Christians—and the Eastern saints perhaps more than the Western—had visions and dreams of angels. An integral Christian life should imply a daily and familiar intercourse with the angelic world. The experiences of Jacob should become ours: "And Jacob went on his way, and the angels of God met him. . . . And there wrestled a man with him until the breaking of the day. . . . And he said: I will not let thee go, except thou bless me. . . . And he dreamed, and, behold, a ladder set up on the earth, and the top of it reached to heaven: and behold the angels of God ascending and descending on it" (Gen. 32.1, 24, 26, and 28.12).

At the summit of the celestial hierarchy is the *Theotokos*, the blessed Virgin Mary and Mother of God incarnate, whom the Orthodox Church, chiefly since the Council of Ephesus (431), has surrounded with a worship exceeding that of the other saints. A special Lent and numerous feasts and hymns are dedicated to her. Since the Gospel is the first and main source of Orthodox piety, the most Orthodox form of piety towards the Mother of the Saviour is undoubtedly the "evangelical" one, i.e. piety towards Mary as it flows from the sacred texts themselves. Four passages seem to us specially important. First, the angelic salutation: "Hail, thou that art highly favoured, the Lord is with thee: blessed art thou among women," and Mary's answer: "Behold the handmaid of the Lord; be it unto me according to thy word" (Luke 1.28, 38). Secondly, the attitude of Mary at the marriage in Cana of Galilee: "The mother of Jesus saith unto Him, They have no wine . . . His mother saith unto the servants: Whatsoever He saith unto you, do it" (John 2.3, 5). Thirdly, the short dialogue between a certain woman and our Lord: "Blessed is the womb that bare Thee. . . . But He said, Yea, rather, blessed are they that hear the word of God and keep it" (Luke 11.27, 28)—a declaration which does not disparage Mary, but points out where her true merit lies. And finally, the words of Jesus on the Cross: "He saith unto His mother, Woman, behold thy son. Then saith He to the disciple: Behold thy mother," with the practical conclusion: "And from that hour that disciple took her unto his own home" (John 19.26, 27). These texts are the roots of true Marian piety.

We must say here a few words about the ikons which occupy such a place in the life of prayer of the Orthodox, chiefly since the defeat of iconoclasm and the institution of the Feast of Orthodoxy (11th March, 843). Let us first notice that the Eastern ikon is not, like the Latin image (either painted or sculptured), a resemblance. The Orthodox Church keeps the precept of the Decalogue: "Thou shalt not make unto thee any graven image or likeness . . ." (Exod. 20.4). The ikon is a kind of hieroglyph, a stylized symbol, a sign, an abstract scheme. The more an ikon tends to reproduce human features, the more it swerves from the iconographical canons admitted by the Church. Far from being the manifestation of a religious sensualism or materialism, the Orthodox conception of the ikon expresses an almost puritanical hostility against the "sensuous." Some recent Orthodox writers (Bulgakov, Ostrogorsky) see another difference between the ikon and the Latin image or statue. While the likeness is for the West a means of evocation and teaching, the Eastern ikon is a means of communion. The ikon is loaded with the grace of an objective presence; it is a meeting place between the believer and the Heavenly World. This is taught by St. Theodore the Studite, and also in certain Greek texts of the ninth century which set the ikon side by side with the Eucharist.[9] But the official documents of the Orthodox Church adopt a somewhat cooler view, which entirely coincides with the attitude of the Latin Church. The Second Council of Nicaea says: "We paint them (the saints) because we would have their virtues to imitate, and we retrace their lives in books . . . for our benefit." The same Council of 787 says again: "The honour paid to the image goes over to the prototype." St. John Damascene compares the ikon to the word or the book: it is a memorial, *hypomnema.* Let us add that ikon-worship, which could not be attacked without heresy, is not as a practice binding on any individual.

As there is an "evangelical piety" towards Mary, there is also an "evangelical piety" towards the saints, and we shall repeat that the most evangelical is always the most Orthodox. The evangelical attitude towards the saints is indicated in John 12.20–22: "And there were certain Greeks . . . that came up to worship at the feast. The same came therefore to Philip . . . saying: Sir, we would see Jesus. Philip cometh and telleth Andrew; and again Andrew and Philip tell Jesus." And in Luke 22.11: "The Master saith unto thee, Where is the guestchamber where I shall eat the passover with my disciples?"

(7) The Stages of the Spiritual Life

The attempt was made very early to distinguish ascending stages in the spiritual life. The distinction between the three ways—purgative, illuminative, unitive—has become classical in the West. Its origin is Eastern: it is due to the pseudo-Dionysius. St. Basil and Cassian discriminate between beginners, proficients and the perfect. The Alexandrines and Diodore of Photike mention three types of Christians: the *eisagogikos*, "introduced" or "approaching," who is mainly concerned with the practice of virtues (*praxis*); then the *mesos* or "middle one," to whom contemplation (*theōria*) and the suppression of passions (*apatheia*) are particularly suitable; at last the *teleios*, "perfect," who is qualified for the true experimental knowledge of God (*theologia*).

Under different names these classifications generally recur, and they contain a nucleus of truth. But none has an absolute value. The various states penetrate each other. The soul rises and falls back from one to the other without following any rule. Moreover these classifications express states of the soul rather than the objective data of God's action. They mark some moments of our own human existence rather than moments of the life of our Saviour. They are anthropocentric rather than theocentric. Finally they represent the interesting views of eminent spiritual writers, but they lack the authority of the Church.

Hence the question: would it be possible to discover an itinerary of spiritual life officially proposed by the Church and emphasizing the divine operation rather than the psychology of the soul *in via*?

Nicholas Cabasilas shows us where the scale of the degrees of sanctification adopted by the Orthodox Church is to be found. He distinguishes three essential moments in spiritual life: Baptism, Chrisma (confirmation by unction), Eucharist. This is not a private view. The official spirituality of the Orthodox Church is consigned in her text-book of sanctification, that is, in the Ritual (Greek *Euchologion*, Slavonic *Trebnik*). The Ritual takes man from his baptism and accompanies him to his burial; it constitutes the most authoritative treatise on the spiritual life. The order in which it presents the holy mysteries expresses the ascending order of the sanctification of the soul according to the mind and intention of the Church.

Therefore one might say that the three holy mysteries of Baptism, Chrisma and Eucharist are the three essential stages in the way that leads to God. The other sacraments and sacramentals may be connected with one or another of these three degrees and mysteries. Penance, the first monastic profession, the second wedding and the unction of the sick are connected with Baptism. The first wedding, the great monastic profession and ordination are connected with the Eucharist. Ordinations and the anointing of Kings (in the Byzantine tradition) are also connected with Chrisma. We shall come back to these points.

Not only the sacraments, or solemn rites respected almost as sacraments, but all the aspects of the life of prayer of the Church, her feasts, her calendar, her hymns, are focussed in these three mysteries. The Holy Liturgy in the strict sense, i.e. the Lord's Supper, sums up their meaning. The first part of our Eucharistic Liturgy is called the Liturgy of the Catechumens, because the candidates for Baptism were allowed to be present. The part of the liturgy called *anaphora*, which culminates in the *epiklēsis* or invocation of the Holy Ghost on the Eucharistic Gifts, is particularly linked with Chrisma as sacrament of the Spirit. The part of the Liturgy constituted by the communion is the Eucharist itself, the meal of the immolated Body and Blood of the Lord Jesus.

Does this mean that our whole spiritual life is merely a ritual life? Chiefly in this field we must guard ourselves against a deadly literalism: "It is the spirit that quickeneth; the flesh profiteth nothing: the words that I speak unto you, they are spirit, and they are life" (John 6.63). We must go beyond the letter, beyond the mere visible celebration of the three sacraments of Baptism, Chrisma and Eucharist, and perceive the invisible graces which they express. Baptism, Chrisma and the Lord's Supper are *signa*, signs. Baptismal grace, Pentecostal grace, Paschal grace are *res*, the realities behind the signs. The signs, it is true, confer the realities, but the realities overflow the signs. It is the realities that matter and that we must strain after. These three graces are given with the corresponding holy mysteries, and are in some way supported by them. The Lord can nevertheless impart them to souls which never receive the sacramental signs. He can also revive them (as in the case of perfect contrition) within souls which received the grace with the sacrament and then lost it, and this revivification is not necessarily accompanied by the performance of sacramental rites. Baptismal grace, Pentecostal grace, and

Paschal grace exist wherever supernatural love exists. They are the very texture of spiritual life.

In the Church Ritual, the Chrisma precedes the Eucharist. It will be objected that Pentecostal grace was given to the Apostles after Paschal grace. This is true only in appearance. At the time of the first Easter the Apostles obtained only an incomplete experience of Paschal grace: they shared in the Lord's Supper and in the joy of the Presence of the Risen Lord, but they did not share in the immolation of Christ. They knew the fullness of Paschal grace only at the end of their life, when their own martyrdom joined with Christ's sacrifice. Pentecost was for them the necessary condition of this full Paschal grace, just as the gift of the Spirit is for us the necessary condition of a full eucharistic life.

The three graces—Baptismal grace, Pentecostal grace, Paschal grace—are but aspects of one and the same divine grace. They can never be kept asunder; they almost coexist. When we say that, in the mind of the Church, they represent an ascending order, we mean that in the course of the normal and untroubled growth of a soul, each of these aspects should predominate in its turn and in its own time.

Symbolically, we could imagine these three theological graces as the *Charites* of ancient Hellas—the three chaste, generous and beautiful maidens who formed an interwoven group, *manibus amplexis*, says Seneca. Or we can think of them as of a cantata for three voices. Each voice dominates in its turn, but the other two never cease to accompany the dominant one. Or again, if we turned to the representations of primitive Christian art, we could say that Baptismal grace finds its expression in the Ichthys, the divine Fish; Pentecostal grace in the descent of the Dove; Paschal grace in the immolation and triumph of the Lamb.

But let us, rather, leave these images aside. We shall go deeper if we understand that these three graces express three moments in the life of our Lord: His own contact with the baptismal waters; His reception and sending of the Paraclete; and finally His Passover. Our own spiritual experiences are but weak reflections of His life. The baptizing Christ (who is also the forgiving and healing Christ), Christ the sender of the Spirit, and Christ the Paschal Lamb, or, rather, our true Passover: such are the aspects of our Lord, the revelation and inner experience of which constitute the spiritual life of the Christian.

Notes

1. II *Contra Arianos*, XLIII.
2. *Adv. Haeres.* V.36.2.
3. *Hom. XII in Hebr.*
4. *Hom. XII in 1 Cor.*

5. In the course of this chapter we reproduce, with the leave of the editor of *Sobornost*, some passages from an article published by us, under the title "On Contemplation" in *Sobornost* of June, 1941.

6. *In Exod. Hom.* XIII, 3.

7. *Orat.* III, 40.

8. *Orat.* 42, *P.G.* IX, 36, 459.

9. See *Roma e l'Oriente,* V, p. 351.

Lutheran Spirituality

Bengt Hoffman

> For I am not ashamed of the gospel: it is the power of God for salvation to every one who has faith, to the Jew first and also to the Greek. For in it the righteousness of God is revealed through faith for faith; as it is written, "He who through faith is righteous shall live."
>
> —Romans 1:16–17

L uther's theology gave rise to two ways of apprehending the *kerygma* in the Bible and in Christian life. They did not and do not always coincide. In fact, one can speak of a bifurcation, a dividing of the ways. On the one hand, there is the legacy of cognitive theologizing around the theme of justification by faith, the dogmatic bulwark building against the heresies of humanism and scholasticism. That tradition is called "Lutheran orthodoxy." On the other hand, there is the line of personal appropriation of that same theme of justification, evidenced not least by Luther's closeness to some mystics in the Catholic Church. Without necessarily lacking in dogmatic stringency, the proponents of personal spirituality in Lutheranism emphasized the experiential side of Christianity. That tradition is referred to as "Lutheran pietism."

Orthodoxy and Pietism

It may not be the easiest thing in the world to discover the experiential strand in Lutheran thought. The reasons are several.

This essay first appeared in *Spiritual Traditions for the Contemporary Church*, ed. Robin Maas and Gabriel O'Donnell (Nashville: Abingdon, 1990), 145–61. Used by permission.

Luther himself, in his theological battles against certain forms of Catholic life and thought, in his fight against the cautious humanism of Erasmus, and in his battle against the prophets of extreme inwardness called "enthusiasts" (or *Schwärmer*), placed a great deal of emphasis on expressions such as "the external word," "righteousness outside us," and "Christ for us." They all point away from the human person to something objective. And when, under these various contingencies, he spoke of "sanctification," he seemed to conceive of it in an exclusively eschatological fashion. Luther brings out the objective and imputative character of faith. "Since righteousness is imputed"—that is to say, *attributed as merit transmitted by another,* namely Christ—"the individual Christian has done nothing about it himself. The Christian is advised to take hold of the promise of forgiveness offered in the word but think nothing of the movements of the soul which, because they fluctuate, are not reliable guides to God."[1]

But in Luther's thought there is

> another category of terms mirroring personal experience and an awareness of non-rational forces active in faith. These terms convey Luther's persuasion that precisely the external in sign and word reaches and is meant for the internal, for "heart" and "feeling." The imputation of God's righteousness is in fact unavailing without the indwelling of Christ which can be experienced "with mystical eyes," in Luther's words.[2]

Take, for example, Luther's comments on Psalm 51:10, "Create in me a clean heart, O God, and renew a right spirit within me." Here he goes to the heart of his theology, to the experiential side of forensic justification. He writes,

> The Holy Spirit is present and works his gift in us. A gift, yes, for the Holy Spirit himself is at work in us. Since I am indeed justified, I know that my sins are forgiven without my merits. But then it is of the essence that I begin to feel [*sentire*] so that I may in some manner understand.[3]

What kind of understanding does Luther mean? He obviously makes a distinction between knowledge as cognition and knowledge as understanding. Later on in his scrutiny of this same passage he explicates: "The truly pure heart . . . does not harbor a false fantasy about God. It boils down to the understanding of the heart which abides in spiritual things."[4]

Or consider the following statements in which Luther's words challenge the cognitive imperialism of Lutheran orthodoxy:

> A theologian is molded by living, no rather by dying and being judged, not by conceptualizing in itself or by study or speculating.[5] Negative theology . . . true cabala, is very rare . . . too perfect . . . beyond every thought. . . . But not even the affirmative theology can be treated by disputation and numerous words. It

rather moves in the highest repose and silence of the mind, as in rapture and ecstasy [*in raptu et extasi*]. That makes for a true theologian.[6]

Like Johann Tauler, one of the medieval mystics he frequently quoted approvingly, Luther makes a distinction between cognitive speculation and feeling-borne knowledge by referring to some scholastics (whom he sometimes called "sophists") as *Lesemeister* ("masters of reading") and to Christians who knew about the presence of God in experiential ways as *Lebemeister* ("masters of living").[7]

This same distinction between ways of knowing cognitively and experientially is evident in two sermons preached on Good Friday 1518 (on Isaiah 53 and Psalm 45), in which Luther claimed that our prayer should be that we might come to see Christ "with the eyes of the soul," and not as Pilate and other onlookers saw him, with their external eyes merely, or "the eyes of those who know according to the flesh," to use Luther's words. All treasures, Luther continues, are "hidden" in Christ (Col. 2:3):

> They are called "hidden" because they can only become visible through mystical and spiritual eyes. In him is love and the fountain of all light through which the feeling [*affectus*] is informed. . . . Christ was made our love to influence our feeling and he was made God's wisdom to help our understanding. Thus, as I have said, we should open our spiritual eyes and lay hold of this beautiful form of Christ which holds in it all virtues, depicted and presented to us in clear, vivid, expressive words and signs.[8]

If we define spirituality as the awareness of the presence of the Holy Spirit mediated by the risen Christ, it is clear from these brief quotations that the tradition emanating from Martin Luther contains an essential element of the inward, personal, and subjective, which is often associated with the term "spirituality."

This inward dimension of Martin Luther's legacy can be termed *sapientia experimentalis*, an expression he himself uses and that may be translated "existential wisdom" or "knowledge by experience." Luther speaks of the "kingdom in us," of the *unio mystica*, of the "mystical Christ," of the spiritual, prayer-borne life that is a paradoxical movement between *gemitus* ("anguish") and *raptus* ("transporting bliss").

So you have, on the one hand, the intellectual interpretation of faith with Luther and interpreters such as Flacius, Calovius, and Quenstedt, and, on the other hand, the "experience theology" that employs the same spiritual vocabulary as many medieval mystics and has its anchorage also in Luther and those of his followers who were later termed "pietists"— Arndt, Spener, and Francke.[9]

The two sides of the gospel proclamation, the Christ-for-us of Lutheran orthodoxy and the Christ-in-us of Lutheran pietism, are integrally related in Luther's thought. But *in practice* the two traditions have gone their separate ways, and in the process, the intellectual structures have prevailed over the inward aspect, so much so that practically all well-known accounts of Luther's Reformation theology, both the ones written within a confessionalistic-orthodox framework and those molded by liberal-rationalistic epistemologies, play down Luther's references to spiritual experience and his kinship with the mystics. Much like the intellectualistic exegesis that accords little theological importance to St. Paul's feeling-laden, shattering encounter with the cosmic, supernatural Lord on the Damascus road and that, instead, derives a theology from an intellectual-theological discourse around the Hebrew notion of Law, these elaborations of Luther's theological thought turn the student's attention away from the experience of God's presence to intellectual-theological deliberations, as though they are capable of standing by themselves.[10]

Spirituality and Knowledge in Lutheran Traditions

Interpretations of Luther's—and the Lutheran—approach to the spiritual depend on the definition one applies to the nature of knowledge. If knowledge as the range of what has been perceived, discovered, or inferred is limited to reason's grasp of the testimonies of the senses, we can speak of a rationalistic-empirical epistemology within which two mutually contradictory propositions cannot both be true. Spirituality as the experience of mystic presence will not find much room within such a context. If, on the other hand, knowledge as the range of what has been perceived, discovered, or inferred is expanded to include the experience involved in intuition, intimation, and spiritual inspiration—exceeding the yardsticks of causality within time and space alone—we can speak of a pneumatic ("spiritual") epistemology within which a purely logical treatment cannot cover what the experiencing person "knows." In that kind of knowledge, two mutually contradictory propositions can indeed be true.

In the wake of the Lutheran Reformation, spirituality as experience of divine presence fared less well inside the rationalistic-empirical framework than within the pneumatic one. This can be seen in three respects. We may, with regard to the place of the spiritual or the mystical, speak of three sorts of censorship.

First, Luther's references to experiences of grace and the presence of the "mystical Christ" have often been—and often are—evaluated only from strictly confessional points of view. The result is that Lutheran orthodoxy, as well as Lutheran liberal theology, tends to view Protestant and Roman Catholic theological thought as antithetical at each essential doctrinal juncture. A spirituality with mystical overtones is considered heretical in many Protestant accounts and is assigned to pietism or Catholicism. The matter of Lutheran spirituality has thus contributed to a censoring Lutheran posture with regard to Catholic doctrine. Out of such a criticism comes a statement like the following: "Only dilettantes in the field of spiritual history can call Luther a mystic." The dictum stems from H. Bornkamm, in this regard echoing A. Harnack.[11] In defense of Protestantism, one endeavors to prove an absolute contradistinction between the Catholic-mystical and the Lutheran-evangelical.

Second, the *gnesio*-Lutheran and Melanchthonian reflection on the gospel often regards as theologically inconsequential Luther's frequent allusions to mystic intimations, especially in expositions on Christology and angelology. The effect of this particular form of censorship is that the term *unio mystica* among the Lutheran schoolmen or scholastics became—and becomes—part of a rational system of propositional truth, the doctrine of imputed righteousness.[12] The term consequently lost—and loses—its intuitive-experiential elements in the name of "objective" verity, firmly set against the "subjectivity" of pietism and mysticism.

Third, spirituality in Lutheran garb has been the object of censoring treatment under the impact of theological thought molded by pragmatic and empirical scientific reasoning. To apprehend this climate of scholarly inquiry, we have to go back to Descartes' (1596–1650) ideas about the absolute centrality of intellectual cognition ("I think, therefore I am"), a philosophy inspired by Newton's (1642–1727) notion of a clockwork universe and Kant's (1724–1804) suggestion that metaphysics, attempting to objectivize reality outside the perception-guiding forms—space and time—cannot be accommodated within the only genuine scientific knowledge there is, namely, pure mathematics and pure natural science. These reflections concerning the nature of human knowledge, so indispensable to the cultural movement called the Enlightenment, have molded much of the epistemology governing theological efforts to understand Luther. The outcome is often a failure to find an organic locus in his thought for spirituality or inward knowledge. As a consequence, the *ordinary*, the *public*, and the *objective* in the life of faith tend to take precedence over or almost occlude their complementary counter-points, the *extraordinary*, the *private-personal*, and the *subjective*.

In both orthodox and liberal Lutheran discourses we therefore frequently find an emphasis on "theological faith" as opposed to "actual change" in heart and mind. (This particular choice of words is found in Gerhard Ebeling's interpretation of Luther.)[13] Theology in the former sense deals with "the *nous*, mind, intelligence . . . and has through its unconscious intellectualism often proved a significant restrictive influence, stifling the work of the Holy Spirit."[14] This third kind of censorship, unconscious to be sure, runs the risk of eclipsing the aspect of spiritual and mystical knowledge *(sapientia experimentalis)* in Luther's and Lutheran thought. One may lose Martin Luther himself, and his theological concern, by that omission.[15]

There are those in the theological community who recognize the somewhat crippling consequences of the reductionism alluded to here. One such interpreter is Jesuit scholar Jared Wicks, who asserts that at least the younger Luther's primary concern was not intellectual, dogmatic rampart building around God's self-disclosure. Rather, Luther was about the business of translating into meaningful theological language a radical spiritual experience of Christ's justifying and loving presence.[16] Luther's positive use of the writings of mystics supports this claim. He often quoted with approval Bernard of Clairvaux, Hugo and Richard of St. Victor, Jean Gerson, Johann Tauler, and the anonymous "Frankfurter" who wrote *Theologia Germanica*, to name a few of his mystical kin. In fact, such references throughout Luther's career suggest to us that the kinship in question endured throughout his years as a mature Reformer.

Luther and the Mystics

Luther used expressions like "the mystical Christ," "mystical incarnation," "mystical theology," and "mystical eyes" when he wanted to depict life in God. When he looked for a definition of the mystical life in God, he found it in Bernard of Clairvaux and quoted with approval his definition of mystical theology. "Mystical theology," wrote Bernard, is of the "experimental and experiential" kind. In other words, mystical theology to Luther is *experience* of God.[17] It is the inner, spiritual side of Christian faith. It is what prayer leads to. It is the awesome and joyful knowledge, beyond purely rational knowledge, that God is present. It is heart rather than head, but never the one without the other.

The trouble with *our* trouble with Luther's mystical utterances—that is, his knowledge that God is indeed not very far from us—is that we let the theoretical understanding, the urge for all-embracing theological-logical theorems, so overwhelm the religious quest that intuition, inspiration, intimation, and feeling are not given their due. Hence we find in a goodly part of Luther scholarship the cliché that Luther's view of God and salvation stands in diametrical opposition to that of the mystic.[18]

It would carry us too far in the context of this discussion to compare Luther's views of the image of God in man, man's will in relation to God, the "marriage" between Christ and the Christian, or his position on sin, with those of the mystics to whom Luther felt close. Suffice it to say here that the experience of justification by faith, perhaps beginning with the so-called tower experience, became the yardstick with which Luther meditated on the mystics. And from that point of view it is clear that he felt the closest kinship with Johann Tauler and the writer of the four-teenth-century tract *Theologia Germanica.* He had the latter work printed, apparently without any editing of the contents.[19]

Luther's frequent use of the adjective "invisible" points to his trusting knowledge that faith always moves into dimensions not approachable by reason and logic but available to inner experience. Like the mystics, he assumes the reality of a supernatural or supernormal realm. This becomes evident, for instance, in his angelology. In this respect, Luther's thought essentially coincides with that of Bernard of Clairvaux—mys-tic, healer, administrator, and theologian—who claimed that to dwell with God in the mystic realm is "as by the hands of angels we both feel the being of God and attribute to angelic ministration whatever simili-tude in which the feeling was conveyed."[20]

It has been alleged that Luther may have been close to the way of the mystics in his younger days but that he abandoned mystical modes in his maturity. This contention is not sustained by the facts.[21] One illustration from his use of the word "invisible" will have to suffice. Luther commented many times in the course of his life on Hebrews 11:1 ("Now faith is the assurance of things hoped for, the conviction of things not seen"). Both in his younger years and in later days when he was battle-scarred and dog-matically much more contentious, he pointed out that when we are involved with God, we are involved with the invisible, with a Christ who knows us from the invisible and with "the dear angels" who draw close for our protection.[22] This attachment to and feeling for the invisible presence of the Holy Spirit is what Luther had in common with some of the mys-tics. We Wittenbergians are certainly not saying anything new in this regard, he exclaims in the foreword to *Theologia Germanica.*[23]

Yes, mystical knowledge *was* part of Luther's spirituality, but it was not free-floating; it was rooted in the justifying *kerygma* of Scripture.

Anchorage in the Biblical Word

The scriptural *Word* is both outward and inward, an external sign and an inner experience. Luther says in a Christmas sermon (1515) that the *Logos* is the inner Word, God himself—his wisdom, his thought, his power, his life, his righteousness. For us to understand and absorb it, the Word must assume concrete shape. God's inner Word must come in flesh. That enfleshment is the external Word, Christ, and all that he says and does. Christ in his Word is God's external Word to man.[24]

Later in life Luther prefers to speak of "the outer and the inner clarity" of the Word of God. The outer Word comes first. Only the *Word* communicates the Spirit. Luther's forensic or imputative notion of justification demands that kind of start, the outward address. But the forensic action remains a dead Word if the Spirit does not begin to speak inside the Word, through the Word, to man's heart. Then dawns the inner clarity. Luther writes, "The word is a divine and eternal power, for although the voice and the speech soon vanish, the innermost kernel remains, that is the insight, the truth, contained in the voice."[25] Luther continues, "I bring to my mouth the goblet in which there is wine but I don't press the goblet down into my throat. So it is with the word that brings the voice. . . . It falls down into my heart and comes alive."[26] At another point Luther says that when God's Word opens up to a person, it happens only through the Holy Spirit. And this, he continues, has to be experienced, tried, and felt. The Law and the cross are "media" in the "school of the Spirit." The Virgin Mary, he adds, is a good example of one who has seen the inner side or clarity of the Word. She was "illumined and taught through the Holy Spirit" that "God . . . breaks what man makes and makes from what is broken."[27]

Some years ago I was casting around for a picture that would give some idea of Luther's view of the workings of the Word, especially the Word *about and by* Christ. I found the illustration I sought among my memories of a tour through East Africa. I got out of the car in the steppe-like Masai country with the intention of taking a picture of the javelin-equipped tribesmen herding their cattle. As they shied away from my camera, it was brought home to me that these Africans are persuaded that if you have a picture of them, you have *them*. The picture of a person emanates the specific character of the one it represents. Since they practice magic—black and white—they are never sure what the intentions are of the one who possesses a photograph or effigy of them.

Luther could not, of course, have used such an analogy to make a point about the power of the Word of God. But I believe that we may allow ourselves such an application. Just as a photo of a person emanates the specific character of that person and no one else, the Word in Scripture "vibrates" the one who spoke it. The Holy Spirit uses in a special way the words about and by Christ. These words are preeminently the receivers and channels of his communication with us. The Word calls forth the divine Presence to the one who seeks. No wonder Luther encouraged Christians to be diligent in their reading and contemplation of Scripture! The Word spoken by and about Christ is a bridge between the Lord and his friends, Luther thought. It offers us an eternal Now.

It is from Scripture also that Luther derives his understanding of faith as both "historical" and "inner."[28] A distinction between historical and inner faith exists, but for Luther they are interlocked and should never be separated. Historical faith is readily prepared to make the concession that the creedal confession—"Christ has suffered and certainly also for me"—is proper and true. But, said Luther, historical faith, if left to its own ways, does not add this feeling-laden experiential knowledge metaphorically conveyed by the marital union, an image of man-God togetherness that Luther derived from the Song of Songs, Isaiah, Jeremiah, Matthew, John, and the book of Revelation, as well as from some mystics. The true faith is the necessary inner, nonrational *affect* that prompts the faithful to exclaim, "My beloved is mine, and I reach out for him with gladness!" This feeling-laden faith is not grounded in our natural capacity for emotion but in our discovery of sinfulness and experience of grace.

The important point in the present context is that spiritual knowledge, the knowledge imparted by faith, is more than the apprehension of Jesus Christ as a kind of mathematical cipher aiding our self-understanding or promising eschatological fulfillment. Faith is also an "experiential knowledge," according to Luther: By *experience* does the justified know.

As for *historical* faith, well, "even the devil believes it," but the devil certainly balks at the *inner* faith. He does not follow us there. His aim is to keep us captive in the outward repetition alone. He is quite satisfied with merely historical faith.[29] We are back, then, with Luther's comment on Psalm 51: "It is of the essence that I begin to feel so that I may in some manner understand." *Sola fide*, faith alone, cannot be understood as a repudiation of mysticism with Luther, as is often maintained. Luther speaks of "the ecstasy of faith" and is thereby close to the mystical concept of *raptus*. He also uses the term *sensus fidei*, the knowledge of faith that includes "heart," feeling, and sometimes even a state that is beyond the feelings of the psyche and the senses. That side of faith carries us off *(translatio)* from all known conditions to God as "totally exalted." "Faith causes the heart to be carried away to dwell in things that are invisible" and also unutterable.[30]

Significantly, Luther makes a similar distinction between the historical Christ and *Christus mysticus*. Christ is historical in the sense that he appeared in history, walked on earthly roads, and is the center of the scriptural record. Anyone can study the record; it is public. Christ has indeed been here. But this same Jesus Christ is also what Luther calls "the mystical Christ." Jesus Christ is more than an influential memory. He is, after the Resurrection, the cosmic Lord and mystical Presence. He is in fact the spiritual Sun behind the visible, external sun. The psalmist does not merely speak of the visible sun—"In the heavens, he has set a tent for the sun which comes forth like a bridegroom" (Ps. 19:4–6)—wrote Luther in refutation of some notions among theologians, but the visible sun is the outward sign for the mystical Christ, "the SUN of righteousness who provides light and energies and is all" in his followers.[31]

This double view of Christ has another aspect. As we saw, orthodox Lutheran dogmaticians, as well as Lutheran systematicians of Newtonian modernity, spoke and still speak of the Christ-*for*-you, the forensic for-you, as the basis of faith and Christ allegiance, almost to the exclusion of a Christ-*in*-you. This follows logically from the assumption that if one wants to elevate God absolutely—to the 100 percent level—man's value necessarily declines to zero. Consequently there cannot be, with such a "low" anthropology, much talk about an indwelling Christ or the possibility of being, as Luther puts it, "formed in Christ" or of "Christ [being] formed in us."[32]

On the other hand, pietistic thinkers emphasized and still emphasize the *in*-you of Christ, almost to the exclusion of the *for*-you. But Luther's theology contained *both* the justifying *for*-you and the sanctifying *in*-you (or "divinizing," to use a mystic term to which Luther did not object when he let *Theologia Germanica* go to print.) Christ was more than an *idea* in Luther's world, yes, more than an eschatological *promise*. He was a loving and protecting *Presence*, often working through his angels.

Worship and Presence

I have underlined the significance of objective and external forms of approaching God in Luther and in Lutheran worship. As early as 1523, Luther drew attention to the importance of the Roman Mass as a historical link. In his pamphlet on the Mass he writes, "The liturgy now in common use everywhere, like the preaching office, has a high, Christian origin." But Luther also found "much that was blameworthy in the service of the mass of his day." The sacrament had been buried under all kinds of additions, and the Mass had become, he thought, "a merciless judge." The sacrifice of the Mass "presumes to save man from the anger of God," but it did not as far as Luther was concerned. To him the Mass had become idolatry. So instead of speaking of "the sacrifice of the mass," Luther spoke of "the mass of Christ." The Mass was not a work of merit, earning grace. It was a gift. The Words of Institution were placed in the center of the Mass, the service was translated into the vernacular, Communion in both forms was introduced for everyone, and the transubstantiation section was removed together with the words about the repetition of Christ's sacrifice.[33]

Order is necessary and useful in worship, said Luther, but do not let it obscure the gospel. He wrote in 1539:

> If the Elector will let the Gospel of Jesus Christ be clearly preached, . . . why, have your procession in the name of God, carry a silver or a golden cross, and wear a chasuble or surplice of velvet, silk, or linen. If your lord the Elector is not content with one chasuble or surplice, put on three of them as did Aaron, the

high priest . . . and if your Electoral Grace is not content with one procession in
which you go around singing and ringing, then go around seven times, as did
Joshua with the children of Israel . . . And if your lord the Elector is so inclined,
let him leap and dance in front with harps, drums, cymbals, and bells, as David
did before the Ark. . . . Such matters, as long as they are not abused, do not add
to or take anything from the Gospel. But they must not be made a matter of
necessity for salvation.[34]

In the very way in which Luther spoke of the "ceremoniacs," we recognize that he did not delimit the range of Christ's presence to established
places and ceremonies. The inner man "is free from rites and laws. . . . The
outer man for the sake of love is bound to order and form."[35] In Luther's
view, we need practice, training, and order, but since God is everywhere,
we can pray to God everywhere. In *The Bondage of the Will* Luther speaks of
God's presence everywhere by positing that if "a tyrant would throw me
into a cesspool and I would not believe that God is close to me until I return
to a stately church," then that would really be both a tragedy and a mistake concerning God.[36] Concerning Christ's presence Luther writes (commenting on Eph. 1:23) that it is right to say "not that He is nowhere but
that He is everywhere . . . bound to no particular place." Yes, Christ is
everywhere, but he deigns to meet us in a special way "in the bread we
break in the Holy Communion." That bread is the "body of Christ."[37]

Finally, to Luther's view of worship and Presence belongs his belief in
and experience of the ministry of the angels and in the power of the lay-
ing on of hands for healing, issues that cannot be dealt with adequately
in this chapter but that are important and deserve mention.

The question naturally arises, How does all this affect our lives as moral
beings?

The Relation of the Spiritual to the Moral in Luther

We can safely state at the outset: The moral life is an integral part of
life in the mystical Christ; the ethical and the spiritual are interlocked,
for as theology is more than mere thought, so ethics is more than mere
rational decision making.

The ground of ethics is not confined to material reality and rational
consciousness about Christ or anything else. These elements play their
necessary parts, but the power, the enabling and the incentive for moral
commitment stem from the transrational presence of Christ.[38]

For Luther, the moral is rooted in the mysterious, numinous presence
of the cosmic Lord, the Sun of Righteousness. The inner union with Christ
that is the mystic element in justification by faith is also the wellspring of
moral life, but the "extraordinary" anchorage of the moral does not exclude

common sharing in the ordinary life of the world. The formation of a Christian life occurs, for Luther, in "conformation to Christ"—the soul being "formed in Christ." From this spiritual communion with Christ comes active service and the doing of justice.

Man's sinfulness is not the total truth, for through Christ we may speak of "the good in us." Let me enlarge a bit on this statement: Commenting on John 15:2, Luther wrote that some people think it is true and smart to contend that "man can do nothing but emit his odor and stench." Luther riposts that one has got to be "a stupid ass" to picture man exclusively this way. One should be able to see the "good in us" and "not only look for and think about that which is bad in us." Moral goodness is not our own doing; Christ is at work. The moral life begins in humility and continues in disciplined action. Luther writes, "Should God bestow His grace and Christ, His Son, on us and then say: 'You need not do anything at all but follow whatever pleases you'?"[39]

In the spiritual union with Christ a paradoxical tension exists between suspension of the moral law and a new confirmation of the moral law. Christ, says Luther, "who is present especially when He cannot be seen," brings about a new moral posture. "When by faith we consciously take hold of Christ himself, we enter into a kind of new law," and Luther adds, "Paul calls grace itself 'Law.'" What has happened here, Luther asserts, is that Christ becomes a living, present Power, a *sacramentum*, and then he acts in a Christian's ethical world as *exemplum*.[40] These words were written between 1517 and 1522; thirteen years later Luther reminds his readers and listeners that a sacramental Christ who is the cosmic Lord, the Sun of Righteousness, works with us in our moral strife as our *exemplum*, our model, our source for imitation. God liberates from Law. Paul knew that, but Paul was certainly no antinomian. Moral deeds are part of the life of the Spirit. If one acts against the Spirit, one "cannot possess the Kingdom of God."[41]

Finally, it is a mystical truth that true Christians play a central moral role in the world. Christian deeds, said Luther, are "the extension of the work that Christ merely initiated." For Christ always remains with his followers in invisible but real and powerful ways. Luther reminds his readers that Christ says to them, "Whatever you ask, I will do it." *Prayer* more than *ideas* empowers Christians to act as upholders of life and moral order. This is a paradox: Christians look like "poor beggars," but (listen to this— it boggles the mind!) it is because of Christians and their prayers and actions that "power, honor and goods" exist among people. The unrepenting world does not understand this and "thanks the Christians poorly for it." When "the Christians' words and wonders cease . . . God will end it all; it will all be consumed by fire." Until that happens, those who are spiritually "glued" to the Lord are called to "suffer the stench" from those who do not know the Christ, "in the same manner as the legs carry the paunch and the reeking belly."[42]

Writings in the Tradition of Lutheran Spirituality

Lutheran piety or spirituality has several roots. When we derive it mainly from Luther's influence, it is largely because the main proponents were anxious to claim a precise allegiance to Luther himself. But it should be added that they were also relating themselves more directly to the Lutheran scholastics of the sixteenth, seventeenth, and eighteenth centuries, because they felt the need of defending themselves against accusations of heresy from such quarters. These so-called pietists also absorbed medieval mystical writers through direct study rather than just through references to them in Luther's legacy. The movements of spirituality in Lutheranism mentioned below are best understood as a reaction against the rationalistic objectivism and institutionalism of the ever-growing confessional bodies.

Johann Arndt (1555–1621) and Christian Scriver (1629–1693) were precursors of what was to be called "pietism." Arndt's *True Christianity* became a much-read and beloved book of Christian nurture and meditation all over northern Europe and is still a spiritual resource in Scandinavia.[43] Scriver wrote *The Soul's Treasure*, which has likewise been widely read in the Lutheran churches of Europe.[44] Both works have, for two centuries, been part of the daily worship in countless Lutheran homes.

The same is true in the case of two great spiritual leaders who made pietism a household word: Spener and Francke. The allusion was originally rather critical and negative; mainline Lutherans did not consider it properly Lutheran to be a pietist. However, the socioethical implications of pietistic teachings eventually gave the term a more positive ring. Both social "inner mission" undertakings and "foreign mission" ventures emanated directly from pietist circles, as in the case of Spener's work.

Philipp Jakob Spener (1635–1705) wrote a foreword to a collection of Arndt's sermons, calling it *Pia Desideria*. In 1675 he published it separately. Besides being a devotional source, it was also a reform program for the Lutheran church. A reform movement grew out of Spener's proposals, but it met with heavy resistance from orthodox Lutherans.

August Hermann Francke (1663–1727) made Halle his center, taught at the university there, served as a much-appreciated pastor, and established many institutions for various groups of underprivileged people. Francke claimed Spener as one of his most influential guides. More than Spener's, Francke's pietism was based on the necessity of sudden conversion, a fact he tended to dogmatize. Like much subsequent pietism, the Halle variety tended to be legalistic.

Parallel with this dogmatically more conservative pietism, there arose on German soil a radical pietism that discounted institutional externality. Gottfried Arnold (1666–1730), its best-known representative, wrote (among other works) *An Impartial History of Churches and Heresies, The Mystery of the Divine Sophia,* and the widely read *True Depiction of Inner Christianity.*

In the eighteenth and nineteenth centuries, movements for spiritual renewal created interest in mission work and in public schools all over Lutheran Scandinavia. Thanks to the influence of pietism, catechetical instruction for confirmation was introduced. Danish hymn writer Brorson, Norwegian revivalist Hauge, Swedish law preacher Rosenius, and the illiterate Finnish farmer Ruotsalainen were prominent leaders of waves of inner awakening that swept over Scandinavian countries in the course of two hundred years. Almost everywhere, but especially in Sweden, these renewals met with stiff and sometimes relentless resistance from the established churches, which often used secular authority to silence pietistic preachers and their extra-ecclesial activities. But it is probably true to say that Lutheran church life has benefited from the erstwhile suspect renewals. In Norway, Finland, and Denmark, pietistic renewals were largely integrated with the traditional church structures, whereas in Sweden they often led to the formation of separate sects or churches. Mission work, public schools, and Sunday schools were inspired by spirituality movements.

In recent times, the charismatic renewals in America have also touched Lutheran churches. It is difficult to say whether Martin Luther would have felt at home in a contemporary Lutheran charismatic meeting, with its emphasis on emotional experience. His situation was different from ours: Whereas he battled against clericalism, we contend with secularism. But it seems clear that he would have seen the significance of the charismatic movement as a reaction against the common theological notion that "the church is institutional, not charismatic." Luther's description of faith as "ecstasy" and "rapture" and his emphasis on *feeling* as part of understanding initiated what we rightfully term Lutheran spirituality.

Notes

1. Bengt Hoffman, *Luther and the Mystics* (Minneapolis: Augsburg, 1976), 13.
2. Ibid., 14.
3. Martin Luther, *D. Martin Luthers Werke,* vols. 1–58, kritische Gesamtausgabe, Weimarausgabe (Weimar: Hermann Böhlaus, 1883–1987), vol. 40, 2; 422, 1–5 (on Psalm 51, 1532).
4. Luther, *Werke,* 40, 2; 423, 6–8 (on Psalm 51, 1532).
5. Luther, *Werke,* 5; 163, 28 (on Psalm 5, 1519–1521).
6. Luther, *Werke,* 3; 372, 13–25 (on Psalm 65, 1513–1516).
7. Luther, *Werke,* 6; 291, 30 (1520). See also Hoffman, *Mystics,* 223–24.

8. Luther, *Werke*, 1; 335–45 (1518).

9. Flacius (1520–1575), Calovius (1612–1686), Quenstedt (1617–1688), Arndt (1555–1621), Spener (1635–1705), Francke (1663–1727).

10. Bengt Hoffman, "On the Relationship between Mystical Faith and Moral Life in Luther's Thought," *Gettysburg Seminary Bulletin* (winter 1975): 23.

11. Hoffman, *Mystics*, 19; Hoffman, "Mystical Faith," 23.

12. Hoffman, *Mystics*, 27–28.

13. Gerhard Ebeling, *Luther: An Introduction to His Thought* (Philadelphia: Fortress, 1964), 260.

14. H. Emil Brunner, *The Misunderstanding of the Church*, trans. Harold Knight (Philadelphia: Westminister, 1953), 48.

15. Hoffman, *Mystics*, 100.

16. Jared Wicks, *Man Yearning for Grace: Luther's Early Spiritual Teaching* (Washington, D.C.: Corpus, 1968), ix, 152, 280; Hoffman, *Mystics*, 126–27.

17. Hoffman, *Mystics*, 15.

18. Ibid., 132–33.

19. Ibid., 120–22 (a discussion of three kinds of mysticism). See also the introduction in Bengt Hoffman, *The Theologia Germanica of Martin Luther*, Classics of Western Spirituality (New York: Paulist, 1980).

20. Hoffman, *Mystics*, 15. Bernard of Clairvaux (1090–1153) was abbot at the Cistercian monastery Clairvaux and became very influential in world affairs during the reign of Pope Eugene III, a former monk of Clairvaux.

21. Ibid., 112–19.

22. Luther, *Werke*, 3; 498, 27–36 (1513–1515); 32; 117, 1–18 (1530); 44; 700, 19–21 (1535–1545).

23. Hoffman, *Theologia*, 54.

24. Luther, *Werke*, 1; 20–25. See also Lef Erikson, *Inhabitatio—Illuminatio—Unio* (Turku, Finland: Abo Academy, 1986), 41–45.

25. Luther, *Werke*, 12; 300, 15–17; Martin Luther, *Luther's Works* (Philadelphia: Fortress, 1958–86), 30:45. A further illustration of the conventional "Newtonian" approach to the exclusive "for-you" understanding of Word and justification is provided by Gerhard O. Forde, "Forensic Justification and Law in Lutheran Theology," in *Justification by Faith: Lutherans and Catholics in Dialogue* (Minneapolis: Augsburg, 1985), 7:278–303. In this article support is sought from Teutonic scholars in the rationalist tradition, such as Iwand and Ebeling. Forde frowns on any "shuttle service" between the objective and the subjective and on "psychologization." According to Forde, Luther proclaims a "fundamental discontinuity" between God and everything in a "fallen world." "The spirit," he says, "is not a secret inner sphere"; further, Luther has "a literal, historical sense of Scripture" and the "livingness" of the Word of God lies in its "use." This insistence on a noninteriority in Luther is widespread in theological circles, and Forde has in that sense many supporters. The question is whether his modern intellectualizing grasps Martin Luther. My (minority) opinion is that it does not.

26. Luther, *Werke*, 12; 300, 17–20 (1523); *Luther's Works*, 30; 45.

27. Luther, *Werke*, 7; 546, 24–30 (The Magnificat, 1521); *Luther's Works*, 21; 299.

28. Luther, *Werke*, 40, 3; 738, 2–4 (1544).

29. Luther, *Werke*, 40, 3; 738, 6–20 (1544).

30. Luther, *Werke*, 57, 3; 185, 1–8 (Hebr., 1517); Luther, *Luther's Works*, 29; 185. Hoffman, *Mystics*, 149–51, 155–59.

31. Among many passages, see, for instance, Luther, *Werke*, 548, 5–8, 14–17 (1519–1521).

32. Luther, *Werke*, 39, 1; 204, 12–13 (note on a dissertation, 1537) and 22; 336, 24–31 (sermon on Matthew 22, 1537). These later texts have been chosen to show how vacu-

ous is the prevailing view among modern Luther scholars that only "young" Luther enter-
tained ideas of a "mystical" or "spiritualizing" nature. This view coincides more with the
mind-set and epistemology of the theological majority than it reflects Martin Luther's
style as a theologian. One really picks up what fits one's framework.

33. Vilmos Vajta, *Luther on Worship* (Philadelphia: Muehlenberg, 1958), 3–57.

34. Ibid., 186–87; Martin Luther, *D. Martin Luthers Werke*, vols. 1–18, Gesamtausgabe, Weimarausgabe, Briefwechsel (Weimar: Hermann Böhlaus, 1930–85), vol. 8;
625, 11–625, 37.

35. Vajta, *Luther*, 177.

36. Luther, *Werke*, 18; 623, 14–20 (*De servo arbitrio*, 1525); *Luther's Works*, 33; 47.

37. Luther, *Werke*, 18; 211, 15–16; 18; 212, 30 (*Against the Heavenly Prophets*, 1525).
Luther's Works, 40; 220–21.

38. The major portion of these remarks about the relationship between the spiritual
and the moral in Luther's thought is contained in my essay "Mystical Faith."

39. Luther, *Werke*, 45; 649, 23–27; 45; 650, 14–15 (1538). *Luther's Works*, 24; 207–8;
24; 254.

40. Luther, *Werke*, 10, 1; 11, 1 (1522); 2; 501, 34–37 (1519); 57, third part of the
vol.; 114, 15–19 (1517). *Luther's Works*, 29; 124.

41. Luther, *Werke*, 39, 1; 526, 1–14; 39, 1; 527, 1–4 (1537–1540).

42. Luther, *Werke*, 45; 531, 32–35; 45; 532, 2; 45; 536, 5–10 (1538). *Luther's Works*,
24; 78–79, 83. *Werke*, 45; 535, 27–29 (1538). *Luther's Works*, 24; 82; *Werke*, 45; 536, 16–29
(1538). *Luther's Works*, 24; 82–83.

43. Peter Erb, trans., *Johann Arndt: True Christianity* (New York: Paulist, 1979), see
esp. 4–6.

44. Christian Scriver (1629–1693), *Seelenschatz*, vols. 1–5. See M. Schmidt, "Christian
Scrivers Seelenschatz als Beispiel vorpietistischer Predigtweise," *Kirche in der Zeit* 17 (1962).

Bibliography

Primary Sources

Arndt, Johann. *True Christianity*. Translated by Peter Erb. New York: Paulist, 1979.

Luther, Martin. "The Magnificat." In vol. 21 of *Luther's Works*, edited by Jaroslav Pelikan,
297–358. St. Louis: Concordia, 1956.

———. "Sermons on the Gospel of Saint John." In vol. 24 of *Luther's Works*, edited by
Jaroslav Pelikan and D. E. Poellot, 5–45 (on John 14:1–6), 405–22 (on John
16:26–33). St. Louis: Concordia, 1961.

———. "A Simple Way to Pray." In vol. 43 of *Luther's Works*, edited by Gustav Wiencke,
193–211. Philadelphia: Fortress, 1968.

Secondary Sources

Hoffman, Bengt. *Luther and the Mystics*. Minneapolis: Augsburg Press, 1976.

———. "On the Relationship between Mystical Faith and Moral Life in Luther's
Thought." *Gettysburg Seminary Bulletin* (winter 1975): 21–35.

Hoffman, Bengt, trans. and comm. *The Theologia Germanica of Martin Luther*. Classics of
Western Spirituality. New York: Paulist, 1980.

Wicks, Jared. *Luther and His Spiritual Legacy*. Wilmington, Del.: Michael Glazier, 1983.
(See esp. chap. 7, pp. 120–53.)

Reformed Spirituality

Howard G. Hageman

The Spirituality of Zwingli

It is difficult, if not impossible, to discuss Reformed spirituality as a single concept. It might be supposed that Reformed spirituality and the spirituality of John Calvin would turn out to be the same, but that is hardly the case. Since Calvin was a second generation reformer, there was a Reformed spirituality in existence before him which his own brand of spirituality was never able completely to replace. Furthermore in the late seventeenth and early eighteenth centuries there were spiritual developments in the Reformed tradition which deeply influenced Reformed piety and took it in quite a different direction from Calvin's understanding.

By common consent, the primary mover in what was to become the Reformed tradition was Ulrich Zwingli (1484–1531). Almost an exact contemporary of Luther's, he came at the question of reformation in a very different way which made it virtually impossible for the two reformers to understand each other when finally they met at Marburg in 1529. A parish priest (though never a member of a religious order), Zwingli was greatly influenced by the Erasmian point of view. His emphasis therefore was much more on a reconstruction of dogma in the light of the best New Testament scholarship than on any inner experience.

This essay first appeared in *Protestant Spiritual Traditions,* ed. Frank C. Senn (Mahwah, N.J.: Paulist, 1986), 55–79. Used by permission of Paulist Press.

Deeply distrustful of anything that could detract from the central position of the Word, Zwingli would gladly have dispensed with everything in the liturgy except preaching. As it was he did away with all forms of church music and reduced public prayer to the barest minimum.[1] His emphasis on the primacy of the Word led him to relegate the eucharist to a quarterly celebration the only purpose of which was to remind the faithful of the atoning death of Christ, though there are some signs that he had begun to rethink his position before his tragic death on the field of battle in 1531.

The piety of a Zwinglian Protestant, therefore, was extremely Biblical. God's Word was the sole source and sustainer of the new life so that familiarity with it was absolutely essential. To facilitate that familiarity, he instituted a week-day service called the *prophesying*, which to Zwingli was as important (if not more so) than the Sunday liturgy. In it the faithful offered their comments on a passage of Scripture while the clergy listened and were silent. It was a kind of adult Bible class in which the members of the congregation shared their understanding of the Word with each other.

But the prophesyings were not intended to be a liturgical exercise for their own sakes, but to be instruments to strengthen the faithful in the Word. Zwingli's own confession here is significant.

> I came at length to trust in no words so much as those which proceeded (from the Bible). And when miserable mortals . . . tried to palm off their own works as God's, I looked to see whether any means could be found in which one could detect whether the works of man or of God were the better, especially as I saw not a few straining every nerve to make the simple-minded accept their own views as divine even though they were at variance with or in direct opposition to the words of God.[2]

It was the same Biblical impulse that led Zwingli at the beginning of Lent in 1519 to abandon the use of the lectionary to preach consecutively on Matthew's gospel with the Greek text in front of him on the pulpit. Roland Bainton has described the excitement of a young member of the congregation, Thomas Platter, who spent every night studying Greek and Hebrew with sand in his mouth so "that the gritting against his teeth might keep him awake."[3]

Although Zwingli's understanding of the eucharist might seem to rob it of all mystery, in the eucharistic liturgy which one of his colleagues, John Oecolampadius, provided for the congregation in Basel, however, the spirituality of this point of view comes through clearly.

> The Shepherd hath died for the lambs; the innocent hath suffered for the sinners, the Head for the members. By ineffable love, the High Priest hath sacrificed himself to the Father as a burnt offering on our behalf, and with his blood hath suffi-

ciently secured and sealed our union with God the Father. Therefore let us hold
these benefits in an everlasting and lively remembrance. His blood touches our
heart! Now we wish to live and aspire unto Christ and not to ourselves, thus to
be incorporated with him as members, redeemed and purified by his blood. Where-
fore we remember with thanksgiving the benefit of his body and blood, even as
he hath willed us to recall by the holiest of all services—his Supper.[4]

That quotation from Oecolampadius indicates the spiritual possibilities
in an understanding of the eucharist that has often been dismissed as a
"bare and naked sign."

By centering so strongly on the Word and drastically removing everything that might be used to seduce people from it, Zwingli developed a
spirituality which had two principal foci. For one thing, Zwingli's insistence
on the centrality of Scripture developed a piety that was largely inward. It
was never his intention to see the value of the Bible as merely intellectual
knowledge; it was to penetrate the soul of the believer and take possession
of it. Jacques de Senarclens has described Zwingli's intention in this way.

(According to Zwingli) the source of the conflicts of the time is found in ignorance. And since all human teaching is vain unless God inwardly enlightens and
draws us, both individually and corporately we must pray fervently that God
may cause the light of his Word to shine and that he may draw us by his grace,
poor and ignorant that we are.[5]

Already in the quotation from de Senarclens a second Zwinglian
emphasis is noticeable. The root of our trouble is *ignorance* which only a
knowledge of Scripture can correct. Implicit in the Zwinglian point of
view is an emphasis on knowledge which is not without an intellectual
cast. In order to be delivered from our misery, we need a right knowledge, and that right knowledge can only be one which is derived from
the Word of God.

These two tendencies, one toward inwardness and the other toward
knowledge, easily became distorted in later Zwinglian piety into an inner
subjectivity and a rational approach to the faith. While certainly the original teaching of Zwingli intended no such results, there can be no question that they began to appear in those areas in the Reformed tradition
where a Zwinglian piety prevailed. Indeed, it could be argued that New
England Puritanism, for example, despite all of its protestations of loyalty to John Calvin, was basically Zwinglian in its approach. The same
could be said for large areas of Dutch Protestantism as well.

Louis Bouyer, no friend of the Zwinglian spirituality, has been quick
to point out the excesses and distortions to which it led.

The first of them was the opposition between the inner and the outer. . . . The
outer, whether it meant Church-as-institution, the sacraments or ascetic prac-

tices was automatically reduced to the role of being no more than an expression (always suspect and dangerous at that) of the inner, or else was condemned outright as materialistic and idolatrous . . . .

It was a religion so reasonable that it was latent rationalism—in spite of seeing itself as a child of the Gospel—and was in fact no more than the last fruit of a scholasticism that had become impenetrable to the Christian mystery, before eliminating religion itself in a free-thought faintly tinged by mystical moralism.

Sincere and moving as piety toward Christ may have been in these Christians who were so biblical in desire but so platonizing and rationalizing in fact, it was a piety that did no more than color with religious emotion and tenderness what otherwise would have been a mere intellectualist ethic.[6]

Bouyer's judgment may seem harsh, but it is interesting to compare it with what Calvin had to say about Zwingli's views on the eucharist. They were those of a *homo profanus*, which perhaps can best be translated as a *secular person*. But whether in their pristine or their distorted form, Zwinglian ideas were the common ones in the Swiss Protestantism to which Calvin came in 1536. The fact that Zwingli had died a martyr's death in 1531 gave his piety an even greater sanctity in the eyes of the Zwinglian faithful. Liturgically, eucharistically, theologically and spiritually, all of the Reformed churches in both German and French speaking Switzerland were Zwinglian when Calvin came to them.

As we shall see, the spirituality of Calvin was something very different, but it had to be imposed not on a *tabula rasa*, but on a spiritual pattern which had already been set for almost twenty years and was sanctified with the memory of a great spiritual hero. That fact has given Reformed spirituality a dual character which it has had from its very beginning. William Farel's Neuchatel liturgy, which was in use in Geneva when Calvin came, contains the following instruction to the preacher.

After the prayer, the preacher commences by taking some text of the Holy Scripture, which he reads as clearly as did our Lord in Nazareth, and having read it, he expounds word for word without skipping, using scriptural passages to clarify the subject which he is explaining. He does not depart from Holy Scripture lest the pure Word of God be obscured by the filth of men, but bears the Word faithfully and speaks only the Word of God. And having expounded his text as simply as possible and without deviating from Scripture, as God gives grace he exhorts and admonishes the hearers, in keeping with the text, to depart from all sin and error, superstition and vanity, and return wholly to God.[7]

Or listen to the clear Zwinglian tone in the following passage from Farel's eucharistic liturgy.

. . . our blessed Savior has abundantly expressed his very great love, by giving his life for us, washing and purging us by his blood. Thus, before he suffered, he instituted his holy Supper in that last meal which he held in this mortal life and which he said he deeply desired. It was his will that in memory of his profound love in which he gave his body for us on the cross and spent his blood for the remission of our sins, we should partake of the same bread and drink of the same cup, without any discrimination, even as he died for all men without discrimination. And he bade all men to take, eat and drink in his Supper.[8]

The Spirituality of Calvin

Such was the spiritual climate in Geneva to which John Calvin came as a young lawyer of twenty-seven in 1536. He has been so modest about his conversion to the evangelical faith that it is not possible to say where he belonged, but it seems reasonable to suppose that he thought of himself as a Lutheran. Doubtless there were many aspects of spirituality which in 1536 he had not yet thought through. It is equally possible that the Zwinglian spirituality of Geneva forced him to consider many questions that were new to him. There is some evidence that as early as 1537 he was already expressing some dissatisfaction with the spiritual situation as he found it in Geneva.

As is well known, Calvin was expelled from Geneva in 1538 and spent his next four years in Strasbourg as minister of the congregation of French refugees there, working under the supervision of Martin Bucer. This pastoral experience under the guidance of a man who was dedicated to finding some kind of common ground between Zwinglian and Lutheran was deeply significant for the growth of Calvin's ideas of spirituality. When he returned to Geneva in 1542, though he had to make some compromises, it was with some well defined ideas about the meaning of spirituality, and it is to these that we shall now turn our attention.

The spirituality of John Calvin is seldom examined. Most of us would feel at home in considering the theology of John Calvin and would almost at once find ourselves wrestling with predestination, the sovereignty of God and all the other theological headlines which have come to be associated with the great reformer's name. But the spirituality of Calvin is something about which it is much harder to get a conversation started, so closely has his name become associated with what we all know as Calvinism.

Wilhelm Niesel, surely one of the best of the modern interpreters of Calvin, has said that the real center of Calvinism as a living faith is not predestination or the eternal decrees. The real center is the *unio mystica*, the union of Christ with the believer. Mingling his own language with that of Calvin, Niesel says:

> For Calvin . . . that joining together of Head and members, that indwelling of Christ in our hearts—in short, that mystical union is fundamental. We do not, therefore, contemplate him outside ourselves from afar in order that his righteousness may be imputed to us, but because we put on Christ and are engrafted

into his body—in short because he deigns to make us one with him. For this reason, we glory that we have fellowship with him.[9]

All of this is to say that Calvin would not have analyzed the various stages
of Christian experience as we tend to, conversion, justification, sanctification, etc. Calvin begins with Jesus Christ and our union with him and
makes that the starting point from which all of his gifts and benefits come.
To quote Niesel once more:

> The distinctive thing in this teaching is that he (Calvin) first of all lays the foun-
> dation, by speaking of our union with Christ, next he deals with the gift of sanc-
> tification and only then develops his doctrine of justification.[10]

If we wish to discuss the spirituality of Calvin, therefore, this must be
our starting point, the mystical union with Christ. (That should provide
no difficulty for those who accept the Heidelberg Catechism as a faithful
witness to the gospel. For it is obviously the starting point of that document as well. The celebrated first question begins with the affirmation that
we belong totally to our faithful Savior, Jesus Christ.) The relationship is
not of our choosing or devising, but one which he has created. But it is the
basic reality from which all other spiritual benefits are derived. "Not only,"
writes Calvin, "does Christ cleave to us by an indivisible bond of fellowship, but with a wonderful communion, day by day, he grows more and
more into one body with us until he becomes completely one with us."[11]

There can be no question but that this living relationship begins with
baptism. Certainly baptism does not create the relationship; baptism is
simply the sign and seal of our acceptance and forgiveness in Christ. But
that fact must not lead us to separate the sign from the thing signified. As
Calvin says, "baptism assures us that we are so united to Christ himself
that we become sharers in all his blessings."[12] But the new relationship
which has been initiated in baptism now has an entire lifetime in which
to grow and develop. We shall consider that growth and development
first and then consider the means which Calvin saw as assisting them.

Before moving to a consideration of these questions, however, we must
notice the extent to which American Reformed Christianity has shifted
the basis of spirituality from that held by Calvin. For him it was the saving act of God in Christ, signed and sealed by the sacrament of baptism.
For a large number in the Reformed Churches today, it is the sign of the
decision of the converted person. That shift has had all kinds of consequences for understanding church and sacraments and is fundamental
for the concept of the Christian life.

But now let us return to consider the meaning of growth and development and the means which assist them.

(a) It is well known that the Lutheran reformation found itself extremely vulnerable at the point of the relation between faith and works. Even though Luther tried to find a place for good works as the fruit of faith, by his heavy emphasis on *justification by faith* alone, he was always open to the charge, which his Roman Catholic opponents did not hesitate to make, that his point of view made all good works unnecessary.

It is much more difficult to make that charge against Calvin. Indeed, Louis Bouyer, the Roman Catholic historian of spirituality, had this to say:

> Calvin, on the other hand, while also maintaining that justification precedes, and is hence independent of any possible works that man may do, added that a faith that did not produce both external works and the progressive sanctification of our whole being was but an appearance of faith and therefore would not have justified us.[13]

(The third section of the Heidelberg Catechism is a good evidence of Calvin's understanding of this point. The second section which deals with our redemption is not complete without the third which deals really with our sanctification.) No one can belong to Christ and not be involved in the style of life which his new relationship demands.

One of the great demands of that new way of life is ethical. From the Calvinist perspective, we have not been redeemed from the law, but made able to obey the law. Calvin never wearies in reminding us that the assurance of our belonging to Christ is to be found not only in our own inward feelings, but in the manner of our outward lives. He would, I think, have been baffled by the later attempt to distinguish between *mysticum* and *practicum*. While valuing the importance of the *mysticum*, he would certainly have maintained that any *mysticum* which did not result in *practicum* was specious. Not even in his liturgical composition will he let us forget that we have been fed at the Table so that we may be more effective agents of the gospel in the world.

We must stress the fact that when Calvin uses the words *justification* and *sanctification*, he does not use them sequentially, as is often the case in many contemporary discussions, nor does he place one above the other as is often done. He sees them rather as dual gifts that come from our relationship with Christ. B. A. Gerrish has put it this way:

> The benefits of Christ, according to Calvin, are ours only as a result of this secret communion that we have with Christ himself. In the *Institutes* he distinguishes two *graces* we receive from Christ; reconciliation (or justification) and sanctification. Neither of the two is given precedence as the supposed center of Evangelical theology, since both look away to the christological point of reference above them. The dominant motif is the *real presence* of Christ with the Christian as the head of the body.[14]

From the time of his baptism on, therefore, the believer through the indwelling of Christ is not only made right with God but is continually enabled to grow into the grace and likeness of his Lord. His being made right with God and his growth into Christ are therefore closely inter-dependent. Bouyer is right; for Calvin there is no being made right with God that is not accompanied by growth in grace; and obviously no growth in grace is possible for those who are not right with God. The locus in which this all takes place is the Church, which is the next topic we must consider in our consideration of Calvin's spirituality.

(b) It might be well to begin our consideration of the Church in Calvin's spirituality by reminding ourselves of the most famous statement he ever made about it. "We cannot have God as our Father if we do not have the Church as our mother." Indeed Book IV of the *Institutes* begins with a chap-ter heading, "The True Church with which as Mother of all the godly we must keep unity." Once again the grudging praise which Louis Bouyer gives to Calvin's ecclesiology is worth quoting.

> Nothing is more revealing of Calvin's neo-Catholic reaction than the space he allotted to the Church in the successive editions of his *Institutes*—from a few pages to a quarter of the work. But still more important is the formal reappearance of a Church that is the mother of believers because the mother of their faith, a Church that is neither the invisible ultra-Augustinian Church of Luther in his first phase, nor the merely religious organization handed over to the supposedly Christian state and depending on its authority alone, such as Luther set up later to combat sectarian anarchy.
> . . . The Calvinist Church had a structure of its own independent of the state, whether Christian or not, and on Calvin's express word it proceeded from the divine will as affirmed in the New Testament.[15]

Niesel has some words which provide a helpful commentary on Bouyer's last point.

> Reformed theology treated with great breadth the doctrine of the Church as a living organically articulated community without losing sight of the individual and with no thought of establishing principles for an authoritarian church, but offering guidance for the assembly of God's people to the praise of God's glory in a world which though lost has been placed under God's promise. . . . Calvin spent his whole life serving this true gathering of God's people in many places, and created the necessary conditions to ensure that the tumults of the Counter-Reformation could not suppress again what had so recently been born of God's Word and Spirit. In the Reformed countries, the Jesuits found not just preach-ing stations, but witnessing and active congregations with well-ordered min-istries and firmly bound together as their Synods showed.[16]

In a word, in Calvin's thinking the Church precedes the individual and not the other way around as has become so popular in contemporary spirituality. It is into the Church that we are brought by baptism and it is in the context of the Church that we grow up into Christ by the use of the means of grace. That is why Calvin can agree with Cyprian that "outside the Church there is no salvation." To be sure, God in his sovereignty is not bound to the Church, but we are.

Calvin is not unaware of the invisible nature of the true Church but he does not give it the exaggerated importance which it has in so many pietist ecclesiologies. Calvin's understanding of the invisible Church is firmly rooted in his understanding of election. The Lord alone knows who are his. But that in no way lessens our obligation to be part of the visible Church since God has willed that she be our mother. We have the promise that where two or three are gathered in my Name, I am in the midst of them, and that promise cannot fail.

This seems to be a good place to observe that our common view of spirituality often suggests the lonely pious individual striving to become more like Christ. That image has little or no place in the spirituality of Calvin. While I am sure that he engaged in private prayer, Calvin has surprisingly little to say on the subject. The Christian joins in the prayers of the people of God on the Lord's Day and in daily services in the Church. But by himself he is not at home praying; he is out in the world engaging in obedient ethical activity. To be sure that ethical activity is nourished and supported by his life in the Church; but, as Abraham Kuyper has reminded us in his classic Stone Lectures on Calvinism, Calvin had a total view of the necessity of self-consciously penetrating the domain of politics, science and art as well as the domain of religion.

B. A. Gerrish has a nice comparison between Luther and Calvin here.

(Luther) preached the Word, slept, and drank his beer; and while he did nothing more, the Word did it all. With Calvin things were quite different. As he lay on his deathbed, he fell to reminiscing about the course of his life and remarked: "When I first arrived in this church, there was almost nothing. They were preaching and that is all. . . . There was reformation."[17]

It is in the Church, therefore, and not in the private closet that Christian growth takes place—and there always as the gift of God in Christ and not as the result of human effort and striving. Certainly any tendency to asceticism as an agent of spiritual growth would have been condemned by Calvin as pure Pelagianism.

(c) Within the Church the primary agent of spiritual growth is for Calvin the preaching of the Word. Indeed, his not so friendly critic, Louis Bouyer, expresses no little surprise at this point.

(The new life) was a life that the Holy Spirit created within us, yes, but the only gift of the Spirit that Calvin seemed willing to enlarge on was the gift of under- standing the Scriptures.[18]

Bouyer's criticism is somewhat exaggerated, but even taken at face value, it really misses what Calvin believed about the preaching of the Word. The French Oratorian is thinking of preaching as commentary on the gospel, the traditional Roman Catholic approach to the question. For Calvin, however, the phrase which contemporary Roman Catholicism uses would have been highly congenial—the real presence of Christ in his Word.

So far from being a mere commentary on the gospel, for Calvin the reading and preaching of the Word is the way in which Christ comes to us and shares himself with us, enlarging our understanding, strengthen- ing our commitment, deepening our assurance. So totally did Calvin see the reading and preaching of the Word as a single indissoluble event (and not one a commentary on the other) that his Liturgy contains no provi- sion for the reading of the Word; it simply assumes that reading and preaching will be a single act.

Because the Word is the instrument through which Christ is given to us, it stands at the very center of the life of the Church and at the very center of the life and growth of the Christian. Listen to part of the prayer which Calvin suggested should be used before the Word on Sunday.

As we look into the face of the Son, Jesus Christ, our Lord, whom (God) has appointed Mediator between himself and us, let us beseech him in whom is all ful- ness or wisdom and light to vouchsafe to guide us by his Holy Spirit into the true understanding of his holy doctrine, making it productive in us of all the fruits of righteousness.[19]

Let me attempt to exegete that prayer as to what it says about preach- ing. I see in it four themes which I should like to discuss briefly.

1. Preaching is the real presence of Christ in his Word. In it, "we look into the face of Jesus Christ our Lord." It is not a speaking about Christ; it is an event in which Christ himself comes to us and offers himself to us in all of his fullness.
2. This presence of Christ in his Word is effected by the Holy Spirit. It is the power of the Spirit that makes Christ who is at the right hand of God present with us in an effective way.
3. As a result of this confrontation with the living Christ, our under- standing of him and his saving presence is enlarged. Our grasp of his gifts to us is increased and strengthened and we perceive more sharply and more meaningfully what he means to us.

BUT . . .

> 4. This increase in knowledge and understanding is not (as it so often became in later Calvinism) merely a head trip as if there were virtue in knowing more about the doctrine. It is functional, enabling us to be more productive of the fruits of righteousness. This, indeed, is the final purpose for which Christ gave himself to us in his Word.

I have done that small piece of exegesis because when we come to consider the eucharist in Calvin's spirituality, we shall have occasion to notice how closely his understanding of it parallels his understanding of preaching.

I do not think that in his understanding of the reading and preaching of the Word there is any basic difference between Calvin and Luther. The only significant difference is the way in which Calvin so definitely links it with our style of life in the world. One suspects that for Luther the assurance of forgiveness would have been the final result of the real presence of Christ in his word, whereas for Calvin it is definitely the empowering for a righteous life.

(d) At this point, I should like to inset a brief consideration of the importance of the liturgy in the spirituality of John Calvin. We often pass by the fact that he composed a liturgy for his congregation in Strasbourg, revising it later for use in Geneva, but even more by the fact that he discouraged any attempts to tinker or tamper with it. Whatever we may think of the liturgical quality of his *Form of Prayers*, Calvin thought it had an important role to play in the life of the Church since liturgy is more than preaching (here he definitely parted company with Zwingli) but also includes prayer, praise and the celebration of the eucharist.

One wonders what Calvin would have to say about many of the liturgical vapidities in the Reformed Churches today. "Those who introduce newly invented methods of worshiping really worship and adore the creature of their own distempered imaginations," wrote Calvin. And while he did not claim final excellence for his own liturgy, he was strongly in favor of one from which ministers should not be allowed to vary. Such a fixed liturgy, he wrote, would limit "the capricious giddiness and levity of such as effect innovations."[20]

In making such observations Calvin was seeking to defend the act of worship against certain destructive tendencies which he saw at work in his own time and which have certainly blossomed like a rose in ours. Briefly put, Calvin wanted to guard worship from becoming a massaging of our own feelings. The real purpose of worship, as he never wearied of saying, is to glorify God. That must put adoration as the central theme of liturgical activity. But, as Calvin also repeatedly said, the real

way to glorify God is to obey him. Liturgical activity has that as a closely
related purpose—the enabling of the people of God to give him glory
in secular service.

Hence one of the most dramatic shifts which Calvin made in traditional
liturgical usage—the use of the Law as an act of thanksgiving after the
announcement of forgiveness. The Calvinist *Gloria in Excelsis* is the Ten
Commandments. I think that that substitution speaks volumes about the
Calvinist idea of spirituality. Here is almost the last word of Calvin's *Liturgy*,
the end of the prayer of thanksgiving after communion. Notice how it
echoes the same theme we have noted.

> Now grant us this other benefit: that thou wilt never allow us to forget these
> things; but having them imprinted on our hearts, we may grow and increase daily
> in the faith which is at work in every good deed. Thus may we order and pursue
> all our life to the exaltation of thy glory and the edification of our neighbor.[21]

Though I have never found any reference to it in Calvin, he must have
considered another factor in his insistence on the value of a virtually unal-
tered weekly liturgy. I refer to the fact that through constant repetition
its language became part of the worshiper's piety. Whether or not that
had been Calvin's intention, it certainly took place in churches which
took his liturgical ideas seriously. My favorite illustration is the case of
Marycke Popinga, a five year old moppet, who startled the congregation of the Dutch Reformed Church in New York in 1698 by perfectly
reciting the Sunday prayer before the sermon, as the domine said, "with
energy and manly confidence." So moved was the congregation, according to the domine, that when Marycke had finished, they said the prayer
together "not without tears." Could there be a better indication of the
way in which repeated usage makes liturgical language part of individual piety and spirituality?[22]

(e) At this point we have to look at a last aspect of Calvin's understanding of spirituality, his idea of the eucharist. We all know that the
place of the eucharist in the life of the Church was one of Calvin's greatest frustrations. Down to the end of his life he protested against the infre-
quency of its celebration, but all in vain. Never was he able to celebrate
it oftener than monthly in Strasbourg, while all during his years in Geneva
a quarterly celebration was the rule.

If Calvin could have spoken about the "real presence of Christ in his
Word," he certainly would not have hesitated to speak about the "real
presence of Christ in his Supper." For to him the Supper was only another
form, though an important form, of the Word, another means by which
Christ comes to share himself with his people. If preaching is the *audible*

form of the Word, the eucharist is the *visible* form. But we need both forms of the Word really to be involved in the wholeness of the gospel.

Despite the fact that Calvin's ideas of the eucharist are contained in almost every Reformed confession, we have largely forgotten the depth of his belief in the real presence and the importance which he assigned to the eucharist in his ideas of spirituality. B. A. Gerrish has put it in this way.

> Once the idea of Christ's living presence, effected through the Word of God, has been presented as the heart of Calvin's gospel, his doctrine of the eucharistic presence is already half stated. The role he assigns to the Lord's Supper in the life of the church is traced to the fact that communion with Christ is not wholly perfect from the very first, but subject to growth, vicissitudes and impediments. He does not think of "receiving Christ" as a crisis decision, but rather as a magnitude subject to variation. . . . The very nature of its symbolism suggests to Calvin that the Lord's Supper is a matter of nourishing, sustaining and increasing a communion with Christ to which the Word and baptism have initiated us.[23]

Gerrish lists seven characteristics of Calvin's understanding of the eucharist which I should like to mention, reducing them to six, although my comments on each one will be much briefer than his.

1. The eucharist is a gift, not a good work. For the Roman Catholic of his time it was a good work, a sacrifice presented by man to God. But it was no less a good work for the Zwinglian who saw in the eucharist only a thankful recollection of Christ's death and recommitment to the Christian community.
2. The gift is Jesus Christ himself. We have already commented on this sufficiently in our discussion of the preaching of the Word.
3. The gift is given through the signs. Again this is aimed at both Roman Catholics and Zwinglians, though in different ways. In medieval Catholicism, the sign became absorbed in the thing signified, while for Zwingli the sign is only a sign.
4. The gift is given by the power of the Holy Spirit—an entire essay could be written on the pneumatology of the eucharist in Calvin's thinking. It is enough to notice here that the gift is not received by the recitation of a formula but by the presence of the Holy Spirit.
5. The gift is given to all who communicate but it is received only by those who have faith. (I have combined Gerrish's fifth and sixth propositions in that statement.)
6. The gift evokes gratitude. We have already noticed this theme in our brief discussion of Calvin's thanksgiving after communion.[24]

No lovelier description of what the eucharist meant to the spirituality of Calvin can be found than in this little confession in the fourth book of the *Institutes*.

> In his sacred supper Christ bids me take, eat and drink his holy body and blood under the symbols of bread and wine. I do not doubt that he himself truly presents them and that I receive them.

It is unfortunate that this very deep faith in the real presence of Christ in the eucharist became obscured in all of the sixteenth century controversies about the mode of the presence, controversies in which Calvin was often an active participant. In those controversies, it is evident that Calvin often felt the limitations of the vocabulary with which he had to work. He was caught up in the dichotomy between body and spirit which was the way in which the sixteenth century thought. He was also limited by the naively geographical way in which Christ was located at the right hand of God, as was the case with all the reformers. Gerrish suggests that in his struggles with a limited vocabulary, Calvin was "moving toward a fresh conception of the substance of Christ's body as precisely its force or power, so that the substance is present, albeit in a nondimensional way."[25] But to enter into that kind of discussion is not only outside our topic, but spoils the air of mystery with which Calvin always viewed the eucharist. I prefer to close this part of the discussion with words taken from Calvin's own eucharistic liturgy.

> Above all therefore, let us believe those promises which Jesus Christ who is the unfailing truth has spoken with his own lips. He is truly willing to make us partakers of his body and blood in order that we may possess him wholly and in such wise that we may live in him and he in us.[26]

What was the spirituality of John Calvin? Once we have been received into God's new people by baptism, we are given everything that Jesus Christ is and has and are enabled to appropriate it in increasing measure by sharing Christ in the preaching of his Word, in the receiving of his Supper, in the liturgical life of his body, the Church. From the power and the strength which we receive in these ways, we are enabled and expected for obedient service to God in the world which is under his promise.

Reformed Spirituality after Calvin

The spirituality of Calvin was by no means accepted in the entire Reformed tradition. Coming, as it did, into a situation already dominated by Zwinglian piety, Calvinist spirituality was never as widely accepted as Calvinist theology or church order. Louis Bouyer has claimed that Calvin had only limited success in trying to convert the Reformed churches to his point of view.

> It is because these churches were later to adopt the practical organization put into effect by Calvin that they are persistently and misleadingly called *Calvinist*. . . . The *Reformed* churches as a whole, and leaving aside the Presbyterian synodal organization and some minority groups of Scottish and Dutch theologians, have always felt the greatest repugnance for the theological theses that properly belonged to Calvinism. It was Zwingli who so excellently expressed the basic mentality of *Reformed* churchmen . . . even if we cannot strictly call them his disciples.[27]

One of the places where the spirituality of Calvin flourished was in seventeenth century Scotland among a group known as the Aberdeen Doctors. Although their loyalty to the Stuart regime had forced them to accept a modified form of episcopacy, the Aberdeen Doctors remained loyal to Calvinist spirituality. G. D. Henderson, the best historian of religion in seventeenth century Scotland, has pointed out the surprising way in which the Aberdeen Doctors and their successors remained loyal Calvinists in spite of their acceptance of episcopacy.

> The great mass of the clergy . . . continued in the Calvinistic faith which had been generally characteristic of Scotland for over a century. Even Robert Leighton, the saintly Bishop of Dunblane and Archbishop of Glasgow, was a Calvinist.[28]

The most celebrated of the later Aberdeen Doctors was Henry Scougal, whose little devotional manual, *The Life of God in the Soul of Man* (which had a great influence on John Wesley), is his most famous work. In a sermon of preparation for the Holy Sacrament, he had this to say about the eucharist.

> This Sacrament doth not only represent a wonder that is past, but exhibits a new. The bread and wine that are received are not bare and empty signs to put us in mind of the death and sufferings of Christ. Our Savior calls them his body and blood and such, without question they are, to all spiritual purposes and advantages.
> . . . These words of our Savior are spirit and life, are to be understood in a spiritual and vital sense; but though these elements be not changed in their nature and substance, yet they undergo a mighty change as to their efficacy and use.[29]

Those interested in tracing the survival of Calvin's spirituality in that of the Aberdeen Doctors will first of all take note of the fact that the very title of Scougal's devotional manual, *The Life of God in the Soul of Man*, is an echo of the Calvinist insistence that the *unio mystica* is central to the Christian faith. What is more, the quotation from his sermon on the eucharist clearly indicates his rejection of the Zwinglian understanding of that sacrament in favor of Calvin's. When he wrote that the "elements undergo a mighty change as to their efficacy and use," he was almost quoting Calvin himself.

Another area in which Calvinist spirituality flourished, as it did in northeast Scotland, was in Puritan New England. Since the spirituality of Puritanism is to be considered elsewhere in this book, we shall not study it in detail here. It is sufficient to point out that Charles Hambrick-Stowe in his definitive work *The Practice of Piety* has pointed out that Puritan piety contained two contradictory strains, one anti-sacramental while the other was much in the spirit of Calvin.

> One thrust of Puritan piety led to sacramental iconoclasm; at the same time the orthodox displayed "a burst of fascination with eucharistic devotional material and sacramental piety." . . . In their public worship New Englanders maintained a doctrine of the real presence that differed little from Calvin.[30]

In his discussion of the Puritan understanding of the eucharist as a vital part of spirituality, Hambrick-Stowe cites a number of New England divines, including such well-known names as John Cotton, Thomas Hooker, Thomas Shepherd and Increase Mather. He also has an extended discussion of the eucharistic poetry of Edward Taylor, the pastor of Westfield. His description of some questions from John Cotton's Catechism, *Milk for Babes*, is filled with echoes of Calvin's spirituality.

> "What is done for you in baptism?" The answer that came back was "the pardon and cleansing of my sins since I am washed not only with water but with the blood and Spirit of Christ." Baptism led "to my ingrafting into Christ and my rising out of affliction and also . . . my resurrection from the dead at the last day. . . ."
>
> Cotton's reply to the same question concerning the Lord's Supper was that the broken bread and the poured wine were "a sign and seal of my receiving the body of Christ broken for me and of his blood shed for me, and thereby of my growth in Christ, of the pardon and healing of my sins, the fellowship of his Spirit, of my strengthening and quickening in grace, and of my sitting together with Christ on his throne of glory at the Last Judgment."[31]

There was one significant American attempt in the nineteenth century to restore the spirituality of John Calvin to its rightful place in the Reformed tradition. The so-called Mercersburg movement took place in the German Reformed Church from about 1845 to 1870. Its leaders were the two theologians from the Seminary in Mercersburg, Pennsylvania, John Williamson Nevin and Philip Schaff. Theirs was a serious effort to take Calvin's ideas of church, ministry, liturgy and sacraments and translate them into nineteenth century terms.

It says much about the validity of Bouyer's assertion about the minority position of Calvinist spirituality within the Reformed churches (quoted earlier in this essay) that when Charles Hodge, the distinguished Princeton Presbyterian theologian, read Nevin's *Mystical Presence* which bears the clear subtitle *A Vindication of the Calvinistic Doctrine of the Eucharist*, he expressed both surprise and horror at the discovery that Calvin could have written such stuff. He tried to argue that when it comes to Sacraments, Zwingli is the responsible Reformed authority.

The same thing happened to Schaff's *Principle of Protestantism* which appeared at about the same time. Because Philip Schaff had asserted that the Reformation was derived from medieval Catholicism, he was tried for heresy by the Classis of Philadelphia. We can be grateful that at that trial the charge was dismissed, but the fact that it could have been brought in the first place indicates how little understanding of Calvinist spirituality there was at that time. In fact, when the Dutch Reformed Church read the Mercersburg theologians, it broke off relations with its German Reformed sister on the grounds that it did not wish to consort with a body so afflicted with "Romanizing tendencies."

Today all that has been forgotten and there is general recognition of the significant contribution which Mercersburg, and especially John W. Nevin, made to the restoration of a largely forgotten area of Calvinist theology and spirituality. Indeed, there is general agreement that Mercersburg theology was one of the most important developments in the history of the American Church.[32]

One of the most important ways in which Calvinist spirituality was threatened in both Europe and America was by the rise of evangelical pietism. Since Pietism is a subject which will be fully discussed in another chapter of this book, there is no need for an extensive discussion here. But it must be noted that with its heavy emphasis on the individual Pietism completely altered traditional Calvinist spirituality. In the Reformed churches on the continent, Pietism seems to have been more churchly in its spirituality. It sought to revitalize the life of the Church by a new emphasis on catechization, pastoral visitation, an interest in missions and the use of hymns as well as psalms in the Sunday liturgy.

But in America the situation was quite different. For one thing, after the American Revolution, the whole model of American life changed from the old pattern of social community to the self-reliant individualist. Social historians, Rowland Berthoff and John Murrin, have this description of what happened.

Freshly released from bonds of social community as well as of feudal lordship, the new democratic individualism harked back to . . . the yeoman freeholder, a figure most typical of the back country settlements of Pennsylvania, the new South-

west and northern New England. Increasingly, he would be taken as the archetype of the American everywhere . . . self-reliant, honest and independent.[33]

Berthoff and Murrin also have pointed out that the rise of the rugged
individualist as the American model replaced older models such as the
tightly knit community of a New England village or the patronal society of the Hudson Valley.

Once the model of the "rugged individualist" began to predominate,
especially on the American frontier, Calvinist spirituality was doomed. It
had already been struggling with the new individualism of the Great Awakening in the new light vs. old light controversies that wracked the Con-
gregational, Presbyterian and Reformed Churches in the colonies. But once
the success of the new republic had crowned the self-reliant individual as
the American pattern, then the new measures of a Charles Finney, as well
as the camp meetings and revivals of Baptist and Methodist origin, became
the new effective pattern. In what they felt was the only way to survive,
traditional Reformed churches tried to adopt Baptist and Methodist spirituality to their own needs. The results are still with us today.

It could be a fitting comment to say that while the spirituality of evangelical pietism probably is still dominant in American Reformed churches
today, the closing half of this century has seen a renewal of Calvinist
spirituality as a result of the ecumenical movement. When Reformed
Churches which had largely abandoned their traditional Calvinist stance
found themselves in dialogue with other Christian traditions, there was
at first a good deal of foundering with questions such as baptism, eucharist
and ministry. So widely had evangelical pietist spirituality spread in
Reformed circles that many were unaware of their own tradition and
thought only in terms of the individual believer and his response to the
gospel. In many instances, it came as a surprise to learn that there was in
the Reformed tradition a carefully articulated churchly spirituality involving liturgy, sacraments and ministry.

It was just this uncertainty that led to the rediscovery and renewal of
Calvinist spirituality within the Reformed tradition. With the Mercersburg movement as the pioneer, there has in recent years been a serious
effort in Reformed circles to update Calvin's ideas, trying to free them
from the concepts and terminology in which they had been locked for
many years. Most recently, the World Council's Lima Document on *Baptism, Eucharist and Ministry* has challenged many Reformed thinkers to critique it from a Calvinist point of view.

A final word must be said about something which pervades all genuine Reformed spirituality whether of the Zwinglian, Calvinist or Pietist
variety. Since Reformed thinking has always emphasized that the Christian life begins with the election of God in Christ, its stress has always

fallen on the divine rather than the human activity. While Calvin has always been known as the theologian of election and predestination, the survival of that idea has been not so much a theological proposition as a "sweet and comforting assurance" to the Christian in his spiritual pilgrimage.

However much Zwingli and Calvin may have differed at other points, they were at one in basing all spirituality on the divine choice and activity. Reformed tradition has always seen the church in Roland Bainton's words as

> . . . the body of the elect, a band of the chosen of the Lord, calling no man sovereign save under God, not worrying about salvation, sustained by the assurance of the unshakable decree, committed not to the enjoyment of the delights of life but only to the illustration of the honor of the sovereign God. . . .[34]

The important thing to notice in Bainton's description is the phrase *not worrying about salvation*. Because salvation was the irreversible decision of a sovereign Lord, there was no point in asking questions about one's status or in being concerned about the state of one's spiritual health. One of the leading Calvinists of the nineteenth century, Herman Friederich Kohlbrügge, urged his congregation in Elberfeld, Germany, not to ask whether or not they possessed the gifts of the Spirit, but to remember that they had a gracious Father. That is the authentic Reformed spiritual voice whether spoken in Zurich, Geneva or Elberfeld.

Steven Ozment has a splendid summary of Reformed spirituality, including a quotation from Calvin himself.

> Man's fallenness obsessed Calvin both in his teaching and his ministry. A large part of the *Institutes of the Christian Religion* is a sad hymn to what man could have been "if Adam had remained upright." A still greater part of the *Institutes* celebrates Christ's redemption of mankind and the possibility for true Christians to recover, gradually and partially, Adam's original righteousness. Calvin believed nothing so much as that "our religion . . . must enter into our heart and pass into our daily living and so transform us into itself that it may not be unfruitful for us." Anything less, for himself or for the citizens of Geneva, was . . . a religion of the tongue and mind, a piety of faith alone.[35]

Notes

1. Bard Thompson, ed., *Liturgies of the Western Church* (Cleveland and New York: Collins, 1962), 147–48.

2. Steven Ozment, quoted in *The Age of Reform* (New Haven: Yale University Press, 1980), 323–24.

3. Cf. Roland Bainton, *The Reformation of the Sixteenth Century* (Boston: Beacon, 1952), 82–83.

4. Thompson, op. cit., 214.

5. Jacques de Senardens, *Heirs of the Reformation* (Philadelphia: Westminster, 1958), 90.

6. Louis Bouyer, *A History of Christian Spirituality* (New York: Seabury, 1982), 3:82–83.

7. Thompson, op. cit., 216.

8. Ibid., 219.

9. Wilhelm Niesel, *Reformed Symbolics* (Edinburgh: Oliver & Boyd, 1962), 182.

10. Ibid., 192.

11. Ibid., 185.

12. Ibid., 268.

13. Bouyer, op. cit., 86.

14. B. A. Gerrish, *The Old Protestantism and the New* (Chicago: University of Chicago Press, 1982).

15. Bouyer, op. cit., 91.

16. Niesel, op. cit., 254–55.

17. Gerrish, op. cit., 258.

18. Bouyer, op. cit., 86.

19. Thompson, op. cit., 209.

20. Ibid., 195.

21. Ibid., 208.

22. J. B. Lyons, *Ecclesiastical Records of the State of New York*, Albany, New York, 2:1240.

23. Gerrish, op. cit., 111–12.

24. Ibid., 112–15.

25. Ibid., 117.

26. Thompson, op. cit., 207.

27. Bouyer, op. cit., 78.

28. G. D. Henderson, *Religious Life in Seventeenth Century Scotland* (Cambridge: Cambridge University Press, 1937), 92.

29. Marion Lochhead, *Episcopal Scotland in the Nineteenth Century* (London: John Murray, 1966), 27.

30. Charles Hambrick-Stowe, *The Practice of Piety* (Chapel Hill, N.C.: University of North Carolina Press, 1982), 125.

31. Ibid., 123–24.

32. For a full discussion of the Mercersburg movement in general and of John W. Nevin in particular, see James H. Nichols, *Romanticism in American Theology;* and Brian A. Gerrish, *Tradition and the Modern World: Reformed Theology in Nineteenth Century.*

33. *Essays on the American Revolution* (Chapel Hill, N.C.: University of North Carolina Press, 1982), 276.

34. Bainton, op. cit., 122.

35. Ozment, op. cit., 380.

Anglican Spirituality
An Ethos and Some Issues

Harvey H. Guthrie

What "Anglican" means is very hard to define. As I think about trying, places and people significantly different from one another—everyone of which is in fact Anglican—come to mind. I think of St. Andrew's Abbey in Denver, Colorado, where going to the liturgy on Sunday not too long ago was to find oneself in a very up to date equivalent of a Benedictine establishment centuries old. Yet, I think also of the cathedral in Sydney, Australia, where there is no altar but a plain, wooden table, and where doctrine and ethos are about as Protestant as can be conceived. I think of the bishop of the recently become independent diocese of Puerto Rico who is very Latin in temperament and style and flair, of the bishop of Maseno South in Kenya who is very African in tribal origin, speech and loyalty, of the archbishop of New Zealand in whom British crispness and Oxford acerbity and Maori astuteness all dwell together, of the primate of the United States whose accent is very southern and who is seen as pretty conservative, of the primate of Canada whose accent is very north-of-the-border and who is seen as fairly liberal. I think of a lawyer in the southwestern part of the United States who goes to a high church mass every day and who has defended civil rights advocates and anti-Vietnam war protesters, of a banker who goes to Morning Prayer only and who would consider protest of any kind as well as prodding into his spiritual life as indecent, of a New England nurse

This essay first appeared in *Anglican Spirituality*, ed. William J. Wolf (Wilton, Conn.: Morehouse-Barlow, 1982), 1–16. Used by permission.

who is a born-again Christian with a well-thumbed Good News Bible in her hands, of a priest who teaches comparative literature and whose spirituality is very Zen, of a nursery school teacher who is a faith healer.

I could go on. Anyone at all familiar with the Anglican churches who thinks about it could come up with a list of contrasts seeming to indicate the impossibility of arriving at any comprehensible definition of "Anglican." I do, however, believe that there is indeed something finally—if vaguely—identifiable as "Anglican" if we will allow that which is being identified to provide the terms of the identification, if we will not presume to impose upon it terms originating in other realities. Furthermore, I believe that other Anglicans, in spite of the vast differences among us, would agree with me that there is something identifiable as "Anglican." We might define it differently, but we would have in common our assumption that there is an "it" to define: an "it" which means a great deal to us both individually and corporately, an "it" which keeps us in the fellowship even when we find ourselves disagreeing with almost every decision taken by the official bodies of our Church, an "it" which has attracted a high percentage of us into one of the Anglican churches out of many different ecclesiastical and secular backgrounds. Moreover, for reasons I shall outline later on, I believe it to be extremely important for those of us who are Anglicans to seek to arrive at a definition of "Anglican" at this point in our history at which so many new realities have to be taken into account.

An Ecclesiastical Typology

Someone, located so far back there in my life that I have forgotten who it was, taught me one of those simplistic lessons easy to remember but probably not adequate to the complicated nature of any reality. The lesson was that there have been, down through Christian history, three basic manifestations of the Church. Upon reflection, I believe that lesson does bear some relation to reality. The lesson had it that those three manifestations of the Church are distinguished from one another by the way in which each of them defines what constitutes membership in the Church.

The first type of church is _confessional_. It holds that what fundamentally makes one a part of the Church is one's confession of the faith which is held by the Church. In the understanding of this type of church, the Church is that body of people which confesses a common faith. The second type of church is _experiential_. It holds that what fundamentally makes one a part of the Church is one's having participated in that experience of conversion through which one's fellow Christians came into the body of those who have been saved by Christ. In the understanding of this type of church, the Church is that body of people who have individually undergone a common religious experience. The third type of church is _pragmatic_. It holds that what fundamentally makes one a part of the Church is one's doing with the Church what the Church does liturgically, sacramentally and empirically. In the understanding of this type of church, the Church is that body of people who have undergone baptism, who participate in the celebration of the Eucharist, who observe the Church's feasts, fasts and ordinances. In the understanding of this type of church individuals may hold various confessional positions, may have undergone differing religious experiences or no particular religious experience at all. The basic thing they have in common is neither a doctrinal position nor a religious experience. It is simply participating in what the Church does as Church.

As I see it, the Anglican churches are fundamentally churches of the third type. And, as I see it, therein lie both the strength and the weakness of Anglicanism. The questions with which Anglicans are characteristically concerned are pragmatic questions. They have to do with whether or not the sacraments are presided over by validly and regularly ordained ministers, with what vestments may properly and legally be worn on occasions of public worship, with whether or not the persons proposing to vote in a parish meeting have been baptized and have received communion at least three times during the past year and have supported the parish financially.

That approach to what constitutes membership in the Church certainly has its weak and trivial side. It produces arid and Erastian situations which drive disciples of the Wesleys to found the Methodist Church and which caused John Henry Newman to turn to the Church of Rome. That approach can result in a church which is theologically flabby, which seems constitutionally incapable of taking a stand on anything significant, which is inarticulate with regard to the demands of Christian faith in some given set of historical circumstances. It can result in a church which neither remembers nor knows any Christian experience which sets it apart from the world in which it exists. It can produce a church which is just the House of Lords or Wall Street or a secular university or some country club at prayer.

That approach also has, however, its steady and comprehensive and inclusive and catholic side. It is not narrowly sectarian. It is capable of transcending the kind of merely intellectual and ideological conceptions of Christianity which keep dividing the Church into more and more numerous groups of believers holding more and more finely defined theological positions. It can thwart that spiritual arrogance which insists that true Christianity must involve only the particular kind of religious experience that I and those like me have undergone. It can allow for difference of opinion—even doctrinal opinion—within one, united Church.

It can conceive of quite different parties being parts of one Christian fellowship. It can provide a place where folk busy with the world's real business and lacking time for theological fine points or rarified spiritual experience can pray in a matter-of-fact, eyes-open, no-nonsense kind of way.

It is that kind of approach which lies at the heart of distinctively Anglican spirituality. Distinctively Anglican spirituality is grounded in the ongoing, corporate, liturgical life of the Church participated in by lay people as well as clergy, by those with occupations in the world as well as those committed to the monastic life. Anglican spirituality arises out of the common prayer of a body of Christians who are united in their participation—through physical presence and liturgical dialogue and sacramental action—in the cult in which the Church identifies itself as Church. It involves a corporate life whose times and seasons and offices and ordinances and readings and sermons are the means of corporate participation, in and through Christ, with God present to and for human beings in history in this world. Private devotion and prayer and meditation on the part of individuals are supports for and means of putting oneself into and extensions of the ongoing, corporate, liturgical life of the Church.

Anglican spirituality is corporate and liturgical and sacramental. That is why, even though the Bible is so central to Anglican spirituality and is read extensively and regularly and serially in the office and the eucharistic liturgy, the Bible per se is not the basis of Anglican spirituality. Indeed, the Bible itself is never, purely and exclusively, the basis of any spirituality, even spiritualities which would think of themselves as biblical. Whether those reading it are conscious of the fact or not, the Bible is always read in some context. The Bible may be read in the context of some doctrinal position centering on the exclusive authority of the Bible. It may be read in the context of some conviction about the way in which the Bible speaks directly to the heart of the individual believer. It may be read in the context of various doctrinal or devotional presuppositions, but it is always read in some context. In Anglicanism that context is the corporate, liturgical, sacramental life of the Church. The Bible is indeed central in Anglican spirituality, is used much more extensively in Anglican liturgy than it is in the worship of many churches more ideologically biblical in their orientation. The Bible itself, however, is not the *basis* of the Anglican spirituality.

Neither is some system of individual devotion or meditation the basis of Anglican spirituality. We are so much the products of the culture in which we live that we are, on the whole, unconscious of the extent to which modern, western anthropology is the framework within which the life of prayer and devotion, the spiritual life, is lived and understood. Modern, western anthropology is fundamentally individualistic and rationalistic. That which makes me what I really am is that which sets me apart from, "individuates" me from, other human beings. Furthermore, that which is most real about things and beings, from atoms to the Almighty, is what I think and feel about them, what they "mean." Those views of what I am and what I deal with have, for the most part quite unconsciously, dominated western spirituality from St. Ignatius and the classic German pietists to contemporary emphases on personal growth. For both Roman Catholic and Protestant spirituality in post-reformation, western Christianity, systems of individual devotion in which "mental prayer" is central have been dominant. The Church's liturgy, its offices and sacraments, have in reality been more resources for individual devotion than the central thing, have become overshadowed by the acts of individual preparation, individual participation and individual thanksgiving emphasized in instruction and manuals and practice.

Anglican spirituality, however, is basically corporate, liturgical and sacramental. That is why its basis is neither the Bible per se nor some system or manual of individual devotion and meditation. That is why the basis of Anglican spirituality is the *Book of Common Prayer*, that book belonging to both clergy and laity which is the means by which the corporate, liturgical and sacramental life of the Church is entered into and participated in by both clergy and laity. The *Book of Common Prayer*, in whatever edition of whatever branch of the Anglican Communion we may choose to examine it, is certainly an exceedingly eclectic collection of materials from many sources and many ages. That is true of both the older Prayer Books and the newer ones which provide various alternatives. Commentaries on the *Book of Common Prayer* go to great lengths to trace the things that make it up back to a thousand different origins, beginning with the Bible itself. That serves to show how rich is the heritage underlying the Prayer Book, as well as to show how the book is the result of a complicated, living history in which many theological and ecclesiastical compromises have taken place.

The Nature of Prayer Book Spirituality

The more basic and important question, however, has to do with what the Prayer Book is in its entirety and not just with where its various parts may have originated. It has to do with the ascetical *genre* of the *Book of Common Prayer*. Though it serves a similar purpose as the *Missale Romanum*, the Prayer Book is more than a missal. Though it serves the same purpose as the Roman breviary, it is more than a breviary. We could go on in the same kind of way about all the various parts of the Prayer Book, the pastoral offices and the ordinal and the psalter and the catechism. What the Prayer Book is consists of more than its various parts and the functions they serve as liturgical manuals. It is more than just a liturgical script for the doing of the Church's offices, ordinances and sacramental actions.

The ascetical *genre* of the *Book of Common Prayer,* as Martin Thornton so aptly observes in his *English Spirituality,* is the same *genre* that finds expression in the Rule of St. Benedict, in Bonhoeffer's *Life Together* which was written as the guide to the corporate life of that underground seminary at Finkenwalde in the time of the Third Reich, in the rule of various Christian communities and monastic establishments. The ascetical *genre* of the *Book of Common Prayer* is that of the *Regulum* which makes it possible for the basis of the spiritual life of a community of Christian people to be the corporate, liturgical, sacramental and domestic life of that community itself. Whether they are explicitly conscious of it or not, that is the fundamental *genre* of the Prayer Book for Anglicans of either the low church or the high church variety, of either the most catholic or the most evangelical persuasion. That is the significance of the *Book of Common Prayer* in a pragmatic Church which *de facto* defines both "Church" and "Christian" in terms of a series of times observed, a set of liturgical actions performed, a sacramental and corporate life together. Anglican spirituality is Prayer Book spirituality in that sense and it is the question of what Prayer Book spirituality is and implies in contemporary culture which must be addressed if Anglicans are to be responsible stewards of the heritage that is theirs. It is to that question that the remainder of this essay will address itself by pointing to a series of issues affecting the spiritual lives of Anglicans today.

Prayer Book Revision and Alternate Rites

One important issue has to do with the Prayer Book itself and the revision it has been undergoing in recent times in almost every branch of the Anglican Communion. Because Anglican spirituality is Prayer Book spirituality, it is a traumatic experience for Anglicans to have to put a much used and familiar book on the shelf and to begin to use a new one. What does it mean to speak of Prayer Book spirituality, if the Prayer Book is subject to radical change? Furthermore, if the Prayer Book is the *Regulum* enabling a community of Christian people to locate its spirituality in its own ongoing life, what are the implications of having a Prayer Book with various alternatives for celebrating the sacraments and observing the Church's ordinances? Given the nature of Anglicanism those are serious questions and advocates of change and modernization should not dismiss them lightly. They are connected with the profound way in which books and writing are so fundamental to the way in which western culture deals with reality and to the way in which the western churches dealt with the issues underlying the Reformation. They are also connected with the disintegration of what Marshall McLuhan, in his *The Medium Is the Message,* called western culture's linear apprehension of reality.

It is tremendously significant that the Reformation and the invention of moveable type by Gutenberg were contemporaneous events. There are many ways in which the Reformation marked the end of an old era rather than the beginning of a new era. As the human community found accustomed social, political, economic and cultural configurations giving way to new ones, as new national identities emerged, the Reformation era was a time in which, in different ways and in different places, Christian people strove to preserve their heritage so that it would not be lost in the new cultural situation. It was a time for seeking what was essentially Christian as the historical structures which had contained Christianity began to disappear, and it was a time for seeking guarantees that the essentials would be maintained. As different as were the classical Protestant, Roman Catholic and Anglican responses to that time, they had one very significant thing profoundly in common: each of them preserved the heritage in a book; each of them sought to guarantee the maintenance of the essentials by identifying the book which contained them.

For the classical Protestant churches that book was the Bible. It is difficult for us to remember, given the place of the Bible as book in western culture, that the Bible as we know it did not exist prior to the Reformation and the invention of moveable type. People knew the contents of the book now so available to everyone as book by hearing the readings in the liturgy, by taking in the narratives pictured in paintings, frescoes and stained glass, through dramatic presentations and the reading of poetry. Furthermore, it was only at the time of the Reformation, when the Bible as book became so important, that explicit and official ecclesiastical decisions were made as to just which writings constituted the sacred book. Of course, going back into the early centuries of the Church's life, a general consensus as to which books were canonical had emerged. No final and explicit decisions had, however, been promulgated, and there was variation as to which writings were included and read. It was in connection with the Reformation's concern to preserve the Christian heritage in a book that the Protestant Churches officially excluded from the Bible those books—the Apocrypha—found in the Greek version of the Old Testament but not in the Hebrew, while the Roman Catholic Church took the official stand that those books were canonical. The Bible as the book which authoritatively defined Christianity was the product of Protestantism's response to the collapse of "Christendom" and Gutenberg's invention of moveable type.

For Roman Catholicism the book was the *Missale Romanum*. Before the era of the Reformation various rites were in existence in the various areas of Europe, and the "scripts" for the parts played in the liturgy by the various ministers existed separately. It was out of the Reformation concern that the heritage be accurately preserved and also the availability of moveable type, that the liturgy in all its parts came to be standardized in one book. It was that Reformation concern and post-Gutenberg printing technology which led to the liturgy's becoming essentially the reading by the priest of a text in a book while the faithful usually engaged in devotions read from their own books.

For Anglicanism the book which emerged from the Reformation was, of course, the *Book of Common Prayer.* What I have just said about the process underlying the creation of the Roman missal was also true of the process by which the Prayer Book came into existence, although all the Church's ordinances rather than just the eucharistic liturgy were included in the one Prayer Book and the book became the common property of both clergy and lay people in a way that the missal and the breviary did not in the Roman Church. Whereas participation in the liturgy had formerly involved seeing, hearing, touching and smelling, Anglicans' participation came characteristically to involve following in the book the text of what was being said.

All that is the background against which western Christian people of all kinds have undergone traumatic experiences in the recent past as historical research has shown how clearly the various books are the products of history and the complex life of the Church, not unconditioned sacred authorities. It is the background against which, to the extent that people do leave behind what McLuhan called linear consciousness, book-centered Christianity becomes an anachronism not really connected with people's modes of apprehending reality. It is the background which explains why revisions of Bibles, missals and Prayer Books result in controversy and resistance. It is the background against which revised Prayer Books containing a collection of doctrinal statements instead of one catechism or set of articles of religion and alternatives for doing the liturgy are confusing and disorienting to Church people.

Anglican spirituality being profoundly Prayer Book spirituality, that issue has to be addressed if we are to be responsible stewards of our heritage as Anglicans at this time in history. One way of addressing it may be to learn anew the significance of the fact that the fundamental *genre* of the Prayer Book is that of a *Regulum,* a rule such as the Rule of St. Benedict which is the basis on which a community of people do the things they do together. A Benedictine community does read and listen to its rule, but reading and hearing the words of the rule is not the essence of its life as a community. The essence of its life is what it *does* as a community liturgically, domestically and socially and at work. The rule does not exist to be read as an end in itself, but exists to lead the community corporately into what it *does* as a community. And that is what the *Book of Common Prayer* is for the Anglican churches. It does not exist to be read as an end in itself, in spite of the extent to which it came to be used in that way in western, "linear" culture. The Prayer Book is the basis on which the Church *does* what it does in things as different as a solemn mass at the abbey in Denver or a celebration at the north end of the communion table in the cathedral in Sydney. The essential thing is not the script and the exact words in the script. The script exists to support the essential thing and to make it possible. The essential thing is the drama itself, the liturgical action, what the Church *does*. What the various churches have in common as Church is the action they have in common, the shape of the liturgy by which they identify themselves as Church, not the reading of the same, exact script in so slavish a way that the script dominates what it came into being to support and serve.

Looking at it that way can help us to understand that Prayer Book revision calculated to allow the action itself to shine through is really quite in the spirit of what the Prayer Book, understood in terms of its *genre*, is all about. It can help us to understand that it is quite fitting that alternative scripts be provided to accompany the action. Indeed, I believe it would have been much more logical for the framers of the *American Prayer Book 1979* to have put *An Order for Celebrating the Holy Eucharist* (page 400) at the very beginning of the provisions for celebrating the Eucharist, and then followed it with Rite One and Rite Two. Then the form of the book would have been saying, "People of God, here is what the Church *does* when it gathers to identity itself liturgically as the Church, and then here are a couple of scripts in varying styles of English to use in doing it." That kind of approach, and this is the point I am concerned to make, can lead us deeper into that Anglican spirituality which is grounded in participating with the Church in what the Church does in the Eucharist, in the Office, in the various sacraments and ordinances. Prayer Book spirituality is not really about the book. It is about the corporate life of the people of God for whom the Prayer Book is God's graciously given *Regulum*.

Personal Devotion and Spiritual Direction

Another set of issues in need of being addressed if Anglican spirituality is to be understood involves individual, personal devotion and spiritual direction. There is widespread interest today in prayer and the life of the spirit and spiritual direction. Given that interest, it is important that spirituality and spiritual direction not be equated with one approach or one tradition, that we be mindful that the Anglican tradition has its own characteristics, is basically corporate, liturgical and sacramental rather than individualistic. In the Anglican tradition personal, individual devotion and spiritual direction are not central. They are not ends in and of themselves. Some system of personal meditation is not the center of the spiritual life. Participation in the corporate, liturgical and sacramental life of the Church is the center of the spiritual life.

Consequently, in the Anglican tradition personal devotions are essentially recollection, in the classical sense of that word in ascetical theology, of Baptism, the Eucharist, the Daily Office and the biblical story in which Baptism, the Eucharist and the Daily Office are grounded. Personal devotions are recollection of what the Church does corporately, of what the present point in the Church's calendar is, of the biblical story the Church is presently hearing in its liturgy. That comes through clearly in such classically Anglican manuals of personal devotion as Andrewes' *Preces Privatae*, Taylor's *Holy Living* and *Holy Dying*, Herbert's *The Temple*, and Donne's prayers and sermons and poems. Those, and we could cite many other examples from Anglican literature, are intimately related to the Prayer Book. They originate in and are not understandable apart from that corporate life of the Church regulated and enabled by the *Book of Common Prayer*. They are embodiments of a tradition in which the prayers and meditation of the individual Christian are basically the results of and musings upon that in which the individual Christian is participating in an ongoing way in the Church.

Personal devotions in the Anglican tradition, moreover, are not "churchy" recollection. The logic of a spirituality which presupposes the presence of God with the historical, human Church in what it does as an historical, human institution also insists on the presence of God in human history in general. If Anglican tradition's coupling of nation and Church, of society and God's kingdom can result in crass Erastianism, it can also result in a piety which discerns God's presence in all of life, in "the daily round and the common task." That is why recollection of the presence of God in life in the world, the discipline of being mindful of that presence in specific situations and persons and needs, is more typical of Anglican spirituality than the kind of self-conscious and structured mental prayer present, for example, in Ignatian spirituality. Anglican spirituality, grounded in faith in the presence of God in the empirical Church and in the givenness of the real world, is not individualistic and subjective. It is ecclesiastical, social and holistic.

That is the reason that spiritual direction in the Anglican tradition is not something which takes place primarily in the relationship between a Christian and an individual director in a one to one relationship. Spiritual direction is, in Anglicanism, a broad based thing, and the term itself

in the sense in which it is presently so widely used is not native to Anglicanism. In the Anglican tradition spiritual direction has to do with a large,
clergy-laity, individual-corporate, private-public dialogue which takes
place in many ways. Direction from God to the individual Christian
comes in the liturgy, in sermons, in catechetical instruction which is an
ongoing and not once-and-for-all process in the Anglican tradition, in
life in the world. To the person looking for direction in living the Christian life, the classical Anglican response would be, "Enter into the life of
the Church with eyes and ears and heart and mind open." The richness
of Anglican spirituality will be missed if spiritual direction is defined as
something taking place between two individuals, if spiritual direction
turns out to be something influenced more than we may consciously realize by clinical and psychological models, if spiritual direction is an enterprise of *mine* for which Church and liturgy and Bible are really only
"resources." The point is this, and it is central and fundamental: in Anglican tradition the Church itself in the totality of its life and liturgy is the
primary spiritual director.

"Mutual Ministry"

Another issue present in that Prayer Book spirituality which is characteristic of Anglicanism has to do with the way in which the life of Christians in the Church—and in the world—is a common enterprise. The
book which contains the *Regulum* is the *Book of Common Prayer*, the property of all the people of God. In the Anglican tradition no special class of
believers is in possession of knowledge or techniques or status to which
common folk do not have access. Neither Eucharist nor Office is, in Anglican tradition, something which is peculiarly the property of the clergy
and those committed to a monastic life. In the earliest version of the *Book
of Common Prayer* the daily office was put into a form calculated to make
the attendance of lay people working in the world possible. Strong Anglican tradition, and in certain provinces explicit canonical provision, insist
that a priest cannot celebrate the sacrament of the Eucharist unless a minimal congregation be there to participate in the celebration. The principle established in the sixteenth century that all parts of the liturgy should
be in the language of the people has continued as the expansion of the
Anglican Communion has resulted in the majority of Anglicans in the
world being no longer white: the Prayer Book has been translated into
many different languages. The tradition that the Church is the whole people of God, laity as well as clergy, has been borne out in the provisions
made for the governance of the Church in the various branches of the
Anglican Communion. Laity not only have a voice and vote along with

clergy, but in important matters have the power to veto decisions voted by bishops and other clergy and vice-versa.

What is true of the Prayer Book and of liturgy and of provisions for ecclesiastical governance is true also of things usually more strictly considered to constitute the life of devotion. Lay-clerical dialogue is typical of the various forms of teaching and spiritual guidance in the Anglican tradition, the catechetical form of question and response itself being significant. From Dame Julian of Norwich in the fourteenth century to such contemporary figures as Evelyn Underhill and C. S. Lewis there has been a constant succession of lay spiritual guides, and it is significant that *priestly* manuals of devotion and prayer do not appear in Anglicanism until the latter part of the nineteenth century when, their own heritage having been obscured in the eighteenth century, many involved in the Catholic revival looked to Rome for guidance and models. Classical Anglican manuals such as those of Lancelot Andrewes, Jeremy Taylor and William Law, however, are clearly written with the people of God as a whole—lay and clerical alike—in mind. That type of clerical devotion which sees the priest's spiritual life as something different from a lay person's, which ties the priest's spiritual life to the liturgical functions performed by a priest and produces such customs as daily masses which are really the priest's personal devotions, is not intrinsically Anglican, nor is the more contemporary custom of "concelebration" which arises out of similar presuppositions.

We have passed through an era in the history of the Church in which both Catholics and Protestants have had it in common that the word "church" was pretty largely equated with "clergy" and the word "ministry" equated with the work of ordained and professional ministers. Now, however, biblical studies and the recovery of the earliest Church's understanding of its life and liturgy indicate the way in which the people of God as a whole, the Church itself as a corporate reality, is God's minister and God's priest to the world. We are coming to see that it is within such a context that the ministries and vocations of *all* members of the Body of Christ have to be understood.

But that is not really something new. The earliest versions of the *Book of Common Prayer* made that radically clear in the sixteenth century against the background of the ecclesiastical and liturgical situation out of which they emerged. The *American Prayer Book 1979* continues to make that clear in its emphasis in many different ways on the participation of all orders of Christian people in the Church's liturgy and life. That emphasis does not represent something new. It is, rather, the recovery of something central in the Anglican tradition of spirituality. It represents the continuation of something fundamental to a tradition in which the common, corporate life of the Church is itself the focus and the basis of the spiritual life. Current discussions of the recovery of the ministry of the diaconate, of the role of the laity in the Church, of what has come to be called "mutual ministry," touch on something central in Anglican Prayer Book spirituality.

Community in a Complex Society

The final issue I shall point to in this essay has to do with a presupposition which underlies all that I have said about the ethos of Anglicanism and the issues to which I have devoted discussion. There is no question but that the kind of Anglican spirituality we have been looking at requires for its very existence a regularly gathered community of Christians. The *Regulum*, which is really what the *Book of Common Prayer* is, has no meaning if it is not lived out liturgically and otherwise in a concrete, corporate human community. That is why Anglican spirituality has found its classical incarnation in the kind of collegial establishment present in English colleges and cathedrals, or in the parish community living geographically together in villages or neighborhoods.

The world has, however, moved on for better or for worse. Changes in the historical, cultural and social realities which constitute the environment in which Christians live have located the lives of Christians elsewhere than in collegial chapels and village churches. Individual Christians who in other times and places might have found themselves existing within the concrete, corporate contexts of collegial chapels and village churches find themselves adrift, existing quite individually and not at all with any sense of corporateness in today's mobile and impersonal urban society. I have lived most of my adult life as part of a seminary community in which daily worship, at office and eucharist, has been in the Anglican tradition. Again and again, however, I have heard expressed the disillusionment of those who found that embodiment of Anglican tradition a wonderful thing, but also a thing left behind when they moved from seminary to life in today's society and today's Church.

The issue to which I am pointing has to be faced. At the beginning of this essay I said that the pragmatic nature of Anglicanism—in which spirituality is connected with the Church's pragmatic, historical and incarnate life—can have its trivial and weak side. One form of that triviality and weakness can be the identification of the Church so completely with one, particular, historical incarnation that it ends up being an antiquarian anachronism, something perceived as utterly irrelevant and without value when social and cultural conditions have changed. That will not, in my view, do. Neither, however, will it do for Anglicans too easily or too quickly to espouse approaches to spirituality which are essentially individualistic and rational, which are—to use my earlier ecclesiastical typology—either confessional or experiential. Because the depth of the crisis which we face is so deep, I see all those alternatives being chosen: a traditional approach which defines the Church in terms of one historical incarnation, an evangelicalism which abandons Anglicanism for a confession of faith which is really more the heritage of other children of the Reformation, a neo-pentecostalism which makes religious experience of one type or another the norm.

My plea is that we do not take the demise of one particular set of structures to be the demise of the Anglican tradition. I believe that the collapse of those given national and geographical structures within which Anglicanism originally defined itself and continued to exist from the Reformation into contemporary times provides an opportunity for the discovery of Anglicanism at a deeper level. The kind of human community for which the reality and existence of the human community itself is primary, both enriched by and taking precedence over the confessional understandings of what it means and the experiences which have brought people into it, is what this pluralistic, contemporary world sorely needs. It is in terms of that kind of human community that Anglicanism, the Prayer Book spirituality and ethos of Anglicanism, have to be understood. The vocation of Anglicans today is to translate such an understanding, in parishes and "at work" and "house church" and all kinds of other embodiments of the Church, into the reality which God has given them as their contribution to the Church Universal.

Methodist Spirituality

David Lowes Watson

I. Wesleyan Foundations

Methodist spirituality begins of course with John Wesley. This is not to say that the spirituality which emerged with a distinctively Methodist imprint did not have roots in the writings by which Wesley was guided and formed in his spiritual pilgrimage; nor yet is it to imply that Methodist spirituality was uniquely Wesleyan.[1] Even so, it was Wesley who gave shape to the Methodist movement, and his spiritual insights provided its bedrock. His genius was to create a theological synthesis between the two major strands of English Protestant spirituality—Anglican holiness of intent and Puritan inward assurance—and apply it in the practical outworking of an accountable discipleship.

1. Anglican Holiness of Intent

By John Wesley's own account, it was while he was a student at Oxford that he began to seek a more disciplined spiritual life by following the advice given by Bishop Jeremy Taylor in *Rules for Holy Living and Dying.* "I began to take a more exact Account than I had done before, of the manner wherein I spent my Time, writing down how I had employed every Hour."[2] He notes that he was "exceedingly affected" by "that part in particular which relates to *purity of intention.* Instantly I resolved to dedicate *all my life* to God, *all* my thoughts, and words, and actions, being thoroughly convinced, there was no medium; but that *every part* of my life (not *some* only) must either be a sacrifice to God or myself, that is, in effect, to the devil."[3]

This essay first appeared in *Protestant Spiritual Traditions,* ed. Frank C. Senn (Mahwah, N.J.: Paulist, 1986), 217–63. Used by permission of Paulist Press.

Taylor is perhaps *the* exemplar of Anglican spirituality. He described the purpose of life as a constant walk with God, so that personal holiness was the necessary concern of the Christian. And since the goal in life was perfection, even the perfection which was in Christ, sin had to be strictly analyzed and overcome. For faith, "if it be true, living and justifying, cannot be separated from a good life. It works miracles . . . and makes us diligently to do, and cheerfully to suffer, whatsoever God hath placed in our way to heaven."[4]

A concern for right intent, however, was not to be pursued in a spiritual vacuum. Taylor saw the continuing life of the visible church, with its sacraments and observances, as at once the setting and the means of implementation for the growth of a personal spiritual life. From the very beginning of the Reformation, liturgy had played an important part in the English church. Drawing on the doctrines and liturgies of the Eastern church, the English reformers had provided corporate spiritual disciplines—as, for example, in the *Book of Common Prayer*. And the touchstone of this spirituality was a concern to avoid any disjuncture between what was holy and what was experienced in the world. The focus of spiritual discernment was to see God at work in the spectrum of daily life.

Nor yet was holiness of intent to be pursued for its own sake, but rather as a means of opening the whole of one's life to the will of God. It was to infuse one's works with divine grace, which alone could ensure that they were good. As Wesley was to note in the opening paragraphs of *A Plain Account of Christian Perfection*, "the giving even *all my life* to God (supposing it possible to do this and go no farther) would profit me nothing, unless I *gave my heart*, yea, *all my heart*, to him. I saw that 'simplicity of intention, and purity of affection,' *one design* in all we speak or do, and *one desire* ruling all our tempers, are indeed 'the wings of the soul,' without which she can never ascend to the mount of God."[5]

Wesley's conviction of the need for inward holiness of intent was further confirmed by his reading of Thomas à Kempis' *Christian Pattern*[6] and William Law's *Christian Perfection* and *Serious Call*.[7] Like Taylor, Law regarded the end of salvation as the regeneration of the *imago Dei*, perfection in the very likeness of God, but with a focus on the will:

> This doctrine does not suppose, that we have no need of divine grace, or that it is in our own power to make ourselves perfect. It only supposes, that through the want of a *sincere* intention of pleasing God in *all our actions*, we fall into such irregularities of life, as by the *ordinary* means of grace, we should have power to avoid.
> And that we have not that perfection, which our present state of grace makes us capable of, because we do not so much as *intend* to have it.[8]

A right intention, marking a transformation of the will, would change Christians, and through them, the world:

And when you have this *intention to please God in all your actions, as the happiest and best thing in the world,* you will find in you as great an aversion to everything that is *vain* and *impertinent* in common life. . . . You will be as fearful of living in any foolish way, as you are now fearful of neglecting the publick Worship.

Now who that wants this general sincere *intention,* can be reckon'd a Christian? And yet if it was amongst Christians, it would change the whole face of the world; true piety, and exemplary holiness, would be as common and visible, as *buying* and *selling,* or any trade in life.[9]

Wesley's relationship with Law continued for some years, exposing him to a High Churchmanship rooted in the patristic writings and traditions. Yet the context of these years of spiritual development was to prove just as important as the expansion of his reading. In 1729, he had returned to Oxford to assume the duties of his fellowship at Lincoln College, and had found himself acting as spiritual mentor to a group of students, known as the "Holy Club," which included his brother Charles. The group had made a commitment to engage in the intentional disciplines of personal and corporate devotions, especially the study of the Scriptures and frequent holy communion, and to pursue an inquiry into the liturgical and devotional practices of the early church.[10] But they were also committed to works of practical charity in the city of Oxford, among the poor, the illiterate, and the imprisoned.

Wesley was thus engaged in a twofold spiritual formation. In his readings, he imbibed some of the greatest writings in the Roman Catholic mystical tradition—those of Pascal, Fenelon, de Renty, and the *Theologia Germanica,* for example—and, through "Macarius the Egyptian," the Byzantine tradition of spirituality, in which the Christian life is seen as a growth toward a goal rather than a static state. But he was also engaged in an active discipleship in the world, which was to have a profound effect on the spiritual leadership which he exercised through the Methodist societies.

2. Puritan Assurance

Yet the very mysticism of Wesley's spirituality was dialectical.[11] He perceived the path to perfection to be a constant tension between the irresistibility of the will of God and the resistance of the human will empowered by prevenient grace.[12] And it was at this point that he drew on the great riches of the Puritan tradition, most particularly on its doctrine of the "inner witness," the assurance that comes from the indwelling Spirit of God.

Wesley was indebted primarily to the Moravians for his introduction to this spiritual heritage. Beginning with a shared voyage to Georgia in 1735, when Wesley was sufficiently impressed by a group of them on board to learn German so that he might converse with them more freely, they brought him to see that a perfectionism of right intent and right endeavor lacked the Augustinian dimension of grace. While William Law's mysticism could instruct in the spiritual self-discipline through which a person could find God, it did little to foster an expectancy of the divine initiative. As opposed to the "stern, objective, moralistic piety of High Churchmanship,"[13] Moravian piety was a discerning of the pattern of God's initiative toward the believer.

During his stay in Georgia, Wesley remained in dialogue with the Moravians, though they would not permit him to join their community. When he pressed them for conditions of acceptance, he was told by one of their members, John Toltschig, that the first step in the spiritual formation which they practiced was to try to "lead people out of themselves," so that the "word of power" might break in on them and "pierce them through." When they were thus "apprehended by grace," their souls were tended so that they might grow in grace from one step to the next. But persons were not admitted into full fellowship until they had "genuine forgiveness of sins" and "peace with God" from which would proceed a "glad and willing submission" to the Moravian discipline.[14]

The wrestling which brought John and Charles Wesley alike to an acceptance of this inward peace is poignantly expressed in the hymn which, as John was to state in his obituary tribute to Charles in 1788, no less a writer than Isaac Watts had described as "worth all the verses he himself had written."[15]

> Come, O thou Traveler unknown,
> Whom still I hold, but cannot see!
> My company before is gone,
> And I am left alone with thee;
> With thee all night I mean to stay,
> And wrestle till the break of day.
>
> • • •
>
> Yield to me now—for I am weak,
> But confident in self-despair!
> Speak to my heart, in blessings speak,
> Be conquered by my instant prayer:
> Speak, or thou never hence shall move,
> And tell me if thy name is LOVE.
>
> • • •
>
> 'Tis Love! 'Tis Love! Thou diedst for me;
> I hear thy whisper in my heart.
> The morning breaks, the shadows flee,
> Pure Universal Love thou art:
> To me, to all, thy bowels move—
> Thy nature, and Thy name, is LOVE.[16]

Wesley came to know this assurance on May 24, 1738, at a religious society meeting in Aldersgate Street, London, where he records that his heart was "strangely warmed."[17] The account he gives of his pilgrimage to that point is a clear indication that he was appropriating what R. Newton Flew has described as the tradition of "the evangelical succession of believers."[18] It was what his father had described as the "inward witness," as had the Puritan scholar, John Preston, a hundred years earlier:

> "If any man love me, and keepe my Commandements, I will shew myself to him;" that is, hee shall have an extraordinary manifestation of my selfe, hee shall have such an expression of love and peace and joy, such a thing that no an knowes but himselfe. Beloved, this is the testimony of the Spirit. I confesse, it is a wondrous thing, and if there were not some Christians that did feele it, and know it, you might beleeve there were no such thing, that it were but a fancie or enthusiasme; but, beloved, it is certaine, there are a generation of men, that know what this seale of the Lord is.[19]

The traditioning may have been Moravian, but Wesley's experience at Aldersgate Street was unmistakably the spirit of Puritanism.[20] When he came to publish the fifty volumes of *A Christian Library*, consisting of "Extracts from, and Abridgements of, the choicest Pieces of practical Divinity which have been published in the English Tongue," the list of Puritan authors was impressive, including Samuel Clarke, Robert Bolton, John Preston, Richard Alleine, John Bunyan, Richard Baxter and Edmund Calamy.[21]

And indeed, the power of this inward assurance led Wesley to turn away from the mystical writers for a time—though not for long. His acceptance of the divine initiative as the *dynamic* of his spirituality did not negate the importance of spiritual disciplines as its *form*. Nor yet did it negate the impact of mystical writers such as Henry Scougal, who defined true religion as "an Union of the Soul with God, a real participation of the Divine Nature, the very image of God drawn upon the Soul, or, in the Apostles' phrase, it is Christ formed within us."[22] The quest for Christlikeness continued to be integral to Wesley's spirituality.

3. Theological Synthesis

The key to Wesley's synthesis of Anglican and Puritan spirituality is discernible first of all in the Oxford Holy Club, where the name "Methodist" seems first to have been used, initially as a term of derision. Wesley himself disliked the name, and frequently preferred to use the phrase "The People Called Methodists." But the occasion of the word is significant. These were young men who took the working out of their faith seriously. They engaged in the study of the Scriptures, in private and public prayer, in frequent Holy Communion, and in works of practical piety among the poor and underprivileged people of Oxford. They may have brought to these outworkings an inner pursuit of holy intent, but the form of their spirituality was sufficiently self-evident for others to discern it to the point of ridicule.

Wesley's appropriation of the evangelical tradition, the inward witness of the Spirit, meant that he could now affirm the assurance of faith as a manifest gift of the Spirit, a divine *elenchos*,

> the demonstrative evidence of things unseen, the supernatural evidence of things invisible, not perceivable by eyes of flesh, or by any of our natural senses or faculties. Faith is that divine evidence whereby the spiritual man discerneth God and the things of God. It is with regard to the spiritual world what sense is with regard to the natural. It is the spiritual sensation of every soul that is born of God.[23]

But he did not equate this assurance with salvation, which was at once a more inclusive and a more extensive work of God. For Wesley, salvation in the fullest sense was enfolded in a catholicity of God's initiatives, "from the first dawning of grace in the soul till it is consummated in glory." It began with "what is frequently termed 'natural conscience,' but more properly 'preventing grace'; all the 'drawings of the Father'; the desires after God which, if we yield to them, increase more and more . . . although, it is true, the generality of men stifle them as soon as possible." It proceeded to justifying grace, "another word for pardon," "the forgiveness of all our sins and, what is necessarily implied therein, our acceptance with God," the immediate effect of which was "a peace that passeth all understanding" and "a rejoicing in hope of the glory of God." And then, even at the very moment of justification, there was a real as well as a relative change in the believer, the beginning of sanctification—an inward renewal by the power of God, "expelling the love of the world [and] changing the 'earthly, sensual, devilish mind' into 'the mind that was in Christ Jesus.'"[24]

The significance of this *ordo salutis* is that Wesley's spirituality was accountable to a disciplined theological reflection, in which he was faithful to the tenets of the English Reformation. From the beginnings of Protestantism in the English Church, its theologians had been concerned to retain the necessary place of good works in the doctrine of salvation. And it is no accident that Wesley, after his return from a visit to the Moravian community at Herrnhut in the fall of 1738, should have begun "more narrowly to inquire what the doctrine of the Church of England is concerning the much-controverted point of justification by faith."[25] The following year, he published editions not only of the Anglican Homilies on salvation, faith and good works, but also a treatise on justification by Robert Barnes, who had been one of the first English scholars to study with Luther at Wittenberg.

Under the scrutiny of Wesley's theological reflection, the spiritualities of right intent and divine illumination were brought together in an out-working of grace which was not optional, nor merely fruitful, but neces-sary. The dynamic of this was a divine initiative which the human will was always able, with the freedom of prevenient grace, to resist. The path to perfection, therefore, was a growth in obedience to the divine initiative—a learning how not to resist the grace of God. And the way to this obe-dience was through the disciplines of right intent.

The scheme is at once awesome and straightforward. By grace, God permits a freedom of choice to the human creature. Yet because of sin, it is not a freedom to choose between good and evil, but rather between resistance or submission to the divine initiative. When the human will ceases to resist, then grace affords a new relationship with God which, moment by moment, is sustained by grace in obedience. Thus the believer grows in grace, and the mind of Christ is formed within.

Wesley's synthesis was especially distinctive, however, in the further step he took to identify a maturity of obedience which renders the believer so in tune with the will of God that love controls every thought, word and deed—truly a Christian perfection. This does not imply a state which can be attained so much as a stage in the process of sanctification. The work of sanctifying grace is of course limitless. But there is a point at which the new relationship with God in Christ is so sealed that we can, by grace, come to love God "with all our heart, mind, soul and strength," in which "all thoughts, words and deeds are governed by pure love." Such a per-fection does not exclude "infirmities, ignorance, and mistake." On this, Wesley was quite clear. The definition of sin which he used in expound-ing the doctrine was that of a "voluntary transgression of a known law"—which is why he resisted the term "sinless perfection," even though the doctrine connoted a cleansing from sin.[26] There is always the possibility of mistake, of "falling away," or "backsliding," because the faith of the believer, however seasoned and mature, is dependent at all times on an openness to grace, for which the believer is responsible.

Of prior importance, therefore, is the relationship of justifying faith. It is this which is the occasion of spiritual growth, which sustains the believer in an obedient discipleship. In short, grace is the occasion of the whole of Christian discipleship: the discreet invitations of God; the imme-diacy of a new relationship with God; and the necessary outworking of this relationship in works of obedience which engendered a transfor-mation in the believer. Rather than a state to be *attained*, spiritual com-munion with God is a relationship to be *sustained* in the midst of a con-stant twofold struggle of the human will: with residual resistance in the individual sinner, and with the resistance of a world which does not yet acknowledge its sovereign God.

The extent to which Wesley worked through these issues and forged the essence of his theological and spiritual synthesis is evident in a short treatise which he published in 1740, entitled *The Principles of a Methodist*.[27] The next step was how to implement it in the rough and tumble of the eighteenth-century England, where the vanguard of spirituality was a religious revival among common people.

4. Accountable Discipleship

The genius of Methodist spirituality lay in the guidance of ordinary people into a discipleship which, empowered by grace and shaped by the doctrines and ordinances of the church, was accountable for good works. Wesley accomplished this with a connectional polity that remains a paradigm of spiritual formation.

Not that Methodist polity was forged *de novo*. Wesley built first of all on the religious societies of the Church of England which had evolved during the latter years of the seventeenth century. Founded in London and thence throughout the country, they were an expression of the religious hunger which had its parallel in German pietism; and in fact, it was an immigrant Lutheran minister, Anthony Horneck, who initially provided guidance for these groups of young men who wanted a more disciplined spiritual life.[28] They met according to a set of rules, by which they prayed together, sang hymns, conversed on matters of practical religion, and took regular collections of money for distribution to the poor. Before the end of the century, the societies had an extensive organization for the relief of debt, visiting the sick, caring for orphans, and providing up to a hundred schools in London and its suburbs alone.[29]

Though they had ceased to be the movement they once were, there were still many of these societies in existence when Wesley began his evangelistic ministry in 1738. They provided him with a structural base, and, more important, a supportive context. The Anglican emphasis was clear: inward holiness of intent applied to practical works in the world, on the assumption that the world is also God's sphere of salvation.

The importance of the Moravians' influence on the form of Wesley's spirituality lay in their intentional analysis of the divine initiative in the life of a believer.[30] Under the religious freedom afforded by Count Ludwig von Zinzendorf on his estates at Berthelsdorf, they had developed in their Herrnhut community a discipline of internal direction within a residential structure, segregated by age, sex and marital status. The members were assessed by the elders of the community as being "dead," "awaked," "ignorant," "willing disciples," and "disciples that have made a progress."[31]

In smaller groupings, known as *bands*, there was intensive confessional inquiry, an exercise regarded as highly important for the spiritual life of the community. Not only did it foster the spiritual growth of each person; it also engendered a spirituality of *koinonia*. Zinzendorf himself was quite specific:

> This day, twenty years ago, whilst the gospel was being preached at Berthels-
> dorf, Herrnhut and elsewhere to an incredible number of people, a gracious wind
> from the Lord was felt, which was the commencement of an uninterrupted work
> of the Holy Spirit in Herrnhut during the remainder of the year. The visit of
> Mary to Elizabeth, which is that day commemorated in the Christian Church,
> gave rise to the idea of bands, or societies; these were established throughout
> the whole community the following week, and have been productive of such
> blessed effects that I believe, without such an institution, the church would never
> have become what it is now. The Societies called bands consist of a few indi-
> viduals met together in the name of Jesus, amongst whom Jesus is; who converse
> together in a particularly cordial and childlike manner, on the whole state of
> their hearts, and conceal nothing from each other, but who have wholly com-
> mitted themselves to each other's care in the Lord.[32]

That Wesley was influenced by the bands as a means of spiritual oversight and nurture is apparent from his account of his ministry in Georgia:

> Not finding, as yet, any door open for the pursuing [of] our main design, we con-
> sidered in what manner we might be most useful to the little flock at Savannah.
> And we agreed (1) to advise the more serious among them to form themselves
> into a sort of little society, and to meet once or twice a week, in order to reprove,
> instruct, and exhort one another. (2) To select out of these a smaller number for
> a more intimate union with each other, which might be forwarded, partly by our
> conversing singly with each, and partly by inviting them all together to our house;
> and this, accordingly, we determined to do every Sunday in the afternoon.[33]

Wesley did not use the word "band" to describe these small groups in
Savannah, nor yet was there an appreciation of the immediacy evinced
by the Moravian fellowship. But clearly he had accepted the importance
of intimate fellowship as a form of spiritual oversight. On his return to
England early in 1738, and largely as a result of his fellowship with a Moravian, Peter Bohler, he helped to form a society at Fetter Lane in London,
which was divided into bands according to the Moravian pattern.

In the months which followed, however, we can discern some reser-
vations in Wesley's attitude toward the Moravian disciplines. There was,
of course, the important experience at Aldersgate Street, where in effect
he ceased to become their pupil, and joined them in their assurance of
the inner witness. But even more significant was his visit to their com-

munity at Herrnhut in the summer of 1738, during which he observed what he felt to be a degree of immaturity in the strict monitoring of their spiritual oversight.[34] He expressed disapproval of this practice in the Fetter Lane Society,[35] and in his own *Rules of the Band Societies,* drawn up in the December of 1738, he stressed the principle of mutual confession and accountability.

In these Band Rules, it was stipulated that the leader, "some person among us," was to "speak his own state first, and then ask the rest, in order, as many and as searching questions as may be," such as:

> Have you the forgiveness of your sins? . . .
> Have you the witness of God's Spirit with your spirit? . . .
> Has no sin, inward or outward, dominion over you? . . .
> Do you desire to be told of all your faults? . . .
> Do you desire that, in doing this, we should come as close as possible, that we should cut to the quick, and search your heart to the bottom?[36]

And at every meeting, there were five questions to be asked of everyone:

1. What known Sin have you committed since our last meeting?
2. What Temptations have you met with?
3. How was [sic] you delivered?
4. What have you thought, said or done, of which you doubt whether it be a Sin or not?
5. Have you nothing you desire to keep secret?

The bands did not, however, become the basic pattern of Methodist spiritual practice, even though they remained as an important dimension of the movement's connectional polity. To understand why this was so, we must be aware of how Wesley was inexorably drawn into the mainstream of the eighteenth century evangelical revival.[37] The turning point was his venture into "field preaching"—proclaiming the gospel in the open air. He agreed to do this with some reluctance, and did so primarily at the urging of George Whitefield, who was making plans to come to North America. But it proved to be a pivotal move, not only in establishing Methodism as a distinctive component of the Revival, but also in determining the shape of Methodist spirituality.

Field preaching ensured that God's gracious initiative reached people with power and effect—ordinary people, who were "utterly inaccessible every other way,"[38] and who were largely neglected by the Church of England. They heard the gospel message in a manner which moved them deeply, and in some instances converted them soundly. The question then became how to nurture these converts in the faith. A sampling of membership lists of the early societies indicates that by and large they were from the artisan stratum of society. This meant that they had little time, even if they were ready, to engage in the intensive spiritual disciplines to which Wesley, with the leisure afforded by years at Oxford, had applied himself.

In a word, Methodist spirituality was honed by the context of its practice—the necessary, though often neglected, Christian discipline of taking the gospel message into the world. To do so was to find that the illumination of faith was indeed available to all—a witness of the Spirit which was not forensic, but dynamic and organic. People were born of the Spirit, but then had to grow in the Spirit; and the intensive mutual searching of the bands presumed too much of those whose spiritual birth was relatively new and sudden.

As Wesley himself described it, those who responded to the preaching of himself and his brother, and who made a commitment to Christian discipleship, found themselves immediately

> surrounded with difficulties;—all the world rose up against them; neighbors, strangers, acquaintances, relations, friends, began to cry out amain, "Be not righteous overmuch; why shouldest thou destroy thyself?" Let not "much religion make thee mad." One, and another, and another came to us, asking what they should do, being distressed on every side; as every one strove to weaken, and none to strengthen, their hands in God. We advised them, "Strengthen you one another. Talk together, as often as you can. . . ."[39]

The implication was clear: the path to perfection did not lie through neutral territory. The disciplines of the spiritual life had to be forged in the immediate reality of a world resistant to its God, in which the Christian had been placed, not to be tested and matured for his or her own sake, but rather as a messenger with the announcement of God's salvation. *Methodist spirituality had a purpose which transcended the personal formation of its practitioners. It was the appropriation and application of those disciplines which equip and empower the believer to be a faithful disciple in the world. The goal of their spiritual pilgrimage was the mind that was in Christ. But their immediate task was to be the ambassadors of God to a sinful and resistant world—of which they were also a part.*[40]

II. The Formation of Methodist Spirituality

1. The Class Meeting: Mutual Accountability

The key to this essentially pragmatic spirituality emerged during a discussion in February, 1742, on how to clear the building debt on the New Room at Bristol. Wesley had personally signed the note, but income had fallen far short of the amount needed; so it was suggested that every member of the society should give a penny a week toward the debt. This seemed to be a good solution, until it was pointed out that not everyone might be able to afford the weekly amount. A retired sea captain, named Foy, then offered to take twelve names, and collect the money personally, putting in himself whatever anyone could not afford. Others offered to do the same, and before long the whole membership had been divided into "little companies, or classes," of twelve according to where they lived, with one person, styled as the leader, to collect the weekly contributions.[41]

As Wesley was to comment in his *Thoughts upon Methodism*, this was the very thing the societies had needed. The class leaders were "the persons who may not only receive the contributions, but also watch over the souls of their brethren."[42] As they made the rounds to collect the weekly contributions, they found themselves involved in the work of spiritual guidance. In some instances, this meant giving advice or even reproof. But more important, the weekly visit was a time of spiritual support and encouragement, for the very reason already cited: that to be a Methodist was not an easy task. Society members were marked persons in the community or the household. They were to be watched, and if possible made to stumble. The society meeting did not always provide a time to give an account of these spiritual battles, but the class leader was there each week to listen and to guide. And in due course, instead of the leader going around to collect the weekly contributions, the members came together to meet with the leader. There had proved to be too many occasions when the leader could not talk with the members alone; besides which, there were misunderstandings which could only be resolved by seeing everyone together, "face to face."[43]

As we might expect from our vantage point of late twentieth-century group dynamics, a sense of Christian fellowship quickly developed. Wesley records that members began to "bear one another's burdens," and to "care for each other." As they now had "a more intimate acquaintance with, so they had a more endeared affection for each other." They felt free to be open with each other, and, "speaking the truth in love, they grew up into Him in all things, who is the head, even Christ."[44]

Many of the classes became as intimate as the bands, especially where the class leader had become skilled and perceptive. It is important to note, therefore, that the bands were by no means neglected. They continued as before, though with significant differences from the classes. The bands were organized according to age, sex and marital status; the classes were divided according to where the members lived. The bands were structured for intensive sharing and mutual confession; the classes were formed around the leaders, whose duties were specified even before the class meetings as such were functioning.

Perhaps the most significant difference was the role of the leader. Indeed, if there is a pivotal figure in early Methodist spirituality, it is the class leader. Wesley acknowledged this by reserving to himself or his assistants the right to appoint or remove them. He was quick to answer their critics by pointing out that God had "blessed their labour,"[45] and there is little question that they developed into as skilled a group of spiritual mentors as the church has ever produced. They combined spiritual discernment with the practical disciplines necessary for accountable discipleship in the world, and it was largely through their office that ordered guidance and oversight in the societies provided a means of growth and maturity among the members.

Class meetings were much less intense than those of the bands, being a mixture of informality and firmness. They would begin with a hymn and a prayer, and would then proceed to a catechesis. The leader, starting with himself or herself,[46] would ask each member to give an account of the past week's spiritual journey, and in response to each account, the leader would clarify what had been said, and then give appropriate guidance.[47] In addition to the weekly catechesis, the members were examined once each quarter by Wesley or one of his assistant preachers, upon satisfactory completion of which, the member was issued a quarterly class ticket, coded in sequence with a letter of the alphabet. This examination was a quiet way of dropping negligent members, and the ticket was an important symbol of identity.

Class leaders were encouraged from an early date to evaluate the spiritual state of their members. For example, one of the leaders at the Foundery society, Abraham Jones, reported to Wesley on December 12, 1742 that his members "do all walk orderly, & keep close to the Word, and the means of grace." One member complained of being "under strong temptations, as to doubt the being of a God, or of ability to hold out, that if the Lord did not destroy the man of sin in her that it would destroy her."[48] Another Foundery leader, John Hague, reported variously on his members in 1747 that there were those who "retain their confidence in the Lord," are "shut up in a fog," are "very dead, and yet very sore," are "earnestly seeking the Lord," and "appear to have a desire, and to be widely seeking something."[49] When class papers were later introduced to record the weekly attendance and contribution of each member, there was a column in which the leader was to insert the letter "a" for one who was "awakened," a period for one who "professed justification," and a colon for one who professed the "perfect love of God."[50] The language may be dated, but the principle was profound: *No dimension of human existence is devoid of the grace of God.*

2. A Catholicity of Grace

It was this very principle which proved to be the occasion of Wesley's rift with the Moravians, causing him to leave the Fetter Lane society and base his London activities at the old Foundery in Moorfields. The issue surfaced initially as a dispute over the efficacy of the means of grace, and in particular whether a person should receive the sacrament without "full assurance of faith." There were those in the Moravian community who advocated a "stillness" in waiting for this gift from God, a "quietism" which might have been practicable in the refined seclusion of Herrnhut, but which for ordinary people in the city of London was leading to damaging self-doubt. Wesley's position was clear:

(1) There are means of grace—that is, outward ordinances—whereby the faith that brings salvation is conveyed to them who before had it not; (2) that one of these means is the Lord's Supper; and (3) that he who has not this faith ought to wait for it in the use both of this and of the other means which God hath ordained.[51]

The implications were to prove significant for the course of Methodist spirituality. Having come to acknowledge, and to receive, the gift of inward assurance, Wesley did not thereby deny the efficacy of grace in the lives of those who had not. The following month, after a long conversation with Philip Molther, the Moravian who was responsible for most of this "quietism" at Fetter Lane, Wesley recorded what he perceived to be their differences:

As to faith, you believe:
1. There are no degrees of faith, and that no man has any degree of it before all things in him are become new, before he has the full assurance of faith, the abiding witness of the Spirit, or the clear perception that Christ dwelleth in him. . . .

Whereas I believe:
1. There are degrees in faith, and that a man may have some degree of it before all things in him are become new—before he has the full assurance of faith, the abiding witness of the Spirit, or the clear perception that Christ dwelleth in him. 2. Accordingly, I believe there is a degree of justifying faith (and consequently a state of justification) short of, and commonly antecedent to, this. . . .

As to the way to faith, you believe:
That the way to attain it is to wait for Christ, and be still—that is, Not to use (what we term) the means of grace; . . . (Because you believe these are not means of grace; that is, do not ordinarily convey God's grace to unbelievers; . . .); Not to do temporal good; Nor to attempt doing spiritual good. (Because, you believe, no fruit of the Spirit is given by those who have it not themselves; . . .)

Whereas I believe:
The way to attain it is to wait for Christ and be still;
In using all the means of grace.

Therefore I believe it right for him who knows he has not faith (that is, that conquering faith),
To go to church;
To communicate;
To fast;
To use as much private prayer as he can, and
To read the Scripture.
(Because I believe these are "means of grace"; that is, do ordinarily convey God's grace to unbelievers; and
That it is possible for a man to use them, without trusting in them.)
To do all the temporal good he can; And to endeavour after doing spiritual good. (Because I know many fruits of the Spirit are given by those who have them not themselves;
And that those who have not faith, or but in the lowest degree, may have more light from God, more wisdom for the guiding of other souls, than many that are strong in faith.)[52]

This statement might well have been a blueprint for *The Nature, Design, and General Rules of the United Societies*, published in 1743. Only one precondition was required of those who wished to join—"a desire to flee from the wrath to come, to be saved from their sins." But it was expected that all who wished to *continue* in a society should give evidence of this desire in three ways: First, "by doing no harm, by avoiding evil in every kind." Second, by "doing good of every possible sort, and as far as possible, to all men." Third, by "attending upon all the ordinances of God. Such are, the public worship of God; the ministry of the word, either read or expounded; the supper of the Lord; family and private prayer; searching the scriptures; and fasting, or abstinence."[53]

In one stroke, Methodist discipleship and spirituality were fused in a catholicity of grace. God awakens, invites, draws a sinner into the way of salvation, the assurance of which is a justifying faith. But because this gift of new life is real, and not forensic, it cannot be regarded as an isolated occurrence.[54] It is preceded by grace, and then nurtured by grace. Wesley could not regard those who were "doing the best they could" as beyond God's plan of salvation any more than he could regard those who were "striving for perfection" as falling short of it.[55]

The class meeting was where all of these variables found a place. Since the means of grace were ordinances of the visible church, and since grace was the dynamic of every level of spirituality, no person, whether beginning the quest for faith or advancing to its fullness, could afford to disregard these basic disciplines. Nor yet could they neglect the works of obedience—doing no harm, and doing every possible good—for these were the outworkings of grace in the world.

3. The Path to Perfection

The bands, on the other hand, continued to function in the Methodist societies as a means of grace for those who wanted and needed some "means of closer union." Band members were those who, "being justified by faith," had peace with God. They "felt a more tender affection than before"; they were "partakers of like precious faith." They

> poured out their souls into each other's bosom. Indeed they had great need so to do; for the war was not over, as they had supposed; but they still had to wrestle both with flesh and blood, and with principalities and powers: So that temptations were on every side; and often temptations of such a kind, as they knew not how to speak in a class; in which persons of every sort, young and old, men and women, met together.[56]

Band members were accordingly held more strictly accountable than the classes. In the December of 1744, Wesley provided them a set of Directions which particularized the General Rules. Their class tickets were marked with the letter "b" in addition to the quarterly code letter, identifying them as those within a society who were firmly committed to the quest for Christian perfection. And there evolved in due course a meeting known as the *public bands*, or the *body band*, when all the band members of a society met together, with a preacher presiding, for a time of intimate mutual sharing.

A further means of grace which at first was the privilege of band members only was the *lovefeast*. Wesley had been introduced to this practice of the early church by the Moravians, and had incorporated it into the rules of the Fetter Lane society. A lovefeast was a common meal, usually consisting of bread distributed by the stewards of the society, and water, or sometimes tea, passed around in a "loving-cup." There would be testimonies from those present, spontaneous prayers, and the singing of hymns; and frequently, when the Spirit moved with power among the company, they would remain in prayer and testimony well into the night.[57]

The quest for Christian perfection was most clearly expressed, however, in the formation of an even more intimate grouping, the *select societies*. Wesley's purpose in forming these groups was to direct those members whom he regarded as "continually walking in the light of God, and having fellowship with the Father, and with his Son Jesus Christ," in the path to perfection. In these meetings, the members learned how to "improve every talent they had received," how to "love one another more, and to watch carefully over each other." And Wesley also notes, with a disarming disclosure of his own spiritual quest, that the select societies consisted of those "to whom I might unbosom myself on all occasions, without reserve; and whom I could propose to their brethren as a pattern of love, of holiness, and of good works."[58] There were no rules for these groups, since they had "the best rule of all in their hearts." They were free to share in their fellowship, speaking openly, with no leader appointed.

It is important to note that the progression to membership of a select society seems frequently to have included a period of "backsliding" and "recovering." Those who "fell from the faith, either all at once, by falling into known, wilful sin; or gradually, and almost insensibly, by giving way in what they called little things," and whose fall was not checked by "exhortations and prayers used among the believers," were classified by Wesley as *penitents*, and given special instruction and advice. Those who "recovered the ground they had lost" proved even stronger in the faith, "being more watchful than ever, and more meek and lowly."[59]

This was another instance where the synthesis of Wesley's spirituality was proved in practice. The striving for perfection was the conscious desire on the part of the band member for holiness of right intent; but the occasion of this striving was justifying grace, the inward assurance. Even though a believer might be advanced in the faith, the relationship could be broken at any time by disobedience, resulting not only in a lack of spiritual progress, but in a breach, however temporary, of the new relationship with God. Christian perfection, therefore, was a consistency of relationship with God in Christ, sustained by disciplined obedience; and those pressing on to perfection were to be accountable no less than those who were awakened. They were to seek the gift of perfect love,

> not in careless indifference, or indolent inactivity; but in vigorous, universal obedience, in a zealous keeping of all the commandments, in watchfulness and painfulness. . . . It is true, we receive it by simple faith; But God does not, will not, give that faith, unless we seek it with all diligence, in the way which he hath ordained.[60]

The center of this perfect love was Christ, and Christ alone; and the path to perfection lay in obedience to Christ, a constant trust in his forgiveness and reconciliation. In the closing months of his life, Wesley could still write: "I do not believe any single person in your Select Society scruples saying, 'Every moment, Lord, I need the merit of thy death.'"[61]

4. The Means of Grace

As we shall see, the doctrine of Christian perfection came to prominence and took on new forms in the spirituality of nineteenth-century Methodism. But in its eighteenth-century origins, the Wesleyan dialectic is clear: Whatever experience of the Holy Spirit might be granted to a person by grace, the means of grace were the necessary structure of that person's spiritual life.

Nowhere is this more clearly articulated than in the tract known as *The Large Minutes*, an abstract of various annual conference minutes, in which Wesley gave definitive shape to Methodist polity, including the spiritual disciplines he enjoined upon his preachers. These are worth excerpting in detail, for they represent as well as anything in his writings the taproot of Methodist spiritual formation.

We might consider those that are with us as our pupils; into whose behaviour and studies we should enquire every day. Should we not frequently ask each, Do you walk closely with God? Have you now fellowship with the Father and the Son? At what hour do you rise? Do you punctually observe the morning and evening hour of retirement? Do you spend the day in the manner which we advise? Do you converse seriously, usefully, and closely? To be more particular: Do you use all the means of grace yourself, and enforce the use of them on all other persons?

They are either Instituted or Prudential:
I. *The Instituted* are,
  (1) Prayer; private, family, public; consisting of deprecation, petition, intercession, and thanksgiving. Do you use each of these? Do you use private prayer every morning and evening? if you can, at five in the evening; and the hour before or after morning preaching? Do you forecast daily, wherever you are, how to secure these hours? Do you avow it everywhere? Do you ask everywhere, "Have you family prayer?" Do you retire at five o'clock?
  (2) Searching the Scriptures by,
    (i) Reading: Constantly, some part of every day; regularly, all the Bible in order; carefully, with the Notes; seriously, with prayer before and after; fruitfully, immediately practising what you learn there?
    (ii) Meditating: At set times? by any rule?
    (iii) Hearing: Every morning? carefully; with prayer before, at, after; immediately putting in practice? Have you a New Testament always about you?
  (3) The Lord's supper: Do you use this at every opportunity? with solemn prayer before; with earnest and deliberate self-devotion?
  (4) Fasting: How do you fast every Friday?
  (5) Christian conference: Are you convinced how important and how difficult it is to "order your conversation right?" Is it "always in grace? seasoned with salt? meet to minister grace to the hearers?" Do not you converse too long at a time? Is not an hour commonly enough? Would it not be well always to have a determinate end in view; and to pray before and after it?
II. *Prudential Means* we may use either as common Christians, as Methodists, as Preachers, or as Assistants.
  (1) As common Christians. What particular rules have you in order to grow in grace? What arts of holy living?
  (2) As Methodists. Do you never miss your class, or Band?

(3) As Preachers. Do you meet every society; also the Leaders and Bands, if any?

(4) As Assistants. Have you thoroughly considered your office; and do you make a conscience of executing every part of it?

These means may be used without fruit: But there are some means which cannot; namely, watching, denying ourselves, taking up our cross, exercise of the presence of God.

(1) Do you steadily watch against the world, the devil, yourselves, your besetting sin?

(2) Do you deny yourself every useless pleasure of sense, imagination, honour? Are you temperate in all things? instance in food: Do you use only that kind and that degree which is best for your body and soul? Do you see the necessity of this?

(3) Do you eat no flesh suppers? no late suppers?

(4) Do you eat no more at each meal than is necessary? Are you not heavy or drowsy after dinner?

(5) Do you use only that kind and that degree of drink which is best for your body and soul?

(6) Do you drink water? Why not? Did you ever? Why did you leave it off? If not for health, when will you begin again? today?

(7) How often do you drink wine or ale? every day? Do you want it?

(8) Wherein do you "take up your cross daily?" Do you cheerfully bear your cross (whatever is grievous to nature) as a gift of God, and labour to profit thereby?

(9) Do you endeavour to set God always before you; to see his eye continually fixed upon you? Never can you use these means but a blessing will ensue. And the more you use them, the more you will grow in grace.[62]

5. The Hymns of Methodism

To all of which, we must add the hymns of early Methodism, in which the means of grace came to matchless expression. Most of them were written by Charles Wesley, though John exercised considerable editorial responsibility, and added a number of important translations, notably of German hymns. Rightly does the preface to the 1933 British Methodist Hymn Book begin with the simple statement, "Methodism was born in song." The Wesleys took the tunes of the day, some by serious composers such as Handel, some popular, some rowdy, and set words to them which gave the society members a ready means of articulating their deepest beliefs.

The definitive edition published in Wesley's lifetime was the 1780 *Collection of Hymns for the Use of the People Called Methodists*. This was for many years the standard referent for every dimension of Methodist spiritual life. It went through countless editions, and was issued in many formats, for use in pocket, pew and pulpit. As I write, I have in front of me the copy which was used by my great-great-grandfather George Watson, of Shotley Bridge, Northumberland, England. It is one of the many popular editions of the mid-nineteenth century, solidly bound, and designed to be carried to and from Sunday worship as well as the weekly class meetings. There is no date of publication, though the inscription is dated January 1, 1856.

The list of contents gives an indication of the breadth and the depth of this distinctively Methodist means of grace:

PART FIRST
SECTION   I. Exhorting Sinners to Return to God
                II. Describing, 1. The Pleasantness of Religion
                                      2. The goodness of God
                                      3. Death
                                      4. Judgment
                                      5. Heaven
                                      6. Hell
                III. Praying for a Blessing

PART SECOND
SECTION   I. Describing Formal Religion
                II.   Inward Religion

PART THIRD
SECTION   I. Praying for Repentance
                II. For Mourners convinced of Sin
                III. For Persons convinced of Backsliding
                IV. For Backsliders recovered

PART FOURTH
SECTION   I. For Believers Rejoicing
                II.   Fighting
                III.   Praying
                IV.   Watching
                V.   Working
                VI.   Suffering
                VII.   Seeking for Full Redemption
                VIII.   Saved
                IX.   Interceding for the World

PART FIFTH
SECTION   I. For the Society Meeting
                II.   Giving Thanks
                III.   Praying
                IV.   Parting

ADDITIONAL HYMNS
On Divine Worship
On the Lord's Supper
On the Resurrection and Ascension of Christ, &c.
Miscellaneous Hymns

SUPPLEMENT
SECTION I. Hymns of Adoration
II. On the Incarnation, Sufferings, &c. of Christ
III. On the Holy Spirit
IV. Penitential Hymns
V. The Experience and Privilege of Believers
VI. The Kingdom of Christ
VII. Time, Death, Judgment and the Future State
VIII. Miscellaneous Hymns

Since the Collection is once again available, and in a new and scholarly edition, this is not the place to cite the hymns in any detail. But one can at least be reproduced as an example of the worldly compassion of Methodist spirituality and the depth of its experience both:

Sinners, obey the gospel word!
Haste to the supper of my Lord,
Be wise to know your gracious day!
All things are ready; come away!

Ready the Father is to own
And kiss his late-returning son;
Ready your loving Saviour stands,
And spreads for you his bleeding hands.

Ready the Spirit of his Love
Just now the stony to remove;
To' apply and witness with the blood,
And wash and seal the sons of God.

Ready for you the angels wait,
To triumph in your blest estate:
Tuning their harps, they long to praise
The wonders of redeeming grace.

The Father, Son, and Holy Ghost,
Is ready, with their shining host:
All heaven is ready to resound,
"The dead's alive! the lost is found!"

Come, then, ye sinners, to your Lord,
In Christ to paradise restored;
His proffer'd benefits embrace,
The plenitude of gospel grace:

A pardon written with his blood,
The favour and the peace of God;
The seeing eye, the feeling sense,
The mystic joys of penitence:

The godly grief, the pleasing smart,
The meltings of a broken heart;
The tears that tell your sins forgiven,
The sighs that waft your souls to heaven:

The guiltless shame, the sweet distress;
The' unutterable tenderness;
The genuine, meek humility;
The wonder, "Why such love to me!"

The' o'erwhelming power of saving grace,
The sight that veils the seraph's face;
The speechless awe that dares not move,
And all the silent heaven of love.[63]

III. The Practice of Methodist Spirituality

Two Biographical Vignettes

In 1778, John Wesley founded the *Arminian Magazine*.[64] As the title suggests, it was intended in part to be a polemical publication, though this purpose was quickly subsumed by Wesley's broader vision of the Christian life. The early issues, and especially those which appeared in Wesley's lifetime, are a goldmine of Methodist spirituality, not least because Wesley asked a number of his early preachers to submit vignettes of their Christian pilgrimages. Many of these accounts were later compiled by Thomas Jackson in *The Lives of Early Methodist Preachers*, one of the classics of Methodist spirituality,[65] from which we shall make two brief selections: an excerpt from the account of John Nelson, one of Wesley's most faithful assistants; and from that of Thomas Rankin, who spent some years in North America as Wesley's superintendent before concluding his ministry in England.

1. John Nelson[66]

John Nelson was born in Yorkshire in 1707, and was trained to be a stone mason, like his father. He had a marked spiritual sensitivity from an early age:

God had followed me with convictions ever since I was ten years old; and whenever I had committed any known sin, either against God or man, I used to be so terrified afterwards that I shed many tears in private; yet, when I came to my companions, I wiped my face, and went on again in sin and folly.

His father, who seems to have been a devout man, reading the Scriptures to the family, and ensuring that his children were instructed in the faith, died when John was aged sixteen. That he died at peace with God made a strong impression on the young boy.

At the age of nineteen, John found himself in "great danger of falling into scandalous sins," and prayed that God would give him a wife, "that I might live with her to His glory." He married shortly thereafter, but although they were happy together, he still "loved pleasure more than God." Looking for work, he traveled to London, where his "concern for salvation increased for some time"; but again,

> I looked at men for example, and fell from my seriousness. The workmen cursed and abused me, because I would not drink with them, and spend my money as they did. . . . But when they took my tools from me, and said if I did not drink with them I should not work while they were drinking, that provoked me, so I fought with several of them; then they let me alone. But that stifled my concern for salvation, and I left off prayer and reading in a great measure.

The ensuing years were unsettled, moving between his home in the North of England, and London, where something seemed to be drawing him. When his friends pressed him about this "wandering," he replied: "I have something to learn that I have not yet learned." Here was a man who was clearly being impelled by the gracious initiatives of the Holy Spirit. He had all that a person of his station in life could want or need, yet still he was unsettled:

> I said to myself, "What can I desire that I have not? I enjoy as good health as any man can do; I have as agreeable a wife as I can wish for; I am clothed as well as I can desire; I have, at present, more gold and silver than I have need of; yet still I keep wandering from one part of the kingdom to another, seeking rest, and I cannot find it." Then I cried out, "Oh that I had been a cow, or a sheep!" for I looked back to see how I had spent above thirty years; and thought, rather than live thirty years more so, I would choose strangling. . . . Yet I thought I would set out once more; for I said, "Surely God never made man to be such a riddle to himself, and to leave him so; there must be something in religion, that I am unacquainted with, [t]o satisfy the empty mind of man; or he is in a worse state than the beasts that perish."

The spiritual quest became more intense. He went from church to church, but "found no ease." The preachers he heard seemed to talk about Christian duty: that God required a man "to do all he could, and Christ would make out the rest." But this was of little comfort, since he knew very well that he had not done all that he could. Indeed, if this was the road to salvation, then "none could be saved but little children."

Then he heard George Whitefield proclaim the gospel in Moorfields, preaching like "a man who could play well on an instrument. . . . I loved the man, so that if any one offered to disturb him, I was ready to fight for him. But I did not understand him. . . ." This brought Nelson closer to the moment of spiritual truth, but clearly there was another step still be taken. He was brought closer yet on Sunday, June 17, when he heard Wesley preach in the same place:

> His countenance struck such an awful dread upon me, before I heard him speak, that it made my heart beat like the pendulum of a clock; and, when he did speak, I thought his whole discourse was aimed at me. When he had done, I said, "This man can tell the secrets of my heart: he hath not left me there; for he hath showed the remedy, even the blood of Jesus." Then was my soul filled with consolation, through hope that God for Christ's sake would save me; neither did I doubt in such a manner any more, till within twenty-four hours of the time when the Lord wrote a pardon on my heart.

Nelson continued to hear Wesley preach, and he had "many flashes of love under the word," when he was at prayer and "at the table of the Lord." His friends tried to persuade him "not to go too far in religion," saying they "should be glad to knock Mr. Wesley's brains out," and avowing that "they would not hear him preach for fifty pounds." But Nelson stood his ground, saying that he intended to "seek to be born again, and experience a spiritual birth."

It was the testimony of an old soldier which brought his search to its crisis. The soldier too had been convicted by Wesley's preaching, and likewise had been discouraged by his friends. They had found him reading the Bible, and had dragged him to an ale-house, where he began to reason with them. But it was not long before they had him as drunk as they were—"how dangerous is it to encounter Satan on his ground!"— and this had brought him to the critical point of surrender. One Sunday morning, at Whitehall Chapel, he had gone to receive the sacrament. And no sooner had he received, than he had "found power to believe that Jesus Christ had shed His blood for me, and that God, for His sake, had forgiven my offences. Then was my heart filled with love to God and man; and since then sin hath not had dominion over me."

This testimony deeply affected Nelson. He found his soul "much refreshed" at the sacrament the Sunday after, and was "mightily encouraged" by Wesley's sermon in the afternoon. During the following week, he "felt an awful sense of God" resting upon him, as his own spiritual pilgrimage reached its critical point of surrender:

> When I went back to my lodging at noon, dinner was ready; and the gentlewoman said, "Come, sit down: you have need of your dinner, for you have eaten nothing today." But when I looked on the meat, I said, "Shall such a wretch as I devour the good creatures of God in the state I am now in? No; I deserve to be thrust into hell." I then went into my chamber, shut the door, and fell down on my knees, crying, "Lord, save, or I perish!" When I had prayed till I could pray no more, I got up

and walked to and fro, being resolved I would neither eat nor drink till had found
the kingdom of God. I fell down to prayer again, but found no relief; got up and
walked again: then tears began to flow from my eyes, like great drops of rain, and
I fell on my knees a third time; but now I was as dumb as a beast, and could not put
one petition, if it would have saved my soul. I kneeled before the Lord some time,
and saw myself a criminal before the Judge; then I said, "Lord, Thy will be done;
damn or save!" That moment Jesus Christ was as evidently set before the eye of my
mind, as crucified for my sins, as if I had seen Him with my bodily eyes: and in
that instant my heart was set at liberty from guilt and tormenting fear, and filled
with a calm and serene peace. I could then say, without any dread of fear, "Thou
art my Lord and my God." Now did I begin to sing that part of the 12th chapter
of Isaiah, "O Lord, I will praise Thee; though Thou wast angry with me, Thine
anger is turned away, and Thou comfortest me. Behold, God is my salvation; I will
trust, and not be afraid: for the Lord Jehovah is my strength and my song; He also
is become my salvation." My heart was filled with love to God and every soul of
man: next to my wife and children, my mother, brethren, and sisters, my greatest
enemies had an interest in my prayers; and I cried, "O Lord, give me to see my
desire on them: let them experience Thy redeeming love!"

We should note in the narrative the worldly context of Nelson's spiritual journey. As with the old soldier who so impressed him, the struggle
was not just with himself, but with the people whom he knew and who
knew him. The inner working of grace was rarely without its testing in
the world. And indeed, shortly after Nelson's conversion (which, as with
so many of these firsthand accounts in the *Arminian Magazine*, took place
in private), he found himself faced with the possibility of being thrown
out of his job because he would not work on the Sabbath. In spite of the
foreman's threats, he stood firm, and found that on the Monday morning
his job was still there. The foreman who had told him on Saturday that
Wesley had made a fool of him, welcomed him back on Monday with
"good words." The character of Methodist spirituality emerges with some
cogency—a quest for obedience to God in the midst of worldly living.

We should also note the importance of the sacrament of the Lord's
Supper in Nelson's spiritual journey as an efficacious means of grace. It
is prominent in Rankin's account also, and it occurs frequently throughout Jackson's *Lives*. Wesley established its priority in Methodist spirituality when he refuted Moravian quietism,[67] and it remained a central focus
of his evangelistic ministry. Moreover, as we shall presently observe, it
figured prominently in the spirituality of the Second Great Awakening
in North America.

Nelson became one of Wesley's most trusted preachers, and the
remainder of his account is noteworthy among other things for his arrest
and impressment into the army in 1744. This was a hazard for all
Methodist preachers, since magistrates could order a man into the military if he did not appear to be gainfully employed—which many clergy

were quick to declare that the Methodist preachers were not. Nelson was released after several months, during which time, of course, he continued to preach to his fellow soldiers and to whoever would hear him in the open air. Quite apart from the spiritual testimony, the episode is a fascinating glimpse of life in eighteenth-century England.

2. Thomas Rankin[68]

Thomas Rankin was born in Scotland, and, like John Nelson, was "early taught the principles of religion." His father catechized the family (and the servants), and he was likewise catechized at school. At the age of eleven or twelve, he was

> deeply affected at a sacramental occasion, being permitted to stay at the administration of the ordinance. When I saw the ministers and people receive the bread and wine, and heard the address from the former to the communicants, I frequently burst into tears.

The occasion of Rankin's first real exposure to the spirit of the Revival was the visit of a company of dragoons to his home town. Among their number were some who had formed religious societies in Germany under the leadership of John Haime.[69]

> The news of soldiers meeting for prayer and praise, and reading the Word of God, soon spread through the town: curiosity led many to attend their meetings, and I was one of that number. . . . It was not long before several were enabled to testify that they had redemption in the blood of Christ, the forgiveness of all their sins. This soon spread abroad, and made a great noise in the town; . . . but I could not understand them when they spoke of God's Spirit bearing witness with their spirits that they were the children of God. . . . My plea was, "that we might be in the favour of God, and not be assured that our sins were forgiven." I granted, "that some very peculiar holy people might be assured of the divine favour; but that it was not the privilege of all the children of God."

This work of prevenient grace was continued, as Rankin joined the society which was formed as a result of the soldiers' witness; and he was further "awakened" by the visit of some Methodist preachers. Even though he did not "remember that [they made] any particular impression" upon him, he did remember a conversation with a woman who belonged to the society, and who took him to task for not attending his class meeting regularly. This brought him sufficiently close to his spiritual crisis to make him leave home to seek a resolution to his dilemma.

> The short of the matter was this: I had a sincere desire to serve God and to save my soul, as also to be thought a religious young man; but I had not learned to "sell all for the pearl of great price."

The point of surrender was brought nearer when Rankin heard George Whitefield preaching in Edinburgh; and the tension heightened when the time came for the sacrament to be administered. He went to the table, receiving the bread "with a broken, melting, and expectant heart." But when the cup was passed to him, a little of the wine was spilt on the floor, and "that very moment Satan suggested that 'Christ's blood was spilt for me in vain!' . . . Hopes and fears alternately prevailed, and thus I went on for several weeks." Finally, he came to "wrestle with God in an agony of prayer."

> I called out, "Lord, I have wrestled long, and have not yet prevailed: Oh, let me now prevail!" The whole passage of Jacob's wrestling with the Angel came into my mind; and I called out aloud, "I will not let Thee go, unless Thou bless me!" In a moment the cloud burst, and tears of love flowed from my eyes; when these words were applied to my soul, many times over, "And he blessed him there." They came with the Holy Ghost, and with much assurance; and my whole soul was overwhelmed with the presence of God. Every doubt of my acceptance was now gone, and all my fears fled away as the morning shades before the rising sun. I had the most distinct testimony that all my sins were forgiven through the blood of the covenant, and that I was a child of God, and an heir of eternal glory. What I now felt was very different from what I had experienced of the drawings of the love of God for several years past, and when I first partook of the sacrament. I had now no more doubt of my interest in the Lord Jesus Christ than of my own existence.

Rankin's association with Methodism in Scotland continued, and when he was asked by a relative to undertake a business trip to South Carolina, he clearly missed the fellowship which the societies had afforded. On his return, he noted that his soul had suffered "a real declension," and he saw as never before "the whole economy of Methodism in the most favourable light—the class and band meetings, meeting of the society, body-bands, lovefeasts . . . ; the whole was calculated to promote the great end for which they were designed—the glory of God in the salvation of souls."

Rankin's account then describes his quest for Christian perfection, which, as with his spiritual birth, came to a point of spiritual crisis:

> [As] I was one evening meeting my class, and happy in my soul, I was all on a sudden seized with such horror as I had never known from the time I knew the pardoning love of God. As soon as the meeting was finished, I went home, and retired to private prayer; but all was darkness and painful distress. I found no intercourse with heaven, and faith and prayer seemed to have lost their wings. For five days and nights I went through such distress of soul as made sleep, and the desire of food, depart from me. I could attend to nothing but my painful feelings, and mourn and weep.
>
> On the fifth day two friends called to see me, and we joined in prayer, and I found more liberty than I had experienced during the time of this painful distress. As soon as my friends were gone, I fell down on my knees, and continued in prayer till I went to bed. I now found a degree of sweetness, and communion

with my Lord once more; and I closed my eyes with the pleasing sensation. I awoke very early next morning, and with a change in my feelings, that I could scarce allow myself time to dress before I fell upon my knees to praise God; and when on my knees, had such a view of the goodness and love of God as almost overcame every power of body and soul.

Soon thereafter, he felt the call to preach, and began to "exhort" at local society meetings. But the call did not come easily. He found that reactions to his preaching were very mixed, and this caused him on a number of occasions "to resolve to preach no more." Yet the spiritual struggle continued, as Rankin sought "the great salvation, deliverance from inbred sin." Finally, in the September of 1761, he records that the Lord gave him such a discovery of His love as he had never known before:

I was meeting with a few Christian friends, who were all athirst for entire holiness, and after several had prayed, I also called on the name of the "Deliverer that came out of Zion, to turn away ungodliness from Jacob." While these words were pronounced with my heart and lips, "Are we not, O Lord, the purchase of Thy blood? let us then be redeemed from all iniquity," in a moment the power of God so descended upon my soul, that I could pray no more. It was

That speechless awe which dares not move,
And all the silent heaven of love![70]

Rankin felt that this was indeed the token of Christian perfection, the "second blessing," which brought him the maturity of perfect love and cleansing from inbred sin. But he continued to have doubts about his calling, and it was Wesley who came to his aid by telling him quite bluntly that he would have no peace until he devoted himself full-time to the work of proclaiming the gospel. He accepted this challenge, became an itinerant Methodist preacher, and then knew the full assurance "that the Lord Jesus has purified my heart by faith in His blood, and that I felt nothing contrary to the pure love of God." He was admitted to a select society, and placed himself at Wesley's disposal.

From 1773–78, Rankin served as Wesley's superintendent in North America,[71] and these years provide us with a convenient introduction to the next phase of Methodist spirituality, which proved to be North American in origin. For some years after his death, Wesley's influence continued to prevail in British Methodism. His joint emphasis on inward witness and the practical outworking of discipleship continued to find expression through the class meeting and other forms of Methodist spiritual practice.[72] But it was not long before the pressures of nineteenth-century English social change, to some extent engendered by Methodist working class leadership, led to polarities and divisions within the movement.[73] As a result, the spirituality of the class meeting in the main body of Wesleyan Methodism became increasingly pietistic to the point of inbred religiosity, while the momentum of social involvement passed to the breakaway groupings. In particular was this true of the Primitive Methodists, whose spirituality owed much to the North American influences we must now examine: the Second Great Awakening, and the interaction between Christian perfection and revivalism which produced the holiness movement.[74]

IV. The Holiness Tradition

1. The North American Context: Revivalism and Camp Meetings

It is clear from Rankin's account of his North American ministry that the doctrine of Christian perfection was a normative dimension of his preaching. On Sunday, July 4, 1773, for example, he "found freedom and tenderness to apply the word in a particular manner to those who were groaning for pardon of sin and for purity of heart." And on Sunday, June 30th, 1776, while preaching from Revelation 3:8 [I know thy works: behold, I have set before thee an open door . . .], "the very house seemed to shake, and all the people were overcome with the presence of the Lord God of Israel. . . . From the best accounts we could receive afterwards, upwards of fifty were awakened and brought to the knowledge of a pardoning God that day; besides many who were enabled to witness that the blood of Jesus had cleansed them from all sin."

Yet the preaching and practice of the doctrine in North American Methodism seems from an early date to have had a characteristic emphasis on the instantaneous experience of the gift of perfect love rather than on the process which led to it. Ironically, it was on this very point that Wesley had found the doctrine to be most controversial in England. In the late 1750s, there had been a sharp increase in the number of society members who professed to have received the gift, and in the early 1760s two of Wesley's preachers, Thomas Maxfield and George Bell, had taken a position which was sufficiently extreme to cause a major reaction against the doctrine altogether.

Wesley's response had been cautious. He had continued to affirm the instantaneous experience of Christian perfection as a gift of grace, but had warned against isolating the experience from its proper grounding in faith and works.[75] And while the conflict had caused him considerable anguish,[76] it had led to serious examination of the doctrine, culminating in the definitive theological treatment of John Fletcher's *Checks to Antinomianism*.[77]

In North America, however, the context of the doctrine was from the beginning the evangelical fervor of revivalism. The Methodist societies were planted in soil already well fertilized by the spirit of the First Great Awakening, in which the preaching of Jonathan Edwards and George Whitefield had focused on the immediacy of decision, and in which the invitation to the sinner was very direct.[78] The evidence of response to this was a divine inruption of grace, changing the will from the way-wardness of sin to God-fearing obedience.[79]

Towards the end of the eighteenth century, there were many in the Congregationalist and Presbyterian Churches who were embarrassed to concede that such an intensive and emotional event could have pro-ceeded from their tradition, which was predominantly Calvinist. Methodist evangelism, on the other hand, was quite openly Arminian. "Whosoever will may come," was the cry. Not only did this adapt well to the revivalist approach to evangelistic outreach; it harmonized well with the democratic theory of the new nation, and was admirably suited to the frontier spirit which stressed enterprise and self-sufficiency.[80] Moreover, by the time the Methodist Episcopal Church was established in 1784, North America was on the threshold of the Second Great Awakening.

Signs of this had begun to emerge in the 1790s, emanating initially from Kentucky—indeed, it was often called "The Great Kentucky Revival."[81] As a movement, it was noted most of all for the camp meet-ing. Not that the idea of bringing people together for an extended week-end of preaching and devotional renewal was new.[82] But to do it with organized accommodations, thereby establishing it as an institutional gathering, was an innovation; and this is what happened when James McGready, a Presbyterian minister, gave advance notice of a sacramen-tal service to be held at Gasper River, Kentucky, in July of 1800. Hun-dreds came from miles around, and many brought their own tents since the crowd was far too large for the Gasper River church to accommo-date. It was followed by an even larger gathering the following year at Cane Ridge, where again the sacrament of the Lord's Supper was announced as the culminating act of worship.

The atmosphere of the camp meeting was to set the tone for the revivalism of the nineteenth century. It retained the directness of the challenge to the sinner, and the necessity of an inruption of divine grace upon the human will; but the focus was on the experience of this inrup-tion, rather than the change it wrought per se. The new birth was now something to be measured by the intensity and impact of its manifesta-tion in the convert. Leaping, shouting and convulsive jerking were nor-mative, and Methodist leaders, such as Francis Asbury, Peter Cartwright and William McKendree, who endorsed camp meetings to the point where they became identified as a Methodist institution, found themselves on the crest of a wave of emotional expression which was highly evocative of scenes at Wesley's early outdoor preaching, and which sometimes were difficult to control.[83]

The descriptions of conversion experiences are predictably vivid, as in the testimony of a little girl at the Gasper River camp meeting:

> O he is willing, he is willing—he is come, he is come—O what a sweet Christ he is—O, what a precious Christ he is—O, what a fullness I see in him—O, what a beauty I see in him—O, why was it that I never could believe! that I could never come to Christ before, when Christ was so willing to save me?[84]

Or in an eyewitness account of the Cane Ridge meeting:

> I attended with 18 Presbyterian ministers; and Baptist and Methodist preachers, I do not know how many; all being either preaching or exhorting the distressed with more harmony than could be expected. The governor of our State was with us and encouraging the work. The number of people computed from 10, to 21,000 and the communicants 828. The whole people were serious, all the conversation was of a religious nature, or calling in question the divinity of the work. Great numbers were on the ground from Friday until the Thursday following, night and day without intermission, engaged in some religious act of worship. They are commonly collected in small circles of 10 or 12, close adjoining another circle and all engaged in singing Watt's and Hart's hymns; and then a minister steps upon a stump or log, and begins an exhortation or sermon, when, as many as can hear collect around him. On Sabbath I saw above 100 candles burning at once and I saw 100 persons at once on the ground crying for mercy, of all ages from 8 to 60 years . . . . When a person is struck down he is carried by others out of the congregation, when some minister converses with and prays for him; afterwards a few gather around and sing a hymn suitable to the case. The whole number brought to the ground, under convictions, were about 1,000, not less. The sensible, the weak, etc., learned and unlearned, the rich and poor, are subjects of it.[85]

Given the pedigree of this critical experience of the indwelling Spirit in Methodist spirituality, it was altogether predictable that Methodism should have embraced and been embraced by the revivalism which received this tremendous second wind at the turn of the century. What provided the distinctive catalyst was the energy and the fervor of a new nation, which rendered the spiritual experience at once a cultural as well as a spiritual phenomenon. As with the common people to whom Wesley had taken the gospel in the previous century, hard labor and long hours perforce rendered their communion with God something which had to be apprehensible in the world where they lived and worked.

The significance of a critical experience in response to the divine initiative cannot therefore be underestimated. There was little time on the frontier for niceties of argument, nor yet for subtleties of spiritual nuance.

When life was lived in a tension of survival, the alternative was all too often death. The revivalist preachers therefore attacked human sin head-on. Resistance was to be broken if grace was to inrupt. And what began in the intensive experience of the camp meeting was replayed and relived throughout the year in pulpits and churches across the land.

2. The Way of Holiness

Even so, the emphasis on critical decision was not distinctively Methodist. Nor had it been in Wesley's England, for that matter, where Methodism was by no means the only component of evangelical revival. Where Methodist spirituality proved distinctive in North America was in the affirmation of a second blessing, a critical experience in which the believer was brought to a "cleansing from sin," a further inruption of grace, marked by an overwhelming sense of God's love. The Christian pilgrimage would thereafter be sustained by a total subjection of the human will to the divine initiative.

While this was preached during the early years of Methodism in North America, and was a dimension of the Methodist contribution to the Second Great Awakening, it does not seem to have been prominent in Methodist spiritual life until the 1840s.[86] As a doctrine, it had been incorporated into the first Discipline of the new Methodist Episcopal Church at Baltimore in 1784, at the urging of Thomas Coke and Francis Asbury, the joint superintendents, and with the firm support of the traveling preachers. Provision had been made for bands and select societies to foster its expectation and to nurture those who were so blessed. Yet it was traditioned during the first half century of the new Methodist church primarily through its literature.

Of the leadership responsible for this, perhaps the most important was that of Nathan Bangs. In his widely read *Letters to Young Ministers of the Gospel*, for example, published when he was head of the Methodist Book Concern, he recommended the British Wesleyan scholars, Adam Clarke and Richard Watson, both of whom assumed the doctrine of Christian perfection to be normative. Clarke in particular stressed the importance of the instantaneous experience of Christian perfection.[87] The influence of these writings, along with many American editions of relevant works by Wesley and Fletcher, began to gather momentum in the 1830s, and in 1839 Timothy Merritt, who had already published a treatise on the subject, started a monthly periodical entitled the *Guide to Christian Perfection*, which in the next thirty years was to reach a circulation of some forty thousand.

As with all aspects of Methodist spirituality, however, the impetus for what became known as the Holiness Movement came from the experiences of Methodists themselves, and perhaps the most influential of these was Phœbe Palmer, wife of a noted New York physician, Dr. W. C. Palmer. In 1835, she and her sister sponsored a joint prayer meeting for women of the Allen Street and Mulberry Street Methodist Churches in New York City, which was subsequently opened to men in 1839. Its specific purpose was to promote entire sanctification, and Phoebe emerged as a leading exponent and exemplar of this form of spirituality, declaring her own experience of entire sanctification in 1837. She published hundreds of tracts, and a number of books, though the most important was *The Way of Holiness* (1846), in which she expounded the discovery by one of "the children of Zion" of the "shorter way of getting into this way of holiness" without the "waiting and struggling with the powers of darkness."

SECTION VII

"They are not of this world, even as I am not of the world. I pray not that thou shouldest take them out of the world, but that thou shouldest keep them from the evil."—The prayer of Jesus for his Disciples.

"Tis done! thou dost this moment save,
With full salvation bless;
Redemption through the blood I have,
And spotless love and peace."

Now that she was so powerfully and experimentally assured of the blessedness of this "shorter way," O, with what ardor of soul did she long to say to every redeemed one, "Ye have been fully redeemed; redeemed from all iniquity, that ye should be unto God a peculiar people, zealous of good works!" . . .

Her now newly-inspired spirit could scarcely conceive of a higher ambition, in the present state of existence, than to be endued with the unction of the Holy One, and then permitted, by the power of the Spirit, to say to every lover of Jesus, "This is the will of God, even *your* sanctification." Jesus, *your* Redeemer, *your* Saviour, waits even now to sanctify you wholly: "and I pray God that your *whole spirit*, and *soul*, and *body*, be preserve[d] blameless unto the coming of our Lord Jesus Christ. Faithful is he that calleth you, who also will do it."

It was in that same hallowed hour when she was first, through the blood of the everlasting covenant, permitted to enter within the veil, and *prove* the blessedness of the "way of holiness," that the weighty responsibilities, and also inconceivably-glorious destination of the believer, were unfolded to her spiritual vision, in a manner inexpressibly surpassing her former perceptions. . . .

Have you brought yourself into this state of blessedness? Is it through your own exertions that this light has been kindled in your heart? were the inquiries which were now urged upon her attention. She deeply felt, as her [heart responded] to these interrogatories, that it was *all* the work of the Spirit; and never before did such a piercing sense of her own demerit and helplessness penetrate her mind as at that hour, while her in[most soul] replied, 'Tis from the "Father of lights," the "Giver of every good and perfect gift," that I have received this precious *gift*. Yes, it is a *gift* from God, and to his name be all the glory![88]

Not that the holiness movement was confined to Methodism. It emerged in other denominations with different emphases, as, for example, in the person of Charles Grandison Finney, whose methods in the 1820s in the northeastern states pioneered many of the methods of modern revivalism.[89] Finney turned to a theological career in the 1830s, and was particularly influenced by Wesley's *Plain Account of Christian Perfection*, which he read in 1836, the year after his appointment to the faculty of the newly founded Oberlin College. It was perhaps inevitable that his presence should have quickened the pace of spiritual life at the college, and he records in his memoirs how, during a revival season in 1839, a student asked whether entire sanctification was possible in this life. The president, Asa Mahan, in what seems to have been a very moving reply, affirmed that indeed it was possible, and from then on, as Finney records it, the faculty members committed themselves to seeking perfection in their own lives. This spiritual blessing, along with the declared purpose of the college to pursue the reform of human institutions, made Oberlin a powerful and distinctive force within the holiness movement.[90]

Indeed, the impact of the holiness movement on society was perhaps its most significant dimension, as it had been with the Second Great Awakening. An important outcome of Finney's work in the 1820s had been a host of societies and associations for the improvement of social life, and as revised editions of his works appear, restoring the excisions of the late nineteenth century editions, it is becoming clear just how committed he was to the work of anti-slavery and social reform. Take, for example, this extract from his "letters on revivals," first published in *The Oberlin Evangelist* in 1846:

> Now the great business of the church is to reform the world—to put away every kind of sin. The church of Christ was originally organized to be a body of reformers. The very profession of Christianity implies the profession and virtually an oath to do all that can be done for the universal reformation of the world. The Christian church was designed to make aggressive movements in every direction—to lift up her voice and put forth her energies against iniquity in high and low places—to reform individuals, communities, and governments, and never rest until the kingdom and the greatness of the kingdom under the whole heaven shall be given to the people of the saints of the most High God—until every form of iniquity shall be driven from the earth.
>
> Now when we consider the appropriate business of the church—the very end for which she is organized and for which every Christian vows eternal consecration, and then behold her appalling inconsistencies everywhere apparent, I do not wonder that so many persons are led to avow that the nominal church is apostate from God. When we consider the manner in which the movement in behalf of the slave has been treated by ecclesiastical bodies, by missionary associations, by churches and ministers, throughout the land, is it any wonder that the Church is forsaken of the Spirit of God? . . .

It is amazing to see what excuses are made by ministers for remaining silent in respect to almost every branch of reform.[91]

It was no coincidence that, as the country came to face its severest crisis over the issue of slavery, much of the momentum for abolition of that "peculiar institution" came from the explosive chemistry of revivalism and perfectionism grounded in a sure sense of social justice.[92]

3. The Test of Methodist Spirituality

In the decades leading up to the Civil War, the question of slavery proved to be the crisis of discipleship for the Methodist Episcopal Church. Increasingly, the experience of revivalism was stressed rather than its social obligations; and even Phoebe Palmer found herself compromised on the issue of abolitionism.[93] As a result, the decades saw divisions in the Methodist Episcopal Church. In 1843–44, under the leadership of Orange Scott, the Wesleyan Methodist Church was organized in protest against the absence of a stand on slavery. And at the General Conference of 1844, the issue was avoided by the agreement to divide the Methodist Episcopal Church between north and south—a portent of the war to come. The Wesleyan Methodists became increasingly a holiness church after their separation, and it was the emphasis on entire sanctification which led to the formation of the Free Methodist Church in 1857 following the expulsion from the Genesee Conference of a minister who had taken a stand on the doctrine.[94]

Most important of all, however, and generative of a spiritual tradition in its own right, were the divisions which had early taken place to constitute the African Methodist Episcopal Church (1816), and the African Methodist Episcopal Zion Church (1820). As the heritage of black spirituality emerges from the liberation of a distinctive Christian identity in our own day, it points us to the radical worldliness of a discipleship which follows a Christ who is always to be found in the midst of suffering and oppression.[95]

This is not the place to chronicle the further developments of the holiness movement.[96] It gathered fresh momentum during the years following the Civil War, and for a time it was embraced by the main body of Methodism as the cutting edge of its evangelism. The Palmers conducted highly successful tours, and in 1867 there was formed the National Campmeeting Association for the Promotion of Holiness. As a result of American initiative, the teaching and practice of entire sanctification were further developed at the Keswick Conventions in England, which met annually after 1875.[97] And in turn, the Salvation Army, which grew from the work of William Booth in the east end of London, spread to the United States.[98]

But the movement, always rich in its diversity, found its connection with mainline Methodism increasingly tenuous. In spite of much effort on both sides to maintain unity, separatist tendencies developed, and in the closing years of the century the holiness groups were seen as a threat to church order.[99] The tensions became polarized, and a number of new denominations were formed, the most significant of which was the Church of the Nazarene.[100] The fractures to the spiritual tradition of Methodism caused by these divisions remain with us to this day.

With the stimulus of a bicentennial celebration in 1984, the United Methodist Church is re-examining its spiritual heritage with vigor. *The Upper Room*, founded as a spiritual devotional guide in 1935, and now published in sixty-one editions and forty-three languages throughout one hundred and twenty-five countries, has become the parent organization for a wide range of spiritual ministries at the General Board of Discipleship of the United Methodist Church.[101] Methodists are also discovering that the mutual accountability of the early class meeting is rich in spiritual potential, with its emphasis on the realities of Christian discipleship empowered by the means of grace.[102] Yet there remains the need for renewed dialogue between United Methodism and the churches which comprise the Methodist traditions—the Free and Wesleyan Methodists, the Nazarenes, and the black Methodist denominations. In company with a number of Pentecostal denominations, they have common roots in the spirituality of entire sanctification, and the disputes which led to these divisions have proved to be mutually impoverishing. Not least among the casualties has been the spirituality which once impelled to service in the world, but which now renders social involvement all too often an optional corollary of the inward witness.

For in the final analysis, Methodist spirituality is nothing if not a responsiveness to the divine initiative. And on this, Wesley's word remains definitive and timely: as we yearn for the Spirit to move in our lives and across the world, let us wait, "not in careless indifference, or indolent inactivity; but in vigorous, universal obedience, in a zealous keeping of all the commandments, in watchfulness and painfulness, in denying ourselves and taking up our cross daily, as well as in earnest prayer and fasting, and a close attendance on all the ordinances of God."[103]

Notes

1. For a full treatment of the spirituality of John Wesley, see the volume edited by Frank Whaling in The Classics of Western Spirituality, *John and Charles Wesley: Selected Writings and Hymns* (New York: Paulist, 1981).

2. *The Journal of the Rev. John Wesley, A. M.*, standard edition, 8 vols., ed. Nehemiah Curnock (London: Robert Culley, 1909), 1:83.

3. "A Plain Account of Christian Perfection," in *The Works of John Wesley*, 14 vols. (London: Wesleyan Conference Office, 1872; repr. ed. Grand Rapids: Baker, 1979), 11:366. Cf. Whaling, *Wesleys*, 299.

4. Jeremy Taylor, "The Rules and Exercises of Holy Living" [1650]; "The Rules and Exercises of Holy Dying" [1651], in *The Whole Works of the Right Reverend Jeremy Taylor*, ed. Reginald Heber, rev. & corr. Charles Page Eden, 10 vols. (London, 1862), 4:183. See also 4:49ff., 132ff.

5. Wesley, *Works*, 11:366; Whaling, *Wesleys*, 299.

6. This was the title of the contemporary translation of the *Imitatio Christi* which Wesley used. See *The Oxford Edition of the Works of John Wesley*, vol. 25, *Letters I: 1721–1739*, ed. Frank Baker (Oxford: Clarendon, 1980), 162 n. 7. See ibid. 9ff. for correspondence between Wesley and his mother on the formative influences of his readings at this time.

7. William Law was a Non-Juror, one of those Anglican clergy whose high view of the church prevented them from taking an oath of allegiance to the king. Initially the Non-Jurors consisted of eight bishops and some four hundred priests who refused to swear loyalty to William and Mary after the ejection of James II in 1688 on the grounds that their oath to the old king was still sacrosanct. For a large part of the eighteenth century, they continued to attract others whose high view of the church engendered similar sympathies—such as William Law, who, having been ordained in 1711 and elected fellow of Emmanuel College, Cambridge, refused to take the oath of allegiance to George I in 1714, and was deprived of his fellowship. As a group, they made a highly significant contribution to Anglican scholarship.

8. William Law, *A Serious Call to a Devout and Holy Life* (London, 1729), 27.

9. Ibid., 18–19.

10. See Richard P. Heitzenrater, *The Elusive Mr. Wesley*, 2 vols. (Nashville: Abingdon, 1984), 1:50ff., 63ff. Cf. "A Scheme of Self-Examination," in Whaling, *Wesleys*, 85–87.

11. *The Bicentennial Edition of the Works of John Wesley*, vol. 1, *Sermons I: 1–33*, ed. Albert C. Outler (Nashville: Abingdon, 1984), 75 n. 27. See also ibid., 66–96, where Outler provides a definitive overview of Wesley's sources. This brilliant statement has set the agenda for Wesley studies for the next generation. See also Albert C. Outler, *John Wesley*, Library of Protestant Thought (New York: Oxford University Press, 1964), 8ff., 252.

12. This is best stated in what is arguably Wesley's most significant theological essay, "Thoughts upon God's Sovereignty," *Works*, 10:361–63.

13. John D. Walsh, "Origins of the Evangelical Revival," in *Essays in Modern Church History: In Memory of Norman Sykes*, ed. G. V. Bennet and J. D. Walsh (London: Adam & Charles Black, 1966), 142. See also John Walsh, "The Cambridge Methodists," in *Christian Spirituality: Essays in Honor of Gordon Rupp*, ed. Peter Brooks (London: SCM, 1975), 255.

14. Cited in Martin Schmidt, *John Wesley: A Theological Biography* (Nashville: Abingdon, n.d.), 1:161ff.

15. *The Oxford Edition of the Works of John Wesley*, vol. 7, *A Collection of Hymns for the Use of the People Called Methodists*, ed. Franz Hildebrandt and Oliver Beckerlegge, asst. James Dale (Oxford: Clarendon, 1983), 250 n.

16. Ibid., 250–52. See also Whaling, *Wesleys*, 192–94.

17. Wesley, *Journal*, 1:475–76.

18. "Methodism and the Catholic Tradition," in *Northern Catholicism: Centenary Studies in the Oxford and Parallel Movements*, ed. N. P. Williams and Charles Harris (London: SPCK, 1933), 526.

19. *The New Covenant, or The Saints Portion. A Treatise unfolding the All-sufficiencie of God, and Mans Uprightnes, and the Covenant of Grace* (London, 1629), 2:155.

20. As Perry Miller has observed, when Puritanism is considered in the broad perspective of human history, it is not a unique phenomenon. It is "one more instance of a recurring spiritual answer to interrogations eternally posed by human existence . . . yet another manifestation of a piety [which I venture to call] Augustinian . . . simply because Augustine is the arch-examplar of a religious frame of mind of which Puritanism is only one instance out of many in fifteen hundred years of religious history." The Puritan frame of mind, suggests Miller, was "a reliance on the moment of aesthetic vision" as opposed to "a dialectical effort to prove the justice of fact" (*The New England Mind: The Seventeenth Century* [Boston: Beacon, 1961], 4–5, 18).

21. For a detailed study of these sources in Wesley, see Robert C. Monk, *John Wesley: His Puritan Heritage* (Nashville: Abingdon, 1966). See appendix I, 255ff., for a listing of the authors as they appeared in the first edition of *A Christian Library*.

22. Henry Scougal, *The Life of God in the Soul of Man; or, The Nature and Excellency of the Christian Religion with Nine Other Discourses on Important Subjects* (London, 1726), 4. Scougal is represented in *A Christian Library*, as are many of the mystical writers Wesley read at Oxford. The circumspection with which the selections for this major publication were made is an indication of the richness and diversity of Wesley's own spirituality.

23. "An Earnest Appeal to Men of Reason and Religion," in *The Oxford Edition of the Works of John Wesley*, vol. 11, *The Appeals to Men of Reason and Religion and Certain Related Open Letters*, ed. Gerald R. Cragg (Oxford: Clarendon, 1975), 46.

24. Sermon, "The Scripture Way of Salvation," in *John Wesley*, ed. Albert C. Outler, 273. Outler notes that if the Wesleyan theology had to be judged by a single essay, this one would do as well as any and better than most (ibid., 171). In addition to the volume already published in the Bicentennial Edition (see above, note 11), three further volumes are in preparation by Outler, to provide a definitive edition of all of Wesley's sermons.

25. *Journal*, 2:101.

26. "A Plain Account of Christian Perfection," in Whaling, *Wesleys*, 327–28. Cf. *Works*, 11:394–96.

27. *Works*, 8:359–74.

28. The standard history of the societies is by Josiah Woodward, *An Account of the Rise and Progress of the Religious Societies in the City of London, &c.* (London, 1698). See also David Lowes Watson, *The Early Methodist Class Meeting: Its Origins and Significance* (Nashville: Discipleship Resources, 1985), where the appendices include all of the various Rules which helped to form early Methodist polity, beginning with those of Anthony Horneck.

29. In 1699, the Society for the Promoting of Christian Knowledge was founded, becoming a resource for the movement with its literature, and in 1701 the Society for the Propagation of the Gospel in Foreign Parts became a missionary wing—helping to sponsor the Wesley brothers in Georgia in 1735.

30. The history of the Moravian communities at Herrnhut, and then in North America, is a study in spirituality in its own right. See Gillian Lindt Gollin, *Moravians in Two Worlds* (New York: Columbia University Press, 1967).

31. Henry Rimius, *A Candid Narrative of the Rise and Progress of the Herrnhuters, Commonly Called Moravians, or, Unitas Fratrum* (London, 1753), 21.

32. Cited in Clifford W. Towlson, *Moravian and Methodist: Relationships and Influences in the Eighteenth Century* (London: Epworth, 1957), 185.

33. *Journal*, 1:197–205. See also ibid., 318–19; and "A Short History of the People Called Methodists," in *Works*, 13:305–6. Wesley regarded the Oxford Holy Club as the "first rise" of Methodism.

34. *Journal*, 2:3–63. Wesley's account of this visit remains a major primary source for Moravian history.

35. *Oxford Edition, Letters I*, 592–93.

36. The *Rules for the Band-Societies* are reproduced in full in Outler, *John Wesley*, 180–81. See also Watson, *Class Meeting*, appendix E.

37. Frank Whaling's identification of five main streams in the Revival is extremely helpful in this regard. See *Wesleys*, 26ff.

38. "A Farther Appeal to Men of Reason and Religion," in *Oxford Edition*, vol. 11, *The Appeals*, 306.

39. "A Plain Account of the People Called Methodists," in *Works*, 8:249.

40. Martin Schmidt makes an important observation in this regard, which may explain why Wesley increasingly found himself at odds with the Moravians: "John Wesley for his part . . . left his followers in their original situations [in contrast with] German Pietism, which set out to make the rebirth or new creation of the whole man and humanity visible in an adequate external form and to extend the work of God into the material sphere, the community of Brethren determining the social structure. Wesley gave full right to the order of creation. . . ." (*John Wesley: A Theological Biography*, vol. 2, pt. 1 [Nashville: Abingdon, 1972], 99).

41. *Journal*, 2:528.

42. *Works*, 13:259.

43. "A Plain Account of the People Called Methodists," *Works*, 8:253.

44. Ibid., 254.

45. Ibid., 254f.

46. Both women and men served as class leaders, except where the class consisted of men only. This was a mark of the role of women in the movement as a whole.

47. The most detailed contemporary account of a class meeting, and of many other early Methodist practices, is in Joseph Nightingale, *A Portraiture of Methodism* . . . (London, 1807), 181ff.

48. *Oxford Edition*, vol. 26, *Letters II:1740–1755*, ed. Frank Baker (Oxford: Clarendon, 1982), 95.

49. *Journal*, 3:449–50.

50. See Watson, *Class Meeting*, appendix L.

51. *Journal*, 2:315.

52. Ibid., 329–30.

53. Outler, *John Wesley*, 177ff.; Whaling, *Wesleys*, 108ff.

54. In a striking analogy, Wesley describes in his sermon, "The New Birth," the similarities between a baby in the womb and a person who has yet to be "born again." See *Works*, 6:69f. This sermon will appear in volume 2 of the *Bicentennial Edition*, ed. Albert C. Outler, forthcoming from Abingdon.

55. "Minutes of the Second Annual Conference, 1745," in Outler, *John Wesley*, 148–53.

56. "A Plain Account of the People Called Methodists," *Works*, 8:257–58.

57. See, for example, Wesley, *Journal*, 1:377; 2:121ff. The best source book on the lovefeast remains Frank Baker's monograph, *Methodism and the Love-Feast* (London: Epworth, 1957).

58. "A Plain Account of the People Called Methodists," *Works*, 8:260.

59. Ibid.

60. "A Plain Account of Christian Perfection," in Whaling, *Wesleys*, 335–36. See also *Works*, 11:402–3.

61. *The Letters of the Rev. John Wesley, A.M.*, standard edition, 8 vols., ed. John Telford (London: Epworth, 1931), 8:254.

62. "The Large Minutes," in *Works*, 8:322–24.

63. *Oxford Edition*, vol. 7, *A Collection of Hymns*, 90–92. Cf. the list of contents, 77f., which differs in some details from the list cited from my personal copy. See also the very good selection of 121 hymns reproduced in Whaling, *Wesleys*, 175–295.

64. *Arminian Magazine: Consisting of Extracts and Original Treatises on Universal Redemption* (London, 1778–97); renamed the *Methodist Magazine*, 1798–1821; further renamed the *Wesleyan Methodist Magazine*, 1822–1913.

65. Thomas Jackson, ed., *Lives of Early Methodist Preachers*, 4th ed., 6 vols. (London: Wesleyan Conference Office, 1871). An expanded edition, edited by John Telford, includes some annotation and additional biographical material, but lacks the fine index of the fourth edition: *Wesley's Veterans: Lives of Early Methodist Preachers Told by Themselves*, 7 vols. (London: Robert Culley; vols. 1 & 2, n.d.; vols 3–7, 1912–14).

66. This follows the narrative in *Wesley's Veterans*, 3:1–197, passages cited passim.

67. "In the ancient Church, every one who was baptized communicated daily. So in the Acts we read, they 'all continued daily in the breaking of bread, and in prayer.'

"But in latter times many have affirmed that the Lord's Supper is not a converting, but a confirming ordinance.

"And among us it has been diligently taught that none but those who are converted, who have received the Holy Ghost, who are believers in the full sense, ought to communicate.

"But experience shows the gross falsehood of that assertion that the Lord's Supper is not a converting ordinance. Ye are the witnesses. For many now present know, the very beginning of your conversion to God (perhaps, in some, the first deep conviction) was wrought at the Lord's Supper. Now, one single instance of this overthrows the whole assertion.

"The falsehood of the other assertion appears both from Scripture precept and example. Our Lord commanded those very men who were then unconverted, who had not received the Holy Ghost, who (in the full sense of the word) were not believers, to do this 'in remembrance of' Him. Here the precept is clear. And to these He delivered the elements with His own hands. Here is example equally indisputable" (*Journal*, 2:360–61).

68. This follows the narrative in *Wesley's Veterans*, 6:113–97, passages cited passim.

69. Haime's ministry among the dragoons, and his subsequent itinerancy as one of Wesley's preachers, is related in *Wesley's Veterans*, 1:11–59.

70. See above.

71. Years which, of course, placed him in the turmoil of the Revolutionary War, though on which he declared it was not his intention "to give a detail, or my judgment . . . suffice it to say, that the business belongs to the historian" (*Wesley's Veterans*, 6:175).

72. On this, see Gordon S. Wakefield, *The Spiritual Life in the Methodist Tradition 1791–1945* (London: Epworth, 1966), 44ff.

73. On this, see Robert Currie, *Methodism Divided: A Study in the Sociology of Ecumenicalism* (London: Faber & Faber, 1968). The relatedness of Methodist spirituality to these social changes remains an area of dispute in nineteenth century historiography. See the excellent introductory chapter in Robert Moore, *Pitmen, Preachers and Politics: The Effects of Methodism in a Durham Mining Community* (London: Cambridge University Press, 1974), 1–27.

74. Wakefield, *Spiritual Life*, 56ff.

75. See, for example, "Thoughts on Christian Perfection" (1760), in Outler *John Wesley*, 283–98; "Cautions and Directions Given to the Greatest Professors [i.e. of Christian Perfection] in The Methodist Societies" (1762), ibid., 298–305; and, of course, "A Plain Account of Christian Perfection" (1766), in Whaling, *Wesleys*, 299–377.

76. See, for example, the letter to his brother Charles in June 1766, cited, with transcriptions from Wesley's shorthand, in Richard P. Heitzenrater, *The Elusive Mr. Wesley*, 2 vols. (Nashville: Abingdon, 1984), 1:198–200.

77. A fine example of Fletcher's craftsmanship can be seen in his exposition of whether Christian perfection is gradual or instantaneous. His answer is disarmingly simple: "Both ways are good." See "The Last Check to Antinomianism," in *The Works of the Rev. John Fletcher, Late Vicar of Madeley*, 8 vols. (London: John Mason, 1846), 5:172ff.

78. Jonathan Edwards' account of this phenomenon in *A Faithful Narrative* made an impression on Wesley when he read it in 1739, and he subsequently published edited versions of several of Edwards' works. See Outler, *John Wesley*, 15f. and note.

79. See, for example, *The Works of Jonathan Edwards*, general editor Perry Miller, vol. 2, *Religious Affections*, ed. John E. Smith (New Haven: Yale University Press, 1959), 205ff.

80. See Bernard A. Weisberger, *They Gathered at the River: The Story of the Great Revivalists and Their Impact upon Religion in America* (Boston: Little, Brown, 1958), 43ff.

81. Theodore L. Agnew, "Methodism on the Frontier," in *The History of American Methodism*, ed. Emory Stevens Bucke, 3 vols. (Nashville: Abingdon, 1964), 1:506.

82. Ibid., 508.

83. Cf. *The Autobiography of Peter Cartwright*, centennial edition, intr. Charles A. Wallis (Nashville: Abingdon, 1956), 45–46; and John Wesley, *Journal*, 2:187–91, 139–40, and passim. See also Sydney G. Dimond, *The Psychology of the Methodist Revival: An Empirical and Descriptive Study* (London: Oxford University Press, 1926).

84. Cited in Weisberger, *They Gathered at the River*, 29.

85. Cited in William Warren Sweet, *The Story of Religion in America* (repr., Grand Rapids: Baker, 1973), 228–29.

86. John Leland Peters, *Christian Perfection and American Methodism* (Nashville: Abingdon, 1956), 97ff. This volume is an important contribution to the study of the doctrine per se, quite apart from its helpful focus on the North American context.

87. Nathan Bangs, *Letters to Young Ministers of the Gospel, on the Importance and Method of Study* (New York: N. Bangs and J. Emory, 1826). Most noteworthy in their writings were Clarke's monumental *Commentary on the Bible*, completed in 1826, and Watson's *Theological Institutes*, published in 1829. Both works have gone through a number of American editions.

88. Phoebe Palmer, *The Way of Holiness* (Kansas City, Mo.: Publishing House of the Pentecostal Church of the Nazarene, n.d.), 34–36. A lengthier extract, comprising sections I and II, can be found in Thomas A. Langford, *Wesleyan Theology: A Sourcebook* (Durham, N.C.: Labyrinth, 1984), 86–90. This volume is a valuable introduction to the writings of many whose names have appeared thus far in our narrative—Wesley, Fletcher, Clarke, Bangs, Watson, Asbury—as well as contemporary Methodist authors.

89. See his *Lectures on Revivals of Religion*, ed. William G. McLoughlin (Cambridge: Harvard University Press, Belknap Press, 1960).

90. Cited in Timothy L. Smith, *Revivalism and Social Reform* (New York: Harper & Row, 1965), 103ff. Cf. George M. Marsden, *Fundamentalism and American Culture: The Shaping of Twentieth Century Evangelicalism 1870–1925* (New York: Oxford University Press, 1980), 72ff.

91. *Reflections on Revival (1845–46)*, comp. Donald Dayton (Minneapolis: Bethany Fellowship, 1979), 113ff. See also Donald W. Dayton, *Discovering an Evangelical Heritage* (New York: Harper & Row, 1976), 15ff.

92. See Smith, *Revivalism*, 148ff., 178ff., 204ff.

93. Ibid., 211ff.

94. See Dayton, *Evangelical Heritage*, 73–84.

95. See the seminal volume by James H. Cone, *The Spirituals and the Blues: An Interpretation* (New York: Seabury, 1972).

96. On this, see Marsden, *Fundamentalism*, 72–101. See also Timothy L. Smith, "The Holiness Crusade," in Bucke, *American Methodism*, 2:608–27; and "A Historical and Contemporary Appraisal of Wesleyan Theology," in *A Contemporary Wesleyan Theology: Biblical, Systematic, and Practical*, ed. Charles W. Carter, 2 vols. (Grand Rapids: Zondervan, Francis Asbury Press, 1983), 1:88–94.

97. See J. C. Pollock, *The Keswick Story: The Authorized History of the Keswick Convention* (London: Hodder & Stoughton, 1964).

98. Dayton, *Evangelical Heritage*, 116ff.

99. The bishops' address to the General Conference of the Methodist Episcopal Church South in 1894 was heavy with innuendo:

"The privilege of believers to attain unto the state of entire sanctification or perfect love, and to abide therein, is a well known teaching of Methodism. Witnesses to this experience have never been wanting in our Church, though few in comparison with the whole membership. Among them have been men and women of beautiful consistency and seraphic ardor, jewels of the Church. Let the doctrine still be proclaimed, and the experience still be testified.

"But there has sprung up among us a party with holiness as a watchword; they have holiness associations, holiness meetings, holiness preachers, holiness evangelists, and holiness property. Religious experience is represented as if it consists of only two steps, the first step out of condemnation into peace, and the next step into Christian perfection. . . . We do not question the sincerity and zeal of these brethren; we desire the Church to profit by their earnest preaching and godly example; but we deplore their teaching and methods in so far as they claim a monopoly of the experience, practice, and advocacy of holiness, and separate from the body of ministers and disciples." (Cited in Peters, *Christian Perfection*, 147–48.)

100. Ibid., 148f.

101. These include: the Academy for Spiritual Formation, for the systematic study of spirituality; the Disciplined Order of Christ, a nationwide organization committed to the spiritual disciplines of the faith; and the United Methodist Renewal Services Fellowship, a network of charismatic groups in the United Methodist Church.

102. See David Lowes Watson, *Accountable Discipleship* (Nashville: Discipleship Resources, 1984).

103. Wesley, "A Plain Account of Christian Perfection," in Whaling, *Wesleys*, 335–36.

Evangelical Spirituality

A Church Historian's Perspective

Richard F. Lovelace

About three decades ago, as I began to study movements of spiritual awakening in Protestantism, I had a scholarly awakening. I woke up to the fact that spirituality was a drastically neglected subject among scholars. Christian experience was treated as an optional dimension of Christian life, a sort of flavor additive that had its place in personal devotion and pastoral work but was marginal as a subject of serious reflection. Scholars focused on the outward shell of the Church's theology and structures but overlooked the vital force that helped make the shell and determine its forms.

Evangelicals did not even have a category of spiritual theology, as Roman Catholics did, dealing with the historical theology of Christian experience. New life in Christ was supposedly the core of our tradition. Where had we mislaid our central heritage?[1]

Roman Catholics, on the other hand, produced mounds of pious literature but not much in the way of solid critical analysis and reflection. One might have expected Thomas Merton to trigger a movement of renewed interest in spirituality. But this did not happen immediately. Merton's own spirituality became increasingly (and healthily) engaged with worldly issues, but the Christian world did not respond by giving greater attention to spirituality.[2]

Now, a generation after Merton, there is a growing crescendo of practical and scholarly reflection on this subject. In the last

This essay first appeared in *Journal of the Evangelical Theological Society* 31 (March 1988): 25–35. Used by permission.

decade scores of works have appeared in spiritual theology from every perspective: Catholic, Orthodox, Lutheran, Reformed, anabaptist, Wesleyan, evangelical, Jungian, liberationist, and even liberal. Spirituality is finally getting the scholarly attention it deserves.

As a Church historian and spiritual theologian, I look at the values and the needs of modern evangelical spirituality against the background of its historical development from the Reformation onward. I see tremendous strengths in this heritage that we ought to recover, along with grievous current weaknesses that we should try to correct.

I. Reformation Spirituality

The spirituality of Luther and Calvin is a reaction against western Catholic spirituality. Let me first point out the features that aroused reaction.

The absence of justification as a theological category separate from sanctification is a dominant factor shaping pre-Reformation spirituality. Luther felt that the spiritual lives of all Catholics, from the monks and nuns to the most retiring layperson, were affected by this justification gap. He also believed that this missing spiritual dimension virtually determined the whole shape of the medieval Church: "Ah, if the article on justification hadn't fallen, the brotherhoods, pilgrimages, masses, invocation of saints, etc., would have found no place in the church. If it falls again (which may God prevent!) these idols will return."[3]

This is an interesting comment on the vital force of theology and spirituality in shaping structures. The core doctrines of spiritual theology determine the shape of spirituality. But spirituality then amplifies the force of these doctrines, and it energizes and projects their shape on the whole of theology and Church structure.

How did the absence of justification lead to dysfunction in medieval spirituality? Catholics believed that they were justified in the process of being sanctified. Since sanctification is never perfect and always in peril during our lifetime, they were imperfectly assured of their salvation. Serious believers could cure this uneasiness by martyrdom, or by the bloodless martyrdom of ascetic spirituality.

Sanctification, bearing an unnatural weight because it was expected to pacify the believer's conscience, was a subject of extraordinary concern. But the ascetic method of sanctification was by amputation, not by healing. If the believer is having trouble with sex, give up sexual relations. If he or she is having difficulty with covetousness, give up private property. If he or she is tempted by power, give up independence. The monastery and the nunnery are sanctification machines that guarantee the surest victory over the sinful use of money, sex and power.[4]

Monasteries are an eastern religious instrument, not a Biblical format. And the medieval view of sanctification was subject to other eastern intrusions. The desert fathers are typically Hellenistic, if not Buddhist, in their assumption that spirit and matter—and especially soul and body—are enemies. "The body kills me," says Macarius, "so I will kill it!"[5]

The western mystical tradition, from Augustine through Bernard and the Rhineland mystics, moved beyond this spiritual masochism to see that mortifying sin was the goal of sanctification and that this was not usually helped by punishing the body. But ascetic mysticism characteristically views spiritual growth as the result of hard work. A central image of this literature is the ladder. One starts at the bottom, and there are thirteen steps that must be climbed, for instance, to move from pride to humility.[6]

Or, at the very least, there are the three steps of the Triple Way: the purging of sin from one's life, then the illumination of the Holy Spirit, and then union with God. There are important lessons for Protestants in this structure, but we must make two observations: (1) that first step (purgation of sin) is a big one; (2) faith in Jesus Christ, and even the mention of the Redeemer, are scarce commodities in this literature. It is overwhelmingly theocentric rather than Christocentric, and it is full of nervous instructions to believers trying to cross the gap between man and God on their own footpaths.

This is not to agree with the common Protestant prejudice that nothing deeply spiritual can be going on among mystics and in monasteries. The problem is somewhat different: Spiritual experiences which for the Catholic doctors seem rare and hard to come by—the awesome summits of acquired or infused contemplation—appear to evangelical Protestants as common and routine possessions found among the laity, part of the birthright acquired by faith in Christ.

And this is the genius of Reformation spirituality. It assumes that the simplest believer leaps to the top of the spiritual ladder simply by realistic faith in Jesus Christ. Consistent Protestants start every day at the top of the ladder, receiving by faith what only God can give and what cannot be achieved by human efforts: assurance of salvation, and the guiding presence of the Holy Spirit. They may slip down a few rungs during the course of the day, but the way up again is not by climbing. It is by the vault of faith.

Similarly Luther stands the *via triplex* on its head. Union with Christ, received by faith, is the foundation of evangelical spirituality, not the final achievement. The illumination of the Holy Spirit then comes in to break up our darkness and show us our sins. Purgation of sin, finally, is a sanctification process in which we are led by the Spirit to recognize, confess and put to death the particular patterns of sin that are present in our characteristic fallen nature.

It seems obvious to evangelicals that this is a Biblical way to look at spiritual growth. The disciples, after all, were not Essene monks any more than Jesus was. They did not wear animal skins and eat locusts, like John. They were clumsy learners and listeners on the track of faith, not chanting monks pursuing solitude. They were annoyingly dense in their spiritual response throughout the gospels. They were cured, however, not by keeping spiritual disciplines but by an infusion of the Holy Spirit, a whirlwind restructuring their minds, imparting a spirituality that they could never have achieved. As Paul puts it: "Did you receive the Spirit by observing the law, or by believing what you heard? Are you so foolish? After beginning with the Spirit, are you now trying to attain your goal by human effort? . . . Does God give you his Spirit and work miracles among you because you observe the law, or because you believe what you heard?" (Gal 3:2–5).

Luther's teaching cut through the Roman Catholic spirituality of achievement by stressing the thing that was most important to Jesus: Christ-centered faith. Evangelical piety is first of all a spirituality of faith as opposed to one of achievement. Responding to an ascetic model of Christian experience, Protestantism adopted an essentially pentecostal or charismatic model. Spirituality comes not through laborious cultivation of the human spirit but through the gracious gift of the Holy Spirit. It is a spirituality that flourishes in the atmosphere of faith. It is not worked up through ascetic exercises but infused directly, as at Pentecost. In Roman Catholic terms, infused contemplation is thus the common inheritance of all laity and clergy and not the private prerogative of those with ascetic vocations.[7]

P. T. Forsyth summarized Luther's approach:

> *Perfection is not sanctity but faith.* . . . It is a perfection of attitude rather than of achievement, of relation more than of realization, of truth more than of behaviour. . . . It is not a matter of our behaviour before God the Judge, but of our relation to God the Saviour. . . . It is a fatal mistake to think of holiness as a possession which we have distinct from our faith. . . . Every Christian experience is an experience of faith; that is, it is an experience of what we have not. . . . Faith is always in opposition to seeing, possessing, experiencing. A faith wholly experimental has its perils. It varies too much with our subjectivity. It is not our experience of holiness that makes us believe in the Holy Ghost. It is a matter of faith that we are God's children; there is plenty of experience in us against it. . . . We are not saved by the love we exercise, but by the Love we trust.[8]

Luther believed that Catholic spirituality imposed a barrier between the believer and God. Because it leaves the believer in partial darkness, unaware of the imputed righteousness of Christ, the theology of Trent

leaves weak Christians feeling distant from the Holy Spirit. It discour-
ages the laity, and wherever it prevails in modern Catholicism the result
is spiritual deadness, as Henri Nouwen has stated.[9]

The Catholic critique of this pentecostal model of spirituality, on the
other hand, is that it too often seems to lead Christians to that life of
casual disinterest in spiritual growth that Dietrich Bonhoeffer defined as
"cheap grace."[10] "Things are admirably arranged," as Heinrich Heine said.
"God likes forgiving sins, and I like committing them."

Catholics could point to another text in Paul that sets up a complementary ascetic model of spirituality: "Do you not know that in a race
all the runners run, but only one gets the prize? . . . Everyone who com-
petes in the games goes into strict training. . . . Therefore I do not run
like a man running aimlessly; I do not fight like a man beating the air.
No, I beat my body and make it my slave so that after I have preached
to others, I myself will not be disqualified for the prize" (1 Cor 9:24–27).
Initial experience of the Spirit may be a gift and not an achievement. But
continued fellowship with him may require effort.

The Reformers shied away from spiritual exercises as a road to growth,
though they did stress the need to hear and read scripture in order to
nourish faith and the need to pray in order to express faith. John Calvin
also balanced Luther's emphasis on justification by an intensive treatment of sanctification. Out of the material in the application sections of
Paul's letters, Calvin carefully drew an understanding of spiritual growth
through mortification of sin and vivification of every aspect of the personality by the Spirit's releasing work. Calvin's later disciple, John Owen,
went so far as to say that "the vigor and power of spiritual life are dependent upon mortification of sin."[11] The Reformed tradition thus made a
strong effort to rule out cheap grace.

II. Puritanism, Pietism and the Evangelical Awakenings

The quotation from Owen brings us to a second stage in the development of evangelical spirituality: the efforts of Calvinist Puritans and
Lutheran pietists to "complete the Reformation" through "reforming our
lives as well as our doctrines." These movements appear to be an ascetic
movement within Protestantism reacting against cheap grace. Puritans
wanted congregations of "visible saints" who were not simply "notionally
orthodox" but were spiritually alive.[12]

Puritans continued to develop Calvin's emphasis on sanctification. Regeneration, the first stage of sanctification, was accented. The "born again"
theme of the anabaptists was integrated into evangelical spirituality.

Gordon Wakefield comments that Catholic spirituality had treated regeneration as a brief baptismal overture to the three-act play of lifelong sanctification. But Puritans identified regeneration with conscious conversion and made conversion into a long first act, to which the rest of Christian growth was almost an epilogue. They insisted on a preliminary "law-work" that marinated the sinner in prolonged reflection on personal sin. Potential converts were searched out and almost pre-sanctified by the time they had found their way to justifying faith.[13]

Assurance of salvation was a crucial focus for Puritans and pietists, a precious gift that could not easily be attained and could easily be lost. Not that salvation itself could be lost, as in the Roman Catholic approach. But Protestants persisting in serious sin were virtually required to lose their assurance.[14]

More legalistic Puritans taught assurance through the inspection of works. More evangelical ones opted for assurance through the inner testimony of the Holy Spirit.[15] Though both approaches have Biblical warrant, Luther would probably have been uneasy with both if pursued apart from an outward-gazing reliance on Christ, grasping salvation through faith alone. Puritans were so unsure that this original thrust of the Reformation was sufficient to guard against cheap grace that they might have called Luther an antinomian if he had appeared among them.

This points to the fact that Puritanism was leaning toward ascetic legalism as it sought to compete with Counter-Reformation piety and to create a distinctive Protestant spirituality that would rule out cheap grace. Puritanism sought to graft patristic and medieval spirituality onto the Reformation base of justification by faith. And there were times when that base was obscured. Max Weber is correct in calling Puritanism "innerweltliche Askese" (inner-worldly asceticism), an effort to turn ordinary Protestant laypersons into married, unenclosed monastics practicing Scriptural mysticism.

There were problems with this venture. Modern fundamentalist spirituality has inherited some of the Tertullianesque casuistry of the Puritans, which ruled out stage plays, cosmetics, dancing, and games of chance.[16]

On the other hand, there was a certain grandeur in the effort to develop a laity as dedicated to religious knowledge and prayer as the better sort of monks and nuns. Modern evangelical spirituality has retained many instruments pioneered during this era. The "quiet time" at the outset of the day springs directly from the Scripture reading and reflection prescribed for Puritan laity. The Puritans added graces at meals, prayer with spouses, and household devotions at the evening meal. Beyond this they recommended continual short prayers during the day, and also "occasional reflections"—mystical insights drawn from the symbolic meaning of events and objects, a devotion tracing back to the medieval Victorine theologians. Puritans invented the use of spiritual diaries as a kind of Protestant substitute for the confessional.

It is not surprising that Puritan writings are saturated with references to patristic authors. There are more references to the fathers than to Luther and Calvin. Puritanism is thus a bridge movement in which modern evangelicals and Roman Catholics may find spiritual common roots. Cotton Mather's omnivorous spiritual appetite smuggled in many Catholic devices: short ejaculatory prayers, vows and intentions of piety, and day- and night-long vigils. Mather also promoted new instruments of Protestant spirituality such as small group meetings for prayer and religious conversation.[17]

Puritanism pioneered the exploration of the neglected field of pneumatology in the massive treatises of John Owen and in Jonathan Edwards' theology of spiritual illumination. The flavor of Puritan spirituality is conveyed in titles like Owen's *The Christian's Communion with the Father, Son and Holy Ghost* and Robert Bolton's *Directions for a Comfortable Walking with God*.

Both Puritanism and pietism define mystical communion with God as a normal occurrence among and for all Christians. Nicholas Byfield says of the Puritan believer:

> The Holy Ghost at some time falls upon him, & sets him all on a fire . . . both of sudden and violent indignation at sinne . . . as also the fire of holy affections. . . . He doth feele his heart oftentimes on a sudden surprised with strange impressions, sometimes of sorrow, sometimes of feare and awefull dread of God; some times of fervent desires after God; some times of strong resolutions of holy duties to be done by him. . . . He feeles at some times the unspeakable and glorious ioyes of the Holy Ghost . . . such as by effect make him more humble, and vile in his owne eies, and doe inflame him to an high degree of the love of God and goodnesse, which illusions can never doe.[18]

This is not a mysticism that is transintellectual in the Pseudo-Dionysian tradition. It is anchored in conscious reflection on Biblical texts. Still, no one can read this literature without thinking immediately of Teresa and John of the Cross. Thomas Goodwin even has a Biblicist version of *The Dark Night of the Soul: A Child of Light Walking in Darkness*, a treatise of "divine desertions."

The goal of Puritan spirituality was "the power of godliness" in opposition to "a form of godliness denying the power thereof." Puritan "live orthodoxy" was equally opposed to lifeless traditionalism on the right and heterodoxy on the left. (Puritans, and especially Lutheran pietists, got attacked from both sides and felt sure they were on the right track when this happened.)[19]

This ethos is carried over into the evangelicalism of the first and second awakenings, which are Puritanism and pietism on the march, replicating their vision of individual spirituality through the conversion of the masses. Awakening spirituality was not simply the perfecting of saintly individuals, however. It involved waiting on God in corporate prayer for pentecostal outpourings of the Holy Spirit, to energize the Church and form it into troop movements assaulting the kingdom of darkness.

Awakening spirituality was consciously ecumenical, recognizing that God has more important goals than refining the perfect theology through this or that small group of elect theorizers. Discernment of the Spirit at work across the boundaries of Calvinism, Lutheranism and Arminianism is a mark of eighteenth- and nineteenth-century evangelicalism.

Count Zinzendorf enlarged the spiritual dimension of community far beyond the anabaptist and Puritan experiments in this area. Corporate prayer for Church-wide spiritual awakening and worldwide missionary outreach was the core of Zinzendorf's Herrnhut community. Herrnhut was an intentional community deliberately designed as an ecumenical symbol, bringing together Lutherans, Moravian Hussites, Calvinists, Catholics and sectarian Protestants in a kind of recapitulation of Acts 1, in which all the types of Christians then existing were gathered for prayer in the upper room. Small groups for mutual confession of sin and intercession broke down the theological partitions between different kinds of Christians, and a round-the-clock prayer—a Protestant equivalent of the monastic canonical hours—paved the way for Herrnhut's experience of "baptism in the Holy Spirit" on August 13, 1727.

Zinzendorf called this event "Herrnhut's Pentecost," and after this the community exploded in mission, producing tentmaking teams for foreign missions and renewal teams visiting the historic denominations. These included Rome, for alone among the Protestant leaders of his time Zinzendorf viewed Catholicism not as antichrist but as just another disordered denomination in need of renewal.[20]

A dimension of evangelical spirituality enlarged during the awakenings was concern for moral and social reform. The Wesleyan movement reached the poor in England and articulated their concerns to the "Evangelical United Front," which included Anglican leaders like John Newton. Evangelical laity—leaders who spent three hours daily in intercessory prayer—sought not only to evangelize individuals but also to change society, to abolish slavery and wage-slavery. A socially progressive mindset, an awakened sensitivity to information, and extensive prayer drove the transforming impact of the second awakening in England and America.[21]

A further development of the Wesleyan impulse was the rise of pentecostal spirituality in the early twentieth century. This continued the characteristic thrust of evangelical spirituality: the activation of the laity.

Belief that every believer has supernatural gifts for building the whole body accented the lay activism of post-Moodyan fundamentalism. Pentecostal and charismatic spirituality kept alive the radical concern for experiencing contact with God that had characterized Puritans and awakeners. More than any other part of modern evangelicalism, this tradition has continued to promote corporate prayer for spiritual awakening in the Church. David Du Plessis continued Zinzendorf's concern for unitive spiritual awakening in the whole visible Church, though few charismatics seem to have understood his concerns.[22]

III. The Spirituality of Modern Evangelicalism

Against this historical background we can make some evaluation of the current state of evangelical spirituality.

Like American liberalism, the modern evangelical movement has a weakened sense of the holiness of God and the depth of personal sin. The Reformation stress on justification has been retained, and also the Puritan motif of the need for regeneration. But the process of being born again is much easier than the Puritans made it: a simple immediate response of faith and commitment, often after a very short presentation of the gospel. The possibility of losing the assurance of one's salvation is not even intimated. In fact, converts are urged to believe they are saved as though this were one of the main doctrines of the faith. The themes of holiness and continued sanctification are very much muted compared to the Puritan and awakening eras. Evangelicals are once again suffering from a sanctification gap.[23]

Modern fundamentalism inherited and emphasized one of the weaker sides of the Puritan tradition, its sectarian legalism. Fundamentalists talk about the authority of Scripture, but their spirituality is captive to revivalist traditionalism.[24]

Neo-evangelicals have developed a better theology of culture, but they generally reflect a rationalistic de-emphasis on spirituality, or even in some cases an active distrust of Christian experience as a source of liberalism. In evangelical parachurch groups and congregations, however, a simplified lay spirituality involving Scripture study and prayer is vigorously promoted.

The charismatic renewal continues to express the mystical spirituality of the Puritan and awakening eras, but often without the rational and theological checks against error and credulity maintained by evangelicals. As a consequence, charismatics have some of the problems of the radical spiritualists in the anabaptist and Puritan left wing. Gifts of the Spirit are more prominent than the call to sanctification. The charismatic garden has a luxuriant overgrowth of theological weeds, including the health-and-wealth gospel, the most virulent form of the American heresy that Christianity guarantees worldly success. A fuzzy and unstructured ecumenism lives side by side with rampant sectarianism.

The division of the evangelical mind in the fundamentalist-modernist controversy has left modern evangelicals with a depressed consciousness of social sin and a weakened prophetic emphasis compared to mainline Protestants and Roman Catholics. Evangelicals are captivated by conservative economic ideologies. The funding structure of the movement is tied to a laity that is not socially progressive, does not pray three hours a day, and does not donate its resources with the generosity of the lay leaders in the second awakening. What was a movement of Christian humanism has become anti-intellectual. The expensive tasks of forming new Christian universities is neglected, and Christian educators, as my readers surely know, are underpaid and overworked.

This limits the spiritual force of evangelicalism in social reform and cultural transformation. Some important moral issues are being addressed by right-wing evangelicals. But the kind of impact made by evangelical Protestants in the nineteenth century is mainly visible in Catholic circles today. Evangelical missionary Guillermo Cook comments that in Latin America, Catholics and Protestants have traded places. Evangelicals are cozying up to dictators and vending a wholly spiritual salvation, while Catholics are breaking the Church's alliance with wealth and military power and developing a Biblical spirituality that stands up against structural injustice.[25]

The sanctification gap has been publicized during the last year through the scandals among media leaders. This election year will continue to expose every spiritual weakness in our movement, as Americans see a reflection of the divided mind of American Protestantism in the campaigns of Pat Robertson and Jesse Jackson. Humanist counterattacks on the religious right are producing the worst public-relations situation the evangelical movement has ever endured—much worse than the discrediting of fundamentalism during the 1920s, of which George Marsden has recently reminded us.[26]

Under these pressures, what can we do to reinvigorate evangelical spirituality? I have three suggestions.

1. *We may need to move back toward the ascetic model of spirituality.* The great spiritual awakenings have come when both the ascetic and pentecostal models have been in force—where there is a balance in the stress on faith and works, on justification and sanctification. During almost every awakening Catholics and Protestants have drawn closer to one another as they are doing now, because they have been moving toward one another's par-

tial models of spirituality to recover Scriptural balance. It now appears
evident that Protestant evangelicalism has drifted off course into cheap
grace. The new interest in spiritual disciplines shows that we are trying
to recover balance. This will be most fruitful if we also begin to explore
the little-known areas of holiness and continued sanctification.

   2. *We may need to challenge more, and comfort less, in our evangelism and disci-*
pleship. We need to make it harder for our people to retain assurance of
salvation when they move into serious sin. The Roman Catholic and
Wesleyan models would call for announcing that they have forfeited
their salvation. The Reformed model that prevails among evangelicals
calls for us to remind them that some plants appear to bear fruit in bad
soil but ultimately wither because they had no deep rootage, because
there was no real conversion in the first place. We need to tell some persons who think they have gotten saved to get lost. The Puritans were
Biblically realistic about this. We have become sloppy and sentimental
in promoting assurance under any circumstances.

   3. *We need to listen hard—because God is speaking to us loudly and clearly about the*
road to recovering the spiritual depth of classical evangelicalism.

   We need to listen carefully to one another. Fundamentalists, evangelicals and charismatics all have preserved parts of the genetic pool of the
evangelical tradition, although usually the good genes are bonded to bad
genes. If we speak the truth in love and listen in humility, we can chip
away one another's deformities and recover some measure of the spiritual
depth our movement used to have.

   We need to listen carefully to other kinds of Christians. Mainline
Protestants, Roman Catholics and Orthodox believers have preserved
Biblical values that we lack. And they often have clear insights about our
faults that could help us toward repentance.

   We need to listen to history—the history of our own movement, and
the body of tradition that has nourished other movements. The early
fathers, the medieval mystics, the spiritual doctors of the Reformation and
Counter-Reformation, the leaders of the awakening eras, the uneven
prophets of liberal social reform—all of these can force us back toward
Biblical balance and authentic spirituality.

   We need to listen to Scripture against this background. Our own stale
and partial contextualizations of the Biblical text need to be broken up as
we discover new implications of truth that our own orthodox self-satisfaction may have obscured.

   Finally, we need to listen to the unfolding record of current events.
Every day may bring new insight into our need for repentance and
renewal, or an encouraging sign of spiritual vigor in places we might not
expect it. Evangelicals have experienced an amazing resurgence in the

past several decades in terms of the multiplication of our leadership. Now God is calling us to get serious in our spiritual lives. I am sobered by our recent failures, but I am still confident that we will respond to that call.

Notes

1. I have reflected more extensively on this problem in the preface to *Dynamics of Spiritual Life* (Downers Grove, Ill.: InterVarsity, 1979).

2. This is not to minimize the solid contributions of P. Pourrat, L. Bouyer, and a few others who have explored the history of Christian spirituality from a Roman Catholic perspective. But in 1980 when I surveyed Roman Catholic educational institutions, most seemed unaware of spiritual theology and few even had functioning analogues in the disciplines of pastoral theology, evangelism, and spiritual formation. It appears that Thomas Merton was able to make the transition from a kind of ascetic, pietistic, Catholic chauvinism to the keen observation of world events through the lens of a well-developed ecumenical sensibility, which we see in works like *Conjectures of a Guilty Bystander*, without losing his spiritual rootage in the Augustinian contemplative tradition. But a whole generation of Catholics seems to have attempted to dive into the world without maintaining any transcendental airhose. Perhaps one of their motivations in exploring the world has been their annoyance with asceticism and other toxic residua in the received tradition. Mainline Protestants and evangelicals after 1960 have had much the same experience in reacting to weaknesses in their own spiritualities.

3. Martin Luther, *Table Talk*, ed. T. G. Tappert (Philadelphia: Fortress, 1967), 340.

4. My favorite analysis of the problems and provisional advantages of asceticism is still H. B. Workman, *The Evolution of the Monastic Ideal* (Boston: Beacon, 1962).

5. *Palladius: The Lausiac History* (Westminster: Newman, 1965), 58–67.

6. The reference here is to Bernard's *Thirteen Steps*.

7. Sister M. Murphy, a Catholic charismatic who has worked closely with George Gallup in recent years, comments that charismatic renewal is simply infused contemplation made available to everybody in the Church. Note that Leo Cardinal Suenens, early in the sessions of the Second Vatican Council, stood up against the traditional teaching that the charismatic gifts had ended with the apostolic era on the grounds that without spiritual charisms broadly available among the laity the priesthood of believers could not be achieved.

8. P. T. Forsyth, *Christian Perfection* (London, 1899), 56, 57–59, 73.

9. H. J. M. Nouwen, *Gracias* (San Francisco: Harper, 1983).

10. D. Bonhoeffer, *The Cost of Discipleship* (New York: Macmillan, 1959), 35–47.

11. J. Owen, *Of the Mortification of Sin in Believers*, in *Works*, ed. T. Russell (London: Richard Baynes, 1823), 7:350.

12. Cf. E. S. Morgan, *Visible Saints* (New York, 1963).

13. G. Wakefield, *Puritan Devotion* (London, 1957), 160–61.

14. *Westminster Confession of Faith* 20.4.

15. Thomas Shepherd is the most famous Puritan favoring assurance through inspection of works. John Cotton and Richard Sibbes exemplify the more evangelical strand who grounded assurance on faith and the internal testimony of the Spirit.

16. For a good account of the roots of modern fundamentalism's dos and don'ts see T. Wood, *English Casuistical Divinity in the Seventeenth Century* (London: SPCK, 1952), 64.

17. For an account of Mather's surprisingly ecumenical piety, see R. F. Lovelace, "The Machinery of Piety," in *American Pietism of Cotton Mather: Origins of American Evangelicalism* (Grand Rapids: Christian University Press, 1979).

18. N. Byfield, *The Marrow of the Oracles of God* (London, 1630), 172–74.

19. See Lovelace, "Live Orthodoxy," in *Dynamics*.

20. For the best study of Zinzendorf as awakener and ecumenist, see A. J. Lewis, *Zinzendorf the Ecumenical Pioneer* (London: SCM, 1962).

21. For the best accounts of the English phase of the second evangelical awakening, see E. M. Howse, *Saints in Politics* (Toronto: University of Toronto, 1952); C. I. Foster, *An Errand of Mercy* (Chapel Hill: University of North Carolina, 1960).

22. A good account of pentecostal spirituality from within this tradition is V. Synan, *In the Latter Days* (Ann Arbor: Servant, 1984).

23. See Lovelace, "The Sanctification Gap," in *Dynamics*.

24. The best witness to this is an attempted defense of modern fundamentalism, *The Fundamentalist Phenomenon*, ostensibly by J. Falwell but actually by E. Hindson and E. Dobson (Garden City: Doubleday, 1981).

25. G. Cook, *The Expectation of the Poor* (Maryknoll, N.Y.: Orbis, 1985).

26. G. Marsden, *Fundamentalism and American Culture* (New York: Oxford University Press, 1980).

Part 4

Spirituality and Theology

One of the major tasks of scholars who work in the field of spirituality today is to define the parameters of this engaging subject, to differentiate it in terms of both content and method from other disciplines in the academy. Integral to this larger process is the task, first of all, of distinguishing spirituality from theology. In this section, then, we will encounter various views on the relation between spirituality and theology and consequently on the place or role that spirituality should have in the academy as well. Is the seminary or church-related college the only appropriate setting for Christian spirituality? Is all Christian spirituality necessarily confessional, and therefore in some sense limited, or does Christian spirituality, in its focus on human *experience*, underscore elements that can characterize all human beings, a fact that would argue for inclusion in the academy?

In the first essay, Charles Bernard explores the nature of spiritual theology by pointing out its association in the past with both asceticism and mysticism. Though he initially highlights the twofold source of spiritual theology as the data of faith and personal experience, Bernard's interest seems to lie elsewhere—not with experience as such but with the "revealed doctrine," which he not only sees as "the basis of spiritual experience" but which he also considers as its ever-present norm. With such a large role assigned to dogmatic theology, it is difficult to see what place the discipline of spirituality would have in a setting other than that of a seminary or church.

Bradley Hanson, for his part, notes that there is "no widespread agreement on the meaning of spirituality," and considers a number of recent definitions offered by scholars, those of Ewert Cousins and Sandra Schneiders among them. Focusing his inquiry on the issues of both subject matter and approach, Hanson maintains that it does not appear that spirituality can qualify as a discipline on the basis of subject matter alone, "for the subject matter is not distinct enough from religion generally or from other fields within religious studies." Beyond this, Hanson points out that the elements of "serious reflection and strongly existential orientation," which distinguish spirituality from the natural sciences, social sciences, and even religious studies (in their intent to be value-neutral and objective) may perhaps render the subject matter of spirituality appropriate for the seminary but not for the university.

In the last essay of this section, Sandra Schneiders illustrates the ambiguity of the term *spirituality* and offers three major referents, as noted earlier in the introduction to this reader: (1) a fundamental dimension of a human being, (2) the lived experience that actualizes that dimension, and (3) the academic discipline that studies that experience. Postulating a different perspective than that of Bernard, Schneiders notes that two basic approaches are possible in understanding spirituality. The first, a "dogmatic position," supplies a definition from above. The second, "the anthropological position," which Schneiders seems to prefer, provides a definition from below, from "the *experience* of consciously striving to integrate one's life in terms not of isolation and self-absorption but of self-transcendence toward the ultimate value one perceives." Here theology (or dogmatic considerations) do not contain or control spirituality as is the case for Bernard. In addition, since the definition of spirituality offered by Schneiders highlights *human* experience, while underscoring the interdisciplinary, holistic, and ecumenical nature of spirituality, the reasons for excluding the discipline from the academy no longer seem to apply.

The Nature of Spiritual Theology

Charles André Bernard, S.J.

n a certain sense one could say that spiritual theology is both old and new; old, because theoretical and practical teaching on the spiritual life can be found in Sacred Scripture and Tradition; new, because it is only in modern times that there has been a need to compose a systematic theology of the spiritual life as lived in the Church.[1]

In examining the manuals of spiritual theology and the programs offered by Institutes of Spirituality, one comes to a very comforting conviction: there is a consensus concerning the concept of spiritual theology. In the Catholic tradition it is admitted by all that the theology of the spiritual life must be based on the data of Revelation and the principles of dogmatic and moral theology. At the same time, one must take into account the data of life as it is lived; that is to say, the experiential aspect.

Preliminary Clarifications

The Problem of Terminology

The most ancient term used for this study was "asceticism," which means any kind of exercise or training, and hence it referred to the efforts by which one strives to make progress in the moral or spiritual life. Granted that effort, and even methodical effort,

This essay first appeared in *Compendium of Spirituality: Volume One,* ed. Emeterio De Cea (New York: Alba House, 1995), 61–76. Used by permission.

is always necessary in the spiritual life, it is not surprising that in some languages, like Italian or German, the word "ascetical" was applied to the entire span of the spiritual life.

Another term used was "mystical," derived from pseudo-Dionysius, who wrote a treatise entitled *Theologia mystica* in the fifth or sixth century. The term was used to designate an experience of God as transcendental and incomprehensible; an experience that is not achieved by our own efforts or intellectual activity, but is a gift from God.

Under the influence of the Quietists, who exalted the mystical way and disdained the practice of bodily mortification and discursive meditation, a dichotomy was established between the two states or stages of the spiritual life. The ascetical way was considered the common and ordinary state of Christians; the mystical way was considered extraordinary. An example of this teaching is found in John Baptist Scaramelli (1687–1752), who composed two distinct treatises: *Direttorio ascetico* and *Direttorio mistico*. Numerous authors of books on prayer followed his example and made the same distinction between ordinary ascetical prayer and extraordinary mystical prayer.

After lengthy disputes, it was decided to adopt a terminology that did not imply an exclusive opposition between the ascetical and the mystical stages of the spiritual life. Ultimately the French word, *spiritualité*, was deemed the most suitable to designate the spiritual life in all its phases. Similarly, the term "spiritual theology," became the title of the systematic study of Christian perfection and the spiritual life.

To designate more precisely the content of spiritual theology, it is necessary to return to the concept of the spiritual life and consider some of the areas that are treated in practically every book of spiritual theology. In the first place, it is evident that the spiritual life is essentially dynamic. It is a sharing in the vital dynamism that is rooted in the grace of Christ and tends toward the plenitude of Christian life that is attainable by all the faithful. This plenitude is nothing less than the holiness to which all are called in Christ.

It is the clear and insistent teaching of the Second Vatican Council that all Christians are called to a holiness that is lived in all the concrete circumstances of life.[2] The vocation to holiness should therefore be the integrating factor of the Christian life which, like all life, is necessarily subject to the laws of growth and development. In this context the spiritual life has been described as a journey (*itinerarium*, e.g., St. Bonaventure), and this concept of a journey connotes the experiential aspect that is proper to spiritual theology and distinguishes it from dogmatic and moral theology.

Spiritual Consciousness

That does not mean, however, that spirituality is compatible with any and every kind of experience, as long as it has a reference to Christ. The Christian spiritual life is born of God's communication of his own divine life through the sacraments of the Church and the active reception of that life by the individual Christian. "He first loved us," says St. John (1 Jn 4:19). He has planted in us the seed of his kingdom, but we must receive it gratefully and cultivate it in docility to the Holy Spirit.

Another feature of the spiritual life is the intimate union that results from the mutual interpersonal relationship between the soul and God. This relationship is fostered and developed by the word of God contained in Sacred Scripture and transmitted by the Tradition of the Church. And since the response to the word of God involves the practice of personal and liturgical prayer, we find here another specific note of spiritual theology, namely, the role of personal experience.

From what has been said, it is evident that spirituality necessarily looks to the common teaching of the Church in order to establish its own principles. All agree that spiritual theology must be subordinated to the teaching of the Church, without being tied to any particular school of theology. As is said today, the indicative of revealed doctrine is the norm for the imperative of moral theology and the basis of spiritual experience.

Having established the objective basis of the spiritual life, we now consider the person who lives that life, i.e., the subjective aspect. We perceive immediately that people are conditioned in a variety of ways by the concrete circumstances of their life. The individual person has a consciousness that is incarnate in a body and endowed with affectivity, but there are numerous factors that must be considered: sensate awareness and the spiritual life, bodily integration, the feminine-masculine duality, etc. Moreover, one's personal experience leaves its stamp on one's character and its development. Finally, one must take into account the social factors, such as family, race, nationality, and church, because these factors produce a particular culture that influences one's perception of the Christian life and the language used to express it. The study of personality and social structure in relation to spiritual theology is very complex; in fact, it requires an interdisciplinary study in order to delineate with precision the components of authentic spiritual experience.

The Emergence of Spiritual Theology

Having marked the boundaries of spiritual theology, we shall now investigate its scientific character. We want to know how it became a specialized branch of theology that treats of the Christian life as known through experience.

Sacred Scripture

We turn first to the perennial source of theological discourse, namely, Sacred Scripture. The message of divine revelation has a basic unity but it also has a twofold aspect: the one, doctrinal, which speaks of God and the implementation of his universal plan of salvation; the other, more practical, comprising the prescriptions of the divine law as well as the cultic regulations and exhortations contained in the Old and New Testaments. Under the practical aspect we also find prescriptions of various kinds that regulate the conduct of the People of God, as well as other texts that describe the life of faith and exhort individuals to live it. We think, for example, of the Psalms, which express the prayer of the people or depict the heroic figures who serve as exemplars for the People of God. We can also point to the Wisdom Books, which state how wisdom can be attained, and to the Book of Job, which is a lengthy meditation on suffering and its relationship to sin.

As regards the New Testament, it suffices to pause at the letters of St. Paul. He did not hesitate to speak of his personal experience and to describe its various aspects; e.g., the warfare between the flesh and the spirit, mystical union with Christ, the meaning of the Church, the apostolic life. It is all a testimony to the life guaranteed by Revelation and offered to each one of us.

The Fathers of the Church

Basing their teaching on Sacred Scripture, the Fathers tried to respond to the various needs of the People of God. When it was a question of refuting the ever-present heresies, the response was doctrinal; when dealing with various personal and community problems in the Church, the answer was based on moral theology; when the faithful needed guidance in the spiritual life, it could be found in the theology of Christian perfection.

The method used by the Fathers was to take a text of Sacred Scripture and explain its application to various levels of the Christian life. Going beyond the literal or historical sense, they developed a "typical" sense, to clarify the relationship between the Old Testament and the teaching of Christ. Then it was easy to discover the "moral" sense, which applies to all, and especially to Christians, who are bound to live according to the law of love.

Much closer to our concept of the spiritual life is the "anagogical" sense, which pertains to the ultimate end of human life in eternity. The elevation of the mind to eternal life enables the contemplative to antic-ipate it to some extent through the practice of faith, hope and charity. This provides a "mystical" sense, which fits in very well with the mate-rial of spiritual theology: the progress of the soul and its prayer life toward the contemplation of God.

It is especially important to mention two Fathers whose influence lasted all through the Middle Ages: Origen and Gregory of Nyssa. Their homi-lies on the Old and New Testaments depict the entire Christian experi-ence as a search for God in Christ. We may rightly see in their expositions the beginning of a spiritual theology, not yet systematic, but rich in con-tent and normative for the centuries that follow. Even in later centuries, when the concept of theology as a science and the use of distinctions pre-vailed, theological study was never considered complete if it did not treat of contemplation or the experiential knowledge of God.

Scholastic Theology

Running parallel to monastic theology towards the end of the twelfth century and throughout the thirteenth century, theology increasingly took on a scientific form. It moved farther and farther away from theology con-ceived as a commentary on the sacred page and an introduction to the experiential knowledge of the divine mystery. The personal assimilation of the mystery of the faith was gradually replaced by a theology that fos-tered a critical understanding of the doctrinal content of the faith. This understanding necessarily came into conflict with other visions of the world, both religious and philosophical. From that time on, there was a distinction between exegetical commentaries or treatises on contempla-tion and disputed questions gathered together in the theological summas.

In responding to the conflicting opinions prevalent at any given time, the speculative theologian had to consider the objective content of the Church's tradition, which is based on Sacred Scripture, and give an objec-tive, scientific response to the questions that had been proposed. His dialectical method eliminated completely the affective and personal dimension of the testimony. What mattered was the elaboration of a the-ology as objective and scientific as philosophy and the other sciences.

This ever more rigorous scientific approach led in time to various schools of theology. Even if the various "summas" presented the whole of theological discourse, didactic necessity introduced a great division between the arts (philosophy) and theology, and in the field of theol-ogy, a further division into various theological disciplines.

Sharing as he did in both monastic theology and speculative theol-ogy, St. Bonaventure exemplifies the ways of doing theology. For him, theology remains a very personal activity on the part of the believer. He even describes theology as an "affective habit" that lies between the speculative and the practical. Its goal is contemplation and personal spiritual progress *(ut boni fiamus)*. He calls this theology "wisdom" because it involves both knowledge and love.[3] In spite of Bonaventure's great authority, theology was increasingly studied and taught as an objective science accessible to all. Hence the division of scientific theology into speculative theology (dogma), practical theology (moral), and affective theology (spirituality).

Mysticism

Spiritual theology treats of an area that is recognized by all as the proper subject matter for this branch of theology, namely, mystical contemplation. The reason is that mystical theology deals with experience; it treats of God, not as an object of human speculation, but primarily, by way of negation, as transcending all particular knowledge, whether sensible or intellectual. This kind of knowledge comes through a passive experience; it is a gratuitous gift of God and not the result of personal effort. The negative knowledge that characterizes the mystical experience is proof of the limitation of our conceptual knowledge and the absolute transcendence of the divine. There is nothing paradoxical about this, however; rather, it is an excellent criterion for theology. Since theological knowledge is valid but intrinsically imperfect, the awareness of its limits is a guaranty of authenticity and scientific honesty. And the area that is proper to spiritual theology is that of experience or, as we would say today, a theology that is lived.

Definition of Spiritual Theology

There is a general consensus concerning the concept of spirituality and, consequently, the concept of spiritual theology. We shall therefore adopt the definition given by Father Aumann and then explain the various terms in a personal way.

Spiritual theology is that part of theology that, proceeding from the truths of divine revelation and the religious experiences of individual persons, defines the nature of the supernatural life, formulates directives for its growth and development, and explains the process by which souls advance from the beginning of the spiritual life to its full perfection.[4]

Theological Principles and Experience

We begin by posing the problem of articulation concerning the twofold source of spiritual theology: the data of the faith and personal experience. The Thomistic tradition generally tends to subordinate spiritual theology to dogmatic theology. Its method is therefore essentially deductive; for example, from the notion of perfection or the doctrine on the priesthood, one deduces the principles of spiritual theology or priestly spirituality. However, some Thomists, e.g., the Spanish Dominicans Arintero and Marín-Sola, treat at length of religious experience, especially that which proceeds from the operation of the gifts of the Holy Spirit. For them the subordination of spiritual theology to dogma is not so immediate; rather, more autonomy is given to the mystical life. Marín-Sola stated as early as 1924 that the affective and mystical way can contribute greatly to the understanding and homogeneous development of Catholic dogma.

The beginning and early stages of the spiritual life constitute the ascetical way, and at this stage certain practices are essential, such as mortification and purgation, spiritual reading, meditation on Sacred Scripture and the life of Christ, etc. But when discussing spiritual maturity and mystical activity, it is necessary to study the experience itself before attempting a systematic elaboration. There are certain factors that must not be separated from the religious experience; for example, a living and personalized faith, the moral predispositions necessary for spiritual progress, the influence of culture and environment, and one's personal spiritual journey.

Moreover, all the methods proper to the human sciences can and should, *mutatis mutandis*, be applied to spiritual theology. This calls for interdisciplinary studies that can integrate the data of Revelation and theology with the scientific data from psychology, sociology, philosophy and linguistics.

Structure of the Christian Experience

Although it is true that Christian spiritual experience falls under the general heading of religious experience, we must nevertheless insist on its uniqueness, a uniqueness that derives from the Christian faith in the historical event of the New Covenant in Christ. The apostles saw clearly the trajectory of the life of Christ, which terminated in the paschal mystery (cf. Ph 2:6–11). In this comprehensive vision one can perceive two constants: first of all, their testimony rests on a concrete history which Jesus lived; secondly, they abstracted a central point in the history of Jesus, namely, the paschal mystery which highlights the historical modality of the Redemption.

Yet another mystery is the Incarnation of the Son of God. In Jesus Christ the history of humanity definitively enters the divine sphere; the wall of separation between the human and the divine has been demolished (Eph 2:14). Christ our peace and our priest has ushered in the time of hope. As a result, there is no room for the Gnostic belief in a material world that cannot be saved; all mankind has been saved and with it the entire universe will be transfigured. The longing for eternal life cannot erase our duty to work in the history of mankind to prolong the effects of the Incarnation of the Son.

The third component of the Christian faith, and most fundamental for the spiritual life, is the revelation of the mystery of the Trinity. This mystery radically transforms the spiritual life of the individual because it reveals our God as a living God. The divine reality is unfolded in the relations among the three Persons: between the Father and the Son the mystery of the communication of life; between the Father and the Son and the Holy Spirit the mystery of love. Through this interpersonal communication, the essential unity and goodness of the three divine Persons become for us the support and criterion of all contemplative and theological activity. The children of God are invited to share in the perfection of the Father by imitating the incarnate Son through the power of the Holy Spirit.

The relationship of the Father to the Son indicates that the Father is the origin and giver of every perfect gift. He has enabled the Son to have life in himself and to communicate that life to the members of his Mystical Body. Reciprocally, the relationship of the Son to the Father signifies the reception of the gift of life from the Father, which is manifested in the perfect obedience of the Servant of Yahweh and his total acceptance of his Father's will. Consequently, the spiritual life of the Christian, which is a sharing in the life of the only-begotten Son, is also a participation in the life of the Trinity.

As the personified love of the Father and the Son, the Holy Spirit leads us by the gift of charity to the only-begotten Son who in turn leads us to the Father, the unique source of every divine and human good. Thus, the participation in the life of the Trinity constitutes the uniqueness of the Christian faith and Christian experience.

The Dynamics of Spiritual Experience

Having seen the elements of the Christian experience, we now discuss its dynamic aspect and its orientation to sanctity as its goal. The Christian experience is imbedded in the vocation to sanctity. God calls us to be saints; consequently, the Christian dedicated to the spiritual life should understand what it involves. Although we seldom make a distinction between "perfection" and "sanctity," the former concept is anthropological: the individual strives for perfection precisely as a human person. The second concept refers to the divine element: God is the only perfect "saint" (*Sanctus*), and we approach sanctity in the measure that we resemble him through a moral and spiritual transformation. Our sanctity is therefore a participation in the sanctity of God (Is 6:3), who wants us to share in his holiness. St. Paul says: "He chose us in him, before the foundation of the world, to be holy and without blemish before him" (Eph 1:4). Our universal vocation to holiness has been stated emphatically by the Second Vatican Council:

> The Church, whose mystery is set forth by this sacred Council, is held, as a matter of faith, to be unfailingly holy. This is because Christ, the Son of God, who with the Father and the Spirit is hailed as "alone holy," loved the Church as his bride, giving himself up for her so as to sanctify her (cf. Eph 5:25–26); he joined her to himself as his body and endowed her with the gift of the Holy Spirit for the glory of God. *Therefore all in the Church, whether they belong to the hierarchy or are cared for by it, are called to holiness, according to the apostle's saying: "For this is the will of God, your sanctification"* (1 Th 4:3; cf. Eph 1:4). [Italics added].[5]

Sanctity cannot pertain to only one part or aspect of our existence; it must permeate the totality of our being. "Be holy yourselves in every aspect of your conduct, for it is written: 'Be holy because I am holy'" (1 P 1:15). Nevertheless, there are tensions in human life, and this raises the question whether sanctity pertains more to one area of the Christian life than to another; for example, the life of prayer or human activity; the love of God or the love of neighbor; life centered in God or in temporal affairs; etc. A clear response was given by the Second Vatican Council:

> The forms and tasks of life are many but holiness is one—that sanctity which is cultivated by all who act under God's Spirit and, obeying the Father's voice and adoring God the Father in spirit and in truth, follow Christ, poor, humble and cross-bearing, that they may deserve to be partakers of his glory. Each one, however, according to his own gifts and duties must steadfastly advance along the way of a living faith, which arouses hope and works through love.[6]

The integration of faith, hope and charity is fostered by two essential elements of an authentic spiritual life. First, a religious attitude, which means that in all one's actions—over and above those that, like the practice of prayer, are already religious activity—the Christian can and should strive to seek God's greater glory. "So whether you eat or drink, or whatever you do, do everything for the glory of God" (1 Cor 10:31). Secondly, the love of God and neighbor, for it is charity that can direct all one's actions to God and lead the Christian to the attainment of sanctity. Sanctity is the fullness of divine life in us; it is manifested by charity and it is increased in us by charity. The Christian life does not allow for a dichotomy between the spiritual life and one's concrete daily life. The latter must always be permeated with charity.

Norms for Spiritual Growth

The religious experience of ordinary Christians as well as that of the saints fully confirms the notion of spiritual growth and development. This is analogous to one's natural human growth from infancy to adulthood. Sins can impede one's spiritual growth, of course, and there are other factors that pose more or less of a problem, but normally there will be a relatively constant growth in persons who have dedicated themselves sincerely to their personal spiritual growth.

There are various ways of charting one's progress in the spiritual life: according to the degrees of charity, the grades of prayer, the degrees of humility, etc. For our purpose it suffices to discuss the one that is best known to most devout Christians: the passage from the stage of beginners to that of proficient or advanced souls and arriving finally at the state of the perfect. For practical purposes the same threefold division has been expressed as the purgative way, the illuminative way and the unitive way.

The first step on the spiritual journey is conversion to the interior life. The beginner seeks a deeper knowledge of God through recollection and the practice of prayer, which usually starts with meditation or discursive prayer. The primary goal at this first stage is purification of the soul by living a moral life that centers especially on the cultivation of the virtues.

After some time, which varies with the intensity of fervor and the degree of purgation needed, the individual enters upon a more peaceful state in which there is more intense divine illumination and no concession is made to any kind of sin. Fervor is very important here so that one's progress will be constant. St. Teresa of Avila states that some souls do not pass beyond this stage because they do not understand the Gospel teaching on self-renunciation and they are not really serious about practicing that renunciation.[7]

This second stage presupposes an authentic interior life; that is, the presence of Christ habitually informs one's judgments, affections and actions. Christ becomes the object of one's personal love, which is made possible by custody of the heart and recollection of spirit. The soul appears to have mastered self, loves silence and is deeply religious. This is the illuminative way of the advanced soul that is completely conformed to Christ and has put on the mind of Christ.

The third and final stage of spiritual growth is that of the perfect, also called the unitive way. The names do not mean that there is no possibility of further progress, however, but that the individual is stabilized in a permanent state of constant sanctification. Father de Guibert describes it this way:

It is customary to distinguish two degrees or stages of perfect souls: (1) the full perfection of charity or heroic charity, which the Church is accustomed to require for the beatification of the servants of God, and which Benedict XIV, after having consulted various definitions offered by theologians, defines as follows: In order to be heroic, Christian virtue must be such that the person who practices it must do so easily, promptly and willingly, in a manner surpassing the ordinary, for a supernatural purpose, with self-abnegation and a surrender of all self-satisfaction. One could also add that the heroic practice of virtue should be so resplendent that the servant of God can be offered as a model to other Christians living in the same conditions.

(2) A perfection of charity that is less intense and resplendent but true and sufficient so that the soul cannot be listed any longer with those who are simply advanced souls. The soul has attained such a degree of self-abnegation and recollection that it is habitually docile to the inspirations of the Holy Spirit and the virtue of charity dominates its entire life, except for some light faults due to human weakness.[8]

Action of God and Activity of the Soul

The problem regarding God's action on the soul and the soul's own activity arises from the fact that the soul is receptive of the grace and gifts of God, but at the same time it must use those gifts in order to share more fully in the divine life. To confine our discussion to the area of religious experience, the precept of charity must be operative in the concrete circumstances of life and the theological virtues of faith, hope and charity should be exercised. But it is commonly agreed that there is also a passive element in the spiritual life, commonly designated as the mystical element. It is in this context that theologians treat of the gifts of the Holy Spirit and the grades of mystical prayer. We shall offer some reflections on the most important aspects of this question without claiming to have treated the matter exhaustively.

All the spiritual writers agree that the beginning of the Christian life demands careful and constant cooperation on the part of the individual. The supernatural gifts are received by a human person, who can, by a free choice, accept or refuse the intervention of the Holy Spirit. Another area in which the individual must remain active is that of contemplative prayer. However evident this may seem, we want to corroborate it with the testimony of St. John of the Cross:

"Never give up prayer, and should you find dryness and difficulty, persevere in it for this very reason. God often desires to see what love your soul has, and love is not tried by ease and satisfaction."[9] Although God can anticipate our efforts and take the initiative, normally there is no deep spiritual life without the constant search for God in the practice of prayer.

There are numerous descriptions of the passive states of prayer. St. John of the Cross has described in great detail the passive purgation of the senses and the spirit, neither of which is our doing but the action of God.[10] For our purposes it suffices to quote St. Teresa of Avila concerning passive prayer:

> Do not think it is a state, like the last, in which we dream; I say "dream," because the soul seems to be, as it were, drowsy, so that it neither seems asleep nor feels awake. Here we are all asleep, and fast asleep, to the things of the world and to ourselves (in fact, for the short time that the condition lasts, the soul is without consciousness and has no power to think, even though it may desire to do so). There is no need now for it to devise any method of suspending the thought.[11]

It is clear from the foregoing that the element of passivity is normally introduced on the level of consciousness. The active grades of prayer begin with an external perception and the exercise of memory, imagination and the discursive intellect, all of which leads to the choice or adhesion of the will. In passive or mystical contemplation, however, the first step is suspension of the faculties; the will is moved directly by divine grace and this activity is accompanied by a general loving knowledge of God, as St. John of the Cross describes it.

Moving beyond the question of prayer, the notion of passivity does not imply the absence of all activity on the level of consciousness. There is, however, a cessation of well-defined and structured discursive activity, which is replaced by a simple gaze on God and the adhesion of the heart. But rather than think of activity and passivity as mutually exclusive, it is better to think of them as two moments in a dialectic relationship in which their predominance will vary according to the degree of development of the spiritual life. There is, in fact, a dialectic from the very beginning, because God's grace is infused in the human nature but respects the operative structure of that nature. But insofar as it implies a radical receptivity before God, it is the practice of prayer that introduces the first moment of the soul's passivity.

There is yet another dialectic: in the order of consciousness, between discursive activity and the simplicity of the contemplative gaze. It is a dialectic that regulates the relationship between knowledge and love. The affective factor becomes predominant and is a decisive element in contemplative perception. Finally, as regards freedom, the sense of adhesion more and more replaces freedom of choice, without, however, totally annihilating that freedom.

Notes

1. Cf. John G. Arintero, *The Mystical Evolution*, trans. J. Aumann, 2 vols. (Rockford, Ill., 1978); Jordan Aumann, *Spiritual Theology* (London: Sheed & Ward; Westminster,

Md.: Glazier, 1980); Reginald Garrigou-Lagrange, *The Three Ages*, trans. T. Doyle, 2 vols. (St. Louis: Herder, 1947).

2. *Lumen Gentium*, n. 41.

3. *I Sent. Proemii*, 3.

4. Jordan Aumann, *Spiritual Theology* (London: Sheed & Ward, 1987, 5th printing), 22.

5. *Lumen Gentium*, n. 39.

6. *Lumen Gentium*, n. 41.

7. St. Teresa of Jesus, *The Interior Castle*, Third Mansions.

8. J. de Guibert, *The Theology of the Spiritual Life*, trans. P. Barrett (New York, 1953), n. 357.

9. "Degrees of Perfection," in *The Collected Works of St. John of the Cross*, trans. K. Kavanaugh and O. Rodriguez (Washington, D.C.: Institute of Carmelite Studies, 1979), 680 n. 9.

10. St. John of the Cross, *The Dark Night*, trans. K. Kavanaugh and O. Rodriguez (Washington, D.C.: Institute of Carmelite Studies, 1979).

11. *Interior Castle*, Fifth Mansions, trans. E. Allison Peers (London: Sheed & Ward, 1946), 2:248.

Spirituality as Spiritual Theology

Bradley C. Hanson

In spite of the fact that *spirituality* is currently a very popular word, it is very difficult to say what is meant by it. What I propose is that the study of spirituality is best understood as spiritual theology or something analogous to it.

A field of study can be distinguished on the basis of two factors: a distinct subject matter and a distinct approach to that subject matter. Most fields of study are distinguished through a combination of these two factors. For instance, on the one hand, New Testament Studies focuses on the New Testament rather than some other piece of literature or subject matter, although it uses methods identical to those employed in Old Testament Studies, other sacred writings, and certain forms of secular literature. Within the study of religion itself, this specific subject matter marks New Testament Studies off from other fields. On the other hand, while a New Testament scholar shares careful attention to the New Testament with the Christian preacher, their approaches to the document are different. What distinguishes the field of New Testament Studies from other fields of inquiry is a combination of subject matter and approach. The same two factors also distinguish music history as a field of study. Among all the many disciplines that employ historical methods, music history has a peculiar subject matter. Among the various disciplines in music such as performance, conducting, and theory, music history alone focuses upon the historical approach.

This essay first appeared in *Modern Christian Spirituality: Methodological and Historical Essays*, ed. Bradley C. Hanson (Atlanta: Scholars Press, 1990), 45–52. Used by permission.

What about spirituality? Can it be distinguished on the basis of its subject matter and approach? We'll begin by examining its subject matter. Since there is no widespread agreement on the meaning of *spirituality*, the best we can do is to consider several proposals for what this subject matter is. One proposal concentrates on the human being as spirit in the sense of self-transcending. Joann Wolski Conn articulates this understanding of spirituality, "From the perspective of the actualization of the human capacity to be spiritual, to be self-transcending—that is, relational and freely committed spirituality encompasses all of life."[1] This is a broad philosophical meaning of the term. "Philosophers speak of our human spirituality as our capacity for self-transcendence, a capacity demonstrated in our ability to know the truth, to relate to others lovingly, and to commit ourselves freely to persons and ideals."[2]

A second proposal for the meaning of spirituality is stated by Ewert Cousins in his preface to the Crossroad series on World Spirituality: "The series focuses on that inner dimension of the person called by certain traditions 'the spirit.' This spiritual core is the deepest center of the person. It is here that the person is open to the transcendent dimension; it is here that the person experiences ultimate reality."[3] What is added to self-transcendence is terminology that points toward the supernatural—"transcendent dimension," "ultimate reality." In other words, the meaning of spirituality in this second proposal is really the same as "religion." Of course, there is also no universal agreement on the meaning of religion, but Cousins' use of the term spirituality is very close to what the history of religions scholar Robert S. Ellwood, Jr. says about religion: "Our basic idea will be that religious thought and activity represents one's acting out, or actualizing, who one thinks he is or she really is deep within. It simultaneously includes the corresponding relationship to our ultimate environment, infinite reality itself."[4] For Ellwood religion includes both a quest for the real self and a relationship to a reality that transcends the material. The fact that for Ewert Cousins spirituality is really another word for religion is borne out by the subtitle of the Crossroad series of which he is general editor: *World Spirituality: An Encyclopedic History of the Religious Quest.* Even the title of the projected twenty-second volume on secular forms is consistent with this: *Spirituality and the Secular Quest;* the title suggests that the secular quest is parallel or analogous to spirituality, not a clear instance of it, similar to the way in which many have spoken of communism as a religion.

A third proposal for the meaning of spirituality is represented in "Theology and Spirituality: Strangers, Rivals, or Partners?" by Sandra Schneiders who says, "[V]irtually everyone talking about spirituality today is talking about self-transcendence which gives integrity and meaning to the whole of life and to life in its wholeness by situating and orienting the person within the horizon of ultimacy in some ongoing and transforming way."[5] This definition further specifies the nature of self-transcendence by adding the feature of ultimacy, yet without the suggestion that the ultimate is supernatural. This idea is familiar to anyone acquainted with the thought of Paul Tillich, for he talked about faith and even religion in a very broad sense as one's ultimate concern. Not just conventionally religious people have faith, but anyone whose life has a master commitment. As Schneiders points out, this faith or master commitment influences all aspects of a person's life, and also serves to unify a person's life by setting up the priorities of one's existence. It might be clearer to say that spirituality in this third sense is faith, and spirituality as a discipline would be faith studies.

A fourth point about the meaning of spirituality does not so much constitute another definition of it as it adds a nuance that could be combined with any of the above definitions. Sandra Schneiders expresses this nuance by emphasizing that spirituality refers to experience. This is echoed in Bernard McGinn's statements that "Christian spirituality is the lived experience of Christian belief" rather than doctrine, and that "Christianity has always insisted upon the primacy of the inner meaning of Christian documents, rituals, and institutions—their spiritual depth. This volume and the two that will follow it in *World Spirituality: An Encyclopedic History of the Religious Quest* are an attempt to present the inner message of Christian belief and practice."[6] Another way of putting this is that spirituality as a study does not focus on the outward forms of religion or faith but on the lived reality. This does not mean that a spirituality can exist without outward forms, but that the outward forms are important as means of inculcating and expressing the inward reality.

Using these four suggestions for the meaning of spirituality, can we discern a subject matter distinct from others in the academic world? In my judgment, the first proposal (the subject matter of spirituality is the human spirit in its multifaceted self-transcending) is too diffuse to be helpful. Conn says spirit is shown in the human ability to know the truth, to give of ourselves to others, and to make free commitments. In his discussion of the human spirit in volume three of his *Systematic Theology*, Paul Tillich sees the free, self-transcending character of the spirit expressed in three broad areas: the area of morality (the centering movement that constitutes the personal self), the area of culture (self-creativity that moves out to produce language, technology, "theoretical" acts of cognition and aesthetics, and human community and persons), and in the area of religion (the self's vertical movement beyond the finite). In short, there is very little that is human in which the human spirit may not be expressed.

This makes it very difficult to have a reasonably clear subject matter called spirituality. While I agree that the human capacity of self-transcendence is an essential ingredient in anything called spirituality, I do not think this very broad meaning of the term is circumscribed enough to be the subject matter of a field of study. This seems analogous to freedom which is also an important human ability and concept, yet while it is worthwhile to clarify the concept, we do not have a distinct field of freedomology; this is probably because freedom has such pervasive influence in human life.

The second suggestion—represented by Ewert Cousins in his Crossroad series preface—also does not mark off a distinct subject matter, for in this case spirituality appears to be just another term for religion.

The third proposal, in which Sandra Schneiders seems to understand a person's spirituality as his or her faith, gains some in distinctness from religion by being more inclusive—in most cases spirituality would coincide with religion but in others it would be a non-religious faith.

Does this and her additional point about spirituality focusing on experience distinguish spirituality as a discipline with its own subject matter? I don't think so. Established disciplines such as religious history, history of religions, and systematic theology already examine faith and often include non-religious forms of faith. Moreover, what one might consider exemplary studies in spirituality do not appear to dwell much on experience. Schneiders' own chapter on "Scripture and Spirituality" in the first Volume of the Crossroad trilogy on Christian spirituality devotes only a few paragraphs to direct discussion of the religious experience of Christians; most of the chapter discusses principles of exegesis until the Middle Ages with special attention to what I would call an existential relation of the interpreter to the Scriptures. This attention to an existential relation to the text points us toward the second major factor in distinguishing an academic discipline—the approach to the subject matter. It does not appear that spirituality can qualify as a discipline just on the basis of its subject matter, for the subject matter is not distinct enough from religion generally or from other fields within religious studies.

Now we must ask whether spirituality as a study has an approach to its subject matter that would help distinguish it from other academic disciplines. Sandra Schneiders says that the methods and approaches of spirituality are:

> irreducibly pluralistic and thoroughly interdisciplinary. Most research projects in spirituality will involve biblical, historical, theological, social, psychological, aesthetic, and comparative approaches. The use of these disciplines will be governed by the methods appropriate to these disciplines themselves but the underlying and guiding philosophical presuppositions for their use are usually

hermeneutical since the fundamental problem in spirituality is always that of interpretation of particulars in order to understand the experience which comes to expression therein.[7]

I have difficulty seeing how this distinguishes spirituality from much else that is done in religious studies. A thorough historical study of the life of Martin Luther such as Roland Bainton's classic *Here I Stand* employs biblical, historical, theological, social, psychological, aesthetic approaches in order to understand Luther's experience and faith. The same thing would be true of much that is done in biblical studies; here too the approach is thoroughly interdisciplinary and hermeneutical. It seems that what is done in history of religions could be described in the same terms.

The element of its approach that I think does make spirituality distinctive is what Schneiders calls "the objectives" of the discipline of spirituality and what I would call the investigator's relation to the subject matter. She points out that the objectives of a study in spirituality are always simultaneously theoretical and practical, and I agree. What I mean is that a spirituality study combines, on the one hand, a rigor of reflection that requires a certain distance of the subject from the object very like that which distinguishes theology from praying and worshipping, and on the other hand, a strongly existential relation to the subject matter in which the subject is seeking in some way either to grow in his or her faith or to help others grow in their faith through this reflection. This combination of serious reflection and strongly existential orientation distinguishes spirituality from all the disciplines in the natural sciences, social sciences, and religious studies that intend to be value neutral and objective, and it also distinguishes spirituality from devotional and homiletical undertakings that aim at growth in a particular faith but do not involve hard reflection. Perhaps this is what Schneiders means by concentrating on experience and what McGinn means by the inner meaning, but I think it is more accurate to speak of an existential relation to the subject matter; it is entirely possible to have a neutral or skeptical attitude toward the experience or inner meaning of another's faith. In fact, many a good study in the history of religions attempts to give an objective description of the inward meaning of a group's religious faith as well as pay attention to its outward forms.

I may sum up my view by saying that I think spirituality is that study whose subject matter is faith and which involves a stance of the subject toward the subject matter that combines hard reflection with a strong existential concern to grow in faith. If this is true, then spirituality will not qualify as a "scientific" discipline among the pantheon of disciplines in religious studies; it belongs to what we in the West have called theology in the broad sense. And even within theology spirituality does not have a clearly demarcated subject matter such as one can see in biblical studies, religious history, ethics, etc., for its topic might be biblical or historical, ethical or doctrinal; what distinguishes it is its reflective, existential approach that seeks to enhance the faith of the scholar or of those the scholar addresses.

I think an appropriate name for this discipline is spiritual theology, although I recognize that this term may have old, unsatisfactory associations. For instance, as a Lutheran I disagree with an older understanding of spiritual theology as the science of perfection. However, the name is rather unimportant. What matters is the stance or orientation that spiritual theology or spirituality represents, a stance that ought to infuse much that is done in biblical studies, systematic theology, and ethics. It may not be a good thing to establish spirituality as a separate discipline within the academy, for the effort to justify spirituality as an academic discipline is likely to be done on terms acceptable to the descriptive, scientific disciplines. The questions Carlos Eire raises come from that Enlightenment perspective. As a short term strategy it is probably necessary to identify certain courses as spirituality, but in the long run spirituality will be a much stronger undertaking if its existential stance pervades much that is done in religious studies.

Given my understanding of spirituality as spiritual theology, I doubt that much of what is labeled "spirituality" today qualifies, since most of it is done from a much more objective stance. For example, in *Christian Spirituality I: Origins to the Twelfth Century* chapters by Jean Leclerq on Western Christian monasticism and asceticism, Thomas Hopko on the trinity in the Cappadocians, Leonid Oupensky on icon and art, and Kallistos Ware on Eastern ways of prayer and contemplation (a random selection) could all just as well fit into an encyclopedia on religion, for while they all do very well in describing a certain expression of Christian faith, there is no hint (except in Ware's final paragraph) of inviting the reader to participate in this expression of faith. Good chapters in an encyclopedic history of religions would do the same.

Ewert Cousins says, "The transmission of spiritual wisdom may be the oldest discipline in human history. Yet this ancient discipline needs to be accorded its own place in academic studies."[8] The "transmission of spiritual wisdom" is a discipline that requires the student's desire to *live* that wisdom and the teacher's intention to help the student in that endeavor. The problem, as I see it, is that in the modern academy this kind of relationship to the subject matter is considered appropriate to the seminary but not to the university class room and its descriptive stance. My hunch is that books labeled "spirituality" often sell well to the public, because people are looking for a spiritual wisdom that they can live and for teachers who will help them live it. I grant that they can find it in the descriptive studies if they have the maturity and insight to dig it out, but I suspect that they are also looking in the text for some spiritual encouragement and direction, and those are generally lacking.

Notes

1. Joann Wolski Conn, *Women's Spirituality: Resources for Christian Development* (New York: Paulist, 1986), 9.

2. Ibid., 3.

3. Ewert Cousins, "Preface to the Series," in *Christian Spirituality*, vol. 1, *Origins to the Twelfth Century*, ed. Bernard McGinn and John Meyendorff, World Spirituality: An Encyclopedic History of the Religious Quest 16 (New York: Crossroad, 1985), xiii.

4. Robert S. Ellwood, Jr., *Introducing Religion: From Inside and Outside* (Englewood Cliffs: Prentice-Hall, 1978), 1–2.

5. Sandra M. Schneiders, I.H.M., "Theology and Spirituality: Strangers, Rivals, or Partners?" *Horizons* 13.2 (1986): 266.

6. Bernard McGinn, introduction to *Christian Spirituality*, 1:xv.

7. Schneiders, "Theology and Spirituality," 272–73.

8. Cousins, preface to *Christian Spirituality*, 1:xiii.

Spirituality in the Academy

Sandra M. Schneiders, I.H.M.

pirituality, despite the fluidity of the term's usage and the general confusion about its meaning, is a subject which can no longer be politely ignored either in a church which would prefer a less "emotional" approach to faith or in an academy which would guard its intellectual precincts from "subjectivism." Since Vatican II, both the Catholic and the Protestant Churches have had to contend with an increasing interest in spirituality on the part of their membership; programs designed to foster the lived experience of the spiritual life have multiplied; and the academy is witnessing (not without apprehension) the birth of a new discipline in its midst.

The contemporary interest in spirituality on the part of the laity, seminary students, and ministers has been documented and analyzed repeatedly in the recent past by scholars, publishers, and cultural commentators.[1] The World Council of Churches, increasingly aware of the thirst for spirituality among its membership as well as the importance of spirituality in the dialogue with non-Christian religions, convened consultations on spirituality in 1984, 1986, and 1987.[2] Academic consultations on spirituality, resulting in published proceedings, have been held at Oxford,[3] Louvain,[4] Villanova,[5] and elsewhere. The American Academy of Religion, the Catholic Theological Society of America, and the College Theology Society now have ongoing seminars on spirituality.[6]

The increasingly serious attitude toward spirituality in the academy[7] is due in no small measure to the fact that the major

This essay first appeared in *Theological Studies* 50 (December 1989): 676–97. Used by permission.

theologians of the conciliar era have made explicit the roots of their constructive work in their own faith experience and their conscious intention that their work should bear fruit in the lived faith of the Church as well as in its speculation and teaching. Karl Rahner's conviction that "the Christian of the future will be a mystic or he or she will not exist at all"[8] has its academic parallel in the evident conviction of such theologians as Mary Collins, Charles Curran, Margaret Farley, Gustavo Gutierrez, Monika Hellwig, Hans Küng, Bernard Lonergan, Rosemary Radford Ruether, Edward Schillebeeckx, and Dorothee Soelle that only a theology that is rooted in the spiritual commitment of the theologian and oriented toward praxis will be meaningful in the Church of the future.[9]

The recognition *that* there exists a vital relationship between faith and spirituality on the one hand and theology and spirituality on the other by no means clarifies either what is meant by the term *spirituality* or what the relationship among faith, theology, and spirituality is.

Before addressing these questions, however, two preliminary observations are necessary. First, the term *spirituality*, like the term *psychology*, is unavoidably ambiguous, referring to (1) a fundamental dimension of the human being, (2) the lived experience which actualizes that dimension, and (3) the academic discipline which studies that experience. Some writers have tried to resolve this ambiguity by reserving the term *spirituality* for the lived experience while referring to the discipline as *spiritual theology*.[10] For reasons that will be given below, I think this solution creates more problems than it solves and I opt for retaining the term *spirituality* for both the experience and the discipline, even though this requires specification whenever the context is not sufficiently clarifying.

Secondly, the term *spirituality* (referring to lived experience) has undergone an astounding expansion in the last few decades. Before Vatican II it was an almost exclusively Roman Catholic term. The term is being gradually adopted by Protestantism, Judaism, non-Christian religions, and even such secular movements as feminism and Marxism, to refer to something that, while difficult to define, is experienced as analogous in all of these movements.[11] A singular indication of how universal the term has become is the title of the 25-volume Crossroad series, only three volumes of which are devoted to Christianity: *World Spirituality: An Encyclopedic History of the Religious Quest*.[12]

Furthermore, the term no longer refers exclusively or even primarily to prayer and spiritual exercises, much less to an elite state or superior practice of Christianity. Rather, from its original reference to the "interior life" of the person, usually a cleric or religious, who was "striving for perfection," i.e. for a life of prayer and virtue that exceeded in scope and intensity that of the "ordinary" believer, the term has broadened to connote the whole of the life of faith and even the life of the person as a whole, including its bodily, psychological, social, and political dimensions.[13]

The academic discipline which studies the lived experience of spirituality has developed rapidly in the past 30 years. Although I will examine this development in a subsequent section, I note here two indications of its power and direction. The first is the proliferation in the academy of courses and programs in spirituality.[14] The graduates of these programs are increasingly being invited to teach in their area of expertise, a sign that interest in the field at the undergraduate level is also increasing.

The second indication of the development of the discipline is the extraordinary burgeoning of publications, especially of research tools, in the field of spirituality. The renowned *Dictionnaire de spiritualité ascétique et mystique*[15] has arrived at the letter S and is now joined by the aforementioned *World Spirituality* encyclopedia and a number of single-volume encyclopedic dictionaries.[16] Introductory volumes such as *The Study of Spirituality*[17] and the *Compendio de teologia spirituale*,[18] extensive bibliographical tools such as the *Bibliographia internationalis spiritualitatis*,[19] which annually indexes approximately 500 publications under eight major headings, introductions to classical texts,[20] as well as a number of series of both critical texts and translations of spiritual classics[21] facilitate work in the field.

Given this extraordinarily broad and deep interest in spirituality on the part of laity, ministerial professionals, and theologians, as well as the rapid development of the academic discipline, it is not surprising that there is also an increasing concern about such basic questions as what the term *spirituality* means, how the discipline of spirituality is related to lived experience of the faith, how the discipline is related to theology on the one hand and other fields of inquiry (such as psychology, anthropology, the arts, and history) on the other, and what role, if any, praxis plays in the study of spirituality. These are the types of questions which any emerging discipline must face early in its development. The purpose of this article is to chart the progress of the discipline in coming to grips with these basic questions, to indicate the areas of continuing confusion, and to suggest directions for further clarification.

The Term "Spirituality" Referring to Experience

Preconciliar Development

Several recent studies have explored the development of the term *spirituality* from its origin in the Pauline neologism "spiritual" (*pneumatikos*), the adjectival form derived from the Greek word for the Holy Spirit of

God (*pneuma*), to its modern use in pre-Vatican II Catholicism.[22] Briefly, the adjective "spiritual" was coined by Paul to describe any reality (charisms, blessings, hymns, etc.) that was under the influence of the Holy Spirit. Most importantly, he used it in 1 Cor. 2:14–15 to distinguish the "spiritual person" (*pneumatikos*) from the "natural person" (*psychikos anthrōpos*). Paul was not contrasting spiritual with material, living with dead, or good with evil, but the person under the influence of the Spirit of God with the merely natural human being.

This theological distinction continued to govern the term *spiritual* and the derivative substantive *spirituality* throughout the patristic period until the 12th century, when a philosophical meaning developed opposing spirituality to materiality or corporeality. In the 13th century a juridical meaning emerged in which spirituality was opposed to temporality to designate ecclesiastical goods and jurisdiction in contrast to secular property or power. It was in the 17th century, the so-called "golden age of spirituality," that the term came to be applied to the interior life of the Christian. Because of the primary emphasis of the term on the affective dimension of that life, the term often carried pejorative connotations. Thus *spirituality* came to be associated with questionable enthusiasm or even heretical forms of spiritual practice (such as quietism) in contrast to *devotion*, which placed a proper emphasis on sobriety and human effort even in the life of the mystic. In the 18th century the elitist emphasis which has been the object of contemporary controversy attached to the word. Spirituality was used to refer to the life of perfection as distinguished from the "ordinary" life of faith, and the role of the spiritual director as the one who possessed the requisite theological expertise to guide the mystic (actual or potential) assumed great importance. By the 19th and early 20th centuries the meaning common just prior to the council, i.e. spirituality as the practice of the interior life by those oriented to the life of perfection, was firmly established.

Contemporary Meaning and Use

As noted above, the term *spirituality* referring to lived experience, i.e. to the reality which the academic discipline studies rather than to the discipline itself, is being used today to denote some experiential reality which characterizes not only Christianity but other religions as well and which, in some analogous fashion, can be predicated of nonreligious or even antireligious phenomena such as secular feminism or Marxism. Arriving at a definition of a term used so broadly has proven extremely difficult. It is possible, however, to discern among authors discussing this issue two basic approaches: a dogmatic position supplying a "definition from above" and an anthropological position providing a "definition from below."

The former is typified by C.-A. Bernard,[23] who equates spirituality in the full sense of the term with the life of the Christian communicated by the Holy Spirit and governed by divine revelation. (This entails, of course, the dependence of the discipline of spirituality on dogmatic theology,[24] a position against which I will argue in my second main section.) The latter is typified by J.-C. Breton[25] who argues, persuasively in my opinion, that spirituality, i.e. the spiritual life, "could be described as a way of engaging anthropological questions and preoccupations in order to arrive at an ever richer and more authentically human life."[26]

For the dogmatic approach spirituality is the life derived from grace and therefore any experience which is not explicitly Christian can be called spirituality only by way of extension or comparison. Humanity, i.e. the anthropological givens of human being, merely supplies the conditions for the reception of grace. For the anthropological approach the structure and dynamics of the human person as such are the locus of the emergence of the spiritual life. Spirituality is an activity of human life as such.[27] This activity is open to engagement with the Absolute (in which case the spirituality would be religious) in the person of Jesus Christ through the gift of the Holy Spirit (in which case the spirituality would be Christian) but is not limited to such engagement. In principle it is equally available to every human being who is seeking to live an authentically human life.[28]

In a recent article Jon Alexander surveyed the definitions of spirituality given by a number of contemporary scholars in the field[29] and concluded that the term is being used by most in an experiential and generic sense,[30] i.e. in a sense consonant with the anthropological rather than the dogmatic approach. In other words, there is a growing consensus in recognizing that Christian spirituality is a subset of a broader category that is neither confined to nor defined by Christianity or even by religion.

The obvious disadvantage of this approach is that it gives the term *spirituality* such a wide application that it is very difficult to achieve the clarity and distinction requisite for a useful definition. Raymundo Panikkar, for example, defines spirituality as "one typical way of handling the human condition."[31] One is tempted to say, "So is alcoholism." The advantages of the anthropological approach, however, outweigh its disadvantages. First, the term is being used this way by increasing numbers of people, both by lay people interested in spirituality as personal experience and by scholars who regard this experience as a subject of study, and there is no way to control the development of language. However vague it may seem, the term is apparently sufficiently connotative to enable people to communicate about the subject matter, and the scholar who insists on a definition which rules out of consideration most of what ordinary people are talking about will find his or her scholarly world largely irrelevant. Second, in our rapidly shrinking world the importance of cross-denominational and interreligious dialogue is rapidly increasing. Scholars like Thomas Merton and Panikkar are not the only thinkers who have insisted that it is not primarily in the area of theology that such dialogue becomes possible and fruitful but in the area of spirituality.[32]

It would seem that the most practical way to arrive at a usable definition of spirituality as experience is to extract from the plethora of current definitions[33] the notes which characterize the contemporary understanding and to construct a definition which includes them. I have attempted this by defining spirituality as "the experience of consciously striving to integrate one's life in terms not of isolation and self-absorption but of self-transcendence toward the ultimate value one perceives."[34] The generally-agreed-upon characteristics included in this definition are the notions of progressive, consciously pursued, personal integration through self-transcendence within and toward the horizon of ultimate concern. If the ultimate concern is God revealed in Jesus Christ and experienced through the gift of the Holy Spirit within the life of the Church, one is dealing with Christian spirituality. But this definition, while excluding the organizing and orienting of one's life in dysfunctional or narcissistic ways (e.g., alcoholism or self-centered eroticism), includes potentially any spirituality, Christian or non-Christian, religious or secular.

At this point, however, it must be realized that while it is possible and, for the reasons given, desirable to define spirituality in such an inclusive way, there is no such thing as "generic spirituality." Spirituality as lived experience is, by definition, determined by the particular ultimate value within the horizon of which the life project is pursued. Consequently, it involves intrinsically some relatively coherent and articulate understanding of both the human being and the horizon of ultimate value (i.e., in Christian terms, theology), some historical tradition, some symbol system, and so on. In order that the discussion may not remain completely formal, through the remainder of this article, unless I specify otherwise, I will be speaking of Christian spirituality. Thus, while theology may not be intrinsic to spirituality as such, it is intrinsic to Christian spirituality and therefore to the academic discipline which studies that experience.

Christian Spirituality as an Academic Discipline[35]

Preconciliar Development

The use of the term *spirituality* to denote an academic discipline which studies Christian spirituality as lived experience is a fairly recent development, and the use is not yet established beyond competition from other terms such as *spirituality theology* or *mystical theology*. However, as Walter Principe correctly observes,[36] and as the titles of research tools in the field increasingly demonstrate, this usage is rapidly gaining ground against its competitors.

Although the term and the discipline are new, they are not without forebears in the history of Christian theology. Recent studies, in the attempt to diagnose and suggest remedies for the "dissociation of sensibility"[37] in theology as well as the "spirituality gap"[38] in Christian experience, have recalled the premedieval unity of the theological endeavor as an intellectual-spiritual pursuit. Patristic theology would today be called biblical theology or more likely biblical spirituality.[39] It consists principally in an exegetically based interpretation of Scripture for the purpose of understanding and living the faith and/or a biblically elaborated theological exploration of spiritual experience.[40]

The roots of the separation of theology from its spiritual matrix were sown in the Middle Ages as philosophy began to rival Scripture in supplying the categories for systematic theology. At the same time the subject matter of spirituality as Christian experience was placed by Thomas Aquinas in Part 2 of the *Summa theologiae*, thereby making it a subdivision of moral theology, which drew its principles from dogmatic theology. In other words, from being a dimension of all theology spirituality began to appear as a subordinate branch of theology. This situation remained essentially unchanged, despite the elaboration of the discipline of spiritual theology itself, until the 1960s.[41]

In the 17th century we meet the first use of the term *ascetical theology* to denote a branch of dogma dealing with the principles of the spiritual life. In the 18th and 19th centuries, following the development during the 17th century of an intense interest in Christian perfection and especially in the mystical life, the spiritual life became the object of study and teaching in its own right. This field of study was called *spiritual theology* and its object was defined as "the science of perfection." It had two branches or subdivisions: *ascetical theology*, which studied the life of perfection (i.e., the spiritual life that had developed beyond the keeping of the commandments and the fulfilment of the ordinary duties of Christian life) in its active premystical phase, and *mystical theology*, which studied the life of perfection subsequent to the onset of passive mystical experience.[42]

The early 20th century saw the publication of the standard textbooks in spiritual theology,[43] which concurred in specifying the proper object of the discipline as the perfection of the Christian life and in situating it as a subdivision of moral theology which draws its principles from dogmatic theology but is superior to both because of its finality in lived holiness. It consisted in a speculative part which explored the doctrinal principles of the Christian life, a practical part which described and prescribed the means by which to develop this life, and the art of applying these principles and means to the individual.

Until the conciliar era most scholars in the field were in basic agreement about the general outline, basic content, and method of the field of spiritual theology. The only real controversy centered on the question, still being discussed today,[44] of the continuity or discontinuity of the mystical life with the life of Christian holiness to which all the baptized are called. In other words, the question is whether mysticism is the normal development of the life of faith or an extraordinary state to which only some, in virtue of a wholly gratuitous vocation, are invited. The modern discussion, especially since Vatican II's stress on the universal call to holiness, has tended more and more to the former position, and this probably has favored the growing preference for the inclusive term *spirituality* as a designation for the field which studies Christian religious experience over the term *spiritual theology* with its division into ascetical and mystical theology.[45]

Contemporary Discipline of Spirituality

VOCABULARY

Dense terminological confusion surrounds the developing academic discipline which studies what we have defined as spirituality. As already noted, the development of language cannot be controlled by fiat. Consequently, all that can be attempted here is to sort out the confusion, pin down the various uses of terms, and suggest a coherent vocabulary. Whether the latter will prevail depends on factors beyond the control of the written word.

There is a historical connection on the one hand between what was called in the 19th century *the life of Christian perfection* and what is today called *Christian spirituality*, and on the other hand between the 19th-century discipline of *spiritual theology* and the contemporary academic discipline of *Christian spirituality*. However, there are obvious and important discontinuities as well.

The expansion of the term *spirituality* to include non-Christian and even nonreligious spiritual experience entails an understanding of the discipline which is not necessarily theological. Thus, since the relation, if any, of theology to a particular spirituality is not determined by the nature of the discipline as such, the question of how the discipline of Christian spirituality is related to theology must be addressed. I have elsewhere proposed that Christian spirituality can be called a theological discipline only if theology is understood as an umbrella term for all of the sacred sciences, i.e. for all religious studies carried out in the context of explicit reference to revelation and explicitly affirmed confessional commitment. But if theology is strictly understood, i.e. as systematic and moral theology, then spirituality is not a theological discipline for the same reasons that church history or biblical exegesis would not be called theological disciplines. Although spirituality and theology in the strict sense are mutually related in that theology is a moment in the study of spirituality and vice versa, theology does not contain or control spirituality. In other words, I have proposed that spirituality is not a subdivision of either dogmatic or moral theology.[46]

Those scholars who defend the opposite thesis, i.e. that spirituality is a subdivision of theology in the strict sense, do so for one of three reasons. A few continue to think that spirituality derives its principles from the systematic elaboration of revelation,[47] i.e. from dogmatic and/or moral theology, of which it is therefore a subdivision. Others consider spirituality a theological discipline in the strict sense because, after describing the data of spiritual experience, the scholar of Christian spirituality judges that experience against a normative faith position.[48] The majority of those who see spirituality as a strictly theological discipline take this position because they are convinced that good theology is rooted in religious experience, reflects upon that experience, and nourishes the religious experience of the theologian and the church community.[49]

Some of the scholars who prefer the term *spiritual theology*, especially those in the last-named category, also tend to use the terms *spiritual theology* and *mystical theology* interchangeably. For two reasons this seems to me an unfortunate terminological move. First, both mystical theology and spiritual theology are terms which have specific historical meanings, and using them for something other than what they historically designated introduces unnecessary confusion into the contemporary discussion. Mystical theology, as it was used in the premedieval period, referred not to systematic theological reflection *on* mystical experience, i.e. to what Rahner correctly calls the "theology of mysticism,"[50] but to the obscure knowledge of God experienced *in and through* mystical experience precisely in contradistinction to the knowledge of God arrived at through systematic theology. As the medieval theologian Jean Gerson said, "[m]ystical theology is experimental knowledge of God through the embrace of unitive love."[51] Merton makes the distinction between mystical and systematic theology well when he says:

> Beyond the labor of argument it [contemplation] finds rest in faith and beneath the noise of discourse it apprehends the Truth, not in distinct and clear-cut definitions but in the limpid obscurity of a single intuition that unites all dogmas in one simple Light, shining into the soul directly from God's eternity, without the

medium of created concept, without the intervention of symbols or of language or the likenesses of material things.[52]

The difference between mystical theology and systematic theology, in other words, is not in *what* is apprehended (the divine Mystery) but in *how* it is apprehended. Systematic theology remains discursive and categorical even when it reflects on mystical experience, including the experience of the theologian himself or herself. And, as Merton says, even mystical theologians usually have recourse to the categories of systematic theology when they want to explain the knowledge received in contemplation.[53]

Spiritual theology, as has been explained, was the technical term used from the 17th century to our own time to denote that branch of theology, subordinate to dogmatics, which studies the Christian life of perfection in its ascetical and mystical realizations. Since we are still very much in the process of trying to liberate the contemporary discipline of spirituality from its tutelage to dogmatics and to broaden its scope to include the whole of the human search for self-transcendent integration and authenticity, it is not helpful to use this historically freighted term to speak of the contemporary discipline.

The second and more serious disadvantage of referring to experientially rooted systematic theology as spiritual (or mystical) theology is that it pre-empts the discussion of the proper relationship between spirituality and theology in favor of subordination of the former to the latter. Obviously, when the spirituality under discussion is religious, Christian or otherwise, theology is integrally involved. But the question of how it is involved is one which must not be decided by a premature subsuming of spirituality under theology.

I find most convincing and clarifying the position that regards spirituality as an autonomous discipline which functions in partnership and mutuality with theology. It is a relationship analogous to that between biblical studies and theology. Theology is a moment within the study of spirituality insofar as it is essential to the full interpretation of Christian spiritual experience.[54] Spirituality, as Keith Egan has explained[55] and William Thompson demonstrated,[56] is a moment integral to theology, both because it raises questions which theology must consider and because it supplies data for theological reflection. Rahner has made this point concretely in relation to the theological study of mysticism. He insists that the empirical mystic supplies data for the theologian which is not available from the traditional sources[57] and that this data is not only useful but necessary for a theological study of the experience.

NAMING THE DISCIPLINE

Throughout the preceding sections I have indicated my conviction that, despite its inherent polyvalence, the term *spirituality* is the most useful name for the emerging discipline. I now offer four reasons for this position.

First, if the emerging contemporary discipline which studies what we have defined as spirituality (in the anthropological sense) is to develop freely in terms of its proper subject matter and the appropriate scholarly approaches, especially in the context of Christian theological scholarship, it is crucial that it distance itself from its 19th-century forebears. Spirituality is related to 19th-century spiritual theology in much the same way that experimental psychology since Freud is related to scholastic rational psychology. The discontinuity, at the moment, is at least as important as the historical link, and new terminology is needed to underscore this point.

Second, by eliminating the term "theology" from the name of the new discipline we can avoid a premature resolution of the question of how spirituality (especially religious spirituality) is related to theology. Even more importantly, we can avoid the subordination of spirituality to theology which would foreclose the very contributions which an autonomous discipline of spirituality is capable of making to the theological enterprise itself.

Third, the term *spirituality*, precisely because it has little history in the academy and is not necessarily a theological term, has great potential for facilitating comparative and cross-traditional inquiry and dialogue. It is truly remarkable that a term which only 20 years ago connoted suspect enthusiasm or mindless piety in Protestant circles and was virtually unknown to Judaism, Eastern traditions, Native American religion, the new religious movements, or secular systems of life integration is now used freely within all of these circles. Even those who know that the term is historically Catholic do not seem to feel that it belongs to Catholicism or that to discuss spirituality is to appear on Catholic turf or to accept Catholic ground rules. It is very interesting that the Crossroad series includes a volume on ancient Greek, Roman, and Egyptian spirituality.[58] Although from a strictly historical perspective this use of the term is clearly anachronistic, it functions well for discussion of a particular dimension of the experience of classical antiquity. In short, by using the term *spirituality* for the discipline, we can identify the subject matter without freighting the discussion with disciplinary, denominational, or ideological presuppositions.

Fourth, spirituality better denotes the subject matter of the discipline than other narrower terms. This is true even when Christian spirituality is the specific area of inquiry. A striking illustration of this occurs in Rahner's essay on the theology of mysticism.[59] He engages the often-discussed question of whether mysticism is a higher state of Christian life to which only some are called, i.e. a nonconstitutive experience in relation to the Christian vocation. He answers that theologically there is no essential difference between ordinary faith experience and mystical experience, but then goes on to recognize that empirically there is a marked difference. He concludes (p. 73):

> When and to what extent such experiences [mystical phenomena of a psychological kind such as altered states of consciousness, paranormal experiences, etc.] occur (to the point of enjoying "essential" differences of a psychological kind), it is the mystic and the experimental psychologist within whose competency an investigation of these phenomena falls, not that of the dogmatic theologian.

In other words, mysticism is the type of subject which, if it is to be studied "in the round" as religious experience, must be explored in an interdisciplinary way. One of the relevant disciplines is theology, but constitutive elements of the phenomenon are outside the competence of theology. A scholar in the field of spirituality would agree with Rahner that one other relevant discipline is psychology, but would also recognize that comparative religion, anthropology, theory of myth and symbolism, history, literary interpretation, and other disciplines are also relevant. Spirituality better denotes the subject matter of this interdisciplinary field than narrower terms such as *spiritual theology*.

DEFINING THE DISCIPLINE

We can now attempt to describe the contemporary discipline which studies "the experience of consciously striving to integrate one's life in terms of self-transcendence toward the ultimate value one perceives." *Spirituality is the field of study which attempts to investigate in an interdisciplinary way spiritual experience as such*, i.e. as spiritual and as experience. I use the expression "spiritual experience" to indicate that the subject matter is not only religious experience in the technical sense but those analogous experiences of ultimate meaning and value which have transcendent and life-integrating power for individuals and groups.

Several characteristics of this emerging discipline should be highlighted, because in combination they help to distinguish it from related fields of study. First, spirituality is essentially an interdisciplinary discipline, or what Van Harvey felicitously called "a field-encompassing field."[60] Although theology is an important moment within the investigation of religious experience (as we saw in the case of mysticism), it is precisely because spirituality is interested in the experience *as* experience, i.e. in its phenomenological wholeness, that it must utilize whatever approaches are relevant to the reality being studied. In the case of Christian spirituality, usually at least biblical studies, history, theology, psychology, and comparative religion must be involved in the investigation of any significant subject in the field.[61]

Second, spirituality is a descriptive-critical rather than prescriptive-normative discipline. Unlike spiritual theology, which aimed to apply unquestioned principles derived from revelation and tradition to the life of the Christian, spirituality wishes to understand religious experience as it occurs. As in any field, the scholar in the field of spirituality will make critical judgments about the adequacy of such experience using norms derived from various disciplines including theology.[62] And spirituality as a discipline has, as one of its ends, to facilitate healthy religious experience in much the same way that the study of psychology is directed toward therapy. But spirituality is not the "practical application" of theoretical principles, theological or other, to concrete life experience. It is the critical study of such experience.

Third, spirituality is ecumenical, interreligious, and cross-cultural. This does not mean that every investigation in the field is comparative in nature but rather that the context within which spiritual experience is studied is anthropologically inclusive. Even the study of Christian spirituality as such does not proceed on the assumption that Christianity exhausts or includes the whole of religious reality or that only Christian data is relevant for an understanding of Christian spiritual experience. A study of Christian mysticism, for example, must be carried on within and in terms of the ongoing cross-cultural and interreligious discussion of mysticism, religious and nonreligious, as a human experience.

Fourth, spirituality is a holistic discipline in that its inquiry into human spiritual experience is not limited to explorations of the explicitly religious, i.e. the so-called "interior life." The psychological, bodily, historical, social, political, aesthetic, intellectual, and other dimensions of the human subject of spiritual experience are integral to that experience insofar as it is the subject matter of the discipline of spirituality.

It is not amiss to remark that the emphasis in spirituality on inclusivity, wholeness, integration, and the validation of experience creates a particular affinity between spirituality and feminism, which embraces as values in both life and scholarship these very characteristics. The volume of writing in feminist spirituality testifies to this affinity.[63] Some authors have even identified feminist sensibility as a characteristic of the contemporary discipline of spirituality.[64]

Aside from these characteristics, the practice of the discipline involves the conjunction of a particular *type of object* (the individual as opposed to the general), a particular *methodological style* (participation), a general "ideal" *procedure* (description–critical analysis–constructive appropriation), and a particular kind of *objective* (plural rather than singular) which further qualifies and distinguishes it.

Paul Ricoeur referred to the study of texts as a "science of the individual,"[65] by which he meant to insist that the logic of probability consisting in the convergence of mutually supportive indices arrived at through a dialectic of explanation and understanding can provide the appropriately scientific knowledge of a reality which is studied and known not as a member of a class or a verification of a principle but precisely as an individual. Spirituality is characteristically involved in the study of individuals: texts, persons, particular spiritual traditions such as Benedictinism, elements of spiritual experience such as discernment, interrelations of factors in particular situations such as the mutual relation of prayer and social commitment, concrete processes such as spiritual direction, etc. While making use of a plurality of specific methods, the discipline itself has no one method of its own.[66] Rather, methods function in the explanatory moment of the hermeneutical dialectic between explanation and understanding.

The methodological style of spirituality as a discipline must be described as participative. It is certainly the case that most, if not all, students in the field come to the discipline out of and because of their personal involvement with its subject matter. And virtually all intend not only to do research and teach in the field when they graduate but to "practice" in the field in some pastoral sense of the word.[67] But the question of the relation of praxis to the discipline is most complicated in regard to the actual "doing" of spirituality.

Like psychology, spirituality deals with material that often cannot be understood except through analogy with personal experience. Spirituality deals with spiritual experience as such, not merely with ideas about or principles governing such experience (although these certainly have a role in the research). Just as one cannot understand anxiety unless one has experienced it, or the therapeutic process unless one has participated in it, it is difficult to imagine that one could understand mysticism, discernment, or spiritual direction without some personal participation in a spiritual life in which these phenomena or their analogues were experienced. Furthermore, as students readily testify, research in the area of spirituality is self-implicating, often at a very deep level, and the transformation experienced through study reverberates in the ongoing research.

All of this raises serious questions about the appropriate objectivity of the discipline, and where there is a mistrust of spirituality in the academy it tends to center on this issue. Some scholars fear that personal spiritual practice will be substituted for research in arriving at conclusions; others that critical judgment will be clouded by religious commitment; others that programs in spirituality will function as clandestine formation programs or evangelization agencies. While these fears are belied by the quality of research and publication of both doctoral students and mature scholars in the field, there is no question that this issue of the participant nature of the discipline requires further investigation and clarification.

Third, studies in spirituality tend to involve a three-dimensional approach which, while not a "method" in the strict sense, does give a recognizable and distinguishing shape to many studies in the field and might eventually permit the type of cumulation of research results that has so far not been possible. The first phase is essentially descriptive and intends to surface the data concerning the experience being investigated. In this phase historical, textual, and comparative studies are of primary importance. The second phase is essentially analytical and critical, leading to an explanation and evaluation of the subject. Here the theological, human, and social sciences are of particular importance. The third phase is synthetic and/or constructive, and leads to appropriation.[68] Hermeneutical theory governs this final phase. Not every study in the field of spirituality will involve all three dimensions nor will they always occur in this order. But experience suggests that this type of approach distinguishes serious studies in the field.

Fourth, spirituality as a discipline seems to have an irreducibly triple finality. While research in the field is aimed first of all at the production of cumulative knowledge, there is no denying that it is also intended by most students to assist them in their own spiritual lives and to enable them to foster the spiritual lives of others. While this triple finality contrasts with the traditional understanding of an academic discipline, it is actually not much different from the objective of the study of psychology or art. And increasingly even speculative theologians are realizing that good theology is not an exercise in abstract thought but reflection on the lived experience of the church community which should affect that life.

Conclusion

No attentive observer of the contemporary cultural scene can fail to recognize the breadth and power of the "spirituality phenomenon" in virtually every part of the world. In the West various theories have been adduced to explain it. Some see it as the natural and even necessary culmination of the psychoanalytic movement inaugurated by Freud. Others attribute it to the final disillusionment with the Enlightenment ideal of progress generated by the wars of the 20th century. Others think it is a response to the meaninglessness of existence in mass society. And some believe it is the proper name for the wholesome breeze that entered through the windows opened by Vatican II. But whatever its cause(s), there is no denying its grip on the contemporary imagination.

Although the interest in spirituality sometimes produces superficial, unhealthy, bizarre, and even evil manifestations, it represents, on the whole, a profound and authentic desire of 20th-century humanity for wholeness in the midst of fragmentation, for community in the face of isolation and loneliness, for liberating transcendence, for meaning in life, for values that endure. Human beings are spirit in the world, and spirituality is the effort to understand and realize the potential of that extraordinary and paradoxical condition.[69]

It is not surprising that scholars have been drawn to study this phenomenon. But what is more than surprising is the speed with which the original interest in charting and even measuring the phenomenon and then in facilitating the spiritual development of laity and ministers has become a serious, critical engagement with the subject matter within the academy. In the space of a couple of decades a new discipline has emerged. Spirituality is by no means a full-grown participant in the academy. Neither its self-definition nor its relationship with other disciplines is clearly established. It has not arrived at a commonly accepted vocabulary nor developed a sufficiently articulated approach to its subject matter to allow for the steady cumulation of research results that marks a mature field of inquiry.

Nevertheless, a steadily increasing number of graduate students are choosing spirituality as an area of specialization. Courses in the discipline are multiplying at the undergraduate and graduate levels. The tools of research and the organs for the communication of research are being developed. Serious and ongoing discussion is being pursued in academic societies and institutions. And some scholars from the traditional mainline disciplines are discovering that their deepest interests can be discussed more freely in the precincts of spirituality and are bringing the expertise of their developed scholarship to the new discussion. Spirituality stands at the junction where the deepest concerns of humanity and the contemporary concern with interdisciplinarity, cross-cultural exchange, interreligious dialogue, feminist scholarship, the integration of theory and praxis, and the hermeneutical turn come together. If the present of spirituality as an academic discipline is somewhat confused, it is also very exciting.

Notes

1. A Protestant, Bradley Hanson, "Christian Spirituality and Spiritual Theology," *Dialog* 21 (1982): 207–12, attributes the upsurge of interest in spirituality to the crisis of meaning generated by the events of the 1960s. Anglican Tilden H. Edwards, "Spiritual Formation in Theological Schools: Ferment and Challenge. A Report of the ATS Shalem Institute on Spirituality," *Theological Education* 17 (1980): 7–52, reports on the

factors accounting for the increased interest in spirituality in seminaries. Among Catholic authors Joann Conn, "Books on Spirituality," *Theology Today* 39 (1982): 65–58, attributes the increased interest in spirituality to the spiritual maturation of Catholics since Vatican II. John Heagle, "A New Public Piety: Reflections on Spirituality," *Church* 1 (1985): 52–55, singles out the increased desire to integrate faith and life, especially the justice agenda. Eugene Megyer, "Theological Trends: Spiritual Theology Today," *The Way* 21 (1981): 55–67, focuses on the factors, especially the biblical and liturgical renewals, on the eve of the council which favored the development of the interest in spirituality. Ewert Cousins, "Spirituality: A Resource for Theology," *Catholic Theological Society of America Proceedings* 35 (1980): 124–37, chronicles the development of interest in spirituality and lists its salient characteristics, while Joseph A. Tetlow, "Spirituality: An American Sampler," *America* 153 (1985): 261–67, notes that 37 million Americans bought books in spirituality during 1985, publishers of spiritual books prospered, and outlets handling publications in spirituality multiplied.

2. Ans J. van der Bent, "The Concern for Spirituality: An Analytical and Bibliographical Survey of the Discussion within the WCC Constituency," *Ecumenical Review* 38 (1986): 101–14, describes the process, beginning in 1948, of the gradual integration of the concern for spirituality into the WCC agenda.

3. Andrew Louth, *Discerning the Mystery: An Essay on the Nature of Theology* (Oxford: Clarendon, 1983) is the volume on the relation of spirituality to theology which resulted from the Oxford program.

4. H. Limit and J. Ries, eds., *L'expérience de la prière dans les grandes religions* (Louvain-la-Neuve: Centre d'Histoire des Religions, 1980) is the acts of a colloquium studying prayer across historical periods and religious traditions, both pagan and Christian.

5. Francis Eigo, ed., *Dimensions of Contemporary Spirituality* (Villanova: Villanova University, 1982), and *Contemporary Spirituality: Responding to the Divine Initiative* (Villanova: Villanova University, 1983).

6. The AAR Seminar on Spirituality meeting at the 1988 national convention was centered on the question, "What Is Spirituality?" and discussed unpublished papers on this topic by Ewert Cousins of Fordham University, Carlos Eire of the University of Virginia, Bradley Hanson of Luther College, Sandra Schneiders of the Graduate Theological Union, and F. Ellen Weaver of the University of Notre Dame. The participants were not in agreement about the nature of either the subject matter or the discipline which studies that subject matter, but as the discussions proceed, it is becoming clearer what questions must be answered.

7. Vernon Gregson, at the 1982 CTSA convention, remarked that "the theological use of spirituality is an obvious and significant change in recent Roman Catholic tradition." See "Seminar on Spirituality: Revisiting an Experiential Approach to Salvation," *Catholic Theological Society of America Proceedings* 37 (1982): 175.

8. Karl Rahner, "The Spirituality of the Future," in *The Practice of the Faith: A Handbook of Contemporary Spirituality*, ed. K. Lehmann and A. Raffelt (New York: Crossroad, 1986), 22. This collection of writings by Rahner on topics related to spirituality includes (313–14) the references to the original location and publication data of each essay.

9. See the excellent article by Regina Bechtle, "Convergences in Theology and Spirituality," *The Way* 23 (1985): 305–14. She discusses the work of Rahner, Lonergan, Pannenberg, Soelle, and the liberation theologians and concludes that their work makes clear that unless theology is grounded in the taste of mystery and in search of God through conversion, it is empty and sterile. But unless spiritual experience is involved in the search for understanding and thus in the movement of reflection, it remains inarticulate for itself and for others.

10. Among the authors who take this position are Hanson, "Christian Spirituality," 212; Cousins, "Spirituality," 126; Megyer, "Theological Trends," 56.

11. Rachel Hosmer, "Current Literature in Christian Spirituality," *Anglican Theological Review* 66 (1984): 425, captures the vagueness of the modern sense of the word: "Spirituality in the broadest sense defies definition. It refers to whatever in human experience is alive and intentional, conscious of itself and responsive to others. It is capable of creative growth and liable to decay." The descriptive definition chosen by the editors of the World Spirituality series is the following: "That inner dimension of the person called by certain traditions 'the spirit.' This spiritual core is the deepest center of the person. It is here that the person is open to the transcendent dimension; it is here that the person experiences ultimate reality. The series explores the discovery of this core, the dynamics of its development, and its journey to the ultimate goal. It deals with prayer, spiritual direction, the various maps of the spiritual journey, and the methods of advancement in the spiritual ascent." Cf. Ewert Cousins, "Preface to the Series," in *Christian Spirituality*, vol. 1, *Origins to the Twelfth Century*, ed. Bernard McGinn and John Meyendorff, World Spirituality: An Encyclopedic History of the Religious Quest 16 (New York: Crossroad, 1985), xiii.

12. World Spirituality, ed. Ewert Cousins, 25 vols. (New York: Crossroad, 1985–).

13. Heagle, "A New Public Piety," 53, succinctly summarizes the major differences between preconciliar and postconciliar spirituality. The former was theoretical, elitist, otherworldly, ahistorical, antisecular, individualistic, concentrated on the "interior life" and "perfection." By contrast, "The emerging spirituality of our age is intensely personal without being private. It is visionary without being theoretical. It is prophetic without being partisan, and it is incarnational without becoming worldly. It emphasizes personal response and interior commitment but it radically changes the context within which this response takes place."

14. E.g., there are doctoral programs in spirituality at the Graduate Theological Union in Berkeley, Duquesne University in Pittsburgh, Fordham University in New York, and at the Pontifical Gregorian University in Rome.

15. M. Viller, F. Cavallera, and J. de Guibert, eds. (Paris: Beauchesne, 1932–).

16. E.g., the *Dictionnaire de la vie spirituelle*, adaptation française par François Vial (Paris: Cerf, 1983).

17. Cheslyn Jones, Geoffrey Wainwright, and Edward Yarnold, eds. (New York: Oxford University Press, 1986).

18. Charles-André Bernard (Rome: Gregorian University, 1976).

19. Juan L. Astigarrago, dir. (Rome: Pont. Inst. Spiritualitatis, 1966–). *The Way, Studies in Formative Spirituality*, and *Nouvelle revue théologique* regularly publish bibliographies and review articles in the field of spirituality. *New Review of Books and Religion* devoted the entire issue 4, April 1980, to books in the field.

20. E.g., Michael Glazier's 12-volume series The Way of the Christian Mystics; Crossroad's Spiritual Classics series; *Christian Spirituality: The Essential Guide to the Most Influential Spiritual Writings of the Christian Tradition*, ed. Frank N. Magill and Ian P. McGreal (San Francisco: Harper & Row, 1988).

21. E.g., Paulist Press's 60-volume series Classics of Western Spirituality and its new series Sources of American Spirituality.

22. The full-length monograph of Lucy Tinsely, *The French Expression for Spirituality and Devotion: A Semantic Study* (Washington, D.C.: Catholic University of America, 1953) was augmented by Jean Leclercq in his article "Spiritualitas," *Studi medievali* 3 (1963): 279–96, which he wrote in response to the study by Italian historian Gustavo Vinay, "'Spiritualità': Invito a una discussione," *Studi medievali* 2 (1961): 705–9. Leclercq's study,

in turn, has been summarized and augmented by Walter H. Principe "Toward Defining Spirituality," *Studies in Religion/Sciences religieuses* 12 (1983): 127–41.

23. Charles-André Bernard, *Traité de théologie spirituelle* (Paris: Cerf, 1986).

24. E.g., Megyer, "Theological Trends," 611–62, says that spirituality is a theological discipline because it derives its principles from revelation; that it is subordinate to dogmatic and moral theology, but is not merely the practical application of these disciplines because it pays particular attention to the personal, historical, and experiential aspects of faith and action. He says that, in a sense, spiritual theology could be called "supernatural anthropology" because its material object is the human being as he or she lives spiritually.

25. Jean-Claude Breton, "Retrouver les assises anthropologiques de la vie spirituelle," *Studies in Religion/Sciences religieuses* 17 (1988): 97–105.

26. Ibid., 101.

27. Ibid., 100.

28. Ibid., 103.

29. "What Do Recent Writers Mean by Spirituality?" *Spirituality Today* 32 (1980): 247–56.

30. See Sandra M. Schneiders, "Theology and Spirituality: Strangers, Rivals, or Partners?" *Horizons* 13 (1986): 265–67, for a summary of Alexander's position and my criticism of it.

31. Raymundo Panikkar, *The Trinity and the Religious Experience of Man: Icon-Person-Mystery* (Maryknoll, N.Y.: Orbis, 1973), 9.

32. See discussion of this point by Cousins, "Spirituality," 124–25, who calls the interaction between Western and Eastern traditions one of the salient features of contemporary spirituality; William Johnston, *The Inner Eye of Love: Mysticism and Religion* (London: Collins, 1978), 60, who says the mystical experience of the Trinity is the meeting ground for the dialogue between Christianity and the great religions of the East.

33. Besides the definitions given in Alexander's article (see n. 29 above), descriptions and/or definitions can be found in the following: Antonio Queralt, "La 'espiritualidad' como disciplina teologica," *Gregorianum* 60 (1979): 334; Hanson, "Christian Spirituality," 207; Principe, "Toward Defining Spirituality," 136; Hosmer, "Current Literature in Christian Spirituality," 425; McGinn, introduction to *Christian Spirituality*, 1:xiv–xvi.

34. Schneiders, "Theology and Spirituality," 266.

35. What is said in this section about Christian spirituality as an academic discipline is applicable, in general and with appropriate modifications, to other spiritualities. While nonreligious spiritualities obviously do not have theologies, they do have ideological structures which function analogously.

36. "Toward Defining Spirituality," 135–36.

37. This expression of T. S. Eliot is used by Bechtle, "Convergences," 305, for what she calls the post-Enlightenment lobotomizing of Western culture, i.e. the separation of thought from feeling, mind from heart, which was reflected in theology as a separation of theology from spirituality or of Christian thought from Christian living. There came to be two paths to God: the way of knowledge/thought/theory and that of love/prayer/action, the first a journey of the mind and the other a journey of the heart. The same phenomenon is discussed by Louth in *Discerning the Mystery*, 1–3. Harvey Egan, "The Devout Christian of the Future Will . . . Be a 'Mystic': Mysticism and Karl Rahner's Theology," in *Theology and Discovery: Essays in Honor of Karl Rahner*, ed. W. J. Kelly (Milwaukee: Marquette University, 1980), 156, remarks that the deeply experiential character of Rahner's theology is "all the more remarkable when one considers the tradition out of which he comes. He had to overcome the radical divorce between spirituality and theology."

38. Richard Lovelace, "The Sanctification Gap," *Theology Today* 29 (1973): 365–66, coined this term to refer to the rationalistic process within the evangelical tradition which so overloaded the conversion process that it left no room for the lifelong process of spiritual growth and resulted in a separation of spirituality from both theological discourse and personal witness.

39. Megyer, "Theological Trends," 56, describes it well as reflection on Christian experience, which led to intensified spiritual life, in contrast to scholastic theology, which was "scientific, theoretical and dry speculation."

40. For a fuller historical treatment of this topic, see Sandra M. Schneiders, "Scripture and Spirituality," in *Christian Spirituality*, 1:1–20.

41. Megyer, "Theological Trends," 58–61, surveys the situation of spirituality under moral theology by such scholars as Congar, Maritain, Vandenbroucke, and Mouroux.

42. G. B. Scaramelli (1867–1952) was the first, apparently, to establish "ascetical and mystical theology" as one of the sacred disciplines, with the distinction between the two in terms of whether the activity of the spiritual life was acquired or infused.

43. E.g., Adolphe Tanquerey, The *Spiritual Life: A Treatise on Ascetical and Mystical Theology*, 2d ed. (Tournai: Desclée, 1930); Reginald Garrigou-Lagrange, *The Three Ages of the Interior Life*, 2 vols. (New York: Herder, 1948).

44. Karl Rahner takes up this issue in "Everyday Mysticism," in *The Practice of Faith: A Handbook of Contemporary Spirituality*, ed. K. Lehmann and L. Raffelt (New York: Crossroad, 1986), 69–70, and decides in favor of the continuity position. Rahner's position is elaborated by Egan in "Mysticism and Karl Rahner's Theology," 149.

45. Megyer, "Theological Trends," 58.

46. Schneiders, "Theology and Spirituality," 271–73.

47. This is Megyer's position in "Theological Trends," 61–62.

48. Principe, "Toward Defining Spirituality," 139–40.

49. Some who take this position are Bechtle, "Convergences," 305–14; Egan, "Mysticism and Karl Rahner's Theology," 140, and elsewhere; Johnston, *The Inner Eye of Love*, 53, 56, and elsewhere; Alan Jones, "Spirituality and Theology," *Review for Religious* 39 (1980): 161–76; M. Basil Pennington, "Spiritual Theology," *America* 155 (1986): 87.

50. Karl Rahner, "The Theology of Mysticism," in *The Practice of Faith*, 70–77.

51. Cited by Jones, "Spirituality and Theology," 170.

52. Thomas Merton, *New Seeds of Contemplation* (New York: New Directions, 1962), 148.

53. "And yet when the contemplative returns from the depths of his simple experience of God and attempts to communicate it to men, he necessarily comes once again under the control of the theologian and his language is bound to strive after the clarity and distinctness and accuracy that canalize Catholic tradition." Ibid., 149.

54. Cf. Harold Hatt, "Christian Experience, Systematic Theology, and the Seminary Curriculum," *Encounter* 36 (1975): 195.

55. Egan's contribution is recorded by Vernon Gregson, "Seminar on Spirituality: Spirituality as a Source for Theology," *Catholic Theological Society of America Proceedings* 38 (1983): 124.

56. In his *Fire and Light: The Saints and Theology: On Consulting the Saints, Mystics, and Martyrs in Theology* (New York and Mahwah, N.J.: Paulist, 1987), Thompson uses specific problems in theology and in spirituality to demonstrate the mutual relationship between the two disciplines.

57. Rahner says that nothing in his position implies that the "theology of mysticism can only be constituted from the same sources and via the same methods as those employed by traditional dogmatic theology (Scripture, the magisterium, Church tradition, and so on)." "The Theology of Mysticism," 74.

58. A. H. Armstrong, ed., *Classical Mediterranean Spirituality: Egyptian, Greek, Roman* (New York: Crossroad, 1986).

59. Rahner, "The Theology of Mysticism," 73.

60. Van A. Harvey, *The Historian and the Believer: The Morality of Historical Knowledge and Christian Belief* (Philadelphia: Westminster, 1966), 54–59.

61. Principe, if I understand him correctly, takes a different view of the pluralistic approach to spirituality. Rather than conceive of the discipline of spirituality as itself interdisciplinary, he takes spirituality as the unitary subject matter, which is then studied historically (history of spirituality), theologically (spiritual theology), in terms of its cultural setting (sociology of spirituality), etc. See "Toward Defining Spirituality," 139–40.

62. Principe distinguishes a history-of-religions approach to spirituality from a theological approach at precisely this point. He says that after describing the spirituality in question, the theologian goes on to evaluate the data against a normative faith position. At this point one is involved in spiritual theology. I believe that the theologically critical moment is integral to the study of the experience under investigation, just as a psychologically critical moment is, without either one translating the study into another field, e.g. theology or psychology.

63. For a brief but excellent introduction to feminist spirituality, see Anne Carr, "On Feminist Spirituality," in *Women's Spirituality: Resources for Christian Development,* ed. Joann W. Conn (New York and Mahwah, N.J.: Paulist, 1986), 49–58.

64. Keith Egan suggested this in the context of the seminar discussion at the 1983 CTSA convention as recorded by Gregson, "Seminar on Spirituality," 124. See also Hosmer, "Current Literature in Christian Spirituality," 426.

65. Cf. Paul Ricoeur, *Interpretation Theory: Discourse and the Surplus of Meaning* (Fort Worth: Texas Christian University, 1976), 79.

66. Edward Kinerk, "Toward a Method for the Study of Spirituality," *Review for Religious* 40 (1981): 3–19, proposes that Lonergan's method can be adapted for the study of spirituality. The problem with his proposal is that he seems to reduce the subject of spirituality to historical studies of spiritualities (in the sense of schools or traditions), whereas the studies in the field are of extremely diverse subjects, e.g. discernment, social-justice involvement, spirituality movements, bodily ramifications of spiritual experience, prayer, mysticism, etc.

67. I say this on the basis of personal experience with doctoral students and am indebted to the students in the doctoral program in Christian spirituality at the Graduate Theological Union for their help in reflecting on this aspect of the issue.

68. I am using the term "appropriation" as Ricoeur does in *Interpretation Theory,* 91–95, to refer to the transformational actualization of meaning.

69. This is the very point which cultural anthropologist Ernest Becker made in his Pulitzer Prize-winning study of the human condition, *The Denial of Death* (New York: Macmillan, 1973). He says toward the end of the book: "The distinctive human problem from time immemorial has been the need to spiritualize human life . . ." (231).

Part 5

Spirituality
and the Trinity

Spirituality and the Christian doctrine of the Trinity are closely related. Accordingly, in the first selection, the late Catherine LaCugna affirms that "who" God is can never be separated from "who we are now and who we are to become." Indeed, not only is relationship the central theme of all trinitarian theology, but also God's "open and dynamic life of giving and receiving" is an emblem of the spiritual journey. Put another way, the "exience" (to use Macquarrie's term) of going outside of oneself to the other is not only the substance of spirituality, but it is also descriptive of the Godhead as understood by the Christian community of faith. Given this understanding, LaCugna argues for a theological shift from "substance ontology" to "relational ontology" and maintains that the communion of God and Christ, according to the doctrine of the Trinity, "does not permit any kind of subordination, inequality or hierarchy."

Building on many of the insights of LaCugna, John Gresham postulates three different ways in which the journey toward union with the trinitarian God has been

understood. He calls the first map or model "contemplative spirituality," and gives as an example Augustine's work, which focused on the divine presence in the soul. Augustine developed a psychological analogy to the Trinity in terms of three elements of the soul: remembrance, love, and knowledge. Eastern theologians, for their part, offered a very different model, which Gresham calls "social spirituality of participation in the Trinitarian fellowship." Here it is not the individual soul or its elements, but the unity of three distinct persons (Peter, James, and John, for example) that provides an illustration of the Holy Trinity. The dominant image here is "not the Trinity dwelling in the human soul, but humanity dwelling in the Trinity." Gresham terms the last model "sacramental/charismatic spirituality of trinitarian missions." This model conceives Christian initiation, in both its sacramental and charismatic dimensions, as "participation in the trinitarian missions of Son and Spirit sent into the world as the Father's gift of salvation."

In the final essay of this section, "Contemplating the Trinitarian

Mystery of Christ," James B. Torrance challenges contemporary Christian worship and practice in light of the doctrine of the Trinity. Torrance contends that much of Christian worship is actually "Unitarian," human-centered, and with no real doctrine of a Mediator. His corrective calls for viewing worship as "the gift of participating through the Spirit in the (incarnate) Son's communication with the Father." His understanding is in agreement with that of the sixteenth-century Reformers and is both trinitarian and incarnational, catholic and evangelical, and beckons all toward participation in the full, rich, and beautiful life of God.

The Practical Trinity

Catherine Mowry LaCugna

The Doctrine of the Trinity has the reputation of being an arcane and abstract theory that has no relevance to the practice of Christian faith. Most people, whether in parish education programs or in advanced theological study, typically avoid this teaching which has played only a peripheral role in Christian thought in the last 15 centuries. This was not always the case; about 1,600 years ago Gregory of Nyssa complained that it was impossible to go into the marketplace to buy bread, or go to the bank, or go to the baths, without getting involved in a discussion about whether God the Son is equal to or less than God the Father. This lively debate, carried on in the most ordinary of settings, would be hard to imagine today. In fact, the late Catholic theologian Karl Rahner once remarked that even if one could show the doctrine of the Trinity to be false, most religious literature could well remain virtually unchanged.

What Rahner said was certainly true 50, 20, even 15 years ago. But recent years have seen an explosion of interest in trinitarian doctrine, due in part to Rahner's own seminal study of the doctrine of the Trinity, complemented by the prominent place Karl Barth gave it in his *Church Dogmatics.* Other factors include changes wrought by the Second Vatican Council, the widespread fascination with spirituality and world religions, new exegetical studies in Christology, and the vital critiques of classical ideas of God made by political, feminist, black, and Latin American liberation

This essay first appeared in *Christian Century* 109.22 (15 July 1992): 678–82. Used by permission of the Christian Century Foundation.

theologians. Although the classical teaching on the Trinity is only in its initial stages of rejuvenation, many significant books and articles have begun to appear that retrieve largely forgotten ideas and persons, and then apply principles gleaned from trinitarian doctrine to current social, political, economic, spiritual or church-related issues. For example, the principle that the divine persons are perfectly co-equal is used to dismantle the patriarchal idea that women are subordinate to men. The idea of God's providential economy as the economics of lavish and superabundant grace is contrasted with human economics driven by scarcity, deprivation and costliness. The idea of the Trinity's loving relation to creation is linked with ecological concerns. And the renewal of interest in the Holy Spirit is becoming a contact point with other religions.

It used to be that a new doctrine of the Trinity meant a new way to explain "God's inner life," that is, the relationship of Father, Son and Holy Spirit to one another (what tradition refers to as the immanent Trinity). But now both Catholic and Protestant theologians who are working to revitalize the doctrine of the Trinity have shifted away from constructing theories about God's "inner life." Instead, by returning to the more concrete images and concepts of the Bible, liturgy and creeds, it has become clear that the original purpose of the doctrine was to explain the place of Christ in our salvation, the place of the Spirit in our sanctification or deification, and in so doing to say something about the mystery of God's eternal being. By concentrating more on the mystery of *God with us, God for us,* and less on the nature of God by Godself, it is becoming possible once again for the doctrine of the Trinity to stand at the center of faith—as our rhetoric has always claimed. The doctrine of the Trinity is being rehabilitated first as the summary of what we believe about God who saves through Jesus Christ by the power of the Holy Spirit, and second as the proper context for the entire theological enterprise, whether in the areas of ecclesiology, sacraments or Christology.

The heart of Christian faith is the encounter with the God of Jesus Christ who makes possible both our union with God and communion with each other. In this encounter God invites people to share in divine life and grace through Jesus Christ by the power of the Holy Spirit; at the same time, we are called to live in new relationship with one other, as we are gathered together by the Spirit into the body of Christ. The personal and communal dimensions of Christian faith are inseparable.

The Letter to the Ephesians (1:3–14) contains a beautiful liturgical hymn that neatly summarizes this basic subject matter of trinitarian theology: God has blessed us from before all eternity; God elected us in Christ so that we would be holy and blameless before God in love; God desires to live with us in the intimacy of a familial relationship. In Jesus

Christ we have been redeemed and our sins forgiven by the blood of the cross; God plans to reunite all things with God, which is why we are sealed with the Spirit of God. We also are told what our vocation is: to live for the praise of God's glory. This is the record of redemptive history, beginning with God turned toward the creature in love, and ending with all things being reunited with God.

Trinitarian theology is about this entire economy (*oikonomia*—dispensation) of providence, election, redemption and consummation. Indeed, the shape of trinitarian doctrine is dictated by the pattern of redemption; everything comes from God, is made known and redeemed through Jesus Christ, and is consummated by the power of the Holy Spirit. Theology as doctrine of God thus is dependent on theology as doctrine of salvation.

In short, the doctrine's subject matter is the mystery of God who acts and is present in the events of history—salvation history. The God of redemptive history comes to be known, loved and worshiped in the course of a yet-to-be-completed relationship between God and God's people. God is discovered first of all in creation—creation as interpreted through the religious history of Israel; the central feature of Israel's history is covenant love, initiated on Sinai and continued through the testimony of the prophets. For Christians the history of God reaches decisive expression in the life, teaching, death and resurrection of Christ. The work of God accomplished in Christ is continued in the ongoing transforming and deifying work of the Spirit, and in the eschatological consummation of creation and the fulfillment of all in God.

Once the close connection between the question of salvation and the question of God becomes apparent, it also becomes clear that the Christian doctrine of God has very little to do with an abstract state of affairs, whether heavenly or earthly. To be sure, "Trinity" is the normative Christian model for understanding who God is; but who God is can never be separated from who we are now and who we are to become. The central theme of all trinitarian theology is relationship: God's relationship with us, and our relationships with one another. The doctrine of the Trinity is not an abstract conceptual paradox about God's inner life, or a mathematical puzzle of the "one and three." The doctrine of the Trinity is in fact the most practical of all doctrines. Among other things, it helps us articulate our understanding of the gospel's demands; how personal conversion is related to social transformation; what constitutes "right relationship" within the Christian community and in society at large; how best to praise and worship God; and what it means to confess faith in and be baptized into the life of the God of Jesus Christ.

The doctrine of the Trinity is therefore naturally linked to the church's confessional and liturgical expressions of "right relationship" such as the one noted in Ephesians. The giving of praise to God is the proper response to what God is accomplishing in salvation history. The content of the doctrine of the Trinity and essential acts of believers—adoration and worship of God—are therefore inseparable. The church confessed in its early creeds, gave thanks for in its eucharistic prayers, and praised in its doxologies *what God had done in Christ.* The original context of trinitarian faith was indeed doxological. Doxology is the living language of faith in which praise is offered to God for the abundance of God's generous love. Through doxology our thoughts and words, hopes and acts, are offered to God and open us up into the reality of the living God. From the beginning Christians offered praise and thanksgiving to God through Jesus Christ. This pattern of prayer signaled a new religious identity. The mediatory prayers offering praise to God through Christ also eventually played a major role in the doctrinal controversies of the fourth century, since some theologians used the prayers to support the view that Christ was less than God.

Liturgy thus shapes trinitarian faith, especially in the sacraments of baptism and Eucharist, and in the recitation of common Christian creeds. Systematic and historical theologies of the Trinity often downplay the extent to which the question of the divinity of Christ (and later, the divinity of the Spirit) was prompted by conflicting interpretations of the early church's liturgical acts. When understood as doxology, trinitarian theology is placed squarely within its proper context, namely, the confessing community of faith. Because trinitarian theology must be moored in the concrete expressions of faith, worship in particular recommends itself as the point of entry into reflection on trinitarian faith.

When the doctrine of the Trinity is presented in a way that is more at home with the concrete language and images of the Bible, creeds and the liturgy, it becomes plain that it is an eminently practical doctrine with far-reaching consequences for Christian faith, ethics, spirituality, and the life of the church. The doctrine of the Trinity is an effort to articulate basic Christian faith: In Jesus Christ, the ineffable and invisible God saves us from sin and death; by the power of the Holy Spirit, God continues to be altogether present to us, seeking everlasting communion with all creatures. Christianity and Christian theology simply cannot do *without* a trinitarian doctrine of God that articulates the heart of this faith.

Two questions seem unavoidable once one recognizes that the doctrine of the Trinity depicts a God who is irrevocably bound to a people and their history; a God resolutely interested in human flourishing, a God intimately present to every creature at every moment. Why has this doctrine played such a minor role in Christian theology and life, and even been regarded as contrary to reason? And what obstacles need to be overcome, what doctrinal adjustments need to be made, so that this profound teaching may once more occupy the center of faith?

Answering the first question requires historical perspective. Briefly, the early church from its very origins struggled to interpret the gospel. It had to answer difficult questions about how Christianity was in continuity with Judaism, about the role of Jesus Christ in our salvation, about whether Jesus was on a par with God or less than God. Within a few decades questions about the Holy Spirit also arose: Is the Spirit distinct from Jesus? Is the Spirit divine? (Not until 381 did the Council of Constantinople affirm the divinity of the Spirit.)

The overriding concern of theologians at this time was precisely the nature of redemption: Who saves us? Is it God who saves? Jesus Christ? The Holy Spirit? Since only God can save, and since God, Christ and the Spirit are all essential to our salvation, are there three gods? The obvious answer was that the one God saves through Jesus Christ by the power of the Holy Spirit. This affirmation was consistent with the New Testament language, and also with the pattern of the church's prayer, since doxologies and early eucharistic prayers were offered in just this pattern—to God through Jesus Christ.

But then the question was posed whether the pattern of the church's prayer and the witness of the New Testament could be interpreted to mean that because Jesus Christ was the mediator of salvation, he is "less than God"—greater, perhaps, than the rest of us, but still less than God. Arius was the main proponent of this view. Theologians at the Council of Nicaea (325) and thereafter (Athanasius and others) reasoned that if Jesus Christ is less than God, then he cannot be truly instrumental in our salvation. Therefore, Jesus Christ must be on a par with God, divine as well as fully human. Trinitarian doctrine was born in the course of this debate, largely through the effort of Athanasius and the Cappadocians (Basil, Gregory of Nazianzus, Gregory of Nyssa) who affirmed that Jesus Christ is essential to our salvation and therefore must be "of the same nature" as God. Likewise with the Holy Spirit.

This was a rather tricky position to maintain. The Cappadocians, and Augustine in the West, used every kind of philosophical idea and term they could think of that might help them make this case. Their initial concern was with our salvation, not with metaphysics. But the strongest way they had to defend their position was to agree with Nicaea that Jesus Christ is "of the same substance" (homoousios) as God. (We say in the creed: God from God; Light from Light, true God from true God, begotten not made, one in being with the Father.)

To some degree this affirmation clashed with Scripture, particularly on the matter of Christ's suffering. It was indisputable from the New Testament that Jesus Christ suffered. However, theologians of the fourth century *assumed without question that God could not suffer.* How then could Christ be God? Their solution was to say that Christ suffered in his humanity, not his divinity. Likewise, his equality with God was according to his divine, not his human, nature. Thus Christ was *homoousios* with God in his divinity, not humanity.

This more metaphysical approach to the Trinity opened up a gap not only between Christ's divinity and humanity, but between what is true at the level of the economy (*oikonomia*) and what is true within God's being (*theologia*). Debates about the equality of Father, Son and Spirit began to sound more like arguments about "intradivine" equality, rather than the equality of the divine persons in our salvation. Trinitarian doctrine was born in this tiny gap between *oikonomia* and *theologia;* the doctrine would also begin to unravel there.

The Bible, liturgy and early Christian creeds do not show any predilection to settle questions of God's "inner" life; they speak only of God's presence in the world through the Son and Spirit. Yet theologians became increasingly concerned with how Father, Son and Spirit are related *to each other.* For many people today, the term "Trinity" evokes just this discussion of God's inner life. The image of the immanent Trinity which perhaps comes to mind most often is of a "heavenly committee" of persons arranged nonlinearly (as in a triangle) or linearly (as in a vertical row). We less frequently connect the idea of "Trinity" with the vision of the author of Ephesians: God's open and dynamic life of giving and receiving in which humanity graciously has been included as partner.

It was no small accomplishment for the Cappadocians and Augustine to figure out how to maintain the co-equality of Father, Son and Spirit, without on the one hand speaking as though there were three gods alongside each other, or on the other hand, three gods arranged in a descending hierarchy. Even so, the effect, however unintentional, was to de-emphasize God's presence *to us* in the economy of redemption. As focus rested more and more on the "inner life" of God—on the self-relatedness of Father, Son, and Spirit to each other—instead of on God's relation to us, eventually the doctrine of the Trinity could speak only of a Trinity locked up in itself, related to itself, contemplating itself perfectly and eternally, but essentially unrelated to us. It is no wonder that so many would find the theoretical explanations for this state of affairs uninteresting and irrelevant.

By the time of medieval theology in the West and Byzantine theology in the East, the trinitarian doctrines of the Cappadocians and Augustine had been hardened into strict metaphysical accounts of God's self-relatedness—or as the tradition would say, of the Trinity *in se* (in itself). In his *Summa Theologiae* Thomas Aquinas (d. 1274) composed a highly sophisticated account of intradivine persons, processions and relations. And Thomas, who wrote a treatise titled *On the One God* and another titled *On the Triune God*, created the impression—although he intended nothing of the sort—that belief in the Trinity was "added on" to belief in the One God. For his part, Gregory Palamas in the East (d. 1359) so emphasized the unknowability and inaccessibility of God as to make the Trinity seem even more distant from us. In the medieval scholastic synthesis the attributes of God—infinity, immutability, impassibility, incorporeality—overtook the biblical presentation of God as someone who initiated relationship with a people, was open to prayer, petition and lament, suffered on account of the suffering of the people, became enfleshed in Christ, and as Spirit is working to bring about the reign of God. It is no small wonder that apart from the efforts of Luther and Calvin to recover the importance of ongoing conversion, personal relationship with Jesus and the centrality of the cross for our salvation, very little happened in theology, East or West, in the area of trinitarian theology—until very recently.

The historical development of the doctrine of the Trinity is impressive from the standpoint of sheer speculative attainment and intellectual vigor. But there were both gains and losses along the way. One gain was the affirmation that Christ and the Spirit are divine. What was lost was the centrality of the mystery of salvation, and hence the connection between trinitarian doctrine and trinitarian faith. The speculative heritage of Christianity must be retrieved where possible only within this nexus of faith and doctrine—a nexus that has pastoral, ethical, spiritual and personal significance. When the doctrine of the Trinity is thus retrieved, theology as a whole becomes much more an act of "confessing faith" in the triune God than an abstract theory that is segregated from the rest of Christian life.

The doctrine of the Trinity, to summarize, is a doctrine about God. But because it is a doctrine about the God who shares life with us in an economy of redemption, it is also a doctrine about salvation. Further, because it uses the idea of "person" and "relation" to affirm that God is essentially personal and relational, the doctrine of the Trinity is also the foundation for a theology of the human person, and a theology of right relationship. Finally, because it affirms that persons, whether divine or human, are made to exist in loving communion with one another, the doctrine of the Trinity is also the foundation for a vision of society and a vision of the church which is to be a sign to the world of the ultimate destiny of all creatures. But even more, out of such a view of the Trinity emerge a number of principles that have a direct bearing on ethics, spirituality, ecclesiology and politics.

First, according to the doctrine of the Trinity elaborated by the Cappadocians, and which is being retrieved today, the ultimate principle of all existence, the Creator of everything, is personal, not impersonal. This is the import of calling God (Father) the Unoriginate Origin. While God comes from no one and from nothing (in the sense that there is nothing more ultimate or primary than God), still God is, by God's very nature, not nonrelated but a person in relation to other persons. It is not as though there is first a God, then there are divine persons. The doctrine of the Trinity insists that God does not exist *except* as Father, Son, Spirit. Apart from the divine persons there is no God. This rules out the search for a definition of God "in and of Godself," or "God unto Godself."

This means that every human being, and indeed every creature, has its origin in a person who by definition is not solitary but in relationship with another. By definition a person is ecstatic, toward-another; we are persons by virtue of relationship to another. Persons know and are known, love and are loved, and express themselves in freedom. To think of a person without thinking of that person in relationship to another person defeats what it means to be a person. Therefore every time we think of God we must think of God not in isolation, "God with God," but in relationship to another person. One of the important features of this shift from a substance ontology to a relational ontology is that it ties theological reflection on God to the economy where the divine persons actually exist and are known in our history.

Second, because God is personal and not impersonal, God exists as the mystery of persons in communion. Communion (*koinonia*) means shared life. Persons who exist together in true communion share happiness, share hope, share suffering, share responsibility. God's life of communion might be described in two ways: first, there is the communion of love of the divine persons for one another. Second, and this is the flip side, there is the communion of the triune God with all creatures in the universe. There is one universal communion; God is both the origin, the sustaining ground, and the final goal of this shared life.

The communion of God and Christ, according to the doctrine of the Trinity, does not permit any kind of subordination, inequality or hierarchy. While every person is unique, no one person is more important than another, no person comes before another. Likewise with the human community. Communion in the Spirit of God means that all persons, while irreducibly unique, exist together as equal partners in Christ.

Third, since God is perfectly personal and relational, and since we are created in the image of God, then we will be most like God when we live out our personhood in a manner that conforms to who God is. To find out the unique characteristics of the divine persons we look to salvation history, where God has revealed Godself, especially in the face of Jesus Christ. Indeed, we say that Jesus Christ is God incarnate. Jesus is God in human form. Jesus is a person the way that God is a person. Therefore, imitating Jesus Christ means being perfected as a human being, and, to go back to Ephesians, the imitation of Christ means fulfilling our vocation as human beings.

The economy of redemption is the arena of the divine-human relationship. God moves toward us through Christ and the Spirit, so that we may come into communion with God and with one another. The Greek word for "economy," *oikonomia*, literally means management of a household. God and all of God's creatures dwell together in a common household referred to in the New Testament as the reign of God, the place where God's life rules. As Jesus Christ revealed in his preaching and teaching, the Samaritan woman, the tax collector and the leper are to be equally at home in God's household.

Orthodoxy means the conformity of theology and faith to the reality of God's glory revealed in Jesus Christ. Orthopraxis means right practice, right acts in response to God's life with us. Just as it would be unorthodox (heretical) to think of God as a solitary, uncaring, aloof authority figure, so it would contravene orthopraxis to exclude the Samaritan woman or the leper from our common household.

Living trinitarian faith thus has two meanings: faith that is alive, and living out one's faith. Faith in the God of Jesus Christ can come alive in the doctrine of the Trinity, provided that this doctrine flows out of the images and intuitions of faith. Living out this doctrine and this faith amounts to living God's life with one another. The extraordinary import of the revelation of God in Christ, affirmed in the doctrine of the Trinity, is that God's life does not belong to God alone: God's life is shared with every creature. Living trinitarian faith entails living as Jesus Christ did: with total confidence in God; as a peaceful, merciful, healing, forgiving presence; praying and praising God constantly; welcoming the outcast and sinner. Living God's life means living according to the power and presence of the Holy Spirit—becoming holy and virtuous, and contributing to the unity of the Christian community and the harmony among all of God's creatures.

Those who live such a faith are known as the church, which in turn is described as the People of God, Body of Christ, Temple of the Holy Spirit. The church's life is to mirror God's life, to be an "icon" of God's life. The church therefore is to embody in its corporate life, in its structures and practices, the nature of God. The church, in other words, should exist as the mystery of persons who dwell together in equality, reciprocity and mutual love.

However, this is only the hope of the church; it is not yet a present reality. Many experience the church's rituals and institutional practices as fostering elitism, discrimination and clericalism. They do not experience the church as the place where the Samaritan woman and the leper are at home. At times the church can seem more a collection of individuals involved in private worship than a truly cooperative association of the baptized, gathered in the Spirit, finding a new basis for unity and harmony. To be the icon of the Trinity the church must give full recognition to the uniqueness of its members and to the diversity that enlivens it.

The church's vocation is to be precisely such a recognizable sign of the ultimate destiny of all of God's beloved creatures, to exist together in harmony and unity. This means that the church should teach, preach and act in ways that accord with the life and teaching of Jesus Christ. Anything that threatens the unity of the Body of Christ or that precludes communion among its members is contrary to the life of the Spirit of God.

The church's mission is expressed in its sacramental life. Sacraments initiate us into the life of God, heal division and sin, and signify service in the reign of God. Regardless of how many sacraments a church includes in its practice, sacramental life is the recognition of the tangible aspects of communion among persons. In baptism we take on ourselves the very name of God; in the Eucharist we receive the Body of Christ and go forward to "love and serve" God and the people of God's household. Through the sacraments we surrender ourselves to transformation by a personal power who promises to restore us to the divine image. As much as we are to become "a new creation" in Christ, so too is the community of Christ to acquire a new profile, one in which "Christ is all, and in all" (Col. 3:11).

The doctrine of the Trinity is then the specifically Christian way of speaking about God. It summarizes our faith in the God of Jesus Christ, and identifies the God whom we worship. This doctrine is not a substitute for God, nor a complete theory about God, but a signpost that points to the shared life of God and God's creation in the economy of providence, election, consummation. The purpose of the doctrine of the Trinity is not to diagnose why God is the way God is, but to remind us to "taste and see the goodness of God" revealed in creation, Christ, and communion with one another in the Spirit.

Three Trinitarian Spiritualities

John L. Gresham, Jr.

Introduction

As an introduction to trinitarian spirituality, we wish to point out three pathways toward a trinitarian experience of God, three different ways in which the journey toward union with the trinitarian God has been mapped.[1] These three expressions of trinitarian spirituality are discovered in an exploration of ancient and modern sources of trinitarian theology and spirituality. It is true that, at one level, all Christian spirituality may be described as trinitarian insofar as there is a basic soteriological pattern whereby one is united to God the Father through Christ in the Spirit.[2] Yet, this trinitarian pattern often remains in the background as one or another of the divine persons, or some particular aspect of divine nature or activity provides the focus of the spiritual life, as in a christocentric spirituality or a creation spirituality. However, there are forms of Christian spirituality in which this trinitarian pattern and content takes a more decisive role in structuring and governing the spiritual life from beginning to end.[3] We will describe three basic types of trinitarian spirituality: a contemplative spirituality of the divine indwelling in the soul, a social spirituality of participation in the divine trinitarian fellowship, and a sacramental/charismatic spirituality of trinitarian missions.

This essay first appeared in *Journal of Spiritual Formation* 15.1 (February 1994): 21–33. Used by permission.

A Contemplative Spirituality of the Divine Trinitarian Indwelling in the Soul

The classic form of trinitarian spirituality in the western church has its roots in Augustine's psychological analogy of the trinity.[4] Augustine's search for analogies to the ultimately ineffable Trinity led him eventually to the divine image in the human soul. The soul as a unity of remembering, knowing, and willing (or loving) reflected its transcendent origin in the divine unity of Father, Son and Spirit. As understood in light of their reflected image in the soul, the Son and Spirit are viewed analogously and by appropriation as the Knowledge and Love of the Father. While sometimes dismissed as a merely speculative theology, Augustine's De Trinitate actually concludes by calling the reader to a contemplative union with the Trinity. While self-remembrance, self-knowledge, and self-love (in which rememberer and remembrance, knower and known, lover and loved, are identical) provides the most consistent analogy to the trinity and unity of God, Augustine does not conclude with that analogy. Rather, he directs the reader toward a fuller understanding of God in the remembrance, knowledge, and love of God wherein the content of one's remembrance, knowledge, and love is no longer the image of the Trinity, but the divine Trinity itself come to indwell the soul. Thus, Augustine's De Trinitate provides the starting point for a contemplative spirituality of the divine trinitarian indwelling. Augustine's spirituality is aptly described as a "mysticism of the trinitarian soul's, search for the trinitarian God."[5]

The Augustinian approach to the Trinity was developed further by Thomas Aquinas. In Thomas's trinitarian spirituality, it is through knowing and loving God that the divine Word and Love (Son and Spirit) indwell the soul, transforming human knowing and loving by conforming the human image to its divine archetype.[6] The Augustinian/Thomistic vision of the soul's transformation through the trinitarian indwelling may also be found in the mysticism of John of the Cross.[7]

The trinitarian teachings of Augustine, Aquinas, and John of the Cross all contributed to the profound trinitarian spirituality expressed in the life and writings of the modern Carmelite, Elizabeth of the Trinity.[8] Elizabeth's trinitarian spirituality begins with her understanding of divine predestination as the destiny, given through baptism to each individual believer, of becoming conformed to the image of Christ in order to offer eternal praise to the triune God. The individual attains this predestined goal by entering into their baptismal union with Christ through negation of self and reception of the Divine Word in silence. This negation of self and receptivity to the Word is achieved through docility to the purifying work of the Spirit. In silence, stillness, and emptiness, the soul receives the Word and Love of God, becoming a house of God, a dwelling place for the holy Trinity.

In this silence, contemplative spirituality encounters the divine silence and darkness in which God communicates with the soul in a manner beyond words or thought. There are mystics, like Meister Eckhart, who interpret this divine silence and darkness as the bare unity of the god-head beyond God in which no distinctions remain, not the distinction between creator and creature, nor even the distinction among Father, Son, and Spirit. In a more thoroughly trinitarian mysticism, such as we find in John Ruusbroec, such pantheistic tendencies are overcome by a trinitarian understanding of divine unity and mystical union with the divine. For Ruusbroec, when the soul reaches the divine silence and dark-ness, it has not passed beyond Trinity, but rather, has found the Father. All does not remain darkness and silence, for the Father eternally utters his Word who brings light.[9] Thus, contemplation in trinitarian spiritual-ity is contemplation of the Word—the Word who comes from the Father and by whom and in whom we return to the Father.[10]

Trinitarian indwelling, therefore, is based upon union with Christ, the Divine Word. This is illustrated in the two prayers to the Son found in Elizabeth of the Trinity's "prayer to the Trinity."[11] Beginning and ending with prayer to the whole Trinity, the heart of Elizabeth's prayer addresses each divine person directly and individually. Significantly, only the Son is addressed twice. First, Elizabeth calls upon Christ as the spouse of her soul with whom she wishes to be united and to whom she wishes to be conformed, giving fervent expression to a Christ-centered bridal mysti-cism. Yet, Elizabeth moves from union with Christ to the indwelling of the whole Godhead, calling upon Christ again, in a second prayer, address-ing him as the divine Word—the Word who brings the whole Trinity to indwell the soul which receives him in empty and silent listening.

Basic to this spirituality is the psychological analogy of the Trinity, in which Son and Spirit are encountered as the Word and Love of God. Christ comes to the soul as the illuminating Word of God. This gives this spirituality its contemplative character—one "listens" that the Word might be heard and welcomed within the heart. Yet, this contemplation is not merely intellectualistic, for the soul's illumination through the indwelling Word is accompanied by an outpouring of the Spirit who enflames the soul with divine love. The divine attribute of love which belongs to God in his essence, and therefore, to each divine person, is appropriated to the Holy Spirit as the Spirit's unique name or title. The Holy Spirit is understood theologically as the hypostatic or subsistent divine love uniting Father and Son and proceeding from them to the world as divine gift. The psychological analogy of the Trinity, whereby

Son and Spirit are envisioned as the Word and Love of the Father, coupled with the trinitarian technique of "appropriation," whereby essential divine attributes such as wisdom and love are singularly embodied in specific divine persons, enables the discovery of distinct relations to the Son and Spirit within the soul. The Son indwells the soul as divine Word illuminating the intellect and the Spirit is present in the soul as the divine Charity enkindling the affections.[12]

The use of this psychological analogy has its value in illuminating this trinitarian presence in the soul, but this analogy has been criticized for leading to a spirituality which restricts the divine image and indwelling to the soul.[13] A more holistic spirituality might conceive the trinitarian image in humanity as reflected in the whole person as body, soul, and spirit[14] rather than the soul as remembrance, knowledge, and love. Such an image lacks the psychological analogy's ability to illuminate the inner distinctions of the divine Trinity with the unique parallels between the soul's knowing and loving and the divine processions of Son and Spirit. It is difficult to find such correspondences between body, soul, and spirit and specific persons of the Trinity. What this analogy lacks in that regard, however, it makes up for in its implications for the spiritual life. This analogy points toward the divine indwelling as tending toward a transformation of the whole person—body, soul, and spirit. Such an analogy envisions the trinitarian indwelling as extending from the divine presence in the mysterious depths of the human spirit to the divine energizing of the human body as a healing foretaste of future glorification. At the center, however, remains the divine presence in the soul through a knowledge and love of God, a response to the divine illumination and inspiration given through the Father's gift of his Son and Spirit. Thus, even if we expand our conception of the triune image and indwelling to encompass body and spirit, the contemplative spirituality of the trinitarian presence in the soul continues to offer light for our journey toward union with the trinitarian God.

Social Spirituality of Participation in the Trinitarian Fellowship

Another trinitarian spirituality has its roots in the Eastern fathers' social analogy of the Trinity, rather than Augustine's psychological analogy. In the Eastern church, it was not the individual human soul but the unity of three distinct human persons which provided illustration for the holy Trinity—not the unity of remembering, knowing, and loving in the soul—but the union of Adam, Eve, and Seth or of Peter, James, and John.[15] These early fathers developed the analogy between divine unity and the unity of three human persons metaphysically, in terms of the unity of nature shared by distinct human persons.[16] Modern theologians have developed this same analogy in terms of the social union of persons in relationship to one another. These modern theologians understand the divine trinity as analogous to a community or fellowship of persons united by their love and shared life.[17] In both Eastern Orthodoxy and in the modern social trinitarians, the social analogy of the Trinity provides the basis for a spirituality of participation through grace in the divine trinitarian fellowship.[18] The dominant imagery of this spirituality is not the Trinity dwelling in humanity, but rather, humanity dwelling in the Trinity. This spirituality is a response to the divine invitation to include humanity in the loving fellowship of the Father, Son, and Spirit.

As in Augustinian trinitarian spirituality, there is a movement from the experience of salvation in Christ to a more comprehensive experience of the whole triune godhead. This salvation in Christ takes place through the divine Son sharing in our humanity in order to make us sharers in his deity. The Son becomes a member of the human community in order to bring humans into the divine community of the holy Trinity. Eastern Orthodoxy expresses this exchange in Athanasius's oft repeated formula, "God became man that man might become God."[19] This does not mean human beings are absorbed in the transcendent divine essence but rather that in Christ we are invited to become members of the divine fellowship, sharing in the divine energies exchanged between Father, Son and Holy Spirit in an eternal circulation of divine life called "perichoresis." Humanity may participate in God through these divine energies extended to the world as deifying grace.[20] Jürgen Moltmann's trinitarian theology emphasizes that not only does the divine Son share our humanity by incarnation, but also, in his abandonment at the cross, the Son shares our "godforsakenness" as sinners. Having fully identified himself with us, Jesus becomes the elder brother of a once godforsaken humanity who can lead his brothers and sisters back into the family of God.[21] The key christological and soteriological concept in this trinitarian spirituality is sonship. By our adoptive sonship in Christ we become children of the Father and share in the loving fellowship between Father and Son in the Spirit.

Leonard Hodgson exemplifies the union of theology and spirituality inherent in this social approach to the Trinity by including in his exposition of trinitarian theology a spiritual method for entering into this experience of participation in trinitarian life.[22] Hodgson's spiritual method is based on his conviction that Jesus' life of communion with the Father and possession by the Spirit is given to Christians through their union with Christ. Jesus' life of fellowship with the Father in the Spirit reveals the social dimension in the eternal Trinity and points to the Christian life as participation in that divine society. The method Hodgson provides for experiencing this trinitarian life consists in consciously realizing our distinct relation to Father, Son and Spirit in Christian prayer and service. Hodgson instructs Christians to pray to the Father as adopted sons and daughters in Christ who are led and inspired by the Spirit; then, to go forth from prayer to serve the Father, in companionship with Christ, continuing Christ's work in the Father's world, empowered and directed by the Spirit. It is by consciously and deliberately living as those who have been made partakers of this trinitarian relation to God that Christians can experientially realize their inclusion in the divine trinitarian fellowship.

This spirituality is nourished by a return to the doxological basis of trinitarian faith. This doxological trinitarianism associated with a social model of the trinity is best expressed in Moltmann's description of the "eucharistic" form of the Trinity.[23] In contrast to the more common "monarchical" form of the Trinity, in which divine action moves from the Father through the Son to completion in the Spirit, the eucharistic form of the Trinity describes an experience of God in which the divine movement begins with the Spirit and reaches through the Son to completion in the Father. This is the movement of praise and glorification in which the Holy Spirit, indwelling and renewing the earth, leads the people of God in worship of the Father in the name of the Son. In Spirit-inspired praise and worship the Church participates in the life of the Trinity by sharing in the Spirit's eternal glorification of the Father and Son.

The social model of the Trinity envisions the eternal life of the Trinity as analogous to a loving dialogue. The Father eternally says to the Son, "You are my beloved," and the Son responds with an eternal, "Yes," to the Father's love. The Spirit eternally glorifies Father and Son with that divine glory and love which unites the three as one. In Christ, the church hears the Father call us his beloved children and through Christ we receive the Spirit. The Spirit unites our "yes" to the eternal "yes" of the Son, that we might share in the Spirit's glorification of Father and Son. Thus, we share in the eternal conversation of the divine trinitarian fellowship.

The social analogy of the Trinity, with its emphasis on an experience of Father, Son and Spirit as distinct divine persons who invite humanity to share in their fellowship, raises a definite danger of tritheism. Yet, this approach to trinitarian theology and spirituality offers such a rich understanding of divine life and our sharing in that life that the risk of tritheism is worth taking. In admitting this risk, we also emphasize the necessity of attempting to express this trinitarian spirituality in such a way that the threat of tritheism is overcome by a clear confession that the interpersonal union of the Father, Son, and Spirit is an expression of their essential unity as one God.[24]

Sacramental/Charismatic Spirituality of Trinitarian Missions

A third approach to trinitarian spirituality understands Christian initiation, in both its sacramental and charismatic dimensions, as participation in the trinitarian missions of Son and Spirit sent into the world as the Father's gift of salvation. This spirituality is based on an understanding of baptism and confirmation (or chrismation) as a liturgical symbol of the distinct but united missions of Son and Spirit.[25] Baptism and confirmation, as two distinct moments in one sacramental initiation, point to the missions of Son and Spirit as two distinct but inseparable aspects of one divine work of salvation. The spirituality which flows from this trinitarian understanding of sacramental initiation is inherently charismatic for it finds the gift of salvation in Christ (baptism) completed through the anointing of the Holy Spirit (confirmation). A charismatic experience of the Spirit was an integral part of the sacramental initiation of Christians through the early centuries of the church and its current recovery can lead toward a spirituality of participation in trinitarian life through the missions of Son and Spirit.[26]

The trinitarian dimensions of the charismatic renewal are suggested by Peter Hocken's trinitarian description of the charismatic experience of "baptism in the Spirit." He describes this experience as the "total immersion of the believer by the agency of the Spirit into the being and mystery of Christ to the glory of God the Father."[27] This sacramental/charismatic trinitarian spirituality we are describing is not limited to the charismatic renewal movement, however. A sacramentally rooted charismatic spirituality of the Trinity such as this can be found in a work on Orthodox spirituality by an anonymous "monk of the eastern church."[28] While the theme of participation in the interpersonal communion of the Trinity, which we have associated with Orthodoxy above, is not absent from this work, the focus lies much more with the sacramental life of the Eastern church. This monk makes a clear distinction between the grace of baptism and the grace of chrismation, even though in Orthodox practice they are not separated in time as in the West. Baptism imparts the grace of new life. This is the grace of regeneration, new creation, forgiveness and healing through union with Christ. Baptismal grace unites us to Christ in his death and resurrection. The presence of the Spirit in baptism is affirmed, as is the presence of the Father and the Son in every action of the Spirit.

Nonetheless, the special character of chrismation as sacrament of the Spirit is equally affirmed. The grace of chrismation is described as "pentecostal" grace. The reference here is not to pentecostalism but rather to the outpouring of the Spirit on the first Pentecost extended through time by the sacrament of chrismation. While upholding the Orthodox belief that the Spirit proceeds only from the Father, this orthodox monk emphasizes that the "sending" of the Spirit is from the Son. In baptism Christ is revealed as the "baptising Christ" whose own baptism sanctified the waters of baptism and made that water the vehicle of deifying grace. In chrismation, Christ is revealed as the "sender of the Spirit." The pentecostal grace of chrismation brings "illumination"—an experiential understanding and even sensation of spiritual reality and introduces one into "charismatic life" wherein Christians share in the anointing of Jesus. The spirituality described by this orthodox monk involves a progressive experiential development or appropriation of the distinct but inseparable gifts of baptism and chrismation. This spirituality is trinitarian for the grace implanted in baptism and chrismation directs one toward the Father through ever deeper union with Christ and ever greater anointing of the Spirit.

A similar distinction between the grace of baptism and chrismation is found in the description of confirmation by the charismatic Catholic theologian, Heribert Mühlen.[29] Mühlen distinguishes between those sacraments which orient the recipient primarily toward God, such as baptism and penance, and those sacraments which orient the recipient toward others, such as confirmation and holy orders. The former bring the grace of salvation to the recipient, the latter equip him or her to minister saving grace to others. Mühlen describes those sacraments which anoint Christians for ministry as "charismatic sacraments." Confirmation, in particular, is described as a "sacramental baptism with the Holy Spirit." For Mühlen then, the charismatic experience called baptism in the Spirit is a renewal of one's confirmation. Like the eastern monk's description of chrismation, Mühlen views the sacrament of confirmation as empowering the Christian with charismatic life for the purpose of ministry. Spiritual life includes ongoing reception of this gift of God. As with this orthodox monk, so for Mühlen, the distinction between baptism and confirmation or chrismation gives Christian initiation two distinct but united foci—new life in Christ and the power of the Holy Spirit. This provides the basis for a spirituality which seeks to experience both the grace of forgiveness in Christ and the charismatic life of the Holy Spirit as two distinct but inseparably united gifts of the Father.

The trinitarian dimensions of this spirituality may be developed further by relating the sacraments of Christian initiation more explicitly to the missions of the Son and Spirit. The interior missions of the Son and Spirit are usually described in relation to the distinct effects of their presence in the soul, without specific mention of the sacraments of Christian initiation.[30] A sacramental approach to these missions views the sacraments as the connecting link between the visible missions of Son and Spirit, in the incarnation of the Son and the Pentecost outpouring of the Spirit, and the interior and invisible missions of Son and Spirit by which the triune God indwells the believing soul. Such a perspective points to the connections between the mission of the Spirit, Pentecost, confirmation, and the charismatic baptism in the Spirit. If the visible coming of the Holy Spirit on the day of Pentecost is perpetuated in the ongoing life of the church through the sacrament of confirmation, then the experiential release of this grace in the baptism in the Spirit must bear an intimate relationship to the interior mission of the Holy Spirit to which the visible flames of Pentecost and the tangible touch of confirmation witness. Similarly, baptism perpetuates the visible coming of the Son in incarnation, atoning death, and lifegiving resurrection, and through the grace of baptism that visible mission of the Son reaches its goal in the invisible mission by which the Son dwells in the Christian. By explicitly relating the sacraments of baptism and confirmation to the missions of the Son and Spirit, Christian initiation is portrayed as an initiation into the life of the holy Trinity.

A spirituality oriented toward realization of the sacramental grace of baptism and confirmation is a trinitarian spirituality—an approach to spiritual life as an ongoing receptivity to Son and Spirit as each indwells the Christian according to their distinct but indivisible missions. In receiving the Son and Spirit, the Father is received as well for each divine person interpenetrates the others in the unity of the Trinity. It is through sending his Son and Spirit that the Father, who dwells in the Son and Spirit, gives himself to us.

The goal of the spiritual life is the indwelling of the holy Trinity through receiving the Son and the Spirit as they are sent into the world— visibly, in the incarnation and Pentecost, sacramentally, in baptism and confirmation, and experientially in new birth and baptism in the Spirit. A sacramental charismatic spirituality with an awareness of the trinitarian depths of its spiritual experience has promise for a spirituality which comprehensively expresses mystical, evangelical, sacramental, ecclesial, and charismatic dimensions of Christian spirituality. The mystical dimension is found by understanding the source of salvation in the trinitarian depths of God. The trinitarian missions by which God comes to us are the prolongation into time of the eternal processions within the very being of God. Our experience of God carries us ultimately back to the trinitarian mystery of God himself. The evangelical dimension is found in a focus on those events in salvation history in which the Son and Spirit came into the world. The incarnation, death, and resurrection of the Son and the Pentecost day outpouring of the Spirit are affirmed in their once-and-for-all character as the decisive salvific events proclaimed in scripture in which the Father gives the Son and Spirit for our salvation. The ecclesial and sacramental dimension of this spirituality is found in an understanding of baptism and confirmation as the channels of grace by which the salvation historical events of Easter and Pentecost are given to each one individually through the mediation of the church. Finally, the experiential, charismatic dimension is found in an emphasis on receiving the grace given sacramentally in the personal appropriation of the gift of the Son and the Spirit in one's own personal Easter of regeneration and one's own personal Pentecost of the baptism in the Spirit. This spirituality may be diagrammed as a movement from God to humanity beginning in the eternal being of God and realizing itself in human experience: Generation of the Son and spiration of the Spirit in eternity (trinitarian processions) > incarnation of the Son and sending of the Spirit in time (trinitarian missions) > Easter and Pentecost (salvation historical events, visible missions) > baptism and confirmation (sacramental initiation) > new birth and Spirit baptism (experiential realization, invisible missions).

One danger in this approach to trinitarian spirituality would be to overstress the distinction between baptism and confirmation, Christ and Spirit, conversion and Spirit baptism so as to imply separation. Relating the experience of Christ and the Spirit to the trinitarian missions, however, enables us to speak of a distinct but not separate presence of the Son and Spirit in the soul.[31] From a trinitarian perspective, not only are these two missions inseparable, but also, the Son is present in the mission of the Spirit and the Spirit is present in the mission of the Son. Thus, any separation between Son and Spirit is denied. At the same time, this trinitarian perspective also explains some of the difficulty in explicating the distinction between the Son and Spirit in the gift of salvation. This difficulty arises for charismatics who attempt to explain the distinction between regeneration and Spirit baptism, and in an exact parallel, for sacramental theologians who attempt to explain the distinction between baptism and confirmation.[32]

In each case, there is an inherent unity between the two in the one total event of Christian initiation, yet the distinction remains. It might be that this difficulty in explaining these distinctions arises because these distinctions find their ultimate basis in the distinction between the missions of the Son and the Spirit. (And these missions find their ultimate distinction as well as their inseparable unity in the still deeper mystery of the inner divine processions of Son and Spirit.) If the distinction between the grace of baptism and the grace of confirmation, or the difference between the experience of new birth in Christ and the baptism in the Holy Spirit, reflects the impenetrable distinction-in-unity of Son and Spirit in the trinitarian missions, it might be the case that these distinctions cannot be theologically explicated as well as they can be sacramentally celebrated and experientially appropriated.

Conclusion

The three trinitarian spiritualities described draw upon different aspects of the trinitarian theological tradition to find illumination and inspiration for the spiritual life. In these spiritualities, theology does not detract from, but rather, contributes to the spiritual life. At the same time, these trinitarian spiritualities can enrich trinitarian theology. In an oft quoted comment, Karl Rahner observed that most contemporary Christians are "mere monotheists" in their experience of God. In order to lead Christians toward a reinterpretation of a fully trinitarian experience of God, Rahner sought to reconnect trinitarian doctrine with its roots in the experience of grace.[33] This turn toward the experience of grace reflects Rahner's awareness that the renewal of trinitarian theology requires a renewal of trinitarian spirituality. This point was made even more explicitly by Anglican theologian Leonard Hodgson. He claimed that the "first task" in teaching the doctrine of the trinity is to teach "trinitarian religion."[34] It is by "trying to live out a trinitarian religion," Hodgson emphasized, "that the doctrine of the Trinity will cease to be for us an abstract and unintelligible theological formula and will become a living reality.[35] Trinitarian spirituality, then, plays a crucial role in trinitarian theology by providing guidance for this living out of trinitarian religion. Theology may describe the mystery of the triune God, but spirituality leads us toward an encounter with that holy mystery as a living reality.

Notes

1. Much of this material was included in my paper, "Charismatic Experience and Trinitarian Spirituality," presented at the 1992 annual meeting of the Society for Pentecostal Studies.

2. See the definition of "trinitarian spirituality" in Columba Cary-Elwes, *Experiences of God: A Dictionary of Spirituality and Prayer* (London: Sheed & Ward, 1986).

3. For other introductions to trinitarian spirituality, see: James Houston, "Spirituality and the Trinity," in *Christ in Our Place*, ed. Trevor Hart and Daniel Thimell (Allison Park, Pa.: Pickwick, 1990); and George Maloney, *Invaded by God: Mysticism and the Indwelling Trinity* (Denville, N.J.: Dimension, 1979).

4. Augustine, *The Trinity*, books 9–14, trans. Stephen McKenna, in *Fathers of the Church*, vol. 45 (Washington, D.C.: Catholic University of America Press, 1963), 269–449.

5. Andrew Louth, "Augustine," in *The Study of Spirituality*, ed. Cheslyn Jones et al. (London: SPCK, 1986), 141.

6. See Noel Molloy, "The Trinitarian Mysticism of St. Thomas," *Angelicum* 57 (1980): 373–88.

7. See John of the Cross, *Spiritual Canticle B*, stanza 39, 3–4, in *Collected Works of St. John of the Cross*, trans. Kieran Kavanaugh and Otilio Rodriguez (Washington, D.C.: Institute of Carmelite Studies, 1979), 558.

8. *Elizabeth of the Trinity, 1880–1906: Spiritual Writings*, ed. M. M. Philipon (New York: Kenedy, 1962); Luigi Borriello, *Spiritual Doctrine of Blessed Elizabeth of the Trinity*, trans. Jor-

dan Aumann (New York: Alba House, 1986); Hans Urs von Balthasar, *Elizabeth of Dijon: An Interpretation of Her Spiritual Mission* (New York: Pantheon, 1956).

9. See Louis Dupre, *The Common Life: The Origins of Trinitarian Mysticism and Its Development by Jan Ruusbroec* (New York: Crossroad, 1984). Ruusbroec (or Ruysbroec) was a fourteenth-century Flemish mystic.

10. See Paul Hinnebusch, *Like the Word: To the Trinity through Christ* (St. Louis: Herder, 1965).

11. This prayer from Elizabeth's *Spiritual Writings* may also be found in Michael O'Carroll, *Trinitas: A Theological Encyclopedia of the Holy Trinity* (Wilmington, Del.: Michael Glazier, 1987), q.v. "Elizabeth of the Trinity." Columba Marmion provides another example in which a deep trinitarian spirituality expresses itself most profoundly in a prayer of consecration to the trinity. See *The Trinity in Our Spiritual Life: An Anthology of the Writings of Dom Columba Marmion*, ed. Raymond Thibaut (Westminster, Md.: Newman, 1953), 1:255–57.

12. Thomas Aquinas, *Summa Theologica*, 1a Q.43 art. 5. E.T., English Dominican Fathers, (Westminster: Christian Classics, 1981), 1:223.

13. Jürgen Moltmann develops this criticism in *God in Creation* (London: SCM, 1985), 234–43.

14. 1 Thessalonians 5:23.

15. For examples of these analogies, see Gregory of Nazianzus, *Fifth Theological Oration (On the Spirit)*, and Gregory of Nyssa, *Not Three Gods*, in *Christology of the Later Fathers*, ed. E. R. Hardy and C. C. Richardson, Library of Christian Classics, vol. 3 (Philadelphia: Westminster, 1965), 200, 256. (The Eastern fathers also use the trinitarian analogy: person, word, breath.)

16. Gregory of Nyssa, for example, argued that even to say, "three men" is philosophically incorrect, for human nature is one. Ibid., 257–58.

17. Examples include Leonard Hodgson, *The Doctrine of the Trinity* (New York: Scribner's Sons, 1944); Jürgen Moltmann, *The Trinity and the Kingdom* (San Francisco: Harper & Row, 1981); Joseph Bracken, *The Triune Symbol: Persons, Process, and Community* (Lanham, Md.: University Press of America, 1985); Leonardo Boff, *Trinity and Society* (Maryknoll, N.Y.: Orbis, 1988).

18. For an Eastern Orthodox example, see John Meyendorff, "Theosis in the Eastern Christian Tradition," in *Christian Spirituality III: Post-Reformation and Modern*, ed. Louis Dupre and Donald Saliers (New York: Crossroad, 1989), 475–76.

19. Athanasius, *On the Incarnation*, 54. E.T. in *Christology of the Later Fathers*, ed. E. R. Hardy and C. C. Richardson, Library of Christian Classics, vol. 3 (Philadelphia: Westminster, 1965), 107.

20. See Kallistos Ware, *The Orthodox Way* (Crestwood, N.Y.: St. Vladimir's Seminary Press, 1980), 167–69.

21. Jorgen Moltmann, *The Trinity and the Kingdom* (San Francisco: Harper & Row, 1981), 80–83, 120–22.

22. Leonard Hodgson, *The Doctrine of the Trinity*, 38–50, 176–81; *How Can God Be Both One and Three?* (London: SPCK, 1960), 17.

23. Moltmann, "Unity of the Triune God," *St. Vladimir's Theological Quarterly* 28 (1984): 163–64.

24. See my forthcoming article, "The Social Model of the Trinity and Its Critics," *Scottish Journal of Theology* (1993).

25. Yves Congar, *I Believe in the Holy Spirit* (New York: Seabury, 1983), 3:222–23.

26. See Killian McDonnel and George Montague, *Christian Initiation and Baptism in the Holy Spirit: Evidence from the First Eight Centuries* (Collegeville: Liturgical Press, 1991), especially their comments on the two equal missions of the Son and Spirit, 321–22.

27. Peter Hocken, "Meaning and Purpose of Baptism in the Spirit," *Pneuma* 7 (1985): 131.

28. A Monk of the Eastern Church, *Orthodox Spirituality: An Outline of the Orthodox Ascetical and Mystical Tradition*, 2d ed. (Crestwood, N.Y.: St. Vladimir's Seminary Press, 1987). The anonymous author is now known to be Lev Gillet, 1893–1980, chaplain to the Anglican-Orthodox Fellowship of St. Alban and St. Sergius.

29. Heribert Mühlen, *A Charismatic Theology: Initiation in the Spirit* (New York: Paulist, 1978), 128–34, 140–43.

30. As in Thomas Aquinas's representation of these missions in terms of the Son illuminating the soul with knowledge as divine Word and the Spirit inflaming the soul with love as the divine Charity, which we described above.

31. The mode of this trinitarian indwelling is a matter of debate in Catholic theology. Some, stressing the unity of the trinitarian "opus ad extra," describe the distinct indwelling of Son and Spirit as appropriations. Others argue for a proper, personal, or hypostatic presence of Son and Spirit in the soul. See O'Carroll, *Trinitas*, q.v. "appropriation," "grace," and "indwelling of the Trinity."

32. "If the Holy Spirit indwells the believer through regeneration, what does it mean to receive the baptism in the Spirit?" Or, "If the Spirit is given in baptism, what is the meaning of confirmation as a distinct rite?"

33. Karl Rahner, *The Trinity*, trans. J. Donceel (New York: Seabury, 1974), 10, 39.

34. Leonard Hodgson, *The Doctrine of the Trinity*, 177.

35. Leonard Hodgson, *Christian Faith and Practice: Seven Lectures* (New York: Scribner's Sons, 1951), 51.

Contemplating the Trinitarian Mystery of Christ

James B. Torrance

D r. James Denney, the beloved Scottish theologian and New Testament scholar, used to say that in the ideal church all our theologians would be evangelists and our evangelists theologians. He was echoing the language of Plato's *Republic*, where Plato said that in the ideal state all politicians would be philosophers and philosophers politicians! We might add that in such a church all our theologians would also be men and women of prayer.

James Houston stands in that noble tradition of Scottish thinkers who have had not only a great desire to reflect theologically on the nature of the Christian gospel, but a passion to communicate it to others. Our lifelong friendship began as undergraduates together in Edinburgh University in the psychology classroom, where we had to observe one another and carry out tests for laboratory purposes! I soon came to see in him not only an able, mature scholar, but a man of prayer, consumed by missionary zeal to share with others the treasures he discovered in the Scriptures—with a vivid awareness of the place of Christ and the Spirit in the Christian life. I shall long remember how almost thirty years ago he came to me in Edinburgh when he was teaching geography in Oxford to expound his vision of a college where lay people from many professions and walks of life could come together in a context of worship and academic study and take

This essay first appeared in *Alive to God: Studies in Spirituality Presented to James Houston*, ed. J. I. Packer and Loren Wilkinson (Downers Grove, Ill.: Inter-Varsity, 1992), 140–51. Used by permission.

degrees in theology to equip them for their witness in their different spheres. That of course was the vision which blossomed into Regent College. I can think of no one better equipped to fulfill there his task of being professor of Spiritual Theology in Regent's ecumenical context of worship, evangelism, missionary concern and academic scholarship.

The Trinitarian Viewpoint

Dr. Houston has grasped clearly the trinitarian nature of Christian spirituality[1] in a day when much religion in the West is in practice deeply subjective and individualistic, indeed narcissistic, preoccupied with self-expression, self-fulfillment, self-realization, and self-esteem, leading at times to a neo-gnosticism where the self is equated with God. The authentic work of the Holy Spirit is to lift us out of all such inverted preoccupation with the self to find the true fulfillment of our humanity in Christ, in the loving heart of the Father. The triune God of grace who has his own true being-in-communion has created us in his image in order that we might find our true being-in-communion with him and one another. The ministry of Christ and the Spirit is to lift us up into this life of communion as members of the body of Christ, participating together in the very triune life of God. Bishop Lesslie Newbigin has commented that when the average Christian in Europe or North America hears the name of God, he or she does not think of the Trinity. After many years of missionary work among Eastern religions, he returned to find that much of the worship in the West is *in practice,* if not in theory, *unitarian.* The "religion" of so many people today is moulded by concepts of God which obscure the joyful witness of the Bible to the triune God of grace. God is conceived of too often as the remote sovereign Individual Monad "out there," the law-giver, the contract-God who needs to be, or can be, conditioned into being gracious by devout religious behavior or by this or that religious act, be it even repentance or prayer. The Reformers were concerned to sweep away these views of God, but in spite of the Reformation, such concepts are alive and highly influential in our day. This is why theologians like Karl Barth, Rahner, Moltmann, Jüngel, Zizioulas, T. Smail and others have in their different ways labored to call the church back to the centrality of the doctrine of the Trinity, not only for a more biblical doctrine of God, but also for a better understanding of worship, as well as for a better concept of the human person and of true community.[2]

Among the Christian churches there are many different forms of worship, Reformed, Lutheran, Presbyterian, Episcopalian, Methodist, Baptist, Pentecostal, Roman Catholic, Eastern Orthodox. Within our different churches there are wide varieties, deriving from different traditions, some more liturgical than others. Today many churches and groups are experimenting with different forms of worship to find relevant ways of communicating the gospel in the context of a changing, increasingly secular world or in response to the challenge of feminism. The question therefore arises with considerable urgency, what is authentic Christian worship whatever form it takes? More specifically, what is the place of Christ and the Holy Spirit in Christian worship?

Two Views of Worship

As we reflect on the wide variety of contemporary forms of worship, it seems to me that we can discern two very different views.[3] The first view—probably the commonest and most widespread—is that worship is something which *we* do, mainly in church on Sunday. We go to church, we sing our psalms and hymns to God, we intercede for the world, we listen to the sermon (too often simply an exhortation), we offer our time and talents to God. No doubt we need God's grace to help us to do it; we do it because Jesus taught us to do it and left us an example as to how to do it. *But worship is what WE do.* In theological language, the only priesthood is our priesthood, the only offering our offering, the only intercessions our intercessions.

Indeed this view of worship is in practice unitarian, has no real doctrine of the Mediator or sole priesthood of Christ, is human-centered, with no proper doctrine of the Holy Spirit, is often non-sacramental, and can easily engender weariness. We sit in the pew watching the minister "doing his thing" and exhorting us "to do our thing," and go home thinking we have done our duty for another week! This kind of "do-it-yourself-with-the-help-of-the-minister" worship is what our forebears would have called "legal worship" as opposed to "evangelical" worship—what the ancient church would have described as "Arian" or "Pelagian," and not truly catholic. It is certainly not trinitarian.

The second view of worship, the view for which the Reformers contended, is that worship is rather the gift of participating through the Spirit in the (incarnate) Son's communication with the Father—the gift of participating, in union with Christ, in what *he* has done for us once and for all by his self-offering to the Father in his life and death on the cross, and in what *he* is continuing to do for us in the presence of the Father, and in *his* mission from the Father to the world. The bread we break, is it not our sharing in the body of Christ? The cup of blessing which we bless, is it not our sharing in the blood of Christ? Our sonship and communion with the Father, are they not our sharing by the Spirit of adoption in Christ's sonship and communion with the Father? Our intercessions and mission to the world, are they not participation in the mission and intercessions of him who is "the apostle and high priest whom we confess" (Heb 3:1)? Is this not the meaning of life "in the Spirit"?

This second view is trinitarian and incarnational, taking seriously New Testament teaching about the sole priesthood and headship of Christ, his self-offering for us to the Father, and our life in union with Christ through the Spirit, with a vision of the church as the body of Christ. It is fundamentally "sacramental"—but in a way which enshrines the gospel of grace, that our Father in the gift of his Son and the gift of the Spirit gives us what he demands—the worship of our hearts and minds—lifting us up out of ourselves to participate in the very life of the Godhead. This is the heart of our theology of the Eucharist—of "holy communion."

The second view is both catholic and evangelical. Whereas the first view can be divisive, in that every church and denomination "does its own thing" and worships God in its own way, the second is unifying, in that it recognizes that there is only one way to come to the Father, namely through Christ in the communion of the Spirit and in the communion of the saints, whatever outward form our worship may take. If the first way can engender weariness, this second way, the way of grace, releases joy and ecstasy, for with inward peace we are lifted up by the Spirit into the presence of the Father, into a world of praise and adoration and fellowship in Christ.

It might be argued that the distinction between these two views is drawn too sharply. Is there not a middle position, as in fact probably most of our good church people suppose? I think this is true, but it is in fact a modification of the first view. It might be stated this way. *Yes, worship is what we do*—but *we* worship God, Father, Son and Holy Spirit, *we* pray to Christ as God, *we* invoke the Holy Spirit, *we* respond to the preaching of the Word, *we* intercede for the world and *we* offer our money, time and service to God.

This view might be defended on the ground of "the priesthood of all believers" and as being trinitarian, but it falls short of the New Testament understanding of participation through the Spirit in what *Christ* has done and is doing for us in our humanity, in his communion with the Father and his mission from the Father to the world. It is a do-it-yourself-in-response-to-Christ worship, and is to this extent a modification of the first view, but with more Christian content. Its weakness is that it falls short of an adequate understanding of the role of Christ and of the Spirit in our worship of the Father. It lacks appreciation of the sole priesthood of Christ as the *leitourgos,* the leader of our worship, as set forth in the epistle to the Hebrews (8:1, 2). It fails to see that *the real Agent in the wor-*

ship is Christ, drawing us by the Spirit into his life of communion with the Father.

This highlights for us the fact that in our understanding of the Trinity in Christian worship, the triune God is not only the *object of* our worship, but paradoxically by grace, this God is the *agent!* That is seen when we consider the place of Christ in worship. In the New Testament, two things are held together. *God* comes to us as person in Christ, and therefore *we pray to Christ as God.* But on the other hand, Jesus as the Word made flesh is our brother, a weak, suffering, tempted, struggling person, *praying for us and with us to the Father,* and uniting us with himself now as our risen and ascended Lord in his communion with the Father and his intercessions for the world. It is because of this that not only is the triune God the *object* of our worship, but our worship is the gift of participating through the Spirit in Christ's own fellowship with the Father. The Christ to whom we pray himself lived a life of prayer, and draws us into his life of prayer, putting his word "Father" onto our lips so that our life might become, in the words of the title of Henry Scougal's devotional classic, "the life of God in the soul of man." By sharing in Jesus' present life of communion with the Father in the Spirit, we are given to participate in the eternal Son's eternal communion with the Father. In Pauline terms, the Father "sent the Spirit of his Son into our hearts, the Spirit who calls out [and we with him] '*Abba,* Father'" (Gal 4:6).

If this account of "two views of worship" in our church today is accurate, we must ask why we have drifted away from the trinitarian view of the great Greek Fathers like Irenaeus, Athanasius, Cyril, and the Cappadocian divines, the view for which the Reformers contended, into this human-centered "unitarian" alternative. Is not the dominance of "the first view of worship" one supreme reason that the doctrine of the Trinity has receded?

Life in Christ

What we have said about the two views of worship can be said about mission, evangelism and the social witness of the church. There are two very different views of each of these. But are these activities primarily ours? Do we engage in them simply because Jesus commanded us to do them and left us an example as to how to do them? Then, no doubt, we would need God's grace to enable *us* to do them. Then God's grace would be conceived of in semi-Pelagian terms as simply "enabling grace," "infused" grace, an "invisible" thing we need, an efficacious impersonal cause (like gasoline to drive our cars!) that is there to make programs work. But in reality, are not mission, evangelism and social action also, like worship, activities in which we are called through the personal activity of the Holy Spirit to participate in Christ's ministry—in the work of the triune God as he establishes his kingdom? In the Bible, grace is always conceived of in personal terms. In grace, the triune God personally stands in for us, gives himself to us and draws us into his inner life. In worship and intercession, Jesus "our great high priest" in our humanity faces the Father with the concerns of the world and all humanity on his heart. In grace, he stands in for us, the One on behalf of the many, and calls us by grace to share in his ministry of intercession as a royal priesthood (1 Pe 2:9). In mission and compassionate service, he faces the world in our humanity with the concerns of his Father (and our Father) on his heart, the apostle as well as the high priest of our profession. Again, in grace he stands in for us, sent by the Father to usher in the kingdom, and anoints us by the Spirit to share his mission to all nations. "And surely I am with you always." In both worship and mission, he baptizes us by the Spirit into his body that we might participate as members of his body in his ministry. "Therefore, holy brothers [and sisters] who share in the heavenly calling, fix your thoughts on Jesus, the apostle and high priest whom we confess" (Heb 3:1).

In our Western pragmatic society, where we are so concerned about questions of "know-how" and "techniques" for mission, evangelism, church growth, and fund-raising, we need to heed Bonhoeffer's plea that we give priority to the "who question" over the "how question" if we would understand the Bible and the biblical meaning of grace. Who is the Father to whom we pray in the name of Christ? Who is the Christ in whose mission we go forth to all nations? Who is the Holy Spirit who draws us into a life of wonderful communion? Only as we know who this triune God of grace is, and what he has done once and for all and is continuing to do for us and with us and in us, can we truly know how to serve.

God's grace is free grace—unconditionally free. But it is also costly grace. We are summoned unconditionally to live a life of costly service, in prayer, mission, and evangelism, to offer ourselves in total obedience (Ro 12:1). How does our ministry relate to Christ's ministry, his once and for all ministry and his continuing ministry? Perhaps the apostle Paul gives us the clue in Gal 2:20: "I no longer live, but Christ lives in me. The life I live in the body, I live by faith in [and by the faithfulness of] the Son of God who loved me and gave himself for me." Is this not "life in Christ," participating by the Spirit in the life and ministry of Christ? Can we not also say, *We* pray, and yet it is not so much we who pray, but Christ and the Holy Spirit who pray for us and with us and in us (Ro 8:26, 27, 34)? Again, we evangelize and seek to carry the gospel of the kingdom to all nations, and yet it is not so much we who do it, but Christ working in us and through us, baptizing people by the Spirit into his kingdom. We exhort people to be reconciled to God and to one another, but it is God in Christ who has by grace reconciled the world to himself in his own person once and for all (Eph 2:8–18), who exercises his continuing reconciling ministry in us and through us today (2 Co 5:18–21). Again, in social concern we seek to give all their humanity, for to hold out Christ to the world in evangelical concern is not only to hold out personal salvation, but to offer authentic humanity to all. But again Christ is the Agent. He has assumed our humanity, sanctified it, realized true humanity for us in his vicarious humanity, and now as the Risen Lord, the Last Adam, he realizes it in us and through us as we give ourselves in compassionate caring concern for all his creatures. What was lost in Adam is restored in Christ and through Christ—full humanity, nothing less.

The Trinitarian Mystery of Christ

Here we see something of the meaning of the New Testament word "mystery," the trinitarian "mystery" of Christ's person and reconciling work, not only in the Pauline epistles, but in our understanding of the Gospels. "The secret of the kingdom of God has been given to you" (Mk 4:11). The prime task of Christian theology is to probe this mystery in the light of revelation, if we would understand aright the nature of Christian worship, mission and evangelism in their unity as different ways of participating in the triune life and ministry of the God of grace in his purposes for the world, and if we would avoid the dualism between theory and practice, academic scholarship and worship, theology and evangelism which has so often characterized and impoverished post-Enlightenment Christianity.[4]

In the New Testament the word μυστήριον, "mystery," is used in four main ways. First of all it refers to the hidden trinitarian purposes of God for all nations in creation and in the election of Israel, the "hidden secret" now revealed in Christ and fulfilled in his reconciling ministry. So Paul writes, "The commission God gave me to present to you the word of God in its fullness—the mystery that has been kept hidden for ages and generations, but is now disclosed to the saints. To them God has chosen to make known among the Gentiles the glorious riches of this mystery, which is Christ in you, the hope of glory" (Col 1:25–27). What is this hidden secret? It is the purpose of the triune God of grace in creating Jews and Gentiles, both men and women, to share his life of loving communion. He does not abandon this purpose, but fulfills it in the election of Israel so that in the fullness of time in Christ, all nations might be called to participate in his triune life by being reconciled to him and to one another. "I will be your God and you will be my people." This is the secret of Paul's apostleship, to make known to the nations (Gentiles) this mystery, this gospel of reconciliation, which was revealed to him on the Damascus road (Col 1:19; Eph 1:9; 3:2–13, 16–21; Ro 16:25–27). The Father revealed his loving purposes in his Son, and calls the church to participate in their fulfillment by life in the Spirit. The doctrine of the Trinity is, so to speak, the grammar of God's mission to the world, as well as the grammar of worship and prayer.

Second, the word "mystery" is used to speak of the Incarnation itself, that God in revealing his divinity to us conceals it in the frail humanity of Jesus, where it is seen by the eye of faith. The hidden mystery is God as human in Jesus Christ. So in 1 Ti 3:16, "Beyond all question, the mystery of godliness is great: He appeared in a body, was vindicated by the Spirit, was seen by angels, was preached among the nations, was believed on in the world, was taken up in glory." The God who reveals himself hides himself in a human body, speaks in parables in human language (Mt 11:22; Mk 4:11; Jn 8:43), and dies on a cross (1 Co 1:21–25). Only through the Holy Spirit can we discern this mystery (Jn 3:3–21; 1 Co 12:3) and see the glory of God in the face of Jesus Christ.

Third, "mystery" is used to speak of our relationship with Christ in his body, the relationship between Christ the head and the members. In being called to know this mystery we are called to participate in it, to find the fulfillment of our destiny in the purposes of God as members of his body where we are brought into union with one another. So the apostle speaks of the relationship between husband and wife as one participatory union. "This is a profound mystery—but I am talking about Christ and the church" (Eph 5:22–33). Christ takes up our relationships, sanctifies them and makes us one in his Body, in union with him. Our mutual loving of one another, as in our love for God, is participatory loving. As the Son indwells the Father, and we dwell in him, so we indwell one another in "perichoretic unity," setting forth the *perichoresis* (mutual indwelling) which is in the triune God. This is the real secret of κοινωνία, "fellowship" (cf. Jn 15:8–17; and our Lord's high priestly prayer in chapter 17).

Fourth, the word "mystery" refers to the eschatological fulfillment of the triune purposes of God in bringing his children to glory in the resurrection and in the kingdom of God—"Christ in you, the hope of glory" (Col 1:27; 1 Co 15:51)—when "the mystery of God will be accomplished" (Rev 10:7).

It is in contemplation of the "hidden mystery" revealed in Christ, and in our reflection on the significance of this for our understanding of worship, mission and the whole of the Christian life, that there unfold the great doctrines of the Trinity, creation, the election of Israel, the Incarnation, the vicarious humanity of Christ, atonement, participation, life in the Spirit, church and sacraments, and our eschatological hope in the kingdom of God.

At the center of the New Testament stands, not our experience, however important that may be, but a unique, absolute relationship between Jesus and the Father, in a life lived in the Spirit, and in that Father-Son relationship we see the disclosure of that communion which is in God himself, and into which we are now drawn by the Holy Spirit. The nature of true ἀγάπη, communion, is defined by that relationship in which we see disclosed, not only the triune God himself, but the inner purpose of creation that we too in the image of the triune God should find our true being-in-communion. Jesus said: "All things have been committed to me by my Father. No one knows the Son except the Father, and no one knows the Father except the Son and those to whom the Son chooses to reveal him" (Mt 11:27). There is given to us in Christ this unique, absolute relationship in which Jesus lives a life of intimate communion with the Father, in his life of worship, mission and service, in which we are called to participate by our life in the Spirit. *He is the Agent* ("Christ in you, the hope of glory"), as he establishes the Father's kingdom and fulfills the trinitarian purposes of God for this world and for all nations.

Trinitarian Contemplation of Christ

In our contemplation of Christ and the mystery of the kingdom of God, as we follow each stage in the life of Christ in the gospel, it is fruitful to focus on four things:

1. The mystery of the presence of the triune God in Christ, as he represents God to humanity and humanity to God.
2. The mystery of incarnation, deity veiled in humanity (God as human), revealed only to the eye of faith.
3. The mystery of "the wonderful exchange," of God as human in Christ in our place, standing in for us, taking what is ours, to give us what is his. This is the mystery of "Christ for us."
4. The mystery of the relationship into which Christ draws us by the Spirit, to participate in his sonship and communion with the Father, and in his mission from the Father to the world. This is the mystery of "Christ in us."

This four-fold contemplation reveals the trinitarian purposes of God in Christ and illumines every stage in the gospel, Jesus' birth of Mary, his baptism in Jordan, his temptation, his ministry and prayer life, the transfiguration on Mt. Tabor, his passion and death, his resurrection and continuing ministry as the high priest and apostle whom we confess. Here we see the heart of a theology of worship and mission.

The story of the birth of Jesus is the story of the Eternal Son "who is in the bosom of the Father [*in sinu patris*]" taking our humanity in the womb of Mary, that he might share with us his sonship and lift us up into the life of God. As Irenaeus puts it: "He takes what is ours to give us what is his." He who is the eternal Son of the Father by nature becomes "Son of Man" that we might become the sons and daughters of God by grace. This is the "wonderful exchange" (*mirifica commutatio*, Calvin calls it) that is consummated in his taking our place on the cross, taking our enmity and death to himself, to give us his love and life in exchange (2 Co 5:18–21).

It has been the mistake of much Western theology, Catholic and Protestant, to limit "substitution" to Christ's death on the cross, to the issue of salvation from sin. The idea has a much wider significance, embracing indeed his whole ministry for us. For example, it is at the heart of our understanding of prayer and the priesthood of Christ. Christ takes our selfish feeble prayers, sanctifies them, and presents them to the Father and in turn puts in his prayer "*Abba*, Father" onto our lips. He stands in for us, intercedes for us and with us and in us, precisely when we do not know how to pray as we ought (Ro 8:26,34; Heb, passim). We have an Advocate with the Father. Substitution, standing in for us, taking what is ours to give us what is his, characterizes every stage of Christ's ministry from the Incarnation to the parousia. Christ's work, as the Scottish theologian John McLeod Campbell used to say, has a retrospective *and* a prospective aspect. Retrospectively, he deals with our past sin, guilt, condemnation, death, wiping out our sins once and for all, carrying our old humanity to the grave. Prospectively his mission from the Father is "to bring many sons to glory," to lift us up into his life of eternal sonship and communion with the Father in the Spirit. These two are never divorced in the New Testament. Jesus rises from the dead to enter into his new ministry of being "the leader of our worship" (λειτουργός), a high priest "forever," "who ever lives to intercede for us." This ministry will be an eternal ministry, continuing when his ministry of saving us from sin and death will have ended (1 Co 15:24). We shall worship the Father through the Son in the Spirit for all eternity. This will be our eternal joy. He is the eternal Mediator of an eternal covenant. In the words of another great Scottish theologian of the thirteenth century, John Duns Scotus, our privilege and high destiny is to be forever *con-diligentes Deo*—"co-lovers with God," participating in the life of mutual love between the Father and the Son, in the life of the man Jesus who is the one true *con-diligens* with the Father.

Trinitarian Participation with Christ

Participation is a key concept in the New Testament. It is in Greek the word κοινωνία, meaning fellowship, communion, sharing, having all in common with one whom we love. There is κοινωνία in the triune God, between Jesus and the Father, and between Christ and the members of his body. This must be carefully distinguished from the Platonic concept of participation, *methexis*, seen in Plato's doctrine of the Forms. For Plato any particular, sensible object is what it is by "participation" in some "form," as we predicate, e.g., Truth, Beauty, Goodness of any particular person or thing. In Platonism the important thing is not the particular thing or person, but the Universal, the Idea. Indeed we do not know particulars as particulars, but only as they participate in Universals. This particular oak tree is an oak in that it participates in the form of an oak. But in the New Testament understanding of participation as κοινωνία, we commune with someone whom we love personally, with the Father, with Jesus Christ, with one another in the Spirit, sharing all, having all "in common." We can see the importance of this distinction in mystical theology in different understandings of the "imitation of Christ." In the Platonic tradition Christ is seen as the ideal Man, the ideal embodiment of Truth and Beauty and Goodness. Then the imitation of Christ (as in aesthetic worship) is motivated by our desire to embody in our spirituality a like Truth and Beauty and Goodness. This is the concept of eros expounded in Plato's dialogue *The Symposium*—the desire for Beauty and Justice and Goodness which motivates the good life. But then our interest would be not so much in Jesus for his own sake, but in the ideals he embodies as our Exemplar. But in the New Testament understanding our relationship with Christ is one of ἀγάπη. We love him for his own sake, and participate in his life and ministry in fellowship with him, and hence in conformity to *him*, not just to his ideals.

Correspondingly, there are two views of "contemplation." The one contemplates the Ideal, abstracted from all particulars, where the soul seeks the beatific vision of Eternal Goodness, in the tradition of Plato's dialogue *Phaedo*, abstracted even from life in the body. This can be a flight from reality. The other is that of this essay where we contemplate the trinitarian mystery of the Person of Christ in loving communion with him in all the historical particularity of his incarnation, death, resurrection and continuing mediatorial ministry, in our desire "to know Christ and the power of his resurrection and the fellowship of sharing in his sufferings" (Php 3:10). It is intensely particular, personal and historical, not a flight from the world but a sharing in his concern for the world.

In similar fashion, we have to distinguish a Platonic from a biblical view of "the one and the many." In the Platonic doctrine of the Forms (as in Hindu mysticism), the interest is in the One, the Universal, the Ideal, but not in the many particulars, the phenomena which participate in the One. But in the Bible, both in the Old Testament interpretation of the election of Israel to be a royal priesthood, the one on behalf of the many, and in the New Testament understanding of Christ as our high priest, giving himself as "a ransom for many," we have a totally different notion (as in Mk 10:45 or Ro 5). Christ is the One for the many, where the many find their fulfillment in loving communion with the One, where Christ's atoning work is for each one of the many and is personalized by the ministry of the Holy Spirit for each person whom he loves in fulfillment of the trinitarian purposes of God. It is in this biblical sense that we speak of "the all-inclusive vicarious humanity of Christ" and his concern for all and see in him our humanity renewed, made righteous, sanctified, offered without spot and wrinkle to the Father, hidden with Christ in God, waiting to be revealed at the last day. It is in that humanity realized for us in Christ, in his priesthood and apostolic ministry, that we are called to participate in a life of worship, prayer, communion and missionary service. It is in his "transforming friendship" that we find eternal joy.

Notes

1. See his beautiful book *The Transforming Friendship: A Guide to Prayer* (Oxford: Lion, 1989).

2. The British Council of Churches in 1983 appointed a "Study Commission on Trinitarian Doctrine Today" with representatives from all main British churches, and in 1989 published the results in two booklets, *The Forgotten Trinity*. A third volume of essays under the same title will appear shortly. They constitute a unanimous ecumenical call to our churches to return to the triune God of grace and to recover a New Testament understanding of the uniqueness of Christ and the Spirit.

3. See my article, "The Vicarious Humanity of Christ," in *The Incarnation: Ecumenical Studies in the Nicene-Constantinopolitan Creed, AD 381*, ed. T. F. Torrance (Edinburgh: Handsel, 1981); "The Place of Jesus Christ in Worship," in *Theological Foundations for Ministry*, ed. Ray S. Anderson (Grand Rapids: Eerdmans, 1979). Cp. J. G. S. S. Thomsan, *The Praying Christ* (Grand Rapids: Eerdmans, 1959); also the third volume of *The Forgotten Trinity*.

4. Cf. Lesslie Newbigin, *Foolishness to the Greeks: The Gospel and Western Culture* (London: SPCK, 1986); idem, *The Gospel in a Pluralist Society* (London: SPCK, 1989); idem, *The Open Secret* (London: SPCK, 1978).

Part 6

Spirituality and Scripture

One of the most important means of grace for nurturing our spiritual lives is Scripture. Indeed, it is the Word of God that addresses us, calls us to account, and invites us to participate in a journey far greater than ourselves. Not only do all Christian traditions (Protestant, Catholic, and Eastern Orthodox) readily acknowledge the revelatory and transforming power of the Bible, but they also cherish this "book of books" through its use in pastoral practice and spiritual discipline.

In our first selection, J. Steven Harper displays the genius of Old Testament spirituality around four key themes: creation, covenant, community, and challenge. The first underscores the sacredness of life as well as the relationship between sexuality and spirituality. Because we are made in the image of God, we can experience intimacy and beauty, even the sublime, in our interpersonal relationships. The second theme reveals the loving bond between God and the children of God, and Harper correctly and courageously notes that within "the Judeo-Christian tradition there is sufficient faith content and experience to render unnecessary any movement toward another religion." Community, as the third theme, militates against the kind of individualism and narcissism that can be found even in some corners of spirituality and the Church. And finally Harper maintains that Old Testament spirituality ever offers us a "challenge," that spirituality is dynamic, never finished, always increasing.

Eugene Peterson in "Saint Mark: The Basic Text for Christian Spirituality" emphasizes the ability of story to call us out of ourselves, to a world larger than we had ever imagined. Peterson points out that the Gospel of Mark is not a text that we master, as if we were in control, but one that actually masters us. We are not the "content" of spirituality; that content is God revealed in Christ. Aberrations, then, can only emerge when we begin to exegete ourselves as the basic and authoritative text. Peterson goes on to argue that asceticism is not life-denying, as some would suppose, but it does strip away all that would prevent us from richly participating in the life of God. And the aesthetic motif of the Gospel of Mark, valuable in so many ways, calls us to nothing less than to spiritual lives in Christ that are marked by beauty and love.

The third selection, by David Dockery on Pauline spirituality, continues several of the themes of the first two selections but places special emphasis on the practical role of the Holy Spirit in the life of the believer and in the community. "Spirituality" then is, in a real sense, life in the "Spirit," under the lead and rule of the Holy Spirit of God. Moreover, viewing spiritual life as remarkably liberating (exactly the opposite of how it is viewed by "outsiders"), Dockery affirms the holiness, the freedom from sin and rebellion, that is displayed in the sixth chapter of Romans where Paul, developing an indicative/imperative tension, beckons his fellow Christians to become what they are. Indeed, this tension between the indicative and the imperative bespeaks of the dynamism of Christian spiritual life, and in its best sense this tension fosters spiritual maturity, a maturity that is deeply satisfying.

Old Testament Spirituality

J. Steven Harper

hristian spirituality is grounded firmly in the Bible. Holy Scripture provides the objective revelation which prevents spirituality from deteriorating into a private and subjective discipline.[1] This objectivity is especially important today when a wide variety of experiences are defined as "spiritual." Everyone from Henri Nouwen to Shirley MacLaine seems to be writing and speaking about "the spiritual life." Spirituality as a human phenomenon is "in," yet it seems that commitment to a spiritual life which is rooted in Scripture is not so popular. Ironically, this is sometimes true of Christians as well as the general public. Those of us who are committed to classical Christianity must examine ourselves at this point. It is easy to let historic traditions of the spiritual life serve as our focal point, and/or to have a particular tradition define our understanding and practice of the spiritual life. While we thank God for the light which tradition provides, it should not become the basis of our spirituality.

Furthermore, it is not unusual to hear people say, "I'm a *New Testament* Christian." This phrase is supposed to bear witness to, and guarantee, a purity of doctrine and experience. But it is a phrase that even Jesus himself would not understand.[2] In terms of a proper view of revelation, it is an unfortunate bifurcation. Omitting the Old Testament from any theological view is a serious mistake. This is particularly true of spirituality.

This essay first appeared in *Asbury Theological Journal* 42.2 (1987): 63–77. Used by permission.

Certainly the focus of Christianity is Christ. But Jesus was a Jew and the Christian faith had its origins in Judaism. It is impossible to separate the New Testament from the Old without violating the message of both. In this article, I hope to show that the Old Testament is an essential and enriching source for the development of a Christian concept of spiritual formation.

It is impossible, however, to provide a complete picture of Old Testament spirituality in one short article. This presentation will be selective, but I also hope it will be representative. At the outset, it is necessary to make two major decisions which will determine the direction and development of the rest of the article.

The first decision relates to the issue of the Old Testament canon itself. It is important to remember that there is no Old Testament spirituality, technically speaking. Because the books were composed over a period of approximately a thousand years, what we really have is a series of Old Testament *spiritualities*.[3] This recognition of a plurality of spiritualities must not be ignored in an in-depth study of the subject.

For this article, I will continue to speak of *an* Old Testament spirituality. The Wesleyan view of canon maintains belief in a certain "connectedness" among the books of the Old Testament. Without this, we could not legitimately speak of *one* testament. There is a real and necessary sense in which the revelatory process occurred in such a way that a larger unity was produced in the midst of plurality. This is not only true within the Old Testament, but also within the New Testament, and between the testaments themselves. Without this belief in a fundamental unity, it makes no sense to talk of *a* Bible.

Secondly, a decision must be made regarding the kind of spirituality described in the Old Testament. It is possible to write this article speaking of "the spirituality of Old Testament times." This approach would emphasize the historical dimension, and would focus upon the faith and practices of ancient Israel. On the other hand, it is possible to write about "the spirituality which is informed and nourished by the Old Testament." In this case, the emphasis would be on the contemporary, and the focus would be on the Old Testament's contribution to a sound spirituality today.[4]

I have chosen the second route. My primary concern is to examine the Old Testament in such a way that our indebtedness to it will be made clear. This is not a license for playing fast and loose with history, but it does mean that a detailed description of the history of Israel will not be the thrust of what is presented. Resources are available to assist us in that kind of approach.[5] Rather, I will take certain historical data and attempt to present it in a way that reveals its significance for contemporary spiritual formation.

There have not been many works written on Old Testament spirituality per se. Two reasons probably account for this. First, the term "spirituality" itself is not a word commonly used by Jews; nor is it a concept given extensive treatment in their religious literature.[6] This is due to their belief that spirituality is too encompassing to ever be properly captured in a word or idea. For the Jew, it is more important to affirm that spirituality *is* than to attempt to describe it. It is a concept whose comprehensiveness and mystery are too great to be analyzed or studied.

I mention this because I generally agree with that belief. Western theology tends to minimize mystery and maximize analysis. If we are not careful, we lose the sense of the sacred which must always attend the theological task. The Jewish perspective is a good one, and it serves as a reminder that we are not writing about something which can be fully captured in words. We are dealing with a mystery too large for our minds or our pens. The preservation of a sense of holiness and reverence about all this is something we dare not lose. To do so would be to turn spirituality into something more akin to an element than an encounter. Having said this, I nevertheless recognize that the task of writing is to attempt as accurate a description as possible.

A second reason for the lack of specific materials on the subject is related to the fact that most of the major aspects of Old Testament spirituality are dealt with extensively under other headings. The task of exploring Old Testament spirituality becomes much easier when specific facets of it are singled out for study. This article is a case study in that approach. It is only when the subject is considered as a whole that a scarcity of materials is noted. This will frustrate anyone who wants to *survey* the subject, but it is not a major obstacle for those who wish to examine the topic in some depth. There is, however room in the discipline of Old Testament studies for reputable scholars to serve the discipline of spiritual formation by providing more general works. As one who teaches in spiritual formation, but who is not a trained Old Testament scholar, I would welcome an increase of materials in this regard.[7]

Let me describe the approach I will take in the rest of this article. First, I will write with a perception of Old Testament spirituality that is roughly analogous to a body's skeleton or a building's superstructure. The topic of Old Testament spirituality will be viewed as present, essential, and describable within the larger flow of revelation, but as a characteristic which does not generally call attention to itself. Second, I will write about Old Testament spirituality under selected categories. I recognize that this approach does some violence to the dynamism of the subject, but I believe it is necessary in an article of this nature. Therefore, I will limit our examination to the following areas: Creation, Covenant, Community and Challenge.

I hope that this article will serve to provide further conviction of the essential role of the Old Testament in the development of a proper spirituality. If it does, it can save us from a truncated view which occurs when we limit our study to the New Testament or to the post-New Testament history of Christian spirituality. We will then have a stronger foundation for discerning truth from error in a time when counterfeit spiritualities abound, and we will have a much richer source from which to draw our own formation.

Creation

It is important that a theology of creation initiates one's reading of the Old Testament. A spirituality rooted in creation is essential. Thus, before we have ventured far into the text of the Old Testament, we encounter some important facts.

First, we learn that the world is from God, and that the world is "good." Against all notions of chance and mindless accident, the Old Testament declares that God is the source of all that is. And against all notions of dualism, it declares that every facet of creation is good and purposeful. The Hebrew word *ṭôḇ*, good, is found seven times in chapter one.

For Christian spiritual formation, this means that the first word in spirituality is "sacred." Whatever else can be said about creation, the starting point is the rightness, goodness, and holiness of it all. Even after the Fall, it is possible to say, "the heavens declare the glory of God and the skies proclaim the work of his hands" (Ps 19:1, NIV). No matter what we do or where we go, we cannot escape or alter the basic "goodness" and Godness of the creation (cf. Ps 139:7–12).

Another important fact discovered in creation is that even if we could escape God's goodness, we would be foolish to do so. For at the heart of creation is Love. The original perfection of creation, its teleology, its majesty and its unity all testify to the goodness of God.[8] In fact, it is this Love which makes it possible to understand other important Old Testament themes such as covenant, prophecy, wisdom, and even eschatology (see especially Deut 7:7–8). The Creator God is so in love with the creation that nothing can cause a cessation of that love or curb its redemptive aspects. Spiritual formation maintains that if we look at the world through the perspective of the Old Testament, we will conclude that God is Love.

This revelation of God forms the foundation for the Old Testament call to worship Yahweh.[9] The biblical account of creation does not fully develop the character of God, or even the concept of monotheism. However, it is worth noting that in the growing religious consciousness of Israel there is no need to abandon the creation's theology of God in order to understand God as the Father of Abraham, Isaac and Jacob. God is personal both in and through nature, as well as in and through human relations.

The creation story tells us that we are loved by a God who is Love. Human beings are the supreme objects of God's love because of the fact that they are created in the image of God. And again, the *imago dei* is a foundational concept on the anthropology of spiritual formation (cf. Gen 1:26–27 and 2:7). For the purposes of this article we will focus on the human dimensions of creation. And when we do, we discover a number of important things about the spiritual life.

First, we see that life is sacred. God is holy, and the fact that we are made in the image of God means that we have a holiness through creation. This is why the murder of Abel by Cain is cited as a serious violation of the order of creation. This comes in time to be further enforced through the Ten Commandments' prohibition against murder. When one human being violates, abuses, or takes the life of another human being, there is a loss of the sacred which God intends (Gen 9:6).

But it goes even deeper than that. Even when physical violence is absent, there is an equal concern for the sanctity of life when a person does violence to another as in adultery or the seemingly lesser evil of a falsification of weights and measures. All this finds its source in a theology of creation which declares that every person, thing and activity is somehow infused with the divine. Only a lifestyle that maintains integrity with this sacredness is acceptable to God.

When we set contemporary perspectives alongside this view of the sacred, we see how we have deteriorated in our acknowledgement of and commitment to holiness. Life has been secularized in large and small ways. A general cheapening of human life characterizes personal and corporate living. The Old Testament plays a valuable role in the formation of Christian spirituality by never allowing us to forget or minimize the sacredness of life.

Second, we learn from creation that our life is specific. There is a general distinctiveness and individuality in the creation of the various species. But this individuality and specificity is amplified and given special attention in the creation of Adam and Eve. The expression of the *imago dei* in sexually distinctive expressions of humanity highlights what Eichrodt calls the creation of "an independent, spiritual I."[10] The value of life is heightened as we see that no person is a duplicate of anyone else. The process of naming further amplifies this fact. Whereas animals may well have been named by order (e.g. giraffe), each human being is given a name which differentiates it from every other human being. Even down to the etchings of our fingerprints, the work of creation bears witness to the uniqueness of each human being.

The uniqueness of self and the preciousness of personality are indispensable elements of Old Testament spirituality. This view of life forms the basis for contrasts between the Israelites and pagan cultures (e.g. infanticide). It stands behind the ethical-behavioral allowances and prohibitions of the Law. It is the foundation of the prophetic call to justice and mercy for even the "least" persons in a society.[11]

Before we leave this idea of specificity as an element in Old Testament spirituality, we need to say more about it as it relates to sexuality. In a society like ours today, we have all but lost knowledge of and appreciation for the relationship between sexuality and spirituality which is presented in the Bible, beginning in and through the creation story.

The sexual differential of human beings into males and females is mystery of the highest order. On a purely logical basis, there is no reason why God had to order creation this way. Even scientifically speaking, such an ordering was not necessary to perpetuate life. Yet, this distinctiveness stands out in creation as a principle of divine significance. Clearly, each man and each woman are made in the image of God. There is no notion of each one having a sort of "half *imago dei*." Much less is there any notion of one having more of the *imago dei* than any other. Even after the differentiation, it is still possible to speak of a kind of completeness within maleness and femaleness.

At the same time, sexual differentiation provides an element in the human order which reflects something God wanted to maintain in the whole of creation, and that is a sense of dependence. We easily see and affirm that God wanted creation to recognize its continual sense of dependence on Him. But we see less easily that this sense of dependency is made visible in the dependence which is set up through the creation of maleness and femaleness. It takes both males and females to describe the full essence of the *imago dei*.[12] Furthermore, there is a holy co-creatorship established between human beings and God, as intercourse between a male and female results in the continuation of creation in history. Further still, there is a dynamic of attraction, love, and relationship which would not be present if human beings were asexual or monosexual—or if each man and woman were absolutely and totally complete in themselves.[13] We end as we began, with mystery, but it is a mystery which embraces sexual differentiation and sexual life as part of the holiness of creation.

The specificity of the "spiritual I" also forms the basis for intimacy of relationship. Because we have been made "like God" we are equipped for relationship with God. In the act of creation, God demonstrated a desire for relationship beyond and outside of the Godhead. By creating human beings with the *imago dei*, God made possible both the desire and ability for every person to relate beyond himself/herself—to others, to every other part of creation, and ultimately to God.[14]

This aspect of relationship is essential if human life is to flourish, even as it was essential if divine life was to flourish. God allows human beings to come close, and God desires to come close to human beings. Yet, this intimacy does not violate the mystery of God or the autonomy of humans.[15] Rather it calls God and humanity into a sacred partnership which maintains God's sovereignty, but which mandates human dominion (cf. Gen 1:28).

Because we are made in the image of God, we can experience intimacy in interpersonal relationships. That intimacy is characterized by respect, service, and love. People are intended to live in peace with one another, and indeed with the rest of creation. Whatever dominion may mean, it does not mean domination or exploitation. The Old Testament is filled with passages that condemn the oppression of people by other people. Morality, fairness, concern, are the standards of interpersonal relations.

Finally, our being made in the image of God has implications for the rest of creation. We are to "have dominion" over creation in the sense of stewardship. The Hebrew concept is that of the faithful discharge of duty. Adam and Eve, and their descendents, are God's representatives on the earth to order and care for it so that it can reflect its own glory. This unity between humanity and the rest of creation is seen in general by the way the creation narratives flow from one stage to another. In a more specific sense, the unity is seen through two specific acts: (1) that the "creeping things" and Adam are both created on the sixth day, and (2) that Adam is given the duty of naming all the animals.[16]

To be made in the image of God means that we are not merely passive receptors of divine destiny. Rather, we are active participators in shaping that destiny. The creation story reveals that God sets forth information about allowances and limits for Adam and Eve, the allowance for authentic choice, and the execution of judgment after failure (judgment only makes sense if responsibility is a reality). The fact that we are created in the image of God means that we are "response-able."

Those in the Wesleyan tradition will immediately see a theology of "natural conscience" as well as a reflection of prevenient grace. Old Testament spirituality as revealed in creation is that amazing and awesome mixture of allowance and accountability, liberty and limitation, freedom and fidelity. Thus our very creation becomes a major element of our spirituality. Such a spirituality saves us from any notions of dualism. Such a spirituality clearly reveals the value and sacredness of life. Through what we might call a spirituality of creation, we see our interconnected-ness, mutual dependency, and moral responsibility. And we recognize that true life is not being swept along by some kind of cosmic energy, but rather is being sustained by an intimate relationship with a personal God.

Covenant

The personal God who creates persons who share in the *imago dei* cannot be satisfied with a generalized relationship. Through the introduction of covenant, the Old Testament reveals an intensification and a particularization of the divine-human relationship. And through the covenant, we learn important things about the spiritual life.

First, the covenant reveals a bonding between God and those who accept the covenant. "I will be their God, and they shall be my people" (e.g. Exod 6:6–7; Lev 26:12). This bonding through covenant begins as early as Gen 9:16 in the covenant between God and Noah. It continues through the patriarchs, climaxing in the national covenant with Israel. Through the covenant, the ideas of closeness and intimacy are amplified. Images of this covenantal bonding run through the Old Testament: sexual intimacy as a symbol of God's intimacy with Israel, a child nursing at a mother's breast, a husband who cannot abandon a whoring wife, a deliverer who releases captives from bondage, etc. One can only conclude that the covenant is God's invitation to "come closer."

This invitation is initiated by God. The shekinah is God's glorious presence with the people. This glory fills the heavens and the earth in a general sense, but comes to reside specifically in the Holy of Holies in the Tabernacle and later in the Temple. It is important to note that this presence is "located" in that place where the worship of God is conducted, where the Law is read and interpreted, and where the people offer their sacrifices and make their responses.[17] But here, as in creation, God maintains intimacy without destroying reverential distance—so that the Creator-creature distinction is preserved. God is not reduced in majesty, and humanity is not absorbed into divinity.[18]

This reverential distance is preserved in two primary ways. First, the "vision of God" which affects and enriches the nation is something reserved for a relatively few people. The experience of Moses is an example. Moses is a reminder of the nearness of God, but Moses is not presented as a model of spirituality available for any and every Jew. Such a universalizing of intimacy, from the Old Testament perspective, must await "the Day of the Lord" (e.g. Joel 2:28–32). And second, Israel's closeness to God is never seen as automatic and guaranteed. Individuals (e.g. Samson) and the nation as a whole experience the *absence* of God.[19] Thus, the bond between God and Israel cannot be assumed or presumed upon. It must be reverently received and conscientiously maintained.

The idea of boundary is related to this. In creation we are given a picture of God's relationship with the world. But in the covenant, there is something of a narrowing of relationship. This is both frustrating and revealing. It is frustrating because we are left to wonder about the precise nature of the relationship between God and other peoples and nations. Once Israel becomes the focus (and even more the New Israel in the New Testament), the Bible never again answers all the questions of God's general relationship with the rest of the world.

Nevertheless, this has some important implications from a spiritual formation perspective. First, it implies that there is some sort of *qualitative* difference between Israel's knowledge of God and that of other people and nations. The idea of covenant implies the enrichment of the divine-human relationship, and enhancement of any less particularized, more cosmological awareness of God.

There is mystery here. It is a mystery which does not allow us to conclude on the one hand that one religion is as good as another, but neither does it allow us to take the other extreme position that Christians are the only ones who have any legitimate light regarding God. In the depths of this mystery, we must allow God to be God in relation to those peoples and nations which are not the focus of the Bible's revelation and natural conscience, both of which do not fully answer our questions.

A second implication of the idea of boundary is that within the Judeo-Christian tradition there is sufficient faith content and experience to render unnecessary any movement toward another religion. Therefore, the task which should consume our time and energy is the cultivation of our relationship with God through Christ to its maximum potential. Dr. Harvey Seifert puts this in perspective by saying, "Going to other world religions for decisively different insights is like carrying a lantern to a neighbor's house to borrow a match. We already have the essential fire in our own keeping."[20]

However, it would be wrong to conclude that living within the covenant is some kind of "end" or goal. To live as God's covenant people is to be engaged in mission and evangelism. In fact, it can be argued that one of the reasons God had to set the New Covenant in motion through the Christian Church was that the Jews did not actualize the missional implications of the Old Covenant. At their best, both Judaism and Christianity have realized that God wants every human being to have a saving relationship with Him. So, the Jews have proselytized and the Christians have catechized. The goal has been to incorporate as many as possible into the covenant community. Thus, to be in covenant is to be reaching out.

For Israel, the idea of boundary was conveyed geographically and legislatively. For the Jews, land and law were two primary means to remind themselves that God did not intend for people to live as they please. Through the land, Israel received a place to cultivate its spiritual life.[21] Through the law, Israel received the information and the perspective to live its life before God.[22] Presence in or absence from the land and obedience or disobedience to the law become two concrete means of assessing the nation's vitality, and the two are interrelated.

The idea of boundary is not an easy one to describe. But it is an observable dimension when the covenant is studied. From a spiritual formation perspective, this element of covenant deserves much further study. The validity and vitality of "the spiritual life" must necessarily have some dimension of boundary to it. This aspect is all the more important as New Age spirituality attracts the attention of more and more people in our society.

Finally, we see in the covenant the motif of blessing, with its flip side of cursing. I state it this way because it seems clear to me that the primary intent of the covenant was to insure the beatitude of Israel. The message of God's judgment more technically belongs to life lived outside the covenant than life lived within it. The covenant itself is a medium of blessing. And it is important to emphasize that even in the Old Testament, the note of "blessedness" is contained and valued.

Traditional Christian spirituality has seen such blessedness clearly in the Beatitudes. The same can be said of the Wesleyan tradition.[23] It is helpful to see that the Old Testament idea of covenant provides the necessary ingredients of substance and accountability as it relates to the blessed life. Again, in our overly-subjectivistic age, we are quick to think of "beatitude" as an essentially private enterprise with a minimal sense (if any) of community or accountability. The Old Testament notion of covenant helps us a great deal in seeing the blessed life in a more proper perspective.

Fundamentally, the idea of covenant blessing is a communal idea. The cultus became the primary medium for describing and interpreting such blessedness.[24] Thus, the blessed life is a life of obedience to and participation in the community of faith, especially in such things as worship, sacrifice and prayer. The idea of blessing was made tangible through the existence of sacred sites, objects, seasons and leaders.

The idea of curse is therefore more nearly the result of disobedience than it is an expression of any type of negative emotion in God. God's wrath and judgment *follow* Israel's breaking of the covenant. In other words, something sacred must be broken or violated if cursing is to result. To be sure, original sin creates a primal rupture in the divine-human relationship which only grace can restore. But here again, the covenant as blessing offers sinful humanity a place to be reconciled. And when that offer is accepted and lived out, blessing is the norm.[25]

I have spent quite a bit of space interpreting the significance of Creation and Covenant in an Old Testament spirituality. I have done so because these are the two elements which have been emphasized most in the history of Christian spirituality. And as we have seen, they have tremendous consequences for the shaping of an authentic spirituality in our time. However, they are not the only notes to be sounded. Therefore, in the remaining pages of this article, I will highlight two more important aspects which are closely related to creation and covenant.

Community

The ideas of Creation and Covenant lead into a discussion of Community, for both speak to us far more of the plural than the singular. And I confess that I have selected community for examination intentionally and in light of our society's fearful drift into unhealthy individualism.

The Old Testament knows nothing of authentic spirituality apart from community, and several Old Testament theologies make "community" the central concern of the OT.[26] Maturity and mission are conceived of only in relation to the community of faith.[27] Here again, we note a significant contrast with contemporary culture and aberrant spiritualities.[28] The Old Testament helps us to set true spirituality in its proper perspective.

Both the law and the prophets are instructions for the people. Spiritual leaders are those who have the nation in their hearts. Private spiritual advancement is not even a minor theme in the Old Testament.[29] The patriarchs, matriarchs, seers, judges, priests, prophets and kings are all people for others. Stepping outside the community to embrace a private experience or a "foreign" entity is anathema. So also is living within the community in ways that violate its ethos. No matter where you are, you are a Jew. Nothing can change that. There is no understanding of faith and life or authentic existence apart from this community perspective.

An examination of the Old Testament shows that Israel had to contend with tribalism and sectarianism. But when the nation was at its best, the tribes and sects saw themselves as part of something far bigger—part of a fellowship and a community. As Jews, they were grounded in the revelation of God as Yahweh (one God), the law (one standard), and the nation (one people). There might be any number of threads, but only one fabric—many colors, but one coat.

In this emphasis on community, we see several important aspects of spirituality. First, we see the formation of identity. Such identity is fueled by a strong sense of national consciousness, which is itself integrally related to sacred actions, sites, objects and seasons.[30] It is an identity which begins in the family and moves outward to embrace the entire nation—and in time, even those in dispersion who live outside the boundaries of the nation. This identity is maintained as the people remember the mighty acts of God, and the certainty of such past acts becomes the grounds for hope.

Second, we see the existence of interdependence. The Old Testament reveals close connections between the king, the priests, prophets and people. A breakdown anywhere along the line causes the whole nation to suffer. And there are times (e.g. Hos 5–7) when nothing short of national repentance will bring healing to the sickness. The theme that "righteousness exalts a nation" is sounded time and again; it is a righteousness which can only be achieved by mutual faithfulness. Holiness exists only where all segments of the nation live properly before God and each other. This helps to explain why immorality, injustice and oppression cannot be tolerated in the community.[31]

Third, the community is sustained and challenged by a divine intuition—a discernment of the word and will of God that comes frequently through the message of Israel's prophets. This word is by no means limited to the prophets. All of Israel's leaders are to be those who walk close to God. And so at various times we see judges, priests and kings expressing the word of God to the people. But when they are not obedient, God raises up prophets so that the people are not without the truth of God in their midst. There can be no genuine community without a sensitivity to God's will and a determination to carry it out. Without this, community is destroyed.[32]

In contemporary spiritual formation, we learn the necessity of community through the witness of the Old Testament. Even by itself, the Old Testament supplies us with all the evidence we need to stand over against the erosion of community in our society. When this biblical revelation is coupled with the witness of the New Testament and the ensuing Christian tradition, we are left with no room to erect any notion of the spiritual life which omits or minimizes community. Community is an essential ingredient for every Christian, regardless of status, maturity, or experience. It is at one and the same time a provider of an essential element in spirituality, and a protector against excesses and pitfalls.

Challenge

All of this culminates in a grand challenge. Old Testament spirituality is never finished. On the one hand, it is a challenge to bring each new generation into the experience of God. And on the other hand, it is a challenge to hold the present generation in a faithful relationship to God. And finally, the spirituality of the Old Testament is one which ultimately looks beyond itself to the coming of the Messiah and the flowering of the People of God.

This means that yesterday's experiences, while valuable, can never become the verifier of present realities. The past cannot sustain the present or guarantee the future. So, the Old Testament has a tone of expectation—a forward look. This tone of challenge is an invitation. Israel is invited to embrace the world as God's creation, themselves as being made in God's image, the covenant as God's bond of love, the leaders as God's appointed servants. The comprehensiveness of the invitation is startling. It is as if God is everywhere declaring His presence, influence and desire to relate intimately with all people.

The essence of the challenge is an increasing closeness and intimacy between God and Israel. Nowhere is this seen any better in the Old Testament than in the Song of Songs. Scholars have given this book a number of different interpretations, but one thing is common—the lover is inviting the beloved, and the beloved is responding to the lover. The result is increasing intimacy. In the process, the Old Testament celebrates such things as spontaneity, longing, fidelity, union, joy and the beauty of nature. In fact, this book has been considered by some to capture the major themes of Old Testament spirituality.[33]

The problem is that the people do not always respond as they are intended. The glorious invitation to intimacy is ignored and/or rejected. And so we see the repeated cycle of repentance/reconciliation. As far back as Adam and Eve, we see the breaking of relationship with God and the need to restore fellowship. God often asks in one way or another, "How long must I bear with you, O Israel?" The law, with its elaborate system of worship and sacrifice, is one means of restoring the nation to God. The prophets are another way through which God seeks to heal the brokenness. The Old Testament does not shield us from a picture of God's ideal intention for all creation, but "Plan B" is usually in operation, thereby keeping God engaged in a perpetual reclamation project.[34]

And once again, at the center of the challenge to intimacy (even in the face of brokenness) is God's inestimable love. The God we meet in the Old Testament has made an indestructible commitment to keep faith with Israel. Nothing can cause God to pull out of that relationship. God's absolute faithfulness is the foundation for everything in the Old Testament. The psalter focuses upon it.[35]

The forward look of this challenge produces a history in which consummation can be celebrated. Israel's history is not meaningless nor haphazard. Looking back, it is possible to trace the activity of God in the midst of the people. Looking forward, it is possible to believe that the future will be directed by God as well. The note of challenge is not only one of experienced intimacy, but also one of anticipated increase.

Interestingly, the present and the future converge to provide a vision of authentic spirituality. Like the two lenses of one's glasses, the present and future each supply a part of the essential clarity. One lens (the future) keeps certainty and ultimacy in view, while the other lens (the present) focuses upon the current tasks of mercy, ministry and mission. We conclude our examination of Old Testament spirituality on a high note of moral and ethical responsibility. The challenge is to live intimately with God in such a way that the future is secure and the present is served.

These major categories of Old Testament theology provide us with numerous insights regarding the nature of spirituality. In creation we are invited to the richness of the cosmos and the sacredness of life made in the image of God. Through the covenant we are encouraged to bond ourselves to the living God, which necessarily calls us into community with all other persons who have done the same. Thus formed, we are challenged to deepen our intimacy with God and to direct our energies toward the service of others.

To be sure, there are many other aspects of Old Testament spirituality which could have been included, and they would have increased our appreciation for the importance of the Old Testament in shaping a biblical spirituality. But these four will serve as irrefutable evidence that a truly spiritual life is informed and formed through the revelation of God as found in the Old Testament. They serve as a reminder that we have not done ourselves or others a service by omitting or minimizing this part of the Story from our theology and experience of the spiritual life.

Notes

1. Bernard McGinn and John Meyendorff, eds., *Christian Spirituality: Origins to the Twelfth Century* (New York: Crossroads, 1985), 23. The objectivity of Judeo-Christian spirituality is rooted in historicity, and this is a notable contrast from contemporary "New Age" spiritualities which are cosmological rather than historical in their nature.

2. Ibid., 7–9. McGinn and Meyendorff provide a brief, but helpful review of the early church's reliance upon the Old Testament in the shaping of Christian spirituality.

3. John F. Craghan, *Love and Thunder: A Spirituality of the Old Testament* (Collegeville, Minn.: Liturgical Press, 1983), ix.

4. Cheslyn Jones, Geoffrey Wainright, and Edward Yarnold, eds., *The Study of Spirituality* (New York: Oxford University Press, 1986), 48.

5. Examples of such resources are cited in the endnotes of this article.

6. Lionel Blue, "Judaism," in *The Westminster Dictionary of Christian Spirituality*, ed. Gordon Wakefield (Philadelphia: Westminster, 1983), 226. Arthur Green makes the same point in his work *Jewish Spirituality: From the Bible through the Middle Ages* (New York: Crossroads, 1986), 7. He writes, "Where a modern employs the term 'spirituality,' an ancient Israelite employs 'yir³at YHWH,' (fear of Yahweh), or 'ꜥavôdat YHWH' (service of Yahweh)."

7. B. S. Childs, *Biblical Theology in Crisis* (Philadelphia: Westminster, 1970), notes that the most difficult, but necessary, task of biblical theology is to "rediscover the Bible as devotional literature" (147).

8. Walter Eichrodt, *Theology of the Old Testament* (Philadelphia: Westminster, 1967), 2:107–13.

9. Green, *Jewish Spirituality*, 13.

10. Eichrodt, *Theology of the Old Testament*, 2:121. Interestingly, this idea is dealt with and confirmed in a work devoted to an examination of human religious experience from a natural science perspective. In *The Spiritual Nature of Man* (Oxford: Clarendon, 1979), Sir Alister Hardy, emeritus professor of zoology of Exeter and Merton Colleges at the University of Oxford, describes the *imago dei* by saying, "I believe that the nature of God is essentially one of personal qualities, and that man's relationship to this presence must be a devotional, personal I-Thou feeling."

11. This view of sacredness makes it impossible to speak of a hierarchy of value in creation. Differences in role and function are inevitable, but an assessment of value based on an attempted hierarchy is unacceptable. There is no attempt to define relative sacredness in relationship to race, sex, or role. Here is at least one reason why the Old Testament sounds a note of *compassion* for the poor and the oppressed. These people are not the sole objects of sacredness, but rather they are a societal test of how complete a view of human sacredness is in operation.

12. Some today attempt to argue that the genderlessness of God (that is, that God contains the fullness of maleness and femaleness) is a case for genderlessness in contemporary society. However, such an argument fails to deal seriously with a theology of creation in which God chose, for whatever reasons, to make the gender differentiation—and called it "good." Christian spiritual formation enables people to accept, celebrate and utilize their sexual specificity as males and females.

13. Craghan, *Love and Thunder*, 213–22.

14. Ibid., 21–25.

15. Jones et al., *The Study of Spirituality*, 56–57.

16. Craghan, *Love and Thunder*, 24–25.

17. Urban T. Holmes, *A History of Christian Spirituality* (New York: Seabury, 1980), 14–15.

18. Blue, "Judaism," 227.

19. Jones et al., *The Study of Spirituality*, 51–52.

20. Harvey Seifert, *Explorations in Meditation and Contemplation* (Nashville: The Upper Room, 1981), 16.

21. Chauncey Holmes, *Christian Spirituality in Geologic Perspective* (Philadelphia: Dourance, 1975). This entire work seeks to show that possession and exile are expressions of the "rhythm" of Israel's spirituality. This has to do both with presence and absence, and also with righteousness and sinfulness. Palestine becomes a stage on which this rhythmic drama is played out.

22. Eichrodt spends hundreds of pages detailing the role of the Law for Israel. See *Theology of the Old Testament*, esp. 1:70–178 and 2:231–496.

23. Dr. Jerry Mercer has recently written an excellent book on the Beatitudes, *Cry Joy!* (Wheaton: Victor, 1987). John Wesley's estimate of the Beatitudes can be found in his *Explanatory Notes upon the New Testament* (Naperville, Ill.: Allenson, 1966), 28–29; and in *Forty Four Sermons*, sermons XVI–XVIII (London: Epworth, 1967), 185–234.

24. Eichrodt, *Theology of the Old Testament*, 1:98–177. Note esp. 173–74.

25. Blue, "Judaism," 226–27.

26. For example, T. C. Vriezen, *An Outline of Old Testament Theology*, 2d rev. English ed. (Newton, Mass.: Branford, 1970). Dr. Gene Carpenter, associate professor of Old Testament at Asbury Theological Seminary, defines the central concern of the Old Testament as, "God's creation of a people in His image, in relationship to Him and to one another, in an appropriate environment."

27. Craghan, *Love and Thunder*, x.

28. William Willimon, "Answering Pilate: Truth and the Postliberal Church," in *Christian Century* 28 (January 1987), 83. Willimon challenges the highly individualistic character of American Christianity and the society's emphasis on self-fulfillment.

29. Jones et al., *The Study of Spirituality*, 48–49.

30. Eichrodt, *Theology of the Old Testament*, 1:101–76.

31. Craghan, *Love and Thunder*, 113–14.

32. The importance of prophecy for Israel is developed in Walter Brueggemann's *The Prophetic Imagination* (Philadelphia: Fortress, 1978); Martin Buber's *The Prophetic Faith* (New York: MacMillan, 1949); and Abraham Heschel's *The Prophets* (New York: Harper & Row, 1962).

33. Craghan, *Love and Thunder*, 215–20.

34. Eichrodt, *Theology of the Old Testament*, 2:457–71.

35. Claus Westermann, *The Praise of God in the Psalms* (Richmond: John Knox, 1965), 81–116. Also, Bernard W. Anderson, *Out of the Depths: The Psalms Speak for Us Today* (Philadelphia: Westminster, 1974).

Saint Mark

The Basic Text
for Christian Spirituality

Eugene H. Peterson

Introduction

A quite remarkable thing has been taking place in this city in the last 25 years; spiritual theology has been named and recognized, appreciated and sought after. Spiritual theology is an honored, central, and ancient concern of the Christian church. But in the last two hundred years with the imperialistic ascendance of rationalism, accompanied by various and sundry reactions of romanticism, spiritual theology virtually disappeared from the scene. Rationalism and romanticism fought for the heart of humankind and between them pretty much divided up the spoils. Spiritual theology, pushed to the sidelines, survived academically in obscure corners of various libraries around the world. Spiritual theology, mostly ignored but sometimes demeaned in both church and world, became the specialty of small and often eccentric coteries of enthusiasts.

Meanwhile here in Vancouver, something quite different has been taking place: spiritual theology has been recovered as a discipline and concern that is basic to the entire Christian enterprise as it is thought through and studied in classrooms, prayed and practised in home and workplace, believed in the church

This essay is based on Dr. Peterson's inaugural lecture as the James M. Houston Professor of Spiritual Theology at Regent College, given October 17, 1993. It was first published in *Crux* 29.4 (December 1993): 2–9, and appeared later in *Subversive Spirituality* (Vancouver, B.C.: Regent College Publishing, 1997), 3–15. Used by permission.

and proclaimed in the world. Both the necessity and the attractiveness of spiritual theology has been worked out and demonstrated among us—an immense gift to both church and world. And a gift most timely, for it is quite clear that our culture, toxic with rationalism and romanticism, is in a bad way and getting worse. Those of us who pray for the salvation of the world cannot do without the rich flocks of wisdom and insight and prayer and maturity to which spiritual theology is shepherd.

The name most associated with this recovery and demonstration is James M. Houston. No one person pulls off an historical and cultural feat like this single-handed. He had, and has, colleagues, friends, and family who were and are part of it in large and small ways. But his name—his focused vision, his sacrificial faithfulness, the clarity of his thinking, the passion of his prayers—his name more than any other identifies this recovery of spiritual theology at this critical time as we approach the third millennium.

Because of what has been taking place in this city in the last 25 years, spiritual theology is no longer confined to the academic pursuits of medievalists. Because of what has been taking place in this city in the last 25 years, spiritual theology now carries the connotation of robust and mature spiritual health instead of being suspect as religious neurosis.

And because James Houston's name is so thoroughly associated with all this, it is fitting that this professorship be distinguished by the title, the James M. Houston Chair of Spiritual Theology.

Saint Mark: The Basic Text

The Gospel of St. Mark is the basic text for Christian spirituality. I use the definite article deliberately, *the* basic text. The entire canon of Scripture is our comprehensive text, the revelation that determines the reality that we deal with as human beings who are created, saved, and blessed by the God and Father of our Lord Jesus Christ through the Holy Spirit. But St. Mark as the first Gospel holds a certain primacy.

1. The Form of the Text

No one had ever written a Christian Gospel before Mark wrote his. He created a new genre. It turned out to be a form of writing that quickly became both foundational and formative for the life of church and Christian. We are accustomed to believing that the Holy Spirit inspired the content of the Scriptures (2 Tim. 3:16), but it is just as true that the form is inspired, this new literary form that we call Gospel. There was nothing quite like it in existence, although Mark had good teachers in the Hebrew storytellers who gave us the Books of Moses and Samuel.

The Bible as a whole comes to us in the form of narrative, and it is within this large, somewhat sprawling narrative that St. Mark writes his Gospel. "We live mainly by forms and patterns," Wallace Stegner, one of our great contemporary storytellers, tells us, ". . . if the forms are bad, we live badly."[1] Gospel is a true and good form, by which we live well. Storytelling creates a world of presuppositions, assumptions, and relations into which we enter. Stories invite us into a world other than ourselves, and, if they are good and true stories, a world larger than ourselves. Bible stories are good and true stories, and the world that they invite us into is the world of God's creation and salvation and blessing.

Within the large, capacious context of the biblical story we learn to think accurately, behave morally, preach passionately, sing joyfully, pray honestly, obey faithfully. But we dare not abandon the story as we do any or all of these things, for the minute we abandon the story, we reduce reality to the dimensions of our minds and feelings and experience. The moment we formulate our doctrines, draw up our moral codes, and throw ourselves into a life of ministry apart from a continuous re-immersion in the story itself, we walk right out of the presence and activity of God and set up our own shop.

The distinctiveness of the form "Gospel" is that it brings the centuries of Hebrew storytelling, God telling his story of creation and salvation through his people, to the story of Jesus, the mature completion of all those stories, in a way that is clearly revelation—that is, divine self-disclosure—and in a way that invites, insists on, our participation.

This is in contrast to the ancient preference for myth-making, which more or less turns us into spectators of the supernatural. It is also in contrast to the modern preference for moral philosophy which puts us in charge of our own salvation. "Gospel story" is a verbal way of accounting for reality that, like the incarnation that is its subject, is simultaneously divine and human. It *reveals*, that is, it shows us something we could never come up with on our own by observation or experiment or guess; and at the same time it *engages*, it brings us into the action as recipients and participants but without dumping the responsibility on us for making it turn out right.

This has great implications for our spirituality, for the form itself protects us against two of the major ways in which we go off the rails: becoming frivolous spectators, clamoring for new and more exotic entertainment out of heaven; or, becoming anxious moralists, putting our shoulders to the wheel and taking on the burdens of the world. The very form of the text shapes responses in us that make it hard to become a mere spectator or a mere moralist. This is not a text that we master, it is one that we are mastered by.

It is significant, I think, that in the presence of a story, whether we are telling it or listening to it, we never have the feeling of being experts—there is too much we don't yet know, too many possibilities available, too much mystery and glory. Even the most sophisticated of stories tends to bring out the childlike in us—expectant, wondering, responsive, delighted—which, of course, is why the story is the child's favorite form of speech; why it is the Holy Spirit's dominant form of revelation; and why we adults, who like posing as experts and managers of life, so often prefer explanation and information.

2. The Content of the Text

We don't read very long in this text by St. Mark before we realize that it is about Jesus Christ, and before we have finished we realize that it is about God revealed in Jesus Christ. This seems obvious enough, but I want to dwell on the obvious for a moment.

I have named St. Mark's Gospel as the basic text for our spirituality. Spirituality is the attention we give to our souls, to the invisible interior of our lives that is the core of our identity, these image-of-God souls that comprise our uniqueness and glory. Spirituality is the concern we have for the invisibility that inheres in every visibility, for the interior that provides content to every exterior. It necessarily deals much with inner-ness, with silence, with solitude. It takes all matters of soul with utmost seriousness.

This would appear to be a wonderful thing, and our initial exclamation is most likely, "Would that all the Lord's people were so engaged!" But twenty centuries of experience in spirituality qualifies our enthusiasm considerably. In actual practice it turns out to be not so wonderful. When you look at our history, it is no wonder that spirituality is so often treated with suspicion, and not infrequently with outright hostility. For in actual practice spirituality very often develops into neurosis, degenerates into selfishness, becomes pretentious, turns violent. How does this happen? The short answer is that it happens when we step outside the Gospel story and take ourselves as the basic and authoritative text for our spirituality; we begin exegeting ourselves as a sacred text. We don't usually throw the Gospel out; we merely put it on the shelf and think that we are honoring it by consulting it from time to time as an indispensable reference work.

Our spiritual guides tell us, "You are wonderful, glorious beings, precious souls. Your aspirations for holiness and goodness and truth are splendid. But you are not the content of spirituality; God revealed in Jesus is that. You need a text to read and study and learn from—here's your text, the gospel of Jesus Christ. Start with St. Mark's Gospel as your basic text."

We open the text and read the story of Jesus. It is an odd kind of story. It tells us very little of what interests us in a story. We learn virtually nothing about Jesus that we really want to know. There is no description of his appearance. Nothing about his origin, friends, education, family. How are we to evaluate or understand this person? And there is very little reference to what he thought, to how he felt, his emotions, his interior struggles.

At some point or other we realize that this is a story about God—and about us. Even though Jesus is the most referred-to person in the story, there is a surprising reticence in regard to Jesus. Jesus is the revelation of God, so we are always being faced in Jesus with what we are faced with in God: most of what is here we don't get, we don't see, don't understand. We don't figure Jesus out, we don't search Jesus out, we don't get Jesus on our terms. It follows that neither do we get God on our terms. As a story, it is a most unsatisfying story.

And then we realize that our attention has been drawn away from ourselves and is on Jesus, God revealed in Jesus. True spirituality, Christian spirituality, takes attention off of ourselves and focuses it on another, on Jesus.

There are others in the story, of course, many others—the sick and hungry, victims and outsiders, friends, and enemies. But Jesus is always the subject. No event and no person appears in this story apart from Jesus. Jesus provides both context and content for everyone's life. Spirituality—the attention we give to our souls—turns out in practice (when we let St. Mark shape our practice) to be the attention we give to God revealed in Jesus. The text trains us in such perception and practice. Line after line, page after page—Jesus, Jesus, Jesus. None of us provides the content for our own spirituality; it is given to us; Jesus gives it to us. The text allows for no exceptions.

3. The Emphasis of the Text

As we read this text we soon discover that the entire story funnels into the narration of the events of a single week of Jesus' life, the week of his passion, death, and resurrection.

And of these three items, death gets the most detailed treatment. If we are asked to say as briefly as possible what St. Mark's Gospel consists of, we must say "the death of Jesus."

That doesn't sound very promising, especially for those of us who are looking for a text by which to live, a text by which to nurture our souls. But there it is. There are sixteen chapters in the story. For the first eight chapters Jesus is alive, strolling unhurriedly through the villages and back-roads of Galilee, bringing others to life—delivering them from evil, heal-ing their maimed and sick bodies, feeding hungry people, demonstrat-ing his sovereignty over storm and sea, telling marvellous stories, gathering and training disciples, announcing that they are poised on the brink of a new era, God's Kingdom, which at that very moment is break-ing in upon them.

And then, just as he has everyone's attention, just as the momentum for life and more life is at its crest, he starts talking about death. The last eight chapters of the Gospel are dominated by death talk.

The death announcement also signals a change of pace. As the story is told through the first eight chapters, there is a leisurely and meander-ing quality to the narration. Jesus doesn't seem to be going anywhere in particular—he more or less drifts from village to village, goes off by him-self into the hills to pray, worships in the synagogues, gives the impres-sion that he has time to take meals with anyone who invites him over, goes boating with his friends on the lake. We do not construe this relaxed pace as aimlessness or indolence, for energy and intensity are always evi-dent. But through these Galilean years, Jesus appears to have all the time in the world, which, of course, he does have.

But with the death announcement that changes: now he heads straight for Jerusalem. Urgency and gravity and destination now characterize the narration. The direction changes, the pace changes, the mood changes. Three times Jesus is explicit: he is going to suffer and be killed and rise again (8:31; 9:31; 10:33).

And then it happens: death. Jesus' death is narrated carefully and pre-cisely. No incident in his life is told with this much detail. There can hardly be any question about the intent of St. Mark: the plot and empha-sis and meaning of Jesus is his death.

It is not as if this death emphasis was an idiosyncrasy of Mark, a mor-bid obsession of his that distorted the basic story, for this sequence and proportion is preserved by St. Mark's successors in Gospel narration, Matthew and Luke. They elaborate St. Mark's basic text in various ways, but preserve the proportions. John, who comes at the story from a quite different angle, dazzling us with images of light and life, actually increases the emphasis on death, giving half of his allotted space to the passion week. All four Gospel writers do essentially the same thing; they tell us the story of Jesus' death, and write their respective introductions to it. And Paul—exuberant, passionate, hyperbolic Paul—skips the narration completely and simply punches out the conclusion, "Christ died for us" (Rom. 5:8); "I decided to know nothing among you except Jesus Christ and him crucified" (1 Cor. 2:2).

But there is far more here than the simple fact of death, although there is that most emphatically—this is a carefully *defined* death. It is defined as voluntary. Jesus did not have to go to Jerusalem; he went on his own volition. He gave his assent to death. This was not accidental death; this was not an unavoidable death.

It is defined as sacrificial. He accepted death that others might receive life, ". . . his life as a ransom for many" (Mark 10:45). He explicitly defined his life as sacrificial, that is, as a means to life for others, when he instituted the Eucharist, "He took a loaf of bread. . . . Take, this is my body. . . . Then he took a cup . . . this is my blood of the covenant, which is poured out for many" (Mark 14:23–24).

And it is defined in the company of resurrection. Each of the three explicit death announcements concludes with a statement of resurrection. The Gospel story as a whole concludes with a witness to resurrection. This doesn't make it any less a death, but it is a quite differently defined death than we are accustomed to dealing with.

Tragedy and procrastination are the words that characterize our culture's attitude to death.

The view of death as tragic is a legacy of the Greeks. The Greeks wrote with elegance of tragic deaths—lives that were caught up in the working out of large, impersonal forces, lives pursued with the best of intentions, but then enmeshed in circumstances that cancelled the intentions, circumstances indifferent to human heroism or hope.

The death of Jesus is not tragic.

The procrastinated death is a legacy of modern medicine. In a culture where life is reduced to heartbeat and brainwave, death can never be accepted as such. Since there is no more to life than can be accounted for by biology—no meaning, no spirituality no eternity—increasingly desperate attempts are made to put it off, to delay it, to deny it.

The death of Jesus is not procrastinated.

It is essential that we counter our culture by letting St. Mark's storytelling shape our understanding of death and eventually come to understand our own death within the rich dimensions and relations of Jesus' story.

4. The Spiritual Theology of the Text

I noted earlier that one of the distinctive qualities of "Gospel story" is that it draws us into participation. The first half of St. Mark's Gospel does that—all sorts of people are drawn into the life of Jesus, experience his compassion, his healings, his deliverance, his call, his peace. We find ourselves implicitly included. In the second half of the Gospel this experience of personal participation becomes explicit.

Right at the center of St. Mark's text is a passage that I am going to designate as the "spirituality" of the text. By using the term spirituality at this juncture I intend to call attention to the place where our concern for our souls, our lives, and Jesus' concern for our souls, our lives, converge. By spirituality I mean the particular way in which St. Mark wrote his Gospel to help us who read him experience truly the message he writes. It goes without saying, I think, that Mark was not a journalist, writing daily bulletins on the first-century activities of Jesus. Nor was he a propagandist, attempting to enlist us in a cause that had designs on history. This is spiritual theology in action, a form of writing that draws us into participation with the text.

St. Mark 8:27–9:9 is the passage. It is set at the center of the Gospel story so that one half of the Gospel, the multiple Galilean evocations of life, falls symmetrically on one side, and on the other side, the single-minded travel to Jerusalem and death.

The passage consists of two stories. The first story, Jesus' call for renunciation as he and his disciples start out on the road to Jerusalem, provides the ascetic dimension in spirituality. The second story, Jesus' transfiguration on Mount Tabor, provides the aesthetic dimension in spirituality.

The stories are bracketed at either end by affirmations of Jesus' true identity as God among us: first, Peter saying, "You are the Christ, the Son of the living God"; second, the voice out of heaven saying, "This is my beloved son, listen to him." Human testimony at one end, divine attestation at the other.

Before we consider the two stories, I want to insist we keep them in context and that we maintain their connection. These stories must never be removed from their context. Their context is the life and death of the God-revealing Jesus. St. Mark's Gospel has Jesus as its subject. Out of context, these stories can only be misunderstood. They do not stand on their own. They do not give us a spiritual theology that we can walk off with and exploit on our own terms.

And these stories are organically connected. They must not be torn apart. They are the two-beat rhythm in a single spiritual theology, not two alternate ways of doing spiritual theology. The two stories bring together the ascetic and aesthetic movements, the No and the Yes that work together at the heart of spiritual theology.

The Ascetic. First the ascetic movement. This is God's No in Jesus. Jesus' words are succinct and stark: "If any want to become my followers, let them deny themselves and take up their cross and follow me" (8:34). The ascetic life deals with life on the road.

The verbs that leap out of the sentence and pounce on us are "deny yourself" and "take up your cross." Renunciation and death. It feels like an assault, an attack. We recoil.

But then we notice that these two negatives are bracketed by the positive verb, "follow," first as an infinitive, then as an imperative. "If anyone wants to follow (*akolouthein*)" opens the sentence; "you follow me (*akoloutheito*)" concludes it. Jesus is going some place; he invites us to come along. There is no hostility in that. It sounds, in fact, quite glorious. So glorious, in fact, that the great verb "follow," sheds glory on the negative verbs that call for renunciation and death.

There is always a strong ascetic element in true spiritual theology. Following Jesus means *not* following your impulses and appetites and whims and dreams, all of which are sufficiently damaged by sin to make them unreliable guides for getting any place worth going. Following Jesus means *not* following the death-procrastinating, death-denying practices of a culture which, by obsessively pursuing life under the aegis of idols and ideologies, ends up with a life that is so constricted and diminished that it is hardly worthy of the name.

Grammatically, the negative, our capacity to say No, is one of the most impressive features of our language. The negative is our access to freedom. Only humans can say No. Animals can't say No. Animals do what instinct dictates. No is a freedom word. I don't have to do what either my glands or my culture tell me to do. The judicious, well-placed No frees us from many a blind alley, many a rough detour, frees us from debilitating distractions and seductive sacrilege. The art of saying No sets us free to follow Jesus.

If we adhere carefully to St. Mark's text, we will never associate the ascetic with the life-denying. Ascetic practice sweeps out the clutter of the god-pretentious self, making ample space for Father, Son, and Holy Spirit; it embraces and prepares for a kind of death that the culture knows nothing about, making room for the dance of resurrection. Whenever we are around someone who is doing this well, we notice the lightness of step, the nimbleness of spirit, the quickness to laughter. H. C. G. Moule wrote that these dominical negatives ". . . may have to carve deep lines in heart and life; but the chisel need never deface the brightness of the material."[2]

The Aesthetic. Alongside St. Mark's ascetic is his aesthetic. This is God's Yes in Jesus. Peter, James, and John see Jesus transfigured before them on the mountain into cloud-brightness in the company of Moses and Elijah, and hear God's blessing, "This is my beloved, listen to him" (Mark 9:7). The aesthetic deals with life on the mountain.

The word "beauty" does not occur in the story, but beauty is what the disciples experienced, and what we find ourselves experiencing—the beauty of Jesus transfigured, law and prophets, Moses and Elijah integrated into the beauty of Jesus, the beautiful blessing, "My beloved . . .": Everything fitting together, the luminous interior of Jesus spilling out onto the mountain, history and religion beautifully personalized and brought into deep, resonating harmony, the declaration of love.

There is always a strong aesthetical element in true spiritual theology. Climbing the mountain with Jesus means coming upon beauty that takes our breath away. Staying in the company of Jesus means contemplating his glory, listening in on this vast, intergenerational conversation consisting of law and prophet and gospel that takes place around Jesus, hearing the divine confirmation of revelation in Jesus. When God's Spirit makes its appearance, we recognize the appearance as beautiful.

Now here's the thing about the transfigured Jesus. Jesus is the form of revelation, "and the light does not fall on this form from above and from outside, rather it breaks forth from the form's interior."[3] The only adequate response that can be made to light is to keep our eyes open, to attend to what is illumined—adoration.

The aesthetical impulse in spiritual theology has to do with training in perception, acquiring a taste for what is being revealed in Jesus. We are not good at this. Our senses have been dulled by sin. The world, for all its vaunted celebration of sensuality, is relentlessly anaesthetic, obliterating feeling by ugliness and noise, draining the beauty out of people and things so that they are functionally efficient, scornful of the aesthetic except as it can be contained in a museum or flower garden. Our senses require healing and rehabilitation so that they are adequate for receiving and responding to visitations and appearances of Spirit, God's Holy Spirit, for as Jean Sulivan says, "The fundamental insight of the Bible . . . is that the invisible can speak only by the perceptible."[4]

These bodies of ours with their five senses are not impediments to a life of faith; our sensuality is not a barrier to spirituality but our only access to it. Thomas Aquinas was convinced that *asensuality* was a vice, the rejection of one's senses too often leading to sacrilege.[5] When St. John wanted to assure some early Christians of the authenticity of his spiritual experience, he did it by calling on the witness of his senses of sight, hearing, and touch—"that which we have heard . . . seen with our eyes . . . touched with our hands concerning the word of life" (1 John 1:1). In his opening sentence, he calls on the witness of his senses seven times.

St. Mark sets this story of glorious affirmation in immediate juxtaposition to his story of stern negation. In company with Jesus, these bodies of ours so magnificently equipped for seeing, hearing, touching, smelling, and tasting, climb the mountain (itself a strenuous physical act), where, in astonished adoration, we are trained to see the light and hear the words that reveal God to us.

This seems simple enough, and it is. St. Mark does not go in for subtleties—he sets it before us plainly. But he also knows that, simple and obvious as it is, it is easy to get it wrong. Peter's initial response in both the ascetic road story and the aesthetic mountain story was wrong.

On the road, Peter tried to avoid the cross; on the mountain, he tried to possess the glory. Peter rejected the ascetic way by offering Jesus a better plan, a way of salvation in which no one has to be inconvenienced. Jesus, in the sternest rebuke recorded in the Gospels, called him Satan. Peter rejected the aesthetic way by offering to build memorials on the mountain, a way of worship in which he could take over from Jesus and provide something hands-on and practical. This time Jesus just ignored him.

Peter's propensity to get it wrong keeps us on our toes. Century after century we Christians keep getting it wrong—and in numerous ways. We get the ascetic wrong; we get the aesthetic wrong. Our history books are full of ascetic aberrations, full of aesthetic aberrations. Every time we get sloppy in reading this text of St. Mark and leave the company of Jesus we get it wrong.

Conclusion

One more thing. These two stories, carefully placed at the center of the gospel story, are not the center of the story. St. Mark's story, remember, is a story about Jesus, not us. In fact, if we deleted this section from the story, the story would still be the same story. Nothing in this road and mountain narrative is essential to understanding the story of Jesus as he lived, was crucified, and rose from the dead. Without this account of the road and the mountain, we would still know everything St. Mark chose to tell us about Jesus as the revelation of God, a full accounting of Jesus' work of salvation.

What happens here is that we are invited into becoming full participants in the story of Jesus and shown how to become such participants. We are not simply *told* that Jesus is the Son of God; we not only *become* beneficiaries of his atonement; we are invited to die his death and live his life with the freedom and dignity of participants. And here is a marvelous thing: we enter the center of the story without becoming the center of the story.

Spirituality is always in danger of self-absorption, of becoming so intrigued with matters of soul that God is treated as a mere accessory to my experience. This requires much vigilance. Spiritual theology is, among other things, the exercise of this vigilance. Spiritual theology is the discipline and art of training us into a full and mature participation in Jesus' story while at the same time preventing us from taking over the story.

And for this St. Mark provides our basic text. The two stories at the center, the road and mountain stories, are clearly proleptic—they anticipate Jesus' crucifixion and resurrection. They immerse us and train us in the ascetic negations and aesthetic affirmations, but they don't leave us there; they cast us forward in faith and obedience to the life that is finally and only complete in the definitive No and glorious Yes of Jesus crucified and risen.

Notes

1. Wallace Stegner, *When the Bluebird Sings to the Lemonade Springs* (New York: Random House, 1992), 181.

2. H. C. G. Moule, *Veni Creator* (London: Hodder & Stoughton, 1890), 104.

3. Hans Urs von Balthasar, *The Glory of the Lord* (San Francisco: Ignatius, 1984), 1:151.

4. Jean Sulivan, *Morning Light* (New York: Paulist, 1988), 18.

5. Quoted by Beldon Lane, *Landscapes of the Sacred* (New York: Paulist, 1988), 81.

An Outline of Paul's View of the Spiritual Life

Foundation for an Evangelical Spirituality

David S. Dockery

ontemporary Christianity is characterized simultaneously by a longing for a deeper relationship with God's Spirit and also a seeming neglect of authentic and developing sanctification. When we look about us, we see many seeking spiritual renewal,[1] some by contemplation,[2] some through community involvement and fellowship groups,[3] and others through signs and wonders.[4] The confusion is compounded by the discussion at the popular level about "prayer in the Spirit," "walking in the Spirit," "life in the Spirit," "baptism in the Spirit," and even "being slain in the Spirit." The terminology is very often used carelessly and without definition. Our purpose is not to address each of these issues, but only to acknowledge the ubiquity of interest in spiritual renewal.

While all of this is true, there yet exists an emptiness in contemporary Christian spirituality evidenced among church members and church leaders by superficiality and busyness. This has resulted in lives characterized by discouragement, frustration, and even problems of immorality.

Some of these problems can be traced to a faulty view of conversion.[5] Others can be linked to our individualistic concept of Christianity.[6] Perhaps underlying all of these matters is the obvious lack of a spiritual theology in Evangelicalism, even in Protestantism at-large. For too long, spiritual theology has been con-

This essay first appeared in *Criswell Theological Review* 3 (spring 1989): 327–39. Used by permission.

sidered the domain of Roman Catholic theology.[7] Recently, however, there have been helpful attempts to fill this void.[8] While our primary focus is not the correction or reshaping of the popular confusion, our theological concerns are always intended to serve the Church.[9] Even without emphasis upon theological and ethical matters, it is hoped that the present investigation will yield fruit for laypeople, as well as the pastoral aspects of the Christian community. This essay will outline Paul's view of the spiritual life which can serve as a foundation for a contemporary evangelical spirituality.

The Pauline view of the spiritual life can best be summarized by the statement in 2 Cor 3:17b, "Where the Spirit of the Lord is, there is liberty." The key concepts in the thought of Paul regarding the Christian life are here expressed: the Spirit, lordship and liberty. The Spirit's activities so widely permeated the apostle's thought that there is hardly any aspect of Christian experience outside of the sphere of the Spirit. We shall examine the main facets of the Spirit's activities by concentrating on both the individual and the community's corporate perspectives of the Christian life. Also matters of freedom will be surveyed, particularly ideas of freedom from sin and from law. We could not do justice to Paul's thought without a brief look at the idea of the spiritual life in tension, including the nature of suffering in relation to life in the Spirit.

I. The Work of the Spirit in the New Life of the Believer

1. *Initiation.* Paul was convinced that it was the responsibility of the Spirit to draw attention to the glories of the risen Christ in the preaching ministry (1 Thess 1:5; 1 Cor 2:1–4). Equally true was the Spirit's task in enabling persons to respond to the message of the glorified Christ. Indeed, it is a fundamental assumption of Paul's theology that all believers are possessors of the Spirit. In other words, "no one can respond to the claims of Christ without being activated and indwelt by the Holy Spirit."[10]

Paul tells the Thessalonians that God has given them the Holy Spirit (1 Thess 4:8). In his first letter to the Corinthians he states that no one can confess Jesus as Lord except by the Holy Spirit (1 Cor 12:13). It can be assumed that all believers have the Spirit since "anyone who does not have the Spirit of Christ does not belong to him" (Rom 8:9). The Spirit has transformed persons from unrighteousness (1 Cor 6:9, 10) to those who are washed, sanctified and justified (1 Cor 6:11). The strong adversative in the passage serves to heighten the contrast between the former life and life in the Spirit and thus focuses attention on the change the Spirit's ministry performs. The point, then, is that a person is regenerated only through the work of the Spirit.[11]

The regenerating work of the Spirit brings about new life in Christ. The new life in Christ is summarized in Paul's classic statement, "If anyone is in Christ, a new creation! The old has passed away, behold the new has come" (2 Cor 5:17). The verse is usually interpreted on the popular level in terms of one's subjective experience, meaning the desires and attitudes of the unregenerate have passed away and have been replaced by a new set of desires and attitudes. The idea of newness, however, in the context of Pauline thought is distinctly eschatological.[12] The new age which has dawned brings a new creation, the creation of a new person.[13] The passing of the old does not mean the end of the old age; it continues until the parousia. But the old age does not remain intact; the new age has broken in.[14] Without discussing the full ramifications of the new age, we can conclude with G. Ladd's appropriate remark, "The underlying idea is that while believers live in the old age, because they *are* in Christ, *they* belong to the new age with its new creation (indicative); thus they *are* to live a life that is expressive of the new existence (imperative)"[15] [emphasis mine]. Having seen that the Spirit is the giver of new life to believers, we now turn our attention to the ministry of the Spirit in the life of the believer.

2. *Adoption and Sanctification.* There are two primary passages which show that the believer's filial consciousness is directly induced by the Holy Spirit (Rom 8:14–17; Gal 4:6). It is the Spirit who leads the children of God to cry out "Abba! Father!"[16] Adoption describes the new relationship into which believers have entered.[17]

D. Guthrie uses the term "sanctification" comprehensively of the overall process by which the new believer moves toward a life of holiness.[18] The standard of sanctification is a holiness acceptable to God, that is, a holiness in line with the Spirit's own character (Rom 15:16; 1 Cor 6:11).

3. *Illumination and Guidance.* The Spirit of God is not only active in revealing the gospel, but is likewise involved in bringing the believer to further understanding (1 Cor 2:13). Paul goes into considerable detail in 1 Cor 2:10–16 in order to establish the distinction between human wisdom and the understanding provided by the Spirit. Paul affirms that without the enablement of the Spirit, a salvific knowledge of God is unattainable. After receiving the gift of the Spirit, there is a capacity for understanding what was previously denied. The Spirit penetrates to the deepest understanding of God in Christ.[19]

The Spirit guides the believer into a new way of thinking and gives her or him a new set of values. Concerning Rom 8:5, "Those who live according to the Spirit set their minds on the things of the Spirit," J. Murray comments that, "the mind of the Spirit is the dispositional complex, including the exercise of reason, feeling and will, patterned after and controlled by the Holy Spirit."[20] The renewal of the mind (Rom 12:2) which was formerly hostile to God (Rom 8:7) can only be achieved by/through the Spirit. The believer's new values come through the leading of the Spirit (Rom 8:14) and cause him or her to walk in the Spirit in opposition to carrying out the desires of the sinful flesh (Gal 5:16; Rom 8:4). The concept of total dependence on the empowering of the Spirit "shows how utterly indispensable the Spirit is for Christian living, and it demonstrates the impossibility of any Christian not possessing the Spirit."[21]

4. *Progress and Development.* Paul speaks in Gal 5:22–23 of the "fruit of the Spirit" as "love, joy, peace, patience, kindness, goodness, faithfulness, gentleness and self-control." These virtues must be compared with the list in Phil 4:8 (cf. Col 3:12–15). These Spirit-prompted virtues go beyond the natural bounds of virtue so that, for example, the believer demonstrates love by loving one's enemies. The outworking of these virtues is a demonstration of the Spirit at work in the believer, but there is not necessarily a one-to-one correspondence between these lists and progress in the Christian life. According to V. Furnish, the virtues are not even designed to portray the pattern of the good person of the Christian ideal toward which all are to strive, but are rather different ways Paul addresses himself to the concrete historical situations to explain how the new life in Christ is to express itself.[22] Yet, it seems to us that they can be seen as evidence of the work of the Spirit in the development of the believer in contrast to "works of the flesh" (Gal 5:19–21). We can say that at least to some extent, they are marks of the Spirit.[23]

5. *Liberation.* One of the key themes which will be discussed later under a separate heading is the theme of freedom. Paul had known the futility of seeking salvation through works and had come to know that liberation comes through the Spirit (2 Cor 3:7–18).[24] An important function of the Spirit is to break shackles which have been carried over from pre-conversion days. Liberty is one of the great outworkings of the Spirit in the new age.

II. The Work of the Spirit in the New Life of the Community

1. *Unity.* Paul viewed the Holy Spirit as the basis for true unity in the body of Christ. Fellowship in the Johannine epistles seems to be with "the Father and the Son" (1 John 1:3), but Paul stresses "fellowship in the Spirit" (Phil 2:1–4; 2 Cor 13:14). The passage in the letter to the Philippians enlarges on the theme of unity and suggests a mutual participation of believers through the common bond of the Holy Spirit. It is the Spirit

who binds Christians together and enables them to be of the same mind, which is the "mind of Christ" (Phil 2:5). The community of faith is to maintain the unity of the Spirit as stated in 1 Corinthians 12 (cf. Eph 4:1–6). The passage emphasizes the unity of the Spirit and diversity of functions and gifts given by the Spirit to the Body. The basis of unity is identified by Paul as the baptism in the Spirit (1 Cor 12:13).

2. *Baptism in the Spirit.* 1 Cor 12:13 is the key passage referring to corporate initiation into new life. While it is much debated in recent times whether the Spirit's baptism is an experience identical with conversion or subsequent to the conversion experience, we find it difficult to support the second stage experience anywhere in the Pauline materials.[25] Guthrie suggests that baptism in the spirit is "no more than another way of expressing the Spirit-dominated character of the (corporate) Christian life."[26] Paul's teaching that "all were made to drink of one Spirit" shows the basic solidarity of all Christians in the Spirit.[27] It is transformation for all believers by which they are placed into the body of Christ. This is made possible by the Spirit.

Although Dunn and Ladd opt for the meaning of baptism as "Spirit baptism" and not water baptism, many scholars believe that baptism refers to water baptism as the means by which the Spirit is imparted to believers.[28] We do not believe that there has to be an either/or answer to the question, "Does Paul mean to say that water baptism is the means of incorporation into the Christian community or that an act of the Holy Spirit is the means of incorporation?" We believe, rather, a both/and answer is more satisfactory. It is the work of the Spirit to form the body of Christ, while water baptism is the outward sphere where this takes place. When men and women believe and are baptized, they become members of the body of Christ. The Spirit has been given by the exalted Christ to form a new people, to join believers together in the baptism of the Spirit constituting the body of Christ.

III. The Spiritual Life as a Life of Freedom

The theme of freedom is seen constantly throughout the Pauline writings. In this section we shall see that Paul is concerned with freedom from sin, freedom from law, and freedom and responsibility, which he discusses from the perspective of the stronger Christian's relationship with the weaker Christian.

1. *Freedom from Sin.* Paul uses the idiom of dying and rising with Christ to express the truth of the believer's union with Christ (Romans 6). Baptism into Christ (Rom 6:4) means union with him in his death, burial with him, which in turn means death to sin, the crucifixion of the "old man," the nul-

lifying of the "body of sin" (Rom 6:6). The positive side means freedom from sin and life to God. In the Romans 6 passage, resurrection with Christ is future and eschatological (vv. 5–7; cf. Eph 2:5–6 which speaks of a present resurrection with Christ).[29]

The baptism into Christ's death is drawing attention to the corporate aspect of Christ's death. As that death was an historical event, so also the incorporation of believers in that death is historical. In other words when Christ died on the cross, all who were to be incorporated in him also died.[30] This implies that when a person puts faith in Christ, he or she is at once identified with a death that has already happened. The identification with death is necessary before there can be a participation in the risen life of Christ, which is life in the Spirit. Ladd comments:

> This is an eschatological fact that every believer should know (Rom. 6:2, 6), and on whose basis he is to consider himself alive to God. It means a change in dominion. In the old aeon, sin reigned (v. 12); but in the new aeon, the dominion of sin has been broken (v. 14). Believers are to recognize this change of dominions, and *for this reason* they are to change their alliance from sin to God (vv. 17, 18, 22). It is because this change has occurred in Christ that believers are exhorted to yield themselves to righteousness (v. 19).[31]

The sixth chapter of Romans highlights Paul's indicative/imperative tension. The command is to become what we are. This is accomplished through yielding to the Spirit. The practical paradox is that freedom from sin comes through slavery to Christ. Even Paul's most affirmative statements about freedom are linked with lordship. Gal 5:1 and 5:13 respectively exhort the Galatians not to return to slavery either of law or licentiousness, but to remain in the Spirit as those who belong to Christ (Gal 5:24). 1 Cor 3:21–23 speaks only of the freedom of those who belong to Christ, who "are Christ's." And 2 Cor 4:12–18 speaks only of the freedom which is "through Christ," "from the Lord" and "of the Spirit." Thus Paul argues that there are only two alternatives: (1) to have sin for one's master or (2) to have God for one's master. For God to be one's master means a life of freedom from sin. True freedom, therefore, comes only through authentic obedience.

2. *Freedom from Law.* Paul views the believer in the age of the Spirit as living under grace and not under Law (Rom 6:14). Paul believed and taught that the Law had been in some sense abrogated by Christ for he is the "end of the Law" (Rom 10:4). The Law is not evil, rather it is "holy, just and good" (Rom 7:12). But what the Law could not do because of the powerlessness of human nature, God did by bringing freedom from Law for all who believe (Rom 8:1–4). Paul, however, disassociates himself from the idea that freedom is power to do for oneself and with one's

life as seems pleasing. Freedom can be misused as a pretext for evil, which is libertinism or antinomianism. True freedom involves obeying the "Law of Christ" (Gal 6:2) which is service to God (1 Thess 1:9) and for humankind (1 Cor 9:19).

The "Law of Christ" seems to mean not only the teaching of Jesus as the embodiment and true interpretation of the will of God (Rom 12–14; 1 Cor 7:10–11), but also the person of the historical Jesus. The life of Jesus served as a tangible portrayal and example of the new divine standard as suggested by the phrase "according to Christ" (Rom 15:5; cf. Eph 4:20–24; Col 2:6–8) and the frequent appeals to the character of Jesus (Rom 15:3, 7, 8; Phil 2:5–11; 1 Thess 1:6).[32] The difference between the law of Christ, which can be identified with the new covenant written upon hearts instead of stone, and the old covenant law is knowing the law as inward principle. F. F. Bruce's comments are extremely helpful in this regard:

> So for Paul there was no substantial difference in content between the "just requirement of the law" which cannot be kept by those who live "according to the flesh" and the just requirement fulfilled in those who live "according to the Spirit." The difference lay in the fact that a new inward power was now imparted, enabling the believer to fulfil what he could not fulfil before. The will of God has not changed; but whereas formerly it was recorded on tablets of stone it was now engraved on human hearts, and inward impulsion accomplished what external compulsion could not.[33]

This is not a new legalism, but a new "nomism." W. D. Davies has suggested that this is a "new torah."[34] There is some difference between *nomos* (the Greek word for "law") and *tôrâ* (the Hebrew term for "law"). *Tôrâ* has the idea of a binding instruction, whereas *nomos* designates a principle. It is also possible for *nomos* to be the equivalent of *tôrâ* in some instances, especially when *nomos* is used with an adjective or article.[35] Only in the atmosphere of spiritual liberty can God's will be properly obeyed and God's *nomos* upheld.[36]

3. *Freedom and Responsibility.* Having been liberated by Christ from the penalty of sin, the believer is challenged to employ this liberty properly in Christian living. Liberty is not to be used as an excuse to satisfy unchristian sinful desires, but to serve others by love.[37] This responsible freedom might be referred to as a law of love. Guidance for the church in questionable areas, so far as Paul is concerned, is provided by the law of love and not by the law of commandments (cf. Eph 2:15).

This topic receives its fullest treatment in Romans 14–15 and 1 Corinthians 8–10. Food sacrificed to idols, for instance, is ethically and religiously indifferent.[38] For Paul, what is important is responsible living so that the effect of one's conduct is an example and not a stumbling block to others.

The law of love becomes, in Paul's thought, the most important motivation for Christian freedom. Love fulfills all the demands of the Law. Therefore, love becomes the solution to the problems raised about food and drink. Love requires that when persons living in freedom find themselves in a situation where the proper exercise of that freedom would truly offend a brother or sister, then freedom is to be set aside. Abstinence is the recommendation, but only when the weaker believer would actually be caused to sin; otherwise the whole standard of conduct in such matters would be decreed by the rigorism of the weak.[39] The basic principle is that personal freedom must be tempered by love for the community. It is clear that "such love is not an emotion, but Christian concern in action."[40]

Responsible freedom, for Paul, also includes a negative, as well as a positive, aspect. The negative teachings are often overstressed in more legalistic environments and understressed in more libertine settings. The Pauline balance must be the goal for believers living in the Spirit. Paul teaches a rigorous self-discipline, self-control and nonconformity (1 Cor 9:27; Rom 12:1–2). Everything is to be done for the glory of God (1 Cor 10:31), and deeds that bring glory to the flesh are to be put to death (Rom 8:13). Paul's nonconformity is not ascetic (Col 2:23). He views the ascetic approach to the Christian life as worldly, because it appeals to human pride and attainment rather than trust in Christ and reliance on the Spirit. The true Pauline view is, "the earth is the Lord's and everything in it" (1 Cor 10:26). In sexual matters, the believer is again not to conform to worldly practices. Paul personally goes beyond this as he was an ascetic in sexual matters (1 Corinthians 7), but only for missionary purposes. Paul recognizes his asceticism as a gift to promote the gospel, not to achieve greater spirituality.[41]

It is beyond the scope of this article to deal with all the lists of vices and virtues which Paul encourages believers to avoid and follow. While his lists are similar to Hellenistic and Jewish lists of virtues and vices, they are not to be overgeneralized to the point that they lose their spiritual significance. We do not believe that Paul considered these lists in any sense as options for life in the Spirit. Rather, they help shape and form what is otherwise a somewhat nonobjective concept. They are part and parcel of normal life in the Spirit. These lists include character qualities to be emulated, and sins to be shunned, which are inconsistent with the spiritual life.[42]

IV. Tension in the Spiritual Life

Life in the Spirit is to be lived out between the polarities of what has been accomplished by the historical achievement of Jesus and what is yet to be fully realized in the consummation of God's redemptive program.[43] The believer lives in this temporal tension. This is characterized by the already/not yet, and indicative/imperative tensions.[44] Christians live in this age, but their life pattern, their standard of conduct, their aims and goals are not those of this age, which are essentially human-centered and prideful, but of the age to come. Yet the struggle with indwelling sin continues (Rom 7:14–25).[45] The flesh continues to war against the Spirit (Gal 5:16–21). The believer's union with Christ must be lived out (Romans 6; 12:1–2). While living in the Spirit as a citizen of the new age (Phil 3:21), it should be remembered that believers will suffer in this age (Phil 1:29–30). Christians are conscious of life "in Adam" (Rom 5:12–21) and "in Christ" (Rom 6:1–11). This life is characterized as a tension between freedom and responsible love (Romans 14). Life in the Spirit awakens believers to the prospects of present and ultimate victories. The basis for life in the Spirit must never be forgotten. It is through the death and resurrection of Jesus Christ that the Spirit applies justification, regeneration, sanctification and ultimate glorification to the lives of believers. Life in the Spirit is living out, by the Spirit's empowerment, what believers are because of Christ.[46]

V. Toward Maturity in the Spiritual Life

It is the fact that for Paul Christianity is essentially "pneumatic" (that is, he interprets Christianity through the category of Spirit) that makes it inevitable that he should also give a greater significance to the ethical aspect of the pneumatic life.[47] Paul's view of life in the Spirit develops shape by the enablement which the Spirit provides for obedience in the midst of struggling and suffering. The most genuine utterance of the Spirit in the assembly of believers is not ecstatic speech, but prophecy, since the intention and criterion of the worship service was that God should become manifest for people (1 Cor 14:23–25). The individual believer experiences the Spirit primarily in prayer when he or she can call upon God in the words of the Lord's prayer, "Abba! Father!" (Gal 4:6; Rom 8:15). The Spirit provides divine enablement for the believer struggling in prayer (Rom 8:26–27). The immediacy of devotion to God does not come forth from innate human capacity, but from the Spirit. The Spirit brings to light an awareness that one has been accepted through the love of God, from which prayer springs forth.[48] When the Spirit reaches to God's children, the love of God reaches out (Rom 5:5). The Spirit ultimately is made known as the consciousness-generating power that creates openness for God, enablement in struggle and openness in prayer.[49] The Spirit is the downpayment of future glory which will be inherited by believers in the eschaton. Until then, the community experiences life in the Spirit in such a way that can be characterized as liberty. Paradoxically, liberty comes about through obedience just as glory comes through suffering.

Conclusion

In this essay we have seen that there is hardly any aspect of the Christian experience that is not influenced by the Spirit's activities. We briefly surveyed the Spirit's work in the life of the individual believer and in the believing community. We observed that the ethical teaching concerning life in the Spirit is shaped by the list of vices and virtues, by the indicative/imperative statements carried out in time of the already/not yet tension. Life in the Spirit brings freedom to the believers in the community.

As the contemporary Church seeks to develop a spiritual theology, it must be primarily grounded in scripture, not just human experience. Paul's view of the Spirit suggests parameters and injunctions by which the confusion in the contemporary Church can be checked. The tendency toward busyness must be balanced by a Spirit-led contemplation. The overstressed themes of triumphalism, so common in the extreme victorious life teachings, as well as the health, wealth and prosperity theologies must be countered by a balanced view of struggle and suffering. False teaching that advocates legalism and asceticism must be replaced by Paul's view of freedom, which is freedom not only from law, but freedom from sin toward obedience, exercised in responsible love. An evangelical spirituality must develop its shape from the Pauline guidelines so that the pneumatic experience is neither totally individualistic, nor is it an out-of-control experience lacking norms or parameters. Instead, an evangelical spirituality must focus upon the corporate experience among believers that stresses worship, mutual commitment and dependency, transparency and authenticity, responsible freedom and loving obedience.

Notes

1. Cf. R. Quebedeaux, *The New Charismatics* (New York: Doubleday, 1976); H. Hobbs, *The Holy Spirit: Believer's Guide* (Nashville: Broadman, 1967); A. A. Hoekema, *Holy Spirit Baptism* (Grand Rapids: Eerdmans, 1972); J. MacArthur, *The Charismatics: A Doctrinal Perspective* (Grand Rapids: Zondervan, 1978); M. Green, *I Believe in the Holy Spirit* (Grand Rapids: Eerdmans, 1975); J. R. W. Stott, *The Baptism and Fullness of the Holy Spirit* (Downers Grove, Ill.: InterVarsity, 1971); J. R. Williams, *Renewal Theology* (Grand Rapids: Zondervan, 1988).

2. Cf. E. Glenn Hinson, "Contemplative Spirituality," in *Christian Spirituality: Five Views of Sanctification*, ed. D. L. Alexander (Downers Grove, Ill.: InterVarsity, 1988);

C. Stanley, *Listening to God* (Nashville: Nelson, 1985). Especially see the article by Bruce Demarest and Charles Raup in *Criswell Theological Review* 3 (spring 1989).

3. H. A. Snyder, *The Community of the King* (Downers Grove, Ill.: InterVarsity, 1977); idem, *The Problem of Wineskins* (Downers Grove, Ill.: InterVarsity, 1975); K. Miller, *The Taste of New Wine* (Waco: Word, 1966); R. F. Webber and R. Clapp, *People of the Truth: The Power of the Worshipping Community in the Modern World* (San Francisco: Harper & Row, 1988).

4. J. Wimber and K. Springer, *Power Evangelism* (San Francisco: Harper & Row, 1986); idem, *Power Healing* (San Francisco: Harper & Row, 1987); J. White, *When the Spirit Comes with Power and Wonders among God's People* (Downers Grove, Ill.: InterVarsity, 1988).

5. See the ongoing discussion in such works as J. MacArthur, *The Gospel according to Jesus* (Grand Rapids: Zondervan, 1988); J. Boice, *Christ's Call to Discipleship* (Chicago: Moody, 1986); Z. Hodges, *The Eclipse of Grace* (Dallas: Redencion Viva, 1985); C. C. Ryrie, *Balancing the Christian Life* (Chicago: Moody, 1969), 170–78; J. I. Packer, *Evangelism and the Sovereignty of God* (Downers Grove, Ill.: InterVarsity, 1961), 89–95; J. R. W. Stott, *Our Guilty Silence* (Grand Rapids: Eerdmans, 1967), 48–50.

6. One of the finest treatments of the Christian life viewed from a corporate perspective can he found in N. H. Ridderbos, *Paul: An Outline of His Theology*, trans. J. R. DeWitt (Grand Rapids: Eerdmans, 1975). Also see the article by Timothy George in *Criswell Theological Review* 3 (spring 1989) which discusses the "priesthood of all believers" from a corporate perspective.

7. R. P. McBrien, *Catholicism* (Minneapolis: Winston, 1981), 903–1099; L. Bouyer, *Introduction to Spirituality* (New York: Desclee, 1961); idem, *Orthodox Spirituality and Protestant and Anglican Spirituality* (London: Burns & Oates, 1969); K. Rahner, *The Dynamic Element in the Church* (London: Burns & Oates, 1964), 84–170.

8. R. Lovelace, *Dynamics of Spiritual Life* (Downers Grove, Ill.: InterVarsity, 1979); J. I. Packer, *Keep in Step with the Spirit* (Old Tappan, N.J.: Revell, 1984). This is reinforced by noting that the 1987 meeting of the Evangelical Theological Society was devoted to concepts and issues involved with evangelical views of spirituality.

9. R. Saucy, "Doing Theology for the Church," in *The Necessity of Systematic Theology*, ed. J. Davis (Grand Rapids: Baker, 1979), 60–67.

10. D. Guthrie, *New Testament Theology* (Downers Grove, Ill.: InterVarsity, 1981), 551.

11. Ibid., 553; cf. J. N. D. Kelly, *The Pastoral Epistles* (London: Black, 1963), 253.

12. G. Ladd, *Theology of the New Testament* (Grand Rapids: Eerdmans, 1974), 479.

13. J. Behm, "καινός," in *Theological Dictionary of the New Testament*, ed. G. Kittel and G. Friedrich; trans. and ed. G. W. Bromiley, 10 vols. (Grand Rapids: Eerdmans, 1964–76), 3:449.

14. F. F. Bruce, "New," in *Interpreter's Dictionary of the Bible*, ed. G. A. Buttrick (Nashville: Abingdon, 1962), 3:542–43.

15. Ladd, *Theology of the New Testament*, 480.

16. J. Jeremias, *The Central Message of the New Testament* (Philadelphia: Fortress, 1981), 18.

17. E. Schweizer, "υἱοθεσία," *TDNT* 8:399.

18. Guthrie, *New Testament Theology*, 554.

19. L. Morris, *Paul's First Epistle to the Corinithians*, Tyndale Commentaries (Grand Rapids: Eerdmans, 1958), 57.

20. J. Murray, *Epistle to the Romans*, 2 vols., NIC (Grand Rapids: Eerdmans, 1959), 1:185.

21. R. Bultmann, *Theology of the New Testament*, ed. K. Grobel, 2 vols. (New York: Scribners, 1951–55), 1:153.

22. V. Furnish, *Theology and Ethics in Paul* (Nashville: Abingdon, 1958), 87.

23. See my discussion of development in Pauline theology related to Galatians 5 in "Pauline Pictures of the Spiritual Life: Developmental or Contextual," in *The Living Word: Essays in Honor of J. H. Greenlee* (forthcoming). Also see R. N. Longenecker, "On the Concept of Development in Pauline Thought," in *Perspectives in Evangelical Theology*, ed. S. Gundry and K. Kantzer (Grand Rapids: Baker, 1979), 195–207.

24. Cf. B. N. Longenecker, *Paul, Apostle of Liberty* (New York: Harper & Row, 1964).

25. For an informative explanation of these differences, see F. D. Brunner, *A Theology of the Holy Spirit* (Grand Rapids: Eerdmans, 1970); and J. D. G. Dunn, *Baptism in the Holy Spirit* (Philadelphia: Westminster, 1970); also E. Schweizer, "πνεῦμα," *TDNT* 6:233–455.

26. Guthrie, *New Testament Theology*, 563.

27. Hoekema, *The Holy Spirit Baptism*, 21.

28. G. R. Beasley-Murray, *Baptism in the New Testament* (Grand Rapids: Eerdmans, 1962), 167; also cf. Stott, *Baptism and Fullness*, 48.

29. Ladd, *Theology of the New Testament*, 485.

30. C. E. B. Cranfield, *A Critical and Exegetical Commentary on the Epistle to the Romans*, 2 vols., ICC (Edinburgh: Clark, 1975–79), 1:295–96.

31. Ladd, *Theology of the New Testament*, 486.

32. R. Longenecker, "Pauline Theology," in *Zondervan Pictorial Encyclopedia of the Bible*, ed. M. C. Tenney, 5 vols. (Grand Rapids: Zondervan, 1975), 4:663. See the provocative view of law and grace in D. Fuller, *Gospel and Law: Contrast or Continuum?* (Grand Rapids: Eerdmans, 1980).

33. F. F. Bruce, *Apostle of the Heart Set Free* (Grand Rapids: Eerdmans, 1977), 199–200.

34. W. D. Davies, *Paul and Rabbinic Judaism*, 4th ed. (Philadelphia: Fortress, 1980), suggests the idea of the spiritual life as a "new torah," while the concept of "nomism" is advanced by Longenecker, *Paul, Apostle of Liberty*.

35. H. H. Esser, "Law," in *The New International Dictionary of New Testament Theology*, ed. L. Coenen, E. Beyreuther, and H. Bietenhard; English translation ed. C. Brown, 4 vols. (Grand Rapids: Zondervan, 1975–86), 2:443; Cranfield, *Romans*, 1:362.

36. J. Blunk, "Freedom," *NIDNTT* 1:717–18.

37. W. H. Mare, "Liberty," *ZPEB* 3:921; cf. W. Longsworth, "Ethics in Paul: The Shape of Christian Life and a Method of Moral Reasoning," *Annual of the Society of Christian Ethics* (1981): 29–56.

38. See the careful exegesis of these chapters in W. Willis, *Idol Meat in Corinth: The Pauline Argument in 1 Corinthians 8 and 10*, SBLDS 68 (Chico, Calif.: Scholars Press, 1985).

39 J. C. Beker, *Paul the Apostle: The Triumph of God in Life and Thought* (Philadelphia: Fortress, 1980), 310–13.

40. Ladd, *Theology of the New Testament*, 524.

41. E. P. Sanders, *Paul and Palestinian Judaism* (Philadelphia: Fortress, 1977), 450; cf. Ladd, *Theology of the New Testament*, 526. It might also be possible to include with the discussion of nonconformity the idea of separation. Paul urges that believers should not be "mismated with unbelievers" (in a disputed passage in 2 Cor 6:14–7:1). This is not to be construed as a breaking of all ties and relationships that believers may have with unbelievers, rather it is directed against close ties that link Christians with unbelievers in pagan ways of thought and action. Separation, properly understood, is a rejection of idolatry and sinful conduct of the old age by one who is a citizen of the age to come.

42. L. Goppelt, *Theology of the New Testament*, trans. J. E. Alsup, 2 vols. (Grand Rapids: Eerdmans, 1982), 2:143–45; also Guthrie, *New Testament Theology*, 920–25; E. Schweizer, "Traditional Ethical Patterns in the Pauline and Post-Pauline Letters and Their Devel-

opment (Lists of Vices and House-tables)," in *Text and Interpretation*, ed. E. Best and R. McL. Wilson (Cambridge: Cambridge University Press, 1979), 195–209.

43. This idea has received its fullest articulation in the work of O. Cullmann, *Salvation in History*, trans. F. Filson (Philadelphia: Fortress, 1951); also cf. A. A. Hoekema, "Already/Not Yet Christian Living in Tension," *Reformed Journal* 29 (1979): 18–20.

44. This has been ably described by Furnish, *Theology and Ethics in Paul*.

45. J. D. G. Dunn, "Romans 7:14–25 in the Theology of Paul," *Theologische Zeitschrift* 31 (1975): 270–81; also D. Dockery, "Romans 7:14–25: Pauline Tension in the Christian Life," *Grace Theological Journal* 2 (1982): 239–57.

46. An extended discussion can be found in Lovelace, *Dynamics of Spiritual Life*.

47. Davies, *Paul and Rabbinic Judaism*, 220.

48. Goppelt, *Theology of the New Testament*, 2:121; G. MacRae, "Romans 8:26–27," *Interpretation* 34 (1980): 288–97.

49. Goppelt, *Theology of the New Testament*, 2:121–22; A. J. M. Wedderburn, "Romans 8:26—Towards a Theology of Glossalalia," *Scottish Journal of Theology* 28 (1975): 369–77; also cf. S. Grenz, *Prayer: The Cry for the Kingdom* (Peabody, Mass.: Hendrickson, 1988).

Part 7

Spirituality and Feminism

Feminism has made its presence felt in many fields that up until now have been dominated by males. Insofar as feminism seeks to transcend the ethnocentrism of group life, the tribalism of patriarchy in particular, it drinks deeply of the discipline of spirituality. But if feminism establishes a new tribalism centered around the interests not of men but of women in an ongoing self-referential way, then it forsakes the hope and promise of a liberating spirituality in all its inclusive and universal possibilities. Put another way, the transcendence to which vibrant spirituality ever invites us is not only the overcoming of personal self-curvature but of group self-curvature as well. That is, there are both personal and social journeys to be considered.

In the first essay that follows, Joann Wolski Conn illuminates the ways in which feminism has challenged the discipline of spirituality to redefine its borders, goals, and consequences. Specifying six tasks for serious feminist scholarship, Conn applies these elements to the promise and hope of spiritual maturity. Beyond this, in a way similar to LaCugna, Conn understands maturity in a trinitarian context where the equality of divine persons sharing life with each other differs from the hierarchical context of the patriarchal father. Maturity, then, is not autonomy or domination, but the experience of deep and *inclusive* love.

Ann Carr maintains in her essay that there are differences between women's and men's spiritualities, while at the same time she rejects the notion of "complementarity" as leading to subordination or inferiority of women. As such, women's spirituality is more related to "nature and natural processes than to culture; more personal and relational than objective and structural; more diffuse, concrete and general than focused, universal, abstract; more emotional than intellectual, etc." Carr is very careful, however, not to overdraw the distinctiveness of women's spirituality nor to impose feminism as yet another ideology "as oppressive as the old obedience to the fathers." And although Carr affirms that Christian feminist spirituality is universal in its vision, when she goes on to observe (apparently in agreement) that some feminists contend that male-female domination is the source of all oppressor-oppressed relationships, she appears to back away from that universality to focus on what can only be a penultimate description of oppression, one that fails to consider the goodness in men and the evil in women. Put another way, the *ultimate* dividing line between oppressor and oppressed lies elsewhere.

Both essays, then, make critical contributions to the discipline of spirituality. They enhance the conversation along lines that need careful and ongoing consideration.

Toward Spiritual Maturity

Joann Wolski Conn

onversations about spirituality happen with unbelievers or nuns, at parties or retreats, with professors or hairdressers. People who never go to church anymore often say they are very interested in spirituality. Graduates of twelve years in Catholic school are surprised to discover that something in their ordinary lives qualifies as a "religious experience." Religious publishers are selling more books about spirituality than any other kind. To base theology on religious experience is now a dominant trend in theological method. Interreligious dialogue focused on spirituality is now the preference of many in conversations that try to bridge East and West. The Association of Spiritual Directors International increased its membership, in three years, from a few hundred to nearly a thousand. Why is spirituality capturing so much attention?

Because spirituality refers both to experience and to an academic discipline, in this chapter I will examine first the different ways the term *spiritual* can refer to life's experience. Then I will explore how the academic field that studies this experience has emerged recently. Finally, using the methodology of academic spirituality, I will examine issues and controversies in the field through one lens: the question of spiritual maturity.

This essay first appeared in *Freeing Theology: The Essentials of Theology in Feminist Perspective,* ed. Catherine Mowry LaCugna (San Francisco: Harper San Francisco, 1993), 235–59. Used by permission.

Spirituality as Experience

Paul's letters describe reality under the influence of the Holy Spirit as "spiritual." There are spiritual blessings, spiritual gifts, spiritual persons. When Paul distinguishes the latter from natural persons he does not mean to contrast spiritual to material or evil, but simply to contrast those who act under the Spirit's influence to those who do not.[1]

This theological denotation for the adjective *spiritual* or the noun *spirituality* continued until the twelfth century when other meanings arose. In philosophy, the spiritual was opposed to the material. In church law, *spiritual* referred to ecclesiastical goods whereas *temporal* designated secular things. In the seventeenth century, *spirituality* came to refer to the interior life of Christians, but often with suspicious overtones of dubious enthusiasm or even heresy. The term *devotion* was preferred; it carried the sense of careful allegiance to the tradition and the exercise of piety within the bounds of standard church practice. By the eighteenth century, *spirituality* referred to the life of perfection that could lead to mysticism, in contrast with the "ordinary" life of faith. By the nineteenth and mid-twentieth centuries, *spirituality* automatically meant the interior life of those striving for perfection. Since the 1950s the meaning of *spirituality* has expanded far beyond a Christian or even religious denotation to refer to the whole realm of experiences and practices involving the human spirit and the soul dimension of existence.

Spirituality is now used in three ways. First, it refers to a general human capacity for self-transcendence, for movement beyond mere self-maintenance or self-interest. Some philosophical, psychological, or anthropological studies use this term. When Jungian psychologists speak of "care of the soul" and of masculine or feminine spirituality, they use the term in this generic sense. When business consultants want to assist personnel to maximize their potential for productive relationships they sometimes speak of a spirituality of work. These uses *may* intend some religious overtones; therefore, it is wise to clarify any meanings that extend beyond the generic. Second, the term *spirituality* can refer to a religious dimension of life, to a capacity for self-transcendence that is actualized by the holy, however that may be understood. Third, it may refer to a specific type of religious experience such as Jewish, Christian, Muslim, or Buddhist.

Self-transcendence is at the core of any definition of spirituality. This does not mean that one transcends or escapes being one's self or stops attending to oneself or caring for oneself. Rather, one acts out of the center or heart of one's self in a way that reaches out in love, freedom, and truth to others and to the unrealized dimensions of one's own capacities. One does this within the horizon of whatever one imagines or judges to be ultimate. Spirituality, then, depends on what is judged to be of ultimate value. Christian spirituality presupposes that ultimacy is God revealed in the death and resurrection of Jesus, known in the sanctifying power of the Holy Spirit poured out in the community. Humanistic spirituality derives from the ultimacy of the individuated self. The definition of spirituality in terms of self-transcendence fits the full range of spirituality, nonreligious as well as religious.

Although the definition of spirituality may be generic, there is no generic spirituality. All spirituality is concrete, embedded in the particularities of experience. These include, for example, symbols and stories, bounds of social awareness, focus of personal authority, modes of knowing and feeling, and range of expectations regarding gender and race. Even though this chapter is focused on Catholic Christian spirituality, there is no generic or uniform Catholic spirituality. Spirituality as experience includes all the complexity and richness of each person's historical and cultural location as well as the particularities of gender, race, class, and psychological development and the unique operation of divine grace within human personality. I will specify these further as I discuss the issues and controversies that are examined by spirituality as an academic discipline.

Spirituality as an Academic Field

Until the High Middle Ages all theology was spiritual theology in the sense that it was reflection upon life "in the Spirit." All theology arose in monastic or pastoral settings as an attempt to convey the experience of faith expressed in Scripture, liturgy, private prayer, communal life, or pastoral care.

When the university rather than the monastery became the primary home of theology, "sacred science" gradually moved away from its explicit foundation in spiritual experience and focused on a foundation in philosophy, logical argumentation, or even in controversy. Reformation theology of the Eucharist, for example, seldom aimed to explicate the religious experience of union or division in Christ; rather, it tried to expose contradictions in its opponents' use of Scripture.

Explicit reflection upon religious experience did continue in monastic and pastoral settings, but this was not considered academically reputable. Julian of Norwich in the fourteenth century gave years of careful attention to her experience of the Trinity and described this in her *Revelations*, yet her book was not studied in the religious academy until recently. Throughout history many careful and even systematic accounts of the spiritual life were written outside of formal theology in many dif-

ferent literary genres: religious rules, commentaries on Scripture, autobiography, letters of spiritual advice, poetry, sermons.

In the eighteenth and nineteenth centuries, academic credibility was
finally granted to the study of the spiritual life, but only by admitting
this field through the side door of moral theology or ethics.[2] Using principles from dogmatic theology and scholastic vocabulary, ascetical and
mystical theology emerged as subdivisions of ethics. The former studied the "purgative way" of ordinary Christians up to the phase of development known as "infused contemplation" or "mysticism." Mystical theology studied the spiritual life from the onset of "the illuminative way"
of passive contemplation up to the "unitive way" characteristic of great
sanctity. As all fields of study mirror the culture that nourishes them, so
this forerunner of academic spirituality reflected its culture's assumptions
about the hierarchy of spiritual stages, the elitism of Christian perfection available primarily to celibate religious, and certitude of dogmatic
conclusions about God and "man."

With the Second Vatican Council's call to return to the sources in Scripture and tradition, the inadequacy of these earlier assumptions became
clear. Out of the aftermath of the Council's impetus to renew Christian
spirituality has come the young academic discipline that studies not only
Christian but all spiritual experience, precisely *as experience.* That is, it aims
to understand spirituality in all its concreteness, in all its complex interaction with its social, cultural, and cosmic setting.

Although spirituality as an academic field is young and its distinctive
nature and methodology are still being debated, some consensus on these
points is emerging. As a field spirituality is understood to be descriptive
and critical rather than prescriptive and normative. Scholars agree also
that the study of spirituality must be ecumenical, interreligious, and cross-
cultural. One of its unique contributions to academic study is its focus
on wholeness. Every aspect of human spiritual experience is integral to
the discipline: bodily, psychological, historical, political, aesthetic, intellectual, social.

Turning from characteristics of spirituality to its practice involves attention to this particular *object,* its *methodological style,* an ideal *procedure,* and its
goal. These distinguish it from other disciplines. The object of spirituality is spiritual experience in its uniqueness, in its messy particularity.

Methodologically the field of spirituality is interdisciplinary; tools from
many disciplines, both religious and secular, are needed to address spiritual experiences both as spiritual and as experience. Methods of study
that involve participation, not merely observation, are appropriate to spirituality for similar reasons that they are found in psychology and anthropology. Spirituality deals with material that cannot be understood—in

the sense of being personally appropriated—except through personal experience or involvement with research data.

This participative style presents a problem regarding the "objectivity" of the discipline, and members of the academy have raised serious questions that reveal their mistrust of spirituality. They fear religious practice may substitute for research or religious commitment may lessen critical judgment or evangelization may be the hidden agenda. I suggest that the real issue behind these questions may not be religious commitment versus objectivity, but the myth of objectivity. The goal of fairness or objectivity in academic disciplines used to be measured by the researcher's distance from the subject matter. I suggest that only when a researcher is critically aware of her or his actual commitments and assumptions, and acts to make them assist rather than prevent insight, can the researcher be objective. This methodological style characterizes the best of contemporary research and scholarship in spirituality.

Regarding *procedure* in the study of spirituality, we find that all serious investigation tends to move in a pattern of three phases. Phase one is descriptive, bringing to our attention the data associated with the experience being investigated. Phase two is analytical and critical, leading to an explanation and evaluation of the subject. In this phase, theological, human, and social sciences are very important. A final phase is synthetic and constructive, leading to the kind of personal knowledge that deeply shifts the scholar's own horizon on the experience studied, as well as on the wider world.

For example, inquiry into strategies of spiritual survival for contemporary Catholic women would begin with a description of their frustration, alienation, and spiritual searching; phase two would explain reasons for these situations and evaluate these reasons according to criteria such as theological or psychological adequacy; phase three would construct creative strategies such as feminist liturgy or feminist reinterpretations of divine mystery or spiritual darkness.

Finally, spirituality as a discipline or field of study has a threefold *goal* or *aim*. Although most people associate spirituality primarily with practical assistance toward a life of greater self-transcendence, the first goal in the study of spirituality is knowledge about religious experience as experience. Only then can it helpfully move to the second and third goals: developing the researcher's own spirituality and fostering the spirituality of others. This triple goal, which includes the aim of changing self and the world, may not be shared by the hard sciences, but it is common to the social sciences, such as psychology, and to the humanities, such as art and philosophy, which aim to liberate humanity from a narrow horizon and free humans for mature relationships.

Spiritual Maturity

Most issues associated with Catholic spirituality as both experience and academic discipline come into focus by attending to a central question: How can we become spiritually mature? That is, how can we realize our spiritual potential? Assuming now that all subsequent discussion comes from a contemporary Catholic viewpoint, notice how reflection upon this one question of experience raises many other issues and suggests the comprehensiveness, complexity, and interdisciplinary nature of spirituality as an academic field. Spiritual maturity is inseparable from issues such as the relationship of grace and nature, growth in prayer, contemplation and action, the role of spiritual darkness. Understanding spiritual maturity is also inseparable from attention to theology, psychology, and history. For example, while all great spiritual teachers say that maturity requires discernment and contemplation rooted in self-knowledge, a psychological climate that insists on conformity to passive female roles allows a very different experience of self-knowledge than a culture that encourages critical questioning. Maturity is also a theological matter. Maturity understood as sharing the trinitarian life of divine persons who are equal in their sharing of life with each other and with all humanity differs from an experience of trinitarian life perceived as flowing in a hierarchical pattern from a patriarchal Father.[3]

An overview of the history of spirituality will afford a glimmer of the richness of the tradition on the question of spiritual maturity and indicate the promise of feminist research that remains to be done. In what follows I apply six tasks of the feminist scholarly agenda[4] to spirituality viewed from the perspective of Christian spiritual maturity. In order to liberate the spiritual tradition from its androcentric bias and make it as inclusive of women's experience as it is of men's, feminist scholars first point out that women have been ignored in the field. For example, Franciscan spirituality ignored Clare until only recently, when she began to be recognized as cofounder, with Francis of Assisi, of the Franciscans. Clare came to be appreciated as the first woman to write a religious rule.

Second, feminist scholars demonstrate that what we do know about women is often accompanied by a high level of diminishment, romanticism, or even hostility. For example, Margery Kempe, an illiterate, medieval woman who left her family to wander the world crying bitter tears, was judged a neurotic eccentric until feminist research disclosed her charism of repentant tears and her vocation to be a pilgrim in a world that assumed women traveling alone were either prostitutes or crazy.[5]

Third, feminist scholars search out and publicize the unknown women in the discipline, in order to add as many figures as possible to an otherwise male pantheon of pioneers and mentors.

Fourth, feminist scholars perform a revisionary reading of the old texts and traditions so that they lose their power to terrorize and exclude women. For example, feminist hermeneutics of Hebrew Scripture and the New Testament has already made a significant scholarly impact on biblical studies and increasingly on spirituality (as exhibited, for instance, in the work of Sandra Schneiders). Revisionist readings challenge the Bible's sexism by revealing its alternative tradition of inclusive language for the divine and its insistence on women's equal discipleship.

Fifth, the discipline of spirituality is challenged methodologically by feminists to redefine its borders, goals, and consequences. For example, Christian ascetical theology used to assume that its foundation rested on a Bible whose inspiration guaranteed its immunity from challenges of sexism and racism. This foundation is now profoundly challenged.

Lastly, scholars work toward a truly integrated field, one not reduced by its prejudices against women, lower classes, variant sexual preferences, or anything else. Future generations may see this accomplished; it is now only emerging. This commitment to integration contributes research on subjects such as the religious experience of poor Hispanic women whose spiritual resources come from "popular religion" (for example, processions, promises to God, concentration on devotion to Mary) and has been derided as superstitious by church authority and theological scholars.

One last word is important regarding assumptions. It is important that insights developed in the present time, such as feminist awareness, not be confused with the fallacy of "presentism." I do not blame the past for not seeing what the present sees as significant, nor do I claim that persons in the past regarded as significant what only recently has become a clear issue. For example, although writers in Christian antiquity almost totally ignored women's experience and generally believed women were inferior humans, the point is not to lay blame, as though they *could* have seen otherwise and freely chose to be blind. Rather, Christians now inherit assumptions about women's humanity that shape the possibilities for their spiritual maturity, and these assumptions require critical evaluation today. For another example, although Hildegard of Bingen used female images for God and was more accomplished in music and healing arts than many women or men in any age, it is inaccurate and inappropriate to call her a feminist. She accepted women's subordination to men and viewed the world as essentially hierarchical; thus she lacks the critical evaluation of patriarchy that is integral to feminism.

Having specified spirituality in terms of six tasks for feminist scholarship, I will apply these tasks to a single issue: spiritual maturity. I will explain maturity and evaluate conclusions about it through an overview of the history of spirituality on the question of Christian maturity. My aim is to clarify spirituality as an academic field by using a topic that integrates psychological issues of personal and social development with theological concerns regarding God's relationship with humanity.

Biblical Spirituality

Feminist biblical scholarship has now demonstrated that even the most basic resource for Christian spirituality, the Bible, must be approached with caution. For some feminists, women and men, the Bible is seen as so pervasively sexist that it can no longer be the revelatory text that grounds their spiritual tradition. These persons have concluded that to sustain personal integrity they must separate from Christianity and seek a spiritual path elsewhere. On the other hand, some feminists are convinced that the hermeneutics of suspicion can reconstruct a biblical theology in which revelation is seen to be a human experience of both sinful sexism and redemptive liberation from all that limits humans or blocks divine love.[6] I write this section from the latter perspective.

We begin our overview of Christian spirituality by looking at early Christian communities of Paul and the gospel writers. Paul's letters reveal that his own religious experience centered on seeing the risen Lord and feeling empowered by the Spirit to witness to God's re-creation of all women and men in Christ, taking down all spiritual barriers between Jew and Greek, slave and free. How this spiritual equality would be worked out in new social structures was a question that Paul's culture could barely grasp. Yet the subversion of that culture's patriarchal assumptions was latent in Christian teaching regarding the new creation.

Paul taught that the experience of daily life in Christ involves bearing one another's burdens, which fulfills the whole law; giving and receiving the Spirit's gifts that build up the body of Christ; eating the meal of unity and love and remembering God's re-creating action in Christ and in us; offering ourselves as living sacrifices of praise and thanksgiving for God's overwhelming love for us in Christ. This is the love that no suffering need separate us from, if we believe that in Christ our struggles continue redemptive love.

This appreciation for the way suffering can reveal that true power resides not in control but in love and relationship to all people is something Paul himself learned from experience. In the beginning of Paul's ministry, his experience of the risen Lord led him to concentrate on proclaiming the power of the resurrection. Later, his experiences of failure and persecution led him to shift his focus and appreciate more deeply the mystery of Christ's passion. His mature experience was one of moving ever more deeply into the entire paschal mystery, of loving trust even unto death so that the power of God manifest in Jesus' weakness might be manifest also in Paul's weakness and in ours.

The religious experience of Mark's community centers on Jesus as the suffering servant messiah because the disciples of Jesus were persecuted and asked, Why is this happening to us? The Gospel replies that if one is a disciple of Jesus, one must expect to follow the master's path of faithful love, giving one's last breath as Jesus did.

Mark portrays the male disciples as particularly fearful and very slow to learn that the true servant of God must love even unto death. Mark taught the community that they too will receive Jesus' patient mercy as they struggle in faith, even as Peter did. Women disciples are noted for their presence at the crucifixion, as well as throughout Jesus' ministry, and they receive the first announcement of Jesus' resurrection. Like all disciples in Mark's Gospel they are portrayed, in the end, as fearful.

Luke's community was a missionary church learning to expand its boundaries of sharing and concern. Only slowly and painfully did they realize that life in Christ called them to care for more than just their own family and friends. As Jesus was impelled by the Spirit to bring the good new of God's covenantal love to the poor and oppressed, so they are called to lives of generosity and service to all. Those in positions of authority were reminded of their responsibility to follow Jesus' path of serving others instead of being served. The story of the prodigal son reveals a divine father who, far from being a controlling patriarch, is prodigal in honoring human choices and in displaying faithful love.

Matthew's community experienced its identity as one of commitment to Mosaic teaching, honoring Jesus as the primary interpreter of the Law, in the face of challenges by other interpreters of the Law. The community meditated upon Jesus, the personification of wisdom, who embodies Israel's righteousness. Mercy, forgiveness, and trust in the midst of persecution come to expression in the Beatitudes. Living according to this teaching means cooperating with God, bringing into being God's new covenant by replacing relationships of domination with those of justice and peace.

John's community experienced unity as well as alienation. More than any other Gospel community, its members realized the depth of Jesus' unity with God and their own indwelling in God through rebirth as God's daughters and sons. They experienced themselves as friends of Jesus and as his sisters and brothers. They lived in relationship to the new Paraclete who lived in them and continued to teach the community the meaning of Jesus' words. Their sense of alienation, stemming from rejection by a very conservative segment of the Jewish community, was so misinterpreted by later generations of Christians that anti-Jewish attitudes came to be legitimated through (mis)use of this Gospel.

At the heart of the apostolic spirituality of the fourth Gospel is the experience of being sent even as Jesus was sent from the Father. Over and over this Gospel echoes the phrase, "As . . . me, so . . . you." All disciples experience, in their own way, the same relationship Jesus has to his Father, the same work as Jesus, the same Spirit, the same joy, the same life.

Finally, Paul and the communities of the Gospels understood their religious experience through Jewish Scripture interpreted in light of their experience of Jesus the Christ. Today, Christians must value their Jewish roots in a way that respects the continuing integrity of revelation in the Hebrew Bible on its own terms. To appreciate this integrity it is wise to include Jewish interpreters.

In summary, the biblical tradition reveals spiritual maturity as an experience of deep and inclusive love. Spiritual maturity is the loving relationship to God, Christ, the Spirit, and to all of humanity that is born of the struggle to discern where and how the Trinity is present in the community, in ministry, in suffering, in religious and political dissension, and in one's own sinfulness. Guidelines for "testing the spirits" do not eliminate the need to trust one's own sense of vocation in the absence of certitude. Maturity is understood primarily as a matter of relationship. Yet the attitudes we now call self-direction and adult freedom are also present in the biblical language of a call to conversion and to fidelity in the midst of spiritual confusion.

Early Christianity

Liturgical and theological texts indicate that Christians, insofar as we can make general judgments from sources that are written entirely by men, understood their lives as personal participation in the mystery of Christ, nourished by sharing in the Lord's Supper and expressed by inclusive love that bore witness to life in the Spirit and drew others to faith. This common faith was experienced in the complexity of the later Roman Empire: both Eastern and Western centers of culture and theology; hierarchical arrangements of gender, race, and class; assimilation and rejection of the dominant culture.[7]

Because Christian spirituality consists of a constellation of integrated elements (God-images, community, asceticism), rearranging one element affects all others, as the history of this period demonstrates. The Sunday Eucharist celebrated in house churches or in larger communities composed of poor and rich, illiterate and educated, women and men, reinforced certain insights, such as the acceptance of diversity, reconciliation, hope, and generous love. Conviction deepened that the community was the primary place to meet the risen Lord.

Initial emphasis on martyrdom also affected all later interpretation of Christian experience. Whereas Paul saw ministry as the imitation of Christ, early martyrs understood a painful death as the closest imitation of Jesus. Praising martyrdom, then, reinforced Greek culture's tendency to deny the body and the world. When martyrdom was no longer possible, complete self-denial was sought through asceticism and monasticism.

Asceticism arose as a countercultural movement against the church that was overly identified with political institutions. Primarily a lay movement, it had a solitary side that tended toward contempt for the flesh and a communal side that stressed simple prayer, that relished Scripture, and that promoted charity and purity of conscience as attitudes needed for proper interpretation of Scripture. Only through asceticism could women overcome men's identification of females with flesh, which was judged as subordinate to spirit, identified with males. That is, women could be equal to men on condition that they renounce the satisfactions of bodily life. Wise ascetics, such as Macrina and Benedict, attracted persons seeking spiritual guidance.

Desert mothers and fathers manifested a profound realization that tradition is not a set formula but a continuity of life lived according to the gospel. Desert wisdom is perennial, yet naturally it mirrors the authoritarian, patriarchal society from which it comes. Christian culture's absorption of ancient learning resulted in a model and method of promoting religious experience that idealized philosophical contemplation centered on the mind. Its method aimed to subject the passions to reason. Virginity, practiced by a minority of women and men, enjoyed a moral and cultural supremacy unchallenged until the Reformation. In ancient Mediterranean society, sexual abstinence was a social convention with negative and positive connotations foreign to modern persons. Negatively, virginity meant fighting against tensions of unfulfilled sexuality. Even more significantly, it meant struggling against the force of social convention that swept a person into her or his supposedly natural social role as a married person whose sexual life was directed toward perpetuating family and kinship. Positively, virginity committed a person to new grounds of social cohesion. For women it meant that what Eve lost through sin the virgin regained through a celibate life. She lived an angelic life that could mediate between the divine and the human. Although this theory was not always practiced, its symbolic power cannot be underestimated. Gradually this theory modified the Platonic ideal of the soul withdrawn from the body, so that the emphasis shifted to withdrawal of the body-self from society's claims regarding the primacy of family and kin. This made a certain type of autonomy possible for upper-class women and for many women in monasteries.

In summary, spiritual maturity in this era continued to be seen as union with God and love of neighbor. However, the influence of surrounding culture added conflicting ideals: love of neighbor was set alongside contempt for the flesh (and, consequently, contempt for women who were identified with flesh); purity of conscience accompanied unquestioning obedience to male authority. Virginity, as an ideal, had a double effect: renunciation of sex as a sacramental way to experience God, along with freedom to renounce the social conventions that restricted women to marriages arranged for the sake of property and family status.

Medieval Spirituality

While the medieval period was innovative in styles of religious life and art, it was not revolutionary because it remained firmly rooted in previous traditions.[8]

Popular spirituality could be distinguished from professional. Mass conversions, low levels of general education, and pastoral neglect promoted the cult of relics, magic under the guise of sacraments, pilgrimages simply for the sake of travel, and thinly veiled paganism. In contrast, the professional spirituality of nuns and monks was informed by study and guidance.

Professional religious life flourished in a variety of forms. While women and men continued to withdraw into solitude, there emerged an urban ministry of clerics devoted to including laity in cathedral liturgy. A central question became: What is the authentic experience of apostolic or evangelical life? Monks concluded that monastic life was the only place in which the image of God could truly be restored to humanity in this life. In contrast, mendicant women and men were convinced that genuine evangelical life was possible outside of monastic structures. Francis of Assisi, for example, believed that anyone could preach who was called by God's Spirit. Francis wandered the countryside, begged for support rather than relying on wealthy benefices, and called all to conversion using metaphors of trade drawn from the experience of the new merchant class. The rule written by Clare of Assisi, who was also attracted by evangelical poverty, reveals not only her originality in stressing women's discretion but also her insistence on radical poverty at a time when Franciscan men were far from this ideal. Her rule also reflects papal decrees that women be secluded.

Beguines were another type of lay group. Independent from men's authority, these women lived at home or in small communities in voluntary poverty and celibacy. With no formal church supervisors, they combined work, common prayer, and life "in the world." Eventually all mendicant preaching was clericalized and all women's religious communities were forced to accept strict cloister.

Although many medieval women and men conveyed their experience of God and of Jesus through maternal imagery, this symbol functioned differently for each sex. Although Julian of Norwich in her *Showings* may be best known for her theology of God's motherhood, she was hardly original since the Bible and patristic writers used feminine images of God. For women, divine motherhood conveyed primarily an experience of receiving unconditional love. For many Cistercian abbots, on the other hand, this image was associated with authority. Out of a need to supplement their male exercise of authority with attitudes such as gentleness and availability, which were considered feminine, they imaged Christ, their model of monk and abbot, as mother and midwife of souls. In the process of infusing authority with love, these men romanticized motherhood, repeated female stereotypes, and imaged Christ as a nursing mother even while they maintained their own separation from and even hostility toward actual women.

Medieval writers described "man" as the image and likeness of God. In *The Cloud of Unknowing*, for example, one finds patristic themes: grace as divinization, human faculties as reflections of the Trinity, the image of God as given from the beginning yet tarnished by sin, and asceticism as the way to develop the true likeness to God. For medieval women and men such as Clare and Francis of Assisi, one became one's true self by conforming to the model of true humanity: Jesus poor, humble, and entirely surrendered to God. Jesus' maleness was not significant; rather, it was his obedience and love that united him to God and to us.

Attachment to Mary was a striking feature of medieval religious experience. During this period the figure of Mary changed from the inspiring mother of Christ to the merciful mother of the people to the queen of heaven and earth who protected her faithful ones. At times her ability to rescue became the focus of exaggerated devotion. The cult of the Virgin reinforced an androcentric image of woman. It praised a woman surrendered to a male divinity, valued entirely on the basis of her abstinence from a sexual life and her devotion to a son's goals. The glorification of this one woman left unaffected the subordinate situation of real women.

In the midst of the wars and religious divisions of this period, some women heeded their inner voices urging them to redirect political affairs. Catherine of Siena admonished the pope and struggled to reconcile warring factions. Joan of Arc led armies to victory, then was betrayed into enemy hands. Joan chose fidelity to her vocation rather than escape, and she was burned at the stake. These saints demonstrate the inseparability of religious and so-called worldly experience.

Eastern Orthodox spirituality in this period is well represented in Gregory Palamas's teaching about hesychasm[9] (silent contemplation) which stressed a theme noted in Western as well as Eastern religious experience: silent prayer of the heart, understood as prayer of the whole person, including the body. Its aim was to be conscious of the grace of baptism already given yet hidden by sin. Its method was probably influenced by Islam's joining of the holy name to the rhythm of breathing. Its wider context was the Eastern understanding of the connection between active and contemplative life. *Active*, for Gregory, referred to the redirection, not suppression, of passions. *Contemplative* referred to silence of the heart, to complete openness and surrender to God. A cloistered nun could be active, while a busy mother could be contemplative if she had silence of heart. Prayer of the heart was considered a type of constant prayer possible for all persons, not just for monks and nuns.

In summary, medieval writers envisioned spiritual maturity as wholehearted conformity to Christ's love and care for all. This care was often conveyed in female images that symbolized different meanings for women and men. New forms of religious life revealed that while men could attain Christian maturity outside of monastic cloister, for several reasons women were presumed to require seclusion. First, unless women were directly attached to men by living in their households, women were defined as "loose," that is, immoral. Second, monastic cloister served in some cases to protect women from male relatives who wanted to force their return to family control. In more cases, however, it symbolized either the conviction that women's humanity was so flawed that it required enforced protective boundaries or it acted as an extension of family control when daughters were put into convents because a suitable marriage was not possible. Writers, both female and male, saw that maturity requires personal judgment in order to discern the appropriate response to new forms of apostolic life and in order to be faithful to contemplative and active aspects of interior development.

Reformation Spirituality

Protestant response to some aspects of medieval tradition led to a new understanding of spirituality. Monasticism was no longer perceived as a special way to experience God. Rather, God was seen as available in all aspects of life, especially where the word of God was preached authentically and the sacraments of baptism and the Lord's Supper were celebrated. Celibacy was no longer the privileged state of life in which to achieve union with God; instead, marriage was particularly valued and in some cases became almost an obligation for clergy. In this movement women lost the advantages of convent life, among them independence from patriarchal marriage and the opportunity for higher education; instead they received a new role expectation: serving as the pastor's wife, which involved total service to the congregation while receiving none of the reverence and rewards bestowed on the clergy.[10]

Catholics and Protestants tended to respond to each other's theology by emphasizing the differences and assuming the other's view had no merit. Contemporary Catholics, however, can now appreciate Luther's insights regarding the importance of Scripture and even notice parallels to the great Spanish mystics that neither Teresa of Jesus (of Avila) nor John of the Cross nor Luther consciously intended.

For Luther, speech about God is speech about absence; God is met only in the cross, in a kind of loneliness in which there are no signs of transcendence, no conceptual neatness, no mystical assurances. Teresa of Jesus and John of the Cross would agree with Luther's conviction that one can neither contain nor control God. Luther and the authentic Catholic contemplative tradition object to the perversion of contemplation into an experience that imprisons God in a set of human feelings or thoughts or impressions. Indeed, John of the Cross in *The Ascent of Mount Carmel* teaches the inevitability of the dark night in which human desire is transformed and human projections onto God eventually are surrendered in order to allow authentic union with God in Christ. John, Teresa, and Luther would agree also that knowledge of God is possible only on God's terms: when humans yield their self-assertive will and respond to God's total self-gift of undeserved love. The affinity between Luther and the great Carmelite reformers does not, however, discount their theological differences over grace, church, and human nature.

Carmelite reform, initiated by Teresa of Jesus and extended to the friars through John of the Cross, was intended to make religious life a community of loving friends, living in poverty and solitude. Its theology of spiritual and human development can assist persons to become completely disposed toward God's action for the sake of the needs of the church and the world. Contemplative transformation, according to Teresa's teaching in *The Interior Castle*, is directed toward one purpose only: "the birth always of good works, good works" (7.4.6).

Teresa's astute interpretation of her own process of religious development, explained first in the *Life* and revised and expanded in *The Interior Castle*, eventually made her a Doctor of prayer for the universal church. Using the "rhetoric of femininity," for example, referring to herself as a weak, ignorant woman to avoid the Inquisition's censure because she dared to teach about spiritual matters, Teresa communicated her experience of deepening prayer through the image of four waters. She explained how her efforts at self-knowledge and honest love (drawing water from a well) yielded a greater capacity for receiving God's love (a wheel turned by a donkey eases the effort of drawing water). Fidelity in the desert of love's purification allowed the full force of God's acceptance and love to inundate her (like a river) with abundant gifts (like rain) of intimacy with the Trinity and of leadership in the church. In the Carmelite tradition, another resource for current feminist concerns is the theology of equality, even with God, that permeates *The Spiritual Canticle* of John of the Cross. Here spiritual maturity is described as complete mutuality with God, as "equality of friendship" (stanza 28.1).

Ignatius of Loyola also distilled his religious experience into guidelines for spiritual growth. His *Spiritual Exercises* are an imaginative method of meditating on and contemplating Scripture. They were designed to assimilate one to the mysteries of Christ and facilitate discernment for a contemplative person in apostolic action. Although they use male-centered examples and military images, the *Exercises* are intended to be adapted to different needs. By expanding the biblical meditations to include women's discipleship and by substituting examples that are truer to women's experience, the *Exercises* can be made effective for women today.

In summary, Reformation spirituality valued what we now call self-direction and intimate relationships. Protestants and Catholics who desired reform called these values fidelity to one's interior call and surrender to God's love. They were considered necessary for both women and men. Religious upheaval reinforced the need to follow an informed conscience, as Martin Luther and Katharina (née von Bora) Luther did. In the midst of uncertainty reformers of this era developed the themes of personal discernment and critical self-knowledge that our own era needs in order to face profound changes.

Modern Spirituality

As the sixteenth century affected later Catholic spirituality through the Spanish mystics, so from the seventeenth century onward French spirituality was also very influential.[11]

Neither monasteries nor universities were the seedbed of this spirituality; rather, it was the parlor of Madame Acarie, known later as the Carmelite Marie of the Incarnation. Her discussion group included Benedict of Canfield and Pierre de Bérulle. They absorbed the Platonic perspective of Denys the Areopagite (sixth century) and reshaped it to support their own understanding of spirituality. Canfield's *Exercises of the Will of God* stressed holiness as accessible to all through an experience of self-emptying that permits participation in the passion of Jesus Christ. Bérulle also taught participation in the mysteries of Christ. In his *Grandeurs of Jesus* the goal of Christian life is imaged as the reproduction on earth of the adoration and servitude of Christ in heaven.

This era was influenced by the exceptional personality of Francis de Sales. A bishop best known for his warmth and sensitivity as a spiritual director, his *Introduction to the Devout Life* became a classic description of how the laity can become holy through the practice of love in ordinary life. Jane de Chantal, Francis's intimate friend, spiritual companion, and cofounder of the Visitation order, was also an outstanding spiritual director. Her *Letters* demonstrate great skill in promoting the integration of spiritual and human maturity. Her unique contributions to Salesian spirituality have become lasting influences.

Jansenism, a complex and controversial combination of theological, political, and economic issues, was named for Cornelius Jansen, whose rigorist presentation of Augustine's theology of grace reinforced certain practices. In confession a penitent should not be given the benefit of the doubt; one should sometimes give up Holy Communion as an act of humility or through mortification; moral life must be strict.

Nineteenth- and twentieth-century spirituality was, like all previous spirituality, a creative response to God's presence discerned in events and ideas. Responses to the Enlightenment, secularism, atheism, and political revolution ranged widely. Thérèse of Lisieux, for example, interpreted her experience of spiritual darkness as redemptive identification with modern struggles for faith. Pierre Teilhard de Chardin reconciled science and faith by interpreting his experience of cosmic unification as *The Divine Milieu*. The concern to restore biblical prayer, share monastic riches with the laity, and reunite spirituality and theology motivated the liturgical movement. Responses to industrialism included the social spirituality of Dorothy Day's and Peter Maurin's Catholic Worker movement in the United States. In Europe, Africa, and the Middle East Little Brothers and Sisters of Jesus, inspired by Charles de Foucauld, began a ministry of evangelical presence as poor workers among workers. Affective, sometimes sentimental, devotion to Mary tended to compensate for Jansenist rigorism and patriarchal religion by promoting Mary as the kind, approachable mediatrix of all grace.

In summary, modern spirituality continued to respond to dramatically new perspectives on faith and doubt, on mission, science, social structures, and world religions. Maturity remained a matter of loving relationships and fidelity to one's vocation. Radical new possibilities for women to found religious congregations, and the Enlightenment critique of religious authority, reinforced the need for a kind of spiritual discernment that demanded one both trust and evaluate personal decisions. Foundresses such as Elizabeth Seton and Cornelia Connelly exemplify the challenges and continuities of modern Catholic spirituality.

Contemporary Spirituality

Western culture is now in the process of a paradigm shift more profound than any since the modern era began. In every field of study and endeavor the standards of "authentic reality" are beginning to change from individualism, hierarchy, and male centeredness to a new paradigm of interdependence, mutuality, and inclusiveness. Yet tremendous pressures resist the emerging paradigm, and Catholic feminism is embedded in this tension as it tries to understand and reach spiritual maturity.

Exploration of this tension will move in three steps: (1) a definition of Catholic feminism; (2) integration of this view with spiritual maturity; and (3) a consideration of the difference it makes to have this perspective.

Recently, a woman who was asked why she was joining the Catholic church when she knew its pervasive sexism replied, "I'm not drawn by the tradition of authority and administration that stays in union with Rome; I'm coming to belong to the great mystical and theological tradition that is still bearing fruit in good works all over the world." Catholicism unites these two aspects that Catholic feminists experience as inseparable yet often in tension.

Catholic feminists also struggle to reconcile two aspects of secular feminism. Individualist feminists argue for the moral equality of women and men whose shared humanity deserves equal rights. Relational feminists also affirm equality yet stress the difference it makes in our culture to be socialized as a woman rather than as a man. They insist that society value the qualities and skills that culture develops in women and grant the same status and rewards to women's contributions that are given to men's. Catholic feminists desire an integration of these two aspects: realization of women's equal human dignity and capacity for all roles in life and church ministry, and just reward for women's unique contributions rather than restriction and abuse. Feminists who identify as Catholic believe they can still find a "usable tradition" within the church.[12]

How is spiritual maturity understood from a Catholic feminist perspective? Because Catholic theology maintains that grace (the Trinity's loving presence) and human nature are intrinsically related, Catholic feminists presume that human and spiritual maturity can be integrated. However, knowing that the tradition has presented a double standard for women and men, they wonder *how* this can be done when women's spiritual maturity is seen so often as self-denial and submission, while men's maturity is presumed to be the standard of human maturity and is described as leadership and heroic resistance in the face of challenge. Given the feminist principles explained above, integration of human or psychological maturity with Christian maturity is possible, then, if and only if the paradigm of maturity is the same for women and men and the same for psychology and spirituality. Everyone strives for maturity in her or his own unique way, so "the same" paradigm means the absence of conflicting values and ideals.

This integration is possible in both theory and practice when a feminist model of psychological development is related to a feminist theology of spiritual development and shown to be identical.[13] In brief, a feminist theology of spiritual development notices that the classical spiritual tradition defines maturity as intimate relationship with the Holy Mystery (ineffable yet named as Source, Word, and Spirit) and with all persons and the cosmos, an intimacy made possible by increasing independence from attachments that block deeper relationship. The desire to affirm women's experience as much as men's leads feminist theologians to notice how both autonomy (traditionally denied or restricted for women) and attachment (culturally reinforced in women) are essential for Christian maturity. In the tradition, autonomy for the sake of relationship is described in the language of detachment for the sake of union with God. That is, the autonomy valued in psychology for its ability to free people for deeper relationship, is spoken of in spirituality traditions as detachment that makes possible union with God. Different cultures have interpreted this detachment in different ways, from renunciation of any pleasure, especially sexual, to letting go of all images of the divine in prayer. Likewise, the language of union with God has been interpreted in immature images of fusion or self-annihilation. Feminist theology finds that the negative connotations of the religious language of detachment and union can be overcome by using feminist structural developmental psychology.

Developmental psychology that gives equal value to women's and men's experience maintains that every phase of human development involves both autonomy and attachment. Greater maturity is a matter of ever greater independence from *fusion* with family, friends, religion, and culture, precisely for the sake of relationships of intimacy that are deeper, more complex, more inclusive of diversity. The self develops through a complex process that includes dying to the old way of interpreting the meaning of oneself and others in order to relate in ways that are ever more authentically intimate and mature. Autonomous persons are free to give themselves in truthful love not only to those who are "like them" but also to those who are different. In order to live from inner self-direction rather than from compulsion or role-conformity, one must "die" to fusion with social roles or to identification with unexamined ways of living. This developmental transformation is a kind of death because it requires facing the radically unknown that is part of facing the fear of failure, anxiety over accepting new ideas, or insecurity in relationships that are more mutual and thus less controlled and predictable. Out of this death comes freedom for relationships that are deeper and more inclusive. In this developmental perspective, autonomy is detachment from restrictive ways of being and relating, precisely so that unbounded love and care for all can arise from ever freer self-donation. Thus union with God and others, in this view, integrates independence with relationship at every phase of development. Unlike models of maturity based on male socialization seeing independence as the goal, this feminist model values independence precisely in terms of its potential for allowing deeper relationship. Thus differentiation for the sake of deeper relationship is the meaning of maturity for both men and women.

This feminist model of human maturity enables the integration of Christian and psychological development in both theory and practice. The Christian language of growth through detachment and spiritual darkness for the sake of union that is more mutual can be recognized as a matter of gaining psychic freedom in order to relate with the intimacy born of equality. In one phase of development it would be freedom from immersion in unexamined relationships to others (including God) in order to *have* relationships rather than simply *be* relationships (women's traditional socialization). In another phase it would be freedom from the need to control relationships (men's traditional pattern and the temptation for feminist individualists) in order to welcome the vulnerability necessary for intimacy and mutuality between equals. The transition from one phase of development to another may feel like death because it is the death of one entire way of being oneself. No wonder spiritual tradition calls this a "dark night" of the senses and the spirit. No wonder, either, that a Catholic feminist would notice how the feminist desire for equality is echoed in the Christian tradition viewing friendship as the school of the spiritual life. As many mystics describe it, using the analogy of friendship, it includes God putting us in God's self, making us God's equal.[14]

What difference does it make to have this feminist perspective? It makes every issue of Catholic spirituality, which is the same as every aspect of life, a struggle for conversion, for a complete change of heart and mind. When feminists desire to identify themselves as Catholic, they face a religious situation of contradiction and conflict. While affirming women as baptized into Christ as fully as men, official church teaching and practice also ignore, demean, and even oppress women. Even while being trivialized or restricted, Catholic feminist women and men (including some bishops) are thinking and acting in creative and courageous ways to convert themselves and others toward the Christian maturity described above. This experience of the patriarchal religious situation in the process of conversion is studied and promoted by the academic study of Catholic spirituality. When we grasp the enormity of this task of transformation in both experience and academic endeavors we may feel frustrated, exhausted, and tempted to quit. Even more, when the feminist critique results in losing past certitudes people feel a profound loss of existential meaning. At times, maintaining a feminist Catholic spirituality feels like a matter of survival. Living with oppressive church structures and male-centered theology is torture, but rejecting Catholic spiritual riches is starvation.[15] Maintaining faith, fidelity, and feminist integrity while the church is converted to genuine inclusiveness requires validation from the spiritual tradition.

How does our Catholic spiritual tradition help us interpret and respond to this contemporary situation? It offers resources that speak directly to the connection between this experience of darkness and the Christian maturity described throughout this chapter. When Catholic spirituality seems profoundly inadequate and therefore our very identity is at stake we have John of the Cross's advice to those struggling with faith: "Because the gold of the spirit is not purified and illumined . . . Wishing to . . . clothe them with the new . . . God leaves the intellect in darkness, the will in aridity, the memory in emptiness, and the affections in anguish, by depriving the soul of the feelings and satisfactions it previously obtained from spiritual blessings."[16]

This "intellect in darkness" well describes the perspective of feminist women and men who must relinquish the entire male-centered theology of God, acknowledge the significant problems with Goddess theology,[17] and labor toward a complete reconstruction of the tradition about the Holy Mystery. Surely, a "memory in emptiness" fits the experience of those whose memory of traditional Christology and sacramental theology brings emptiness at the realization of their profound inadequacy or brings pain when they are used to restrict or oppress women. Knowing that maturity requires letting go of all that blocks wider truth and deeper union, feminists are invited to believe that "although the [person] has not the support of any particular interior light of the intellect or of any exterior guide . . . love alone . . . is what guides and moves [the person] and makes [her or him] soar to God in an unknown way. . . ."[18] The creative love manifest in this book is just one witness to the spiritual energy working to liberate the world for a still unknown spiritual maturity.

Notes

1. For a fuller historical treatment of this term, see Sandra M. Schneiders, "Spirituality in the Academy," *Theological Studies* 50.4 (1989): 684–87.

2. Schneiders has made the most original contribution to defining spirituality as an academic field and to specifying its methodology. See, for example, "Spirituality in the Academy," 676–97. Schneiders's position is represented here.

3. See Catherine Mowry LaCugna, *God for Us: The Trinity and Christian Life* (San Francisco: Harper San Francisco, 1991).

4. These six tasks were first named and developed by Mary Jo Weaver, *New Catholic Women* (San Francisco: Harper & Row, 1985), 154–55.

5. Clarissa W. Atkinson, *Mystic and Pilgrim: The Book and the World of Margery Kempe* (Ithaca: Cornell University Press, 1983).

6. For a concise treatment and further resources see Sandra M. Schneiders, *Beyond Patching* (New York: Paulist, 1991), 37–71.

7. Useful resources for this period include Peter Brown, *The Body and Society: Men, Women, and Sexual Renunciation in Early Christianity* (New York: Columbia University Press, 1988); Elizabeth A. Clark, *Women in the Early Church* (Wilmington, Del.: Michael Glazier, 1983); Douglas Burton-Christie, *The Word in the Desert: Scripture and the Quest for Holiness in Early Christian Monasticism* (New York: Oxford University Press, 1993).

8. Useful resources for this period include volumes in the Classics of Western Spirituality series, such as Julian of Norwich, *Showings* (New York: Paulist, 1797); Francis and Clare of Assisi, *The Complete Works* (New York: Paulist, 1982); *Clare of Assisi: Early Documents*, ed. and trans. Regis J. Armstrong (New York: Paulist, 1988), benefits by the collaboration of Margaret Carney; Carolyn Walker Bynum, *Jesus as Mother: Spirituality of the High Middle Ages* (Berkeley and Los Angeles: University of California Press, 1982).

9. Kallistos Ware, "hesychasm," in *Westminster Dictionary of Christian Spirituality*, ed. G. S. Wakefield (Philadelphia: Westminster, 1983).

10. Resources for this period include primary sources in translation from the Institute for Carmelite Studies (Washington, D.C.) and volumes of The Classics of Western Spirituality on Luther and Ignatius of Loyola; Rowan Williams, *Christian Spirituality* (Atlanta: John Knox, 1979), and *Teresa of Avila* (Harrisburg, Pa.: Morehouse, 1991).

11. Resources for this era include volumes from The Classics of Western Spirituality such as *Bérulle and the French School*; Francis de Sales and Jane de Chantal, *Letters of Spiritual Direction*; Louis Dupré and Don F. Saliers, eds., *Christian Spirituality: Post-Reformation and Modern* (New York: Crossroad, 1989); Jill Raitt, ed., *Christian Spirituality: High Middle Ages and Reformation*, vol. 17 of *World Spirituality: An Encyclopedic History of the Religious Quest* (New York: Crossroad, 1987).

12. For further development see Joann Wolski Conn, "New Vitality: The Challenge from Feminist Theology," *Proceedings of the Catholic Theological Society of America* 46 (1991): 70–74.

13. Joann Wolski Conn, *Spirituality and Personal Maturity* (New York: Paulist, 1989).

14. Constance FitzGerald, "A Discipleship of Equals: Voices from Tradition—Teresa of Avila and John of the Cross," *Proceedings of the Theology Institute of Villanova University*, ed. Francis A. Eigo, O.S.A. (Villanova, Pa.: Villanova University Press, 1988), 63–97.

15. Mary Jo Weaver, *Springs of Water in a Dry Land: Spiritual Survival for Catholic Women Today* (Boston: Beacon, 1992), xii.

16. "The Dark Night," bk. 2, chap. 3, no. 3, in *The Collected Works of St. John of the Cross*, trans. Kieran Kavanaugh and Otilio Rodriguez (Washington, D.C.: Institute of Carmelite Studies, 1973).

17. Contemporary Goddess religion is a complex phenomenon that claims its roots in primal matriarchal societies that were centered on Goddess worship. Its practitioners sometimes describe it as a foreshadowing of feminism. Problems with it include (1) no written evidence for the existence of primal matriarchies or the Great Goddess; (2) reliance on secondary literature for overstated conclusions; (3) reliance on the psychic reality for its adherents while ignoring historical problems; (4) a focus on a utopian poetic and a theology untested by even one generation; (5) an uncritical attitude toward its own tradition while dismissing traditional Christianity as unredeemably sexist. These issues are explained in Rosemary Radford Ruether, *Gaia and God: An Ecofeminist Theology of Earth Healing* (San Francisco: Harper San Francisco, 1992); and Mary Jo Weaver, *Springs of Water in a Dry Land.*

18. "The Dark Night," bk. 2, chap. 25, no. 4.

For Further Reading

Classics of Western Spirituality. New York: Paulist, 1980. A library of original texts translated and introduced by outstanding scholars associated with each author or tradition. Some introductions include feminist concerns.

Conn, Joann Wolski, ed. *Women's Spirituality.* New York: Paulist, 1986. An anthology of essays integrating feminist theology and psychology; explains how women's spirituality may be feminist, feminine, or neither.

Conn, Joann Wolski, and Walter F. Conn, eds. *Horizons on Catholic Feminist Theology.* Washington, D.C.: Georgetown University Press, 1992. Explains and illustrates six tasks of feminist theology.

Fischer, Kathleen. *Women at the Well.* New York: Paulist, 1988. A discussion of spiritual direction from a feminist perspective; includes attention to issues of power and violence.

McGinn, Bernard. *The Foundations of Mysticism.* New York: Crossroad, 1991. The first of three projected volumes; the appendix on theological, philosophical, comparative, and psychological approaches to mysticism outlines all the controversies of the twentieth century.

Meehan, Brenda. *Holy Women of Russia: The Lives of Five Orthodox Women Offer Spiritual Guidance for Today.* San Francisco: Harper San Francisco, 1993. Against the rich backdrop of nineteenth-century Russia, the author—a leading expert in Russian history and especially the history of religion in Russia—charts the forgotten lives of five holy women who each modeled a distinctive spiritual path and inspired the vibrant spirituality that lived on underground among communities of women in our century.

Miles, Margaret. *Practicing Christianity.* New York: Crossroad, 1988. Critical perspectives for an embodied spirituality.

New Dictionary of Catholic Spirituality. Edited by Michael Downey. Collegeville, Minn.: Liturgical Press, 1993. Uses contemporary scholarship, incorporates feminist perspectives.

Plaskow, Judith, and Carol P. Christ, eds. *Weaving the Visions: New Patterns in Feminist Spirituality*. San Francisco: Harper & Row, 1989. Explains new patterns in feminist spirituality, but has an uncritical view of research on Goddess religion.

Ruether, Rosemary Radford. *Gaia and God: An Ecofeminist Theology of Earth Healing*. San Francisco: Harper San Francisco, 1992. Examines patriarchal and ecofeminist religious visions of creation.

Sheldrake, Philip. *Spirituality and History*. New York: Crossroad, 1992. A full-scale contemporary exploration of the role of history in the study of Christian spirituality.

Weaver, Mary Jo. *Springs of Water in a Dry Land*. Boston: Beacon, 1992. Gives strategies for spiritual survival for Catholic women today. It includes a clear, balanced critique of Goddess religion.

World Spirituality. General editor, Ewert Cousins. New York: Crossroad, 1985–. An encyclopedic history of the religious quest. Women are vastly underrepresented.

On Feminist Spirituality

Anne Carr

Discussion about women and spirituality can range from romanticized claims of special privilege to insistence that equality means sameness. Some typical questions focus the issues. "What is a women's spirituality?" "How is it different from male spirituality?" "What is spirituality, anyway?" And, "what is a feminist spirituality?" "Is it androgynous?" "Is it a stage on the way to something else?"[1]

Spirituality

Spirituality can be described as the whole of our deepest religious beliefs, convictions, and patterns of thought, emotion, and behavior in respect to what is ultimate, to God. Spirituality is holistic, encompassing our relationships to all of creation—to others, to society and nature, to work and recreation—in a fundamentally religious orientation. Spirituality is larger than a theology or set of values precisely because it is all-encompassing and pervasive. Unlike theology as an explicit intellectual position, spirituality reaches into our unconscious or half-conscious depths. And while it shapes behavior and attitudes, spirituality is more than a conscious moral code. In relation to God, it is who we really are, the deepest self, not entirely accessible to our comprehen-

This essay first appeared in *Women's Spirituality: Resources for Christian Development,* ed. Joann Wolski Conn (Mahwah, N.J.: Paulist, 1986), 49–58. Used by permission.

sive self-reflection. In a Christian context, God's love goes before us in a way we can never fully name.

Spirituality can be a predominantly unconscious pattern of relating seldom reflected on, activated only in certain situations, as at Sunday Mass or during a personal crisis. As such it is a dimension of life for the most part unexamined, resting on convention, upbringing, or social expectations. But spirituality can also be made conscious, explicitly reflected on, developed, changed, and understood in a context of growth and cultivation of the fundamental self in a situation of response and relationship. Christian spirituality entails the conviction that God is indeed personal and that we are in immediate personal relationship to another, an Other who "speaks" and can be spoken to, who really affects our lives.

Although it is deeply personal, spirituality is not necessarily individualistic, because within the relationship to the ultimate, to God, it touches on everything: our relations to others, to community, to politics, society, the world. Spirituality can be consciously oriented toward the inclusive social context in which we live.

Spirituality is expressed in everything we do. It is a style, unique to the self, that catches up all our attitudes: in communal and personal prayer, in behavior, bodily expressions, life choices, in what we support and affirm and what we protest and deny. As our deepest self in relation to God, to the whole, and so literally to everything, spirituality changes, grows, or diminishes in the whole context of life. Consciously cultivated, nourished, cared about, it often takes the character of struggle as we strive to integrate new perceptions or convictions. And it bears the character of grace as we are lifted beyond previous levels of integration by a power greater than our own.

Spirituality is deeply informed by family, teachers, friends, community, class, race, culture, sex, and by our time in history, just as it is influenced by beliefs, intellectual positions, and moral options. These influences may be unconscious or made explicit through reading, reflection, conversation, even conversion. And so spirituality includes and expresses our self-conscious or critical appraisal of our situation in time, in history, and in culture.

As a style of response, spirituality is individually patterned yet culturally shaped. Implicit metaphors, images, or stories drawn from our culture are embodied in a particular spiritual style; these can be made explicit through reflection, journal keeping, conversations with friends, or therapy. We each live a personal story that is part of a wider familial, cultural, racial, and sexual myth. When our myths are made conscious, we can affirm or deny them, accept parts and reject others, as we grow in relationship to God, to others, to our world. Personal, familial, religious, cultural, racial, sexual stories answer the great questions: Where do I come from? How should I live? What is the meaning of the end, of death? Making myths explicit means that we have already moved beyond them and that they become available for criticism.

Women's and Men's Spiritualities

Even with affirmations of equality between women and men, of a single-nature anthropology in contrast to a dual-nature view,[2] it seems clear that there are differences between the sexes in basic style of understanding and relationship. Thus there are probably differences in women's and men's spiritualities. Recognition of difference, while admitting real equality, need not entail subversive notions of complementarity that really means subordination or inferiority of one in relation to the other. What are these differences, prescinding from the question (unanswerable, I think) of whether these are the result of nature or nurture?

In a helpful book, *Women's Reality,*[3] Anne Wilson Schaef describes the differences between what she calls the White Male System and an emergent Female System on the basis of her consultant work with both women and men. The White Male System is the dominant one in our culture. While there are other systems (Black, Native American, Hispanic) the White Male System, she argues, views itself as (1) the only one, (2) innately superior, (3) knowing and understanding everything, and (4) believing that it is possible to be totally logical, objective, and rational. Schaef lists a set of contrasts that might help us get at differences in women's and men's spiritualities. These contrasts, of course, describe abstract types; no one is completely one type or another. And some men are in fact in the Female System, while some women are in the White Male System. The following indicate some of these different gender based perspectives:

Issues	White Male System	Female System
Time	Clock	Process
Relationships	Hierarchy	Peer
Center of focus	Self and work	Relationship (self-others)
Sexuality	Central	Part in whole
Intimacy	Physical	Verbal
Friendship	Team effort	Knowing and being known
Power	Zero sum (scarcity)	Limitless
Money	Absolute, real	Relative, symbolic
Leadership	To lead	To enable
Negotiation	Fun = winning	Fun = creativity

In sum, the White Male System is analytic, concerned with definition, explanation, either/or, and is goal-centered. The Female System is synthetic, concerned with understanding, both/and, and is process-centered.

Feminist consciousness, as critical of religious and cultural ideologies which reach into our very perception, thought, and language, must be a little suspicious here. Rather than delimiting a female spirituality to one side of the list, would not a critical feminist consciousness try to hold elements of both sides together, in critical correlation with one another? Do we not need to preserve the values of traditional female characteristics while recognizing certain values in the traditional male traits?

Schaef performs an exercise with her groups (male, female, mixed) in which she asks participants to list characteristics of God (whether they believe in God or not) and of humankind; then characteristics of male and female. Invariably, she writes, the lists look like this:

God	Humankind	Male	Female
male	childlike	intelligent	emotional
omnipotent	sinful	powerful	weak
omniscient	weak	brave	fearful
omnipresent	stupid/dumb	good	sinful
eternal	mortal	strong	like children

She concludes that male is to female as God is to humankind. And this, she argues, is the mythology of the White Male System, whose basic hierarchical structure is God—men—women—children—animals—earth, in a system of dominance. Schaef says our traditional theology supports this myth. Clearly feminist theology, and other forms of contemporary theology, do not.

Feminist Spirituality

A feminist spirituality would be distinguished from any other as a spiritual orientation which has integrated into itself the central elements of feminist consciousness. It is the spirituality of those who have experienced feminist consciousness raising.

Feminist spirituality is thus different from women's spirituality, that is, the distinctive female relationship to the divine in contrast to the male. Women's spirituality might be studied across particular historical periods, or within particular religions, or racial or cultural groups (e.g., puritan, Muslim, Black or, as above, White, middle class, Western) and certain "female" characteristics delineated. For example, in contrast to male spirituality, women's spirituality might be described as more related to nature and natural processes than to culture; more personal and relational than objective and structural; more diffuse, concrete, and general than focused, universal, abstract; more emotional than intellectual, etc.

A specifically feminist spirituality, on the other hand, would be that mode of relating to God, and everyone and everything in relation to God, exhibited by those who are deeply aware of the historical and cultural restriction of women to a narrowly defined "place" within the wider human (male) "world." Such awareness would mean that we are self-consciously critical for the cultural and religious ideologies which deny women full opportunities for self-actualization and self-transcendence. This critical stance is both negative and positive. Negatively, it bears a healthy suspicion and vigilance toward taken-for-granted cultural and religious views that, in a variety of subtle ways, continue to limit the expectations of women to passive, subordinate, auxiliary roles and rewards. Positively, this critical stance includes a vision of the world in which genuine mutuality, reciprocity, and equality might prevail. A fully developed feminist spirituality would bear the traces of the central elements of feminist consciousness, integrated within a wider religious framework.

Such a spirituality would affirm and be deeply at home in the reality of sisterhood. It would recognize the importance of the supportive network among women of all ages, races, and classes and would espouse non-competitive, non-hierarchical, non-dominating modes of relationship among human beings. As critical, it would recognize the competitive and non-supportive ways in which women have sometimes related to one another in the past and would consciously struggle to achieve authentic, interdependent modes of relationship. As religious, and as Christian, such a spirituality would strive to integrate the model of feminist sisterhood into a wider vision of human community with men as brothers. Thus it would be open to all people and would not cease calling the brothers to task for their failings and to wider vision of human mutuality, reciprocity, and interdependence before a God who wills our unity and community.

As feminist, such a spirituality would encourage the autonomy, self-actualization, and self-transcendence of all women (and men). It would recognize the uniqueness of each individual as she tells her own story (there is no universal women's experience) and affirm each one as she strives to make her own choices. As critical, it would recognize the cultural and religious limitations placed on women in the past and present; and as self-critical, the temptation of the feminist group to impose another ideology as oppressive as the old obedience to the fathers. Feminist spirituality would consciously struggle to free itself from ideologies in favor of the authentic freedom of the individual and the group as it attempts to be faithful to its own experience. As religious, and as Christian, a feminist spirituality would strive for an ever freer, but always human, self-transcendence before a God who does not call us servants but friends.

In its encouragement of sisterhood and autonomy, feminist spirituality understands the wider dimensions of human oppression, especially the relationships of racism, classism, sexism, and elitism in our society, and affirms the liberation of all oppressed groups. As critical, it would resist limiting the women's movement to a luxury only the affluent can afford, but would embrace the plight of women of all colors and all classes, that is, be genuinely self-critical. As religious, and as Christian, such a spirituality would strive to become global in its concerns, in its prayer as in action, to become truly inclusive of the whole of God's world, to pray and to act with the inclusive mind of God, that is, to be self-transcendent.

A Christian feminist spirituality is universal in its vision and relates the struggle of the individual woman—black, brown, yellow or white, rich or poor, educated or illiterate—to the massive global problems of our day. For in recognizing the problem (the sin) of human exploitation, violence, and domination of male over female, rich over poor, white over color, in-group over out-group, strong over weak, force over freedom, man over nature, it sees the whole through the part. Such a spirituality strives to be not elitist but inclusive. It invites men, and all the other oppressor groups, to conversion. Yet it remains critical, on guard against the easy cooptation that can dim its radical vision of human mutuality and cooperation. Wise as a serpent, cunning as a dove, Christian feminist spirituality resorts to prayer as the only hope for its vision even as it struggles to act, here and now, to bring it into reality.

Given the possible scope of feminist spirituality as it views the whole through the lens of women's situation, what can be said about female and male spirituality? That each has its values and limitations. That the emergent female spirituality has strong humanistic and corrective elements for contemporary society. The feminist spirituality is, I think, new. With the exception perhaps of the 19th century Protestant feminists, the feminist spirituality I have described differs not only from male spirituality, past and present, but from a good deal of female spirituality as well. Clearly, it would be available for everyone, male and female. And clearly, it would be androgynous, if by the term is meant focus on the person as integrating the full range of human possibilities, with choices dependent on talents and attractions rather than the stereotypes of race, class, and sex. (The oppressors are oppressed, too, by limited horizons.) Strictly feminist spirituality, with its particular stress on female bonding in sisterhood, affirmation of the self-actualization and self-transcendence of women, and interrelationships among sexism, racism, and classism, is, one hopes, a temporary stage on the way to a fuller human spirituality.

In the present, however, it remains a stage that has only begun to be explored. Analogies with the experience of other oppressed or minority groups might be helpful. One who has worked in and with any of these groups, shared in their struggle and their prayer, even if she is not a member of the group can to some extent know what that experience is, can be "converted." So, too, any man who has identified with the struggle of women can participate in the feminist experience, share in a feminist spirituality. Given the massive distortions of both the religious and the cultural traditions, I would say that in truth any man should. All the spiritualities of liberation, notwithstanding the distinctive and never to be totally assimilated experience of the "minority," do have a convergent unity. But it is precisely through the particularities of the individual group that some purchase on the broader vision can be had.

The feminist experience is unique in that it potentially covers the world, every human group. It is this that has led some feminists to maintain that male-female domination is not only the oldest, but the source of all oppressor-oppressed relationships. And because of the close familial, personal, ethnic, and class ties involved, it is also often seen as the most difficult to deal with. And yet that very closeness of male-female, in whatever group, may offer stronger possibilities for overcoming the split, for healing the wound, particularly in the religious context that spirituality encompasses. For here, in the Christian framework at least, human beings understand themselves in relation to a God who is ultimate, yet incarnate, whose name is love, who calls us to unity, whose revelation is in the death and resurrection of Jesus, who is among us in the Spirit (our experience of spirituality) that our joy may be complete. The Spirit is advocate, comforter, clarifier of sin and of truth.

A feminist spirituality, with its sources in women's experience of friendship and sisterhood, might express the experience of joy in the divine-human relationship, as suggested by Judith Plaskow in her study of Protestant theologies of sin and grace in relation to the experience of women. This is the experience of grace or the Spirit which is neither "shattering" (Niebuhr) as by an authoritarian father-judge nor a quietistic "acceptance" as by an understanding mother (Tillich), neither "subordination nor participation which threatens the boundaries of the individual self." It is an experience of grace or the Spirit "best expressed in words using the prefix 'co'—co-creating, co-shaping, co-stewardship; and in non-objectifying process words, aliveness, changing, loving, pushing, etc."[4] The suggestion is similar to one made by Elisabeth Schüssler Fiorenza about the metaphor of friend/friendship in relation to God.[5]

What if one were to envision God as friend, even as a feminist friend, rather than father or mother? What if God is friend to humanity as a whole, and even more intimately, friend to the individual, to me? A friend whose presence is joy, ever-deepening relationship and love, ever available in direct address, in communion and presence? A friend whose person is fundamentally a mystery, inexhaustible, never fully known, always surprising? Yet a friend, familiar, comforting, at home with us: a friend who urges our freedom and autonomy in decision, yet who is present in the community of interdependence and in fact creates it? A friend who widens our perspectives daily and who deepens our passion for freedom—our own and that of others? What if? Jesus' relationship to his disciples was that of friendship, chosen friends; he was rather critical of familial ties. His friendship transformed their lives—both women and men—expanded their horizons; his Spirit pressed them forward. Can we pray to the God of Jesus, through the Spirit, as friends?

Notes

1. An earlier version of these reflections was presented at a seminar on feminist spirituality organized by Mary Jo Weaver of Indiana University, Bloomington, in October 1981, and supported by a grant from Lily Endowment.

2. See Research Report: *Women in Church and Society*, ed. Sara Butler, M.S.B.T. (Mahwah, N.J.: Catholic Theological Society of America, 1978), 32–40.

3. Minneapolis: Winston, 1981.

4. *Sex, Sin and Grace: Women's Experience and the Theologies of Reinhold Niebuhr and Paul Tillich* (Washington, D.C.: University Press of America, 1980), 172.

5. "Why Not the Category Friend/Friendship?" *Horizons* 2.1 (spring 1975): 117–18.

Where Do We Go from Here?

In the twenty-first century, we can expect that spirituality will continue to prosper as both a practice and a discipline of study. Three areas show particular promise. First, scholars will no doubt continue to define the parameters of spirituality with an eye toward full inclusion of this field within the larger academy. Before this goal is achieved, however, much more philosophical work needs to be done to articulate and make room for the kind of truth that spirituality evidences. Many of the "facts" of spirituality are unlike those of scientific empiricism, with the result that attentiveness to an appropriate methodology for spirituality, and one that is not reductionistic, becomes all the more important. Beyond this, a "metaphysics of spirituality," a description of what is deemed "real," should be undertaken by leading scholars in the field, especially in light of postmodernism's critique of Enlightenment objectivity and reductionism. Spiritual truth represents a distinct dimension of human experience not easily reduplicated or communicated to another. It is a dimension, not of "objects" and "objectivity," but of persons, transcendence, and relationality.

Second, Bradley Hanson has raised the question of spirituality and evil in his critique of some basic definitions of spirituality. Sandra Schneiders, for example, has defined spirituality as "the experience of consciously striving to integrate one's life in terms not of isolation and self-absorption but of self-transcendence toward the ultimate value one perceives."[1] Hanson, however, replies: "This ability of spirit can be realized for good or evil. So I do not think it is legitimate simply by definition to rule out of bounds the unwholesome actualizations of the human spirit in isolation or self-absorption."[2]

In my reckoning, Schneiders's inclusion of the infinitive "to integrate" in her definition precludes the issue of evil simply because transcending into evil "ultimate" values, such as Nazi racism, leads *over time* not to integration on a personal or social level but to chaos. Nevertheless, Hanson still has a point; for is it not true that some spiritualities offered to the Christian community during the Middle Ages, for example, were morbid and destructive in their consequences, while still others were inimical to the interests of women? And if such spiritualities were evil in their effects, at least in part, must we then conclude that they weren't really spiritualities after all? Or can we acknowledge the actual evil of some spiritual programs and disciplines that, although they lead to a measure of transcendence and integration, may yet result also in dissolution and destruction? In other words, are spirituality and evil mutually exclusive, or can they overlap? More important, is there a spirituality of evil? If so, must we then consider a distinction between real goods and apparent goods as well as the possibility of deception when lured by the multifarious "evoking subjects" of extant spiritualities? Moreover, is the evil entailed in being called forth by what is penultimate—whether it be jingoistic nationalism or unthinking ethnocentrism—a deception that may be evident only over time? These and other questions must be grappled with seriously in the days ahead.

Third, there seem to be some strong similarities between spirituality and the task of critical thinking.[3] Indeed, these disciplines are perhaps most similar in their challenge to egocentrism and ethnocentrism as the most significant obstacles to wisdom, truth, and progress. Thus, just as critical thinking exposes the self-interest that prevents one from seriously entertaining opposing views, so too does spirituality question the pervasive self-concern that undermines the love of God and neighbor. Again, just as critical thinking critiques the ethnocentrism that can be championed by some thinkers as they participate in groups and as they attempt to get what they want at the expense of others, so too does spirituality call for going beyond the limited perspective of a particular group to a genuinely universal dimension of love that acknowledges the dignity of all human beings. In other words, the self-interest present in all human beings, which is compounded at the group level, often thwarts a serious consideration of "the other" and therefore detours an evenhanded pursuit of truth or an approach toward the transcendent.

In light of the preceding parallels, which are not on the periphery but are at the very heart of these respective disciplines, it seems that a critical thinker who is able to move beyond the stereotypes of religion and spirituality often found in American culture may be drawn to the rigors and orientation of spiritual life as elements that are not only amenable to, but also conducive to, a basic search for truth. Likewise, the spiritually earnest—sensing the importance of careful and evenhanded thinking, as exemplified, for instance, in the life and thought of Cardinal Newman and others—may be drawn to critical thinking as one of the more important ways to be conscious of the prejudice and bias that affects us all and that, unfortunately, has the capacity to stop a spiritual journey dead in its tracks.

It is hoped, then, that in the future—although much more work needs to be done—key leaders will emerge both in the critical thinking movement and in the church who will recognize each other as kindred spirits, who will courageously go beyond the stereotypes, and who will seek to hold together the very best operations of the mind with the seriousness and depth of the human heart, leaders who in the words of Charles Wesley will wed "knowledge and vital piety." This is the task that awaits philosopher and saint alike. This is the hope that challenges us all.

Notes

1. Sandra M. Schneiders, "Theology and Spirituality: Strangers, Rivals, or Partners?" *Horizons* 13 (1986): 266. See also Schneiders's essay in this reader.

2. Bradley Hanson, "Theological Approaches to Spirituality: A Lutheran Perspective," *Christian Spirituality Bulletin* 2.1 (spring 1994): 5.

3. Kenneth J. Collins, "Spirituality and Critical Thinking: Are They Really So Different?" *Evangelical Journal* 16.1 (spring 1998): 30–44.

Index